CASE CLOSED™

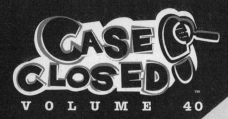

VOLUME 40

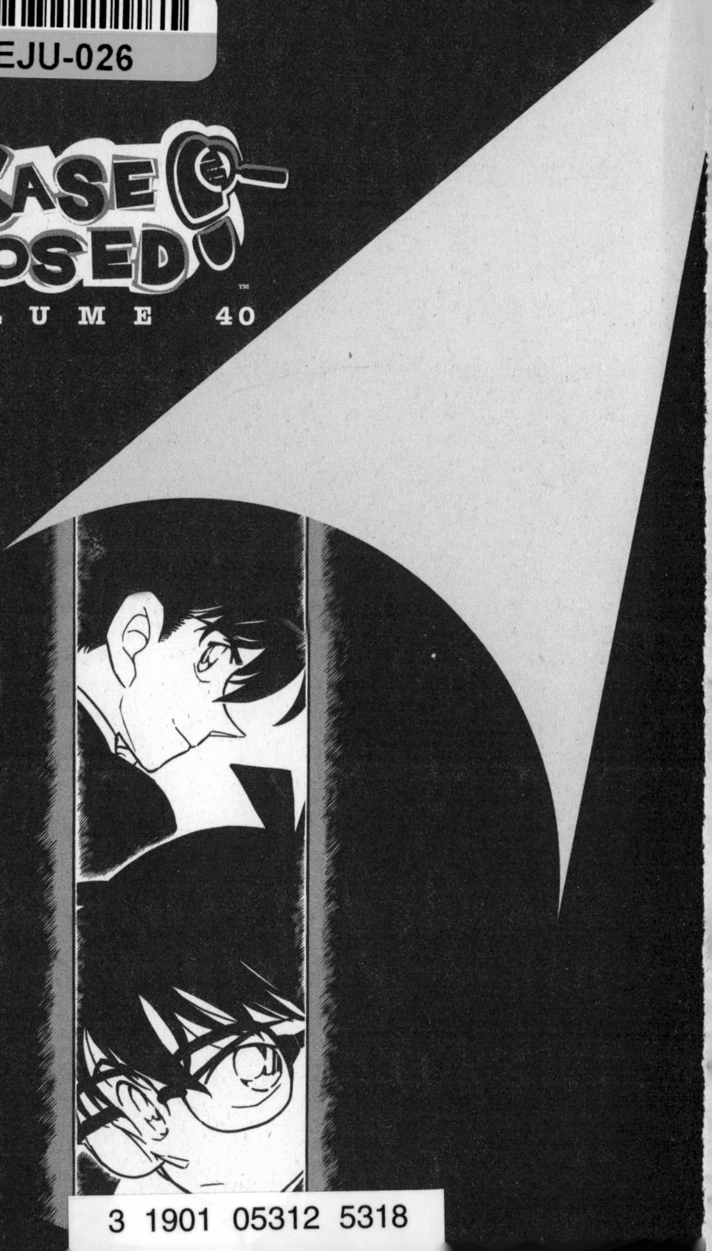

Case Briefing:

Subject:
Occupation:
Special Skills:
Equipment:

Jimmy Kudo, a.k.a. Conan Edogawa
High School Student/Detective
Analytical thinking and deductive reasoning, Soccer
Bow Tie Voice Transmitter, Super Sneakers,
Homing Glasses, Stretchy Suspenders

The subject is hot on the trail of a pair of suspicious men in black when he is attacked from behind and administered a strange substance which physically transforms him into a first grader. When the subject confides in the eccentric inventor Dr. Agasa, they decide to keep the subject's true identity a secret for the safety of everyone around him. Assuming the new identity of first-grader Conan Edogawa, the subject continues to assist the police force on their most baffling cases. The only problem is that most crime-solving professionals won't take a little kid's advice!

Table of Contents

CONFIDEN

CASE CLOSED

Volume 40
Shonen Sunday Edition

Story and Art by **GOSHO AOYAMA**

Original Japanese edition "MEITANTEI CONAN" published by SHOGAKUKAN Inc.

Translation
Tetsuichiro Miyaki

Touch-up & Lettering
Freeman Wong

Cover & Graphic Design
Andrea Rice

Editor
Shaenon K. Garrity

Printed in Canada

Published by VIZ Media, LLC
P.O. Box 77010
San Francisco, CA 94107

10 9 8 7 6 5 4 3 2 1
First printing, October 2011

WWW.SHONENSUNDAY.COM

RATED T+ FOR OLDER TEEN

PARENTAL ADVISORY
CASE CLOSED is rated T+ for Older Teen and is recommended for ages 16 and up. This volume contains realistic and graphic violence.

ratings.viz.com

www.viz.com

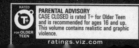

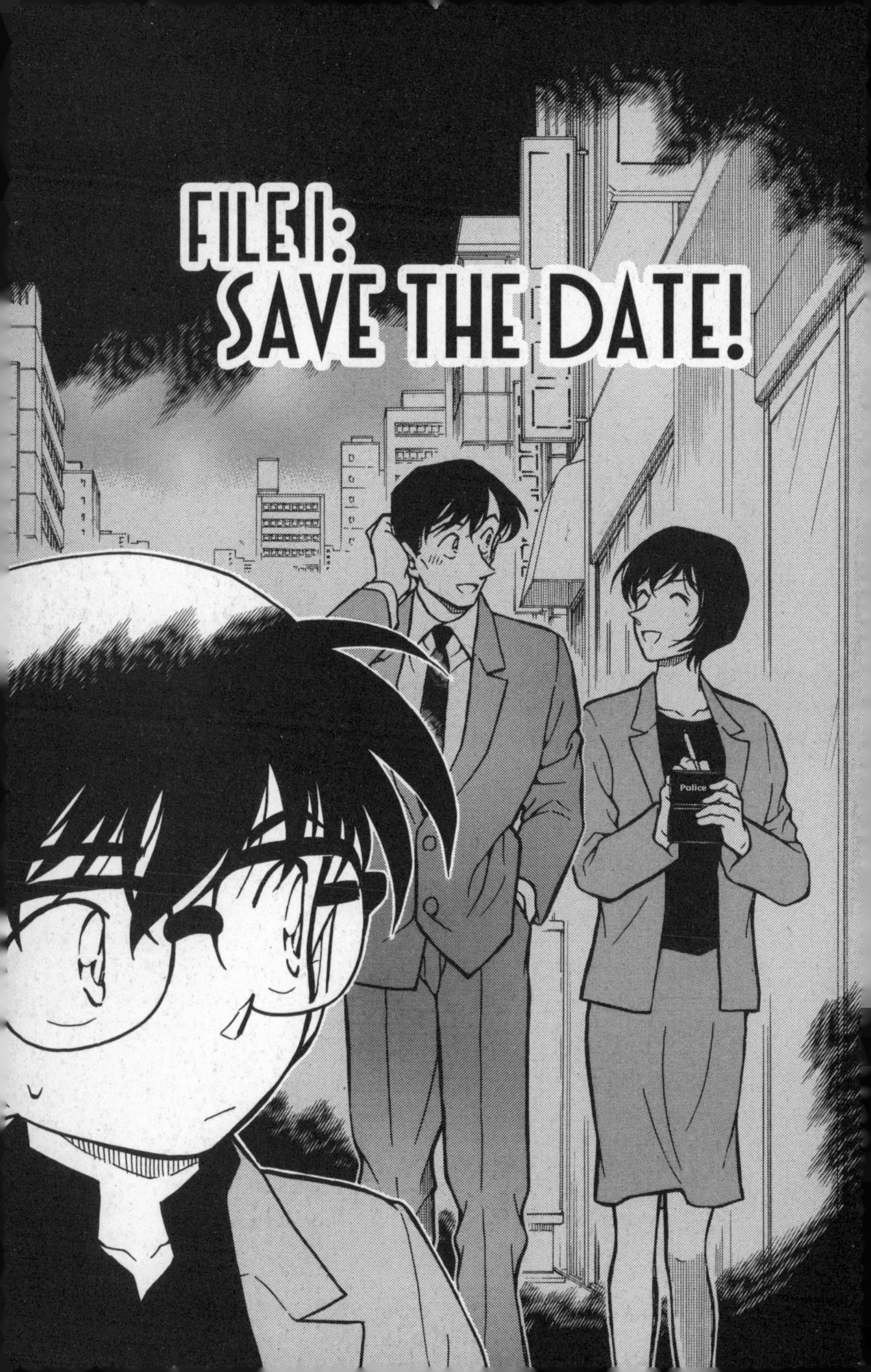
FILE 1:
SAVE THE DATE!
Police

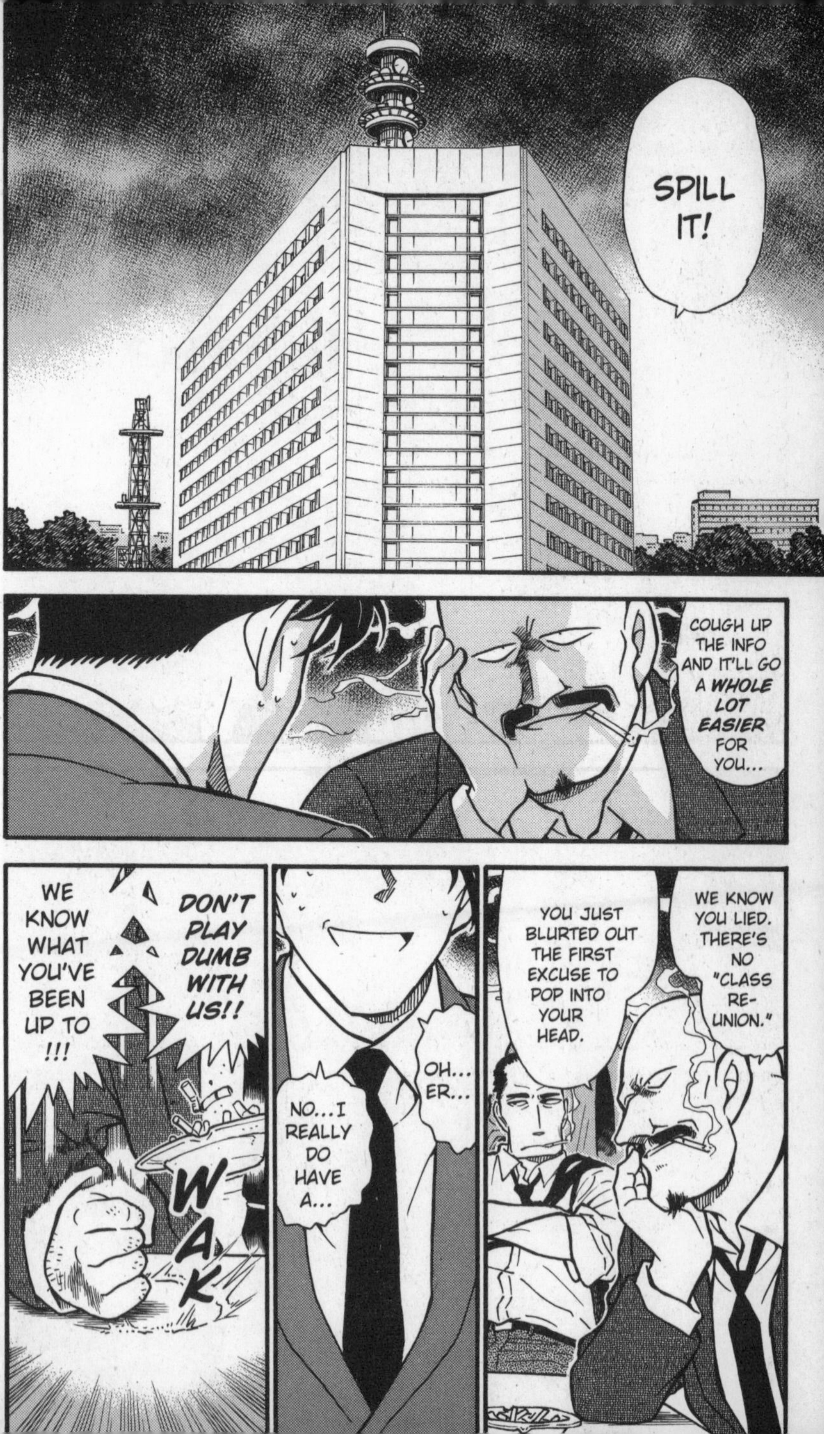
SPILL IT!
COUGH UP THE INFO AND IT'LL GO A ***WHOLE LOT EASIER*** FOR YOU...
WE KNOW YOU LIED. THERE'S NO "CLASS RE-UNION."
YOU JUST BLURTED OUT THE FIRST EXCUSE TO POP INTO YOUR HEAD.
OH... ER...
NO...I REALLY DO HAVE A...
DON'T PLAY DUMB WITH US!!
WE KNOW WHAT YOU'VE BEEN UP TO !!!
WAK

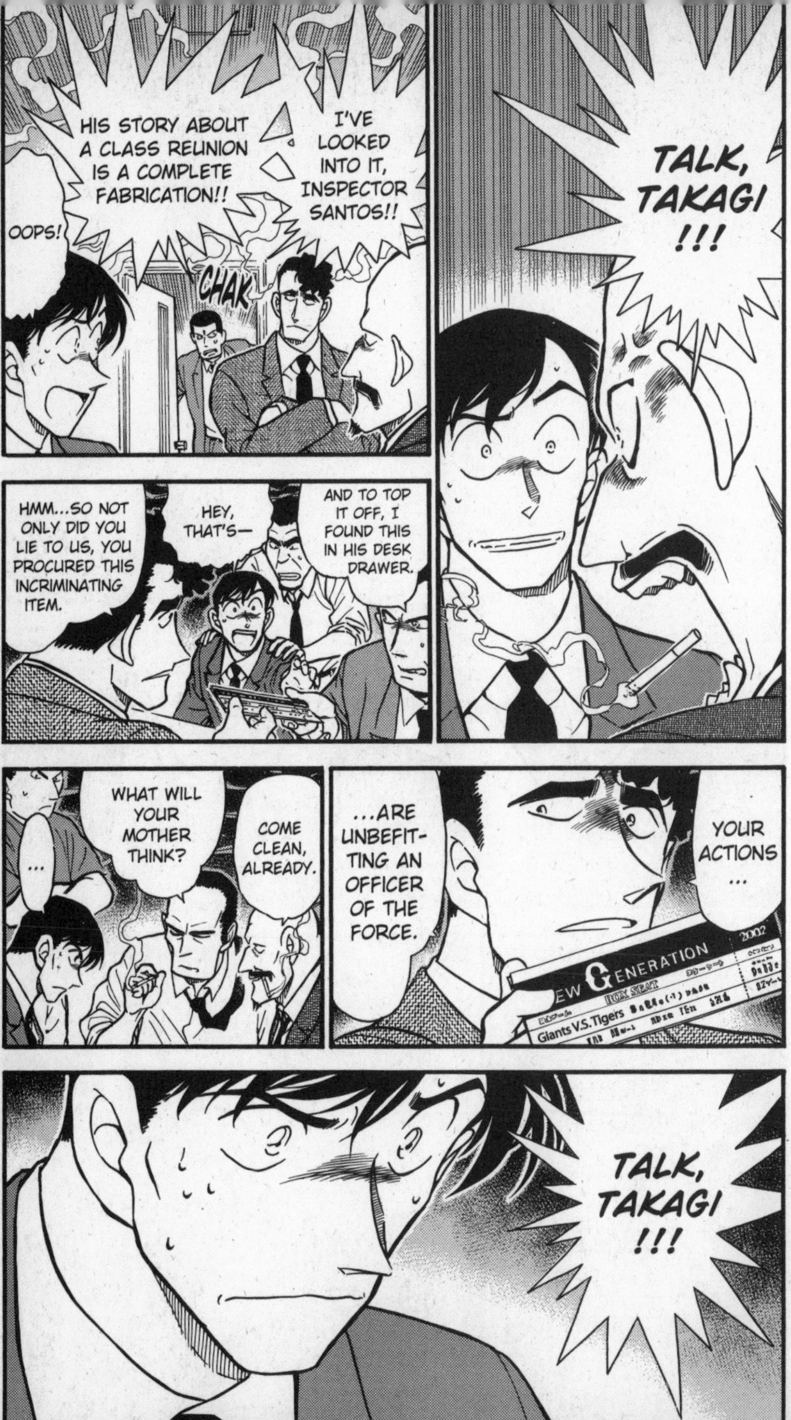
TALK, TAKAGI!!!
I'VE LOOKED INTO IT, INSPECTOR SANTOS!!
HIS STORY ABOUT A CLASS REUNION IS A COMPLETE FABRICATION!!
OOPS!
CHAK
AND TO TOP IT OFF, I FOUND THIS IN HIS DESK DRAWER.
HEY, THAT'S—
HMM...SO NOT ONLY DID YOU LIE TO US, YOU PROCURED THIS INCRIMINATING ITEM.
YOUR ACTIONS...
...ARE UNBEFIT-TING AN OFFICER OF THE FORCE.
2002
EW GENERATION
BOX SEAT
Giants V.S. Tigers
COME CLEAN, ALREADY.
WHAT WILL YOUR MOTHER THINK?
...
TALK, TAKAGI!!!

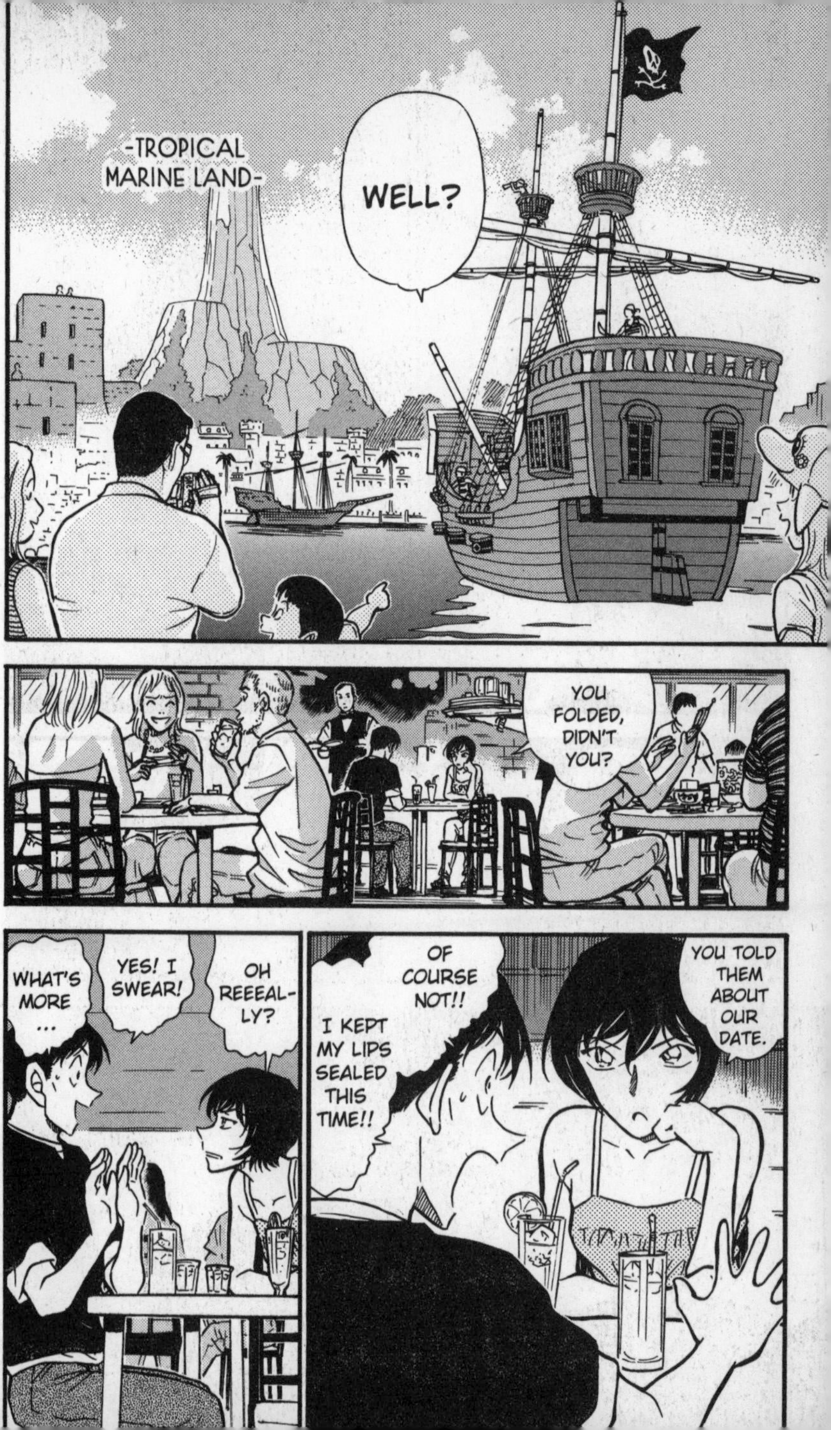
WELL?
-TROPICAL MARINE LAND-
YOU FOLDED, DIDN'T YOU?
YOU TOLD THEM ABOUT OUR DATE.
OF COURSE NOT!!
I KEPT MY LIPS SEALED THIS TIME!!
OH REEEAL-LY?
YES! I SWEAR!
WHAT'S MORE ...

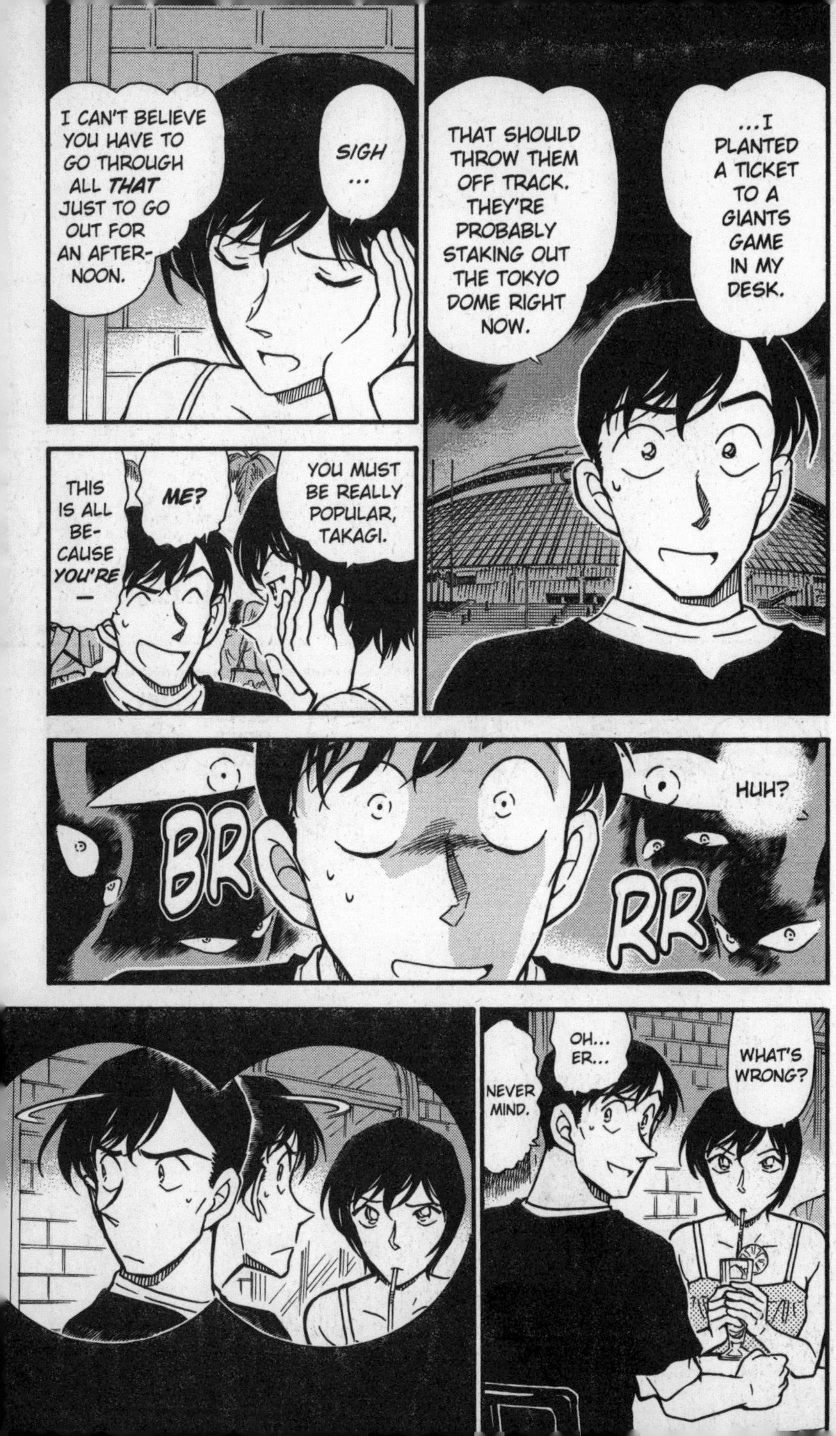
...I PLANTED A TICKET TO A GIANTS GAME IN MY DESK.
THAT SHOULD THROW THEM OFF TRACK. THEY'RE PROBABLY STAKING OUT THE TOKYO DOME RIGHT NOW.
SIGH ...
I CAN'T BELIEVE YOU HAVE TO GO THROUGH ALL *THAT* JUST TO GO OUT FOR AN AFTER-NOON.
YOU MUST BE REALLY POPULAR, TAKAGI.
ME?
THIS IS ALL BE-CAUSE *YOU'RE* —
HUH?
BR RR
WHAT'S WRONG?
OH... ER...
NEVER MIND.

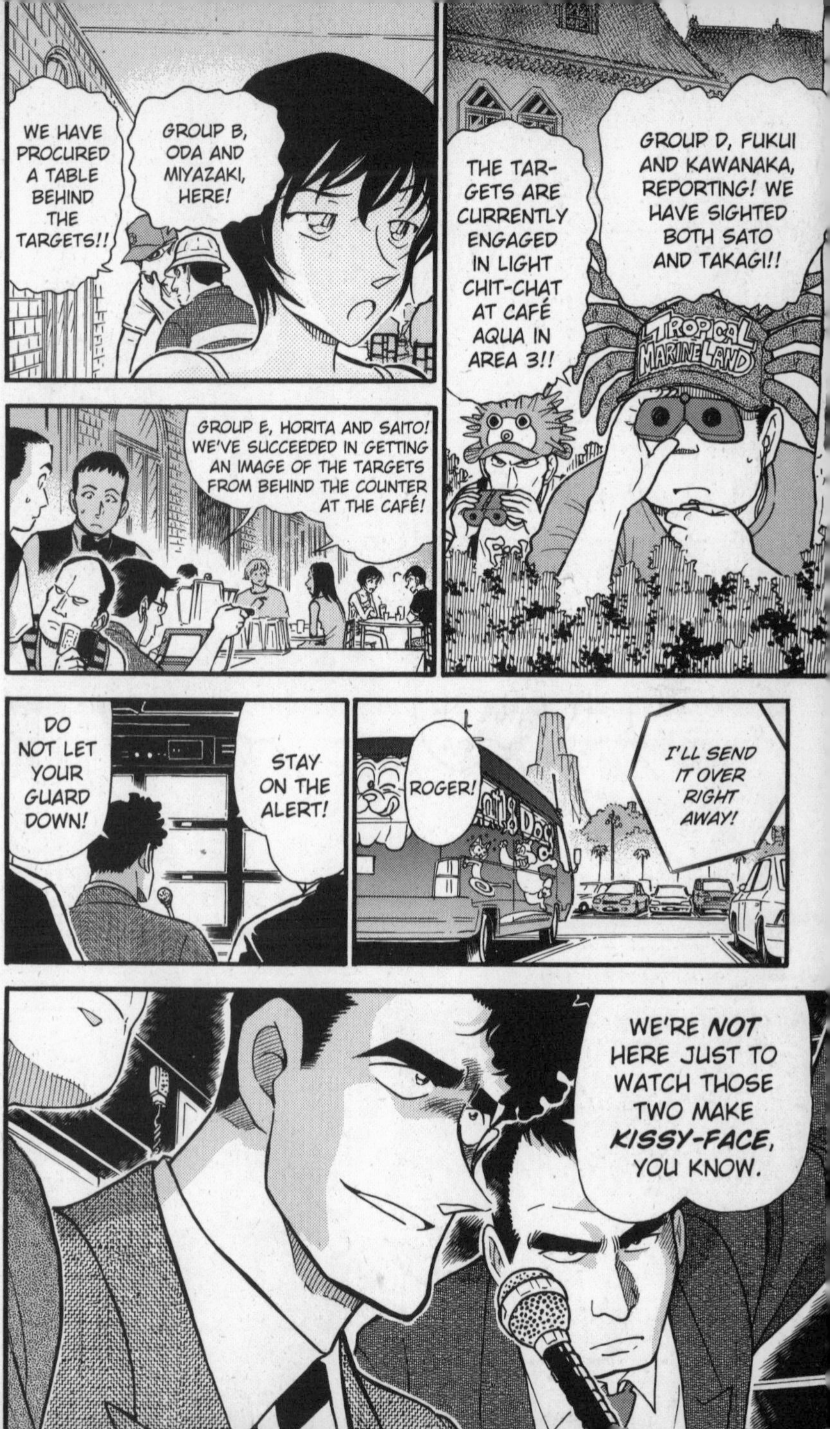
GROUP D, FUKUI AND KAWANAKA, REPORTING! WE HAVE SIGHTED BOTH SATO AND TAKAGI!!
THE TAR-GETS ARE CURRENTLY ENGAGED IN LIGHT CHIT-CHAT AT CAFÉ AQUA IN AREA 3!!
TROPICAL MARINELAND
GROUP B, ODA AND MIYAZAKI, HERE!
WE HAVE PROCURED A TABLE BEHIND THE TARGETS!!
GROUP E, HORITA AND SAITO! WE'VE SUCCEEDED IN GETTING AN IMAGE OF THE TARGETS FROM BEHIND THE COUNTER AT THE CAFÉ!
I'LL SEND IT OVER RIGHT AWAY!
ROGER!
STAY ON THE ALERT!
DO NOT LET YOUR GUARD DOWN!
WE'RE ***NOT*** HERE JUST TO WATCH THOSE TWO MAKE ***KISSY-FACE***, YOU KNOW.

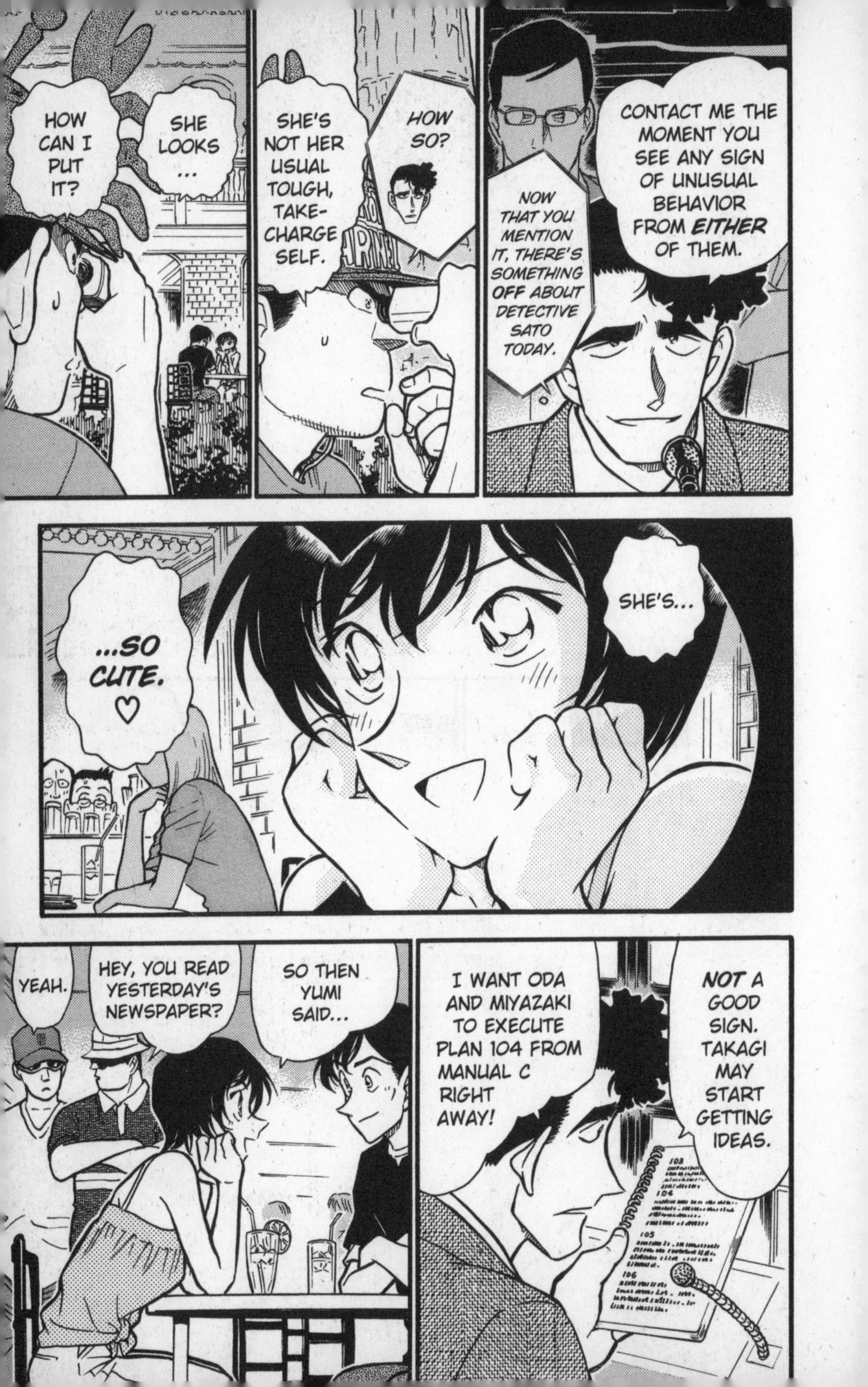
CONTACT ME THE MOMENT YOU SEE ANY SIGN OF UNUSUAL BEHAVIOR FROM *EITHER* OF THEM.
NOW THAT YOU MENTION IT, THERE'S SOMETHING *OFF* ABOUT DETECTIVE SATO TODAY.
HOW SO?
SHE'S NOT HER USUAL TOUGH, TAKE-CHARGE SELF.
SHE LOOKS ...
HOW CAN I PUT IT?
SHE'S...
...SO CUTE. ♡
NOT A GOOD SIGN. TAKAGI MAY START GETTING IDEAS.
I WANT ODA AND MIYAZAKI TO EXECUTE PLAN 104 FROM MANUAL C RIGHT AWAY!
SO THEN YUMI SAID...
HEY, YOU READ YESTERDAY'S NEWSPAPER?
YEAH.

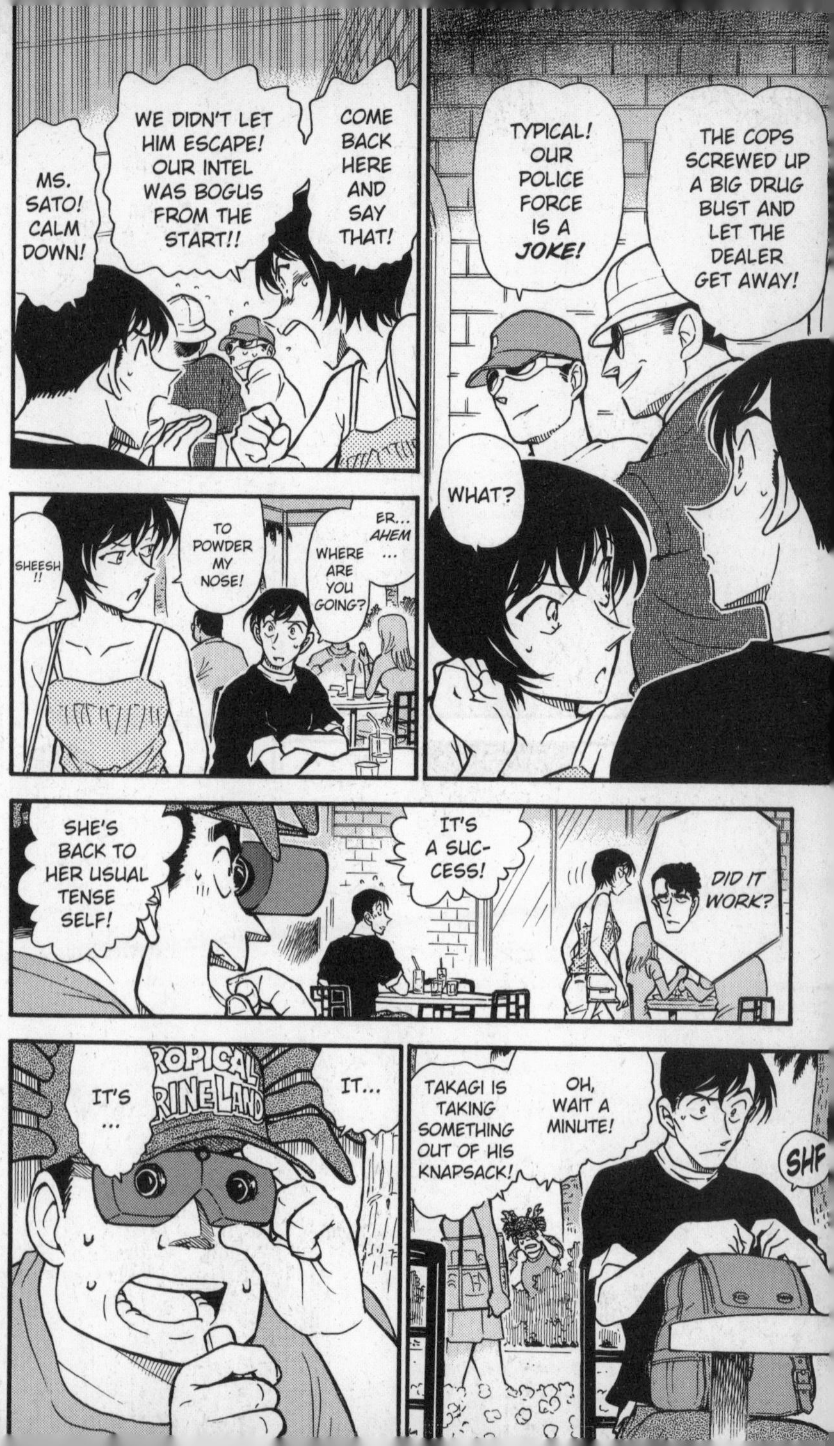
THE COPS SCREWED UP A BIG DRUG BUST AND LET THE DEALER GET AWAY!
TYPICAL! OUR POLICE FORCE IS A *JOKE!*
WHAT?
COME BACK HERE AND SAY THAT!
WE DIDN'T LET HIM ESCAPE! OUR INTEL WAS BOGUS FROM THE START!!
MS. SATO! CALM DOWN!
ER... *AHEM* ... WHERE ARE YOU GOING?
TO POWDER MY NOSE!
SHEESH!!
DID IT WORK?
IT'S A SUC-CESS!
SHE'S BACK TO HER USUAL TENSE SELF!
SHF
OH, WAIT A MINUTE!
TAKAGI IS TAKING SOMETHING OUT OF HIS KNAPSACK!
IT...
IT'S ...

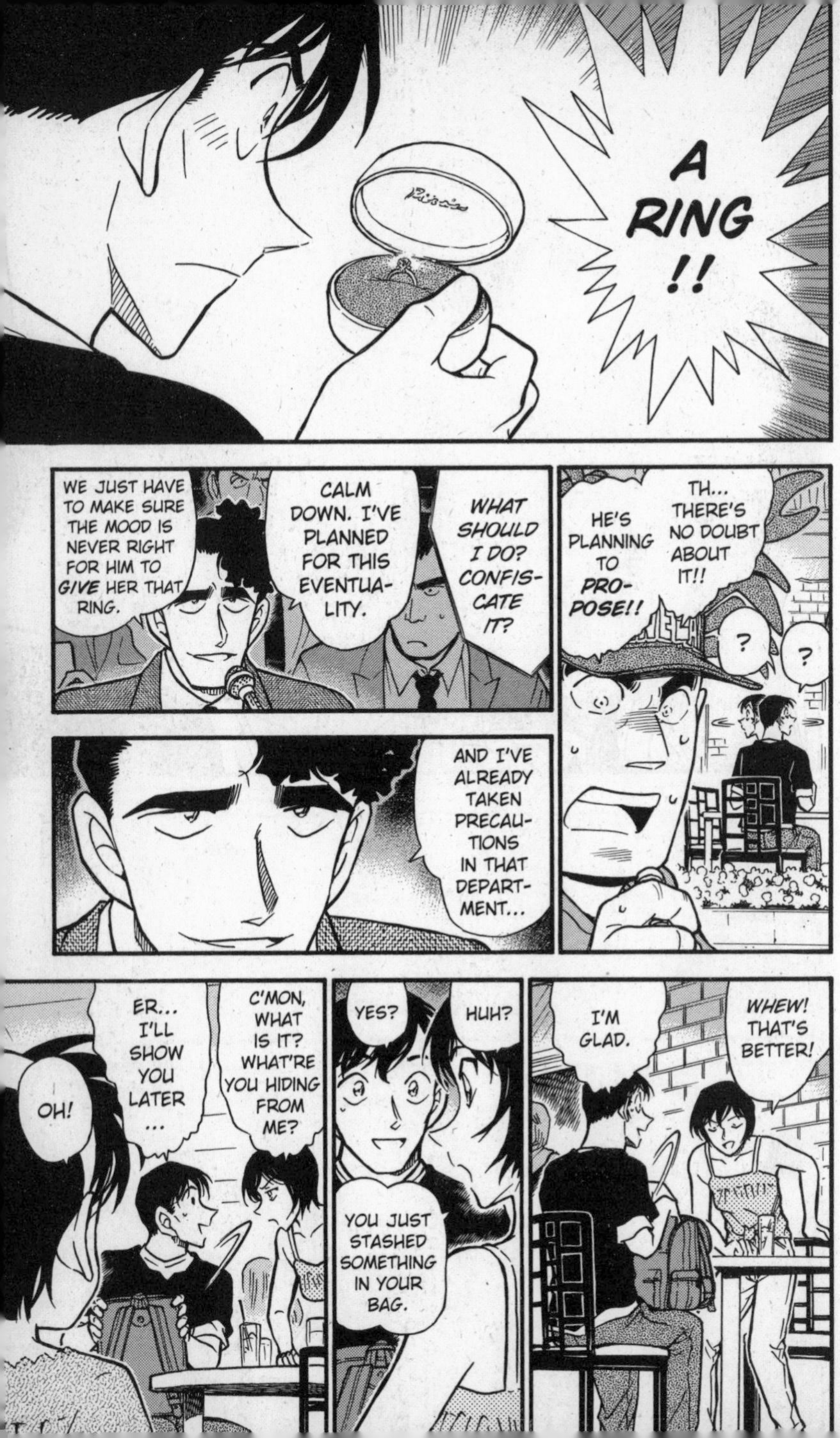
A RING!!
TH... THERE'S NO DOUBT ABOUT IT!!
HE'S PLANNING TO PROPOSE!!
?
?
WHAT SHOULD I DO? CONFISCATE IT?
CALM DOWN. I'VE PLANNED FOR THIS EVENTUALITY.
WE JUST HAVE TO MAKE SURE THE MOOD IS NEVER RIGHT FOR HIM TO GIVE HER THAT RING.
AND I'VE ALREADY TAKEN PRECAUTIONS IN THAT DEPARTMENT...
WHEW! THAT'S BETTER!
I'M GLAD.
HUH?
YES?
YOU JUST STASHED SOMETHING IN YOUR BAG.
C'MON, WHAT IS IT? WHAT'RE YOU HIDING FROM ME?
ER... I'LL SHOW YOU LATER...
OH!

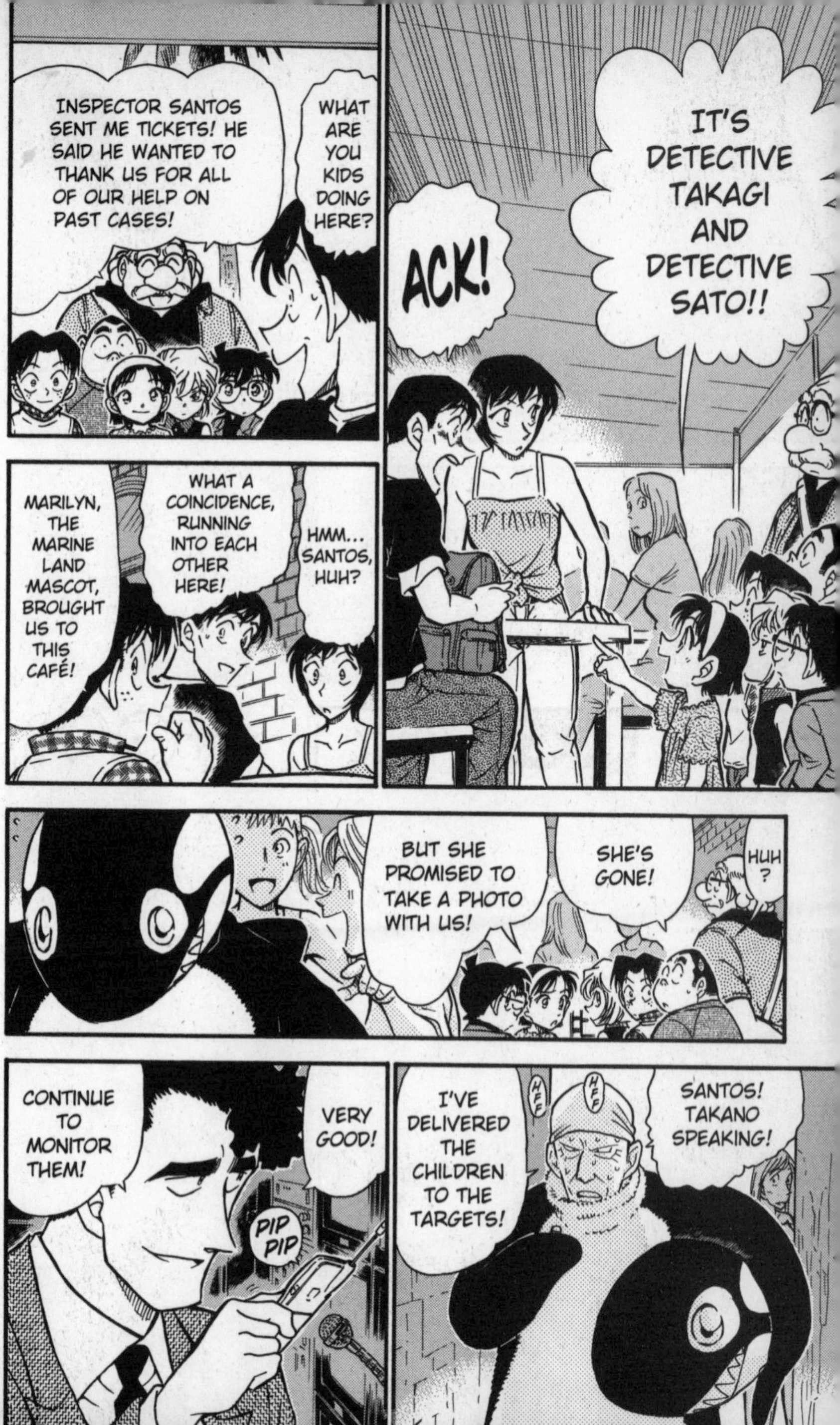
IT'S DETECTIVE TAKAGI AND DETECTIVE SATO!!
ACK!
WHAT ARE YOU KIDS DOING HERE?
INSPECTOR SANTOS SENT ME TICKETS! HE SAID HE WANTED TO THANK US FOR ALL OF OUR HELP ON PAST CASES!
HMM... SANTOS, HUH?
WHAT A COINCIDENCE, RUNNING INTO EACH OTHER HERE!
MARILYN, THE MARINE LAND MASCOT, BROUGHT US TO THIS CAFÉ!
HUH?
SHE'S GONE!
BUT SHE PROMISED TO TAKE A PHOTO WITH US!
SANTOS! TAKANO SPEAKING!
HFF
HFF
I'VE DELIVERED THE CHILDREN TO THE TARGETS!
VERY GOOD!
PIP PIP
CONTINUE TO MONITOR THEM!

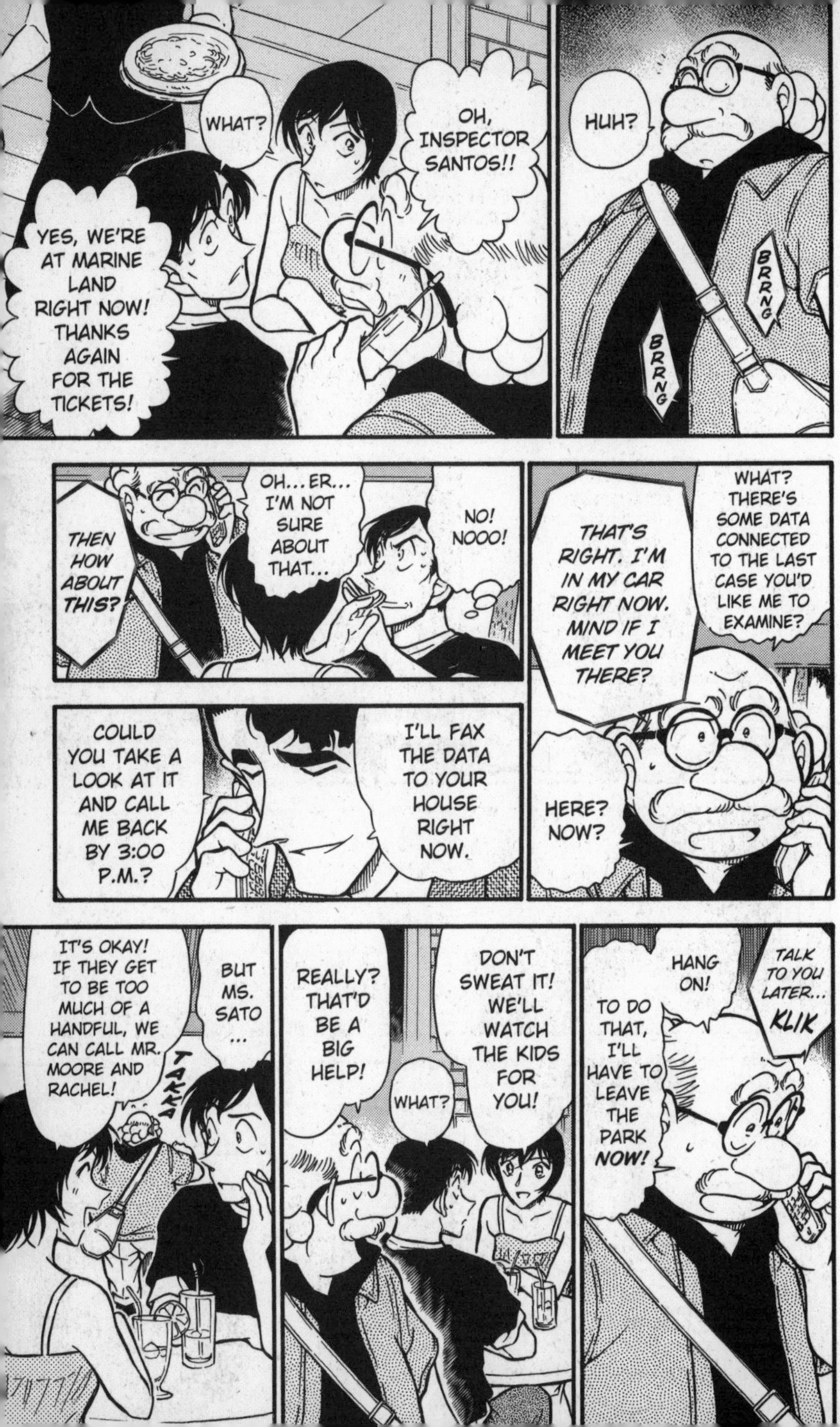
HUH?
BRRNG
BRRNG
OH, INSPECTOR SANTOS!!
WHAT?
YES, WE'RE AT MARINE LAND RIGHT NOW! THANKS AGAIN FOR THE TICKETS!
WHAT? THERE'S SOME DATA CONNECTED TO THE LAST CASE YOU'D LIKE ME TO EXAMINE?
THAT'S RIGHT. I'M IN MY CAR RIGHT NOW. MIND IF I MEET YOU THERE?
HERE? NOW?
NO! NOOO!
OH... ER... I'M NOT SURE ABOUT THAT...
THEN HOW ABOUT THIS?
I'LL FAX THE DATA TO YOUR HOUSE RIGHT NOW.
COULD YOU TAKE A LOOK AT IT AND CALL ME BACK BY 3:00 P.M.?
TALK TO YOU LATER... KLIK
HANG ON!
TO DO THAT, I'LL HAVE TO LEAVE THE PARK NOW!
DON'T SWEAT IT! WE'LL WATCH THE KIDS FOR YOU!
REALLY? THAT'D BE A BIG HELP!
WHAT?
BUT MS. SATO ...
IT'S OKAY! IF THEY GET TO BE TOO MUCH OF A HANDFUL, WE CAN CALL MR. MOORE AND RACHEL!
TAKKA

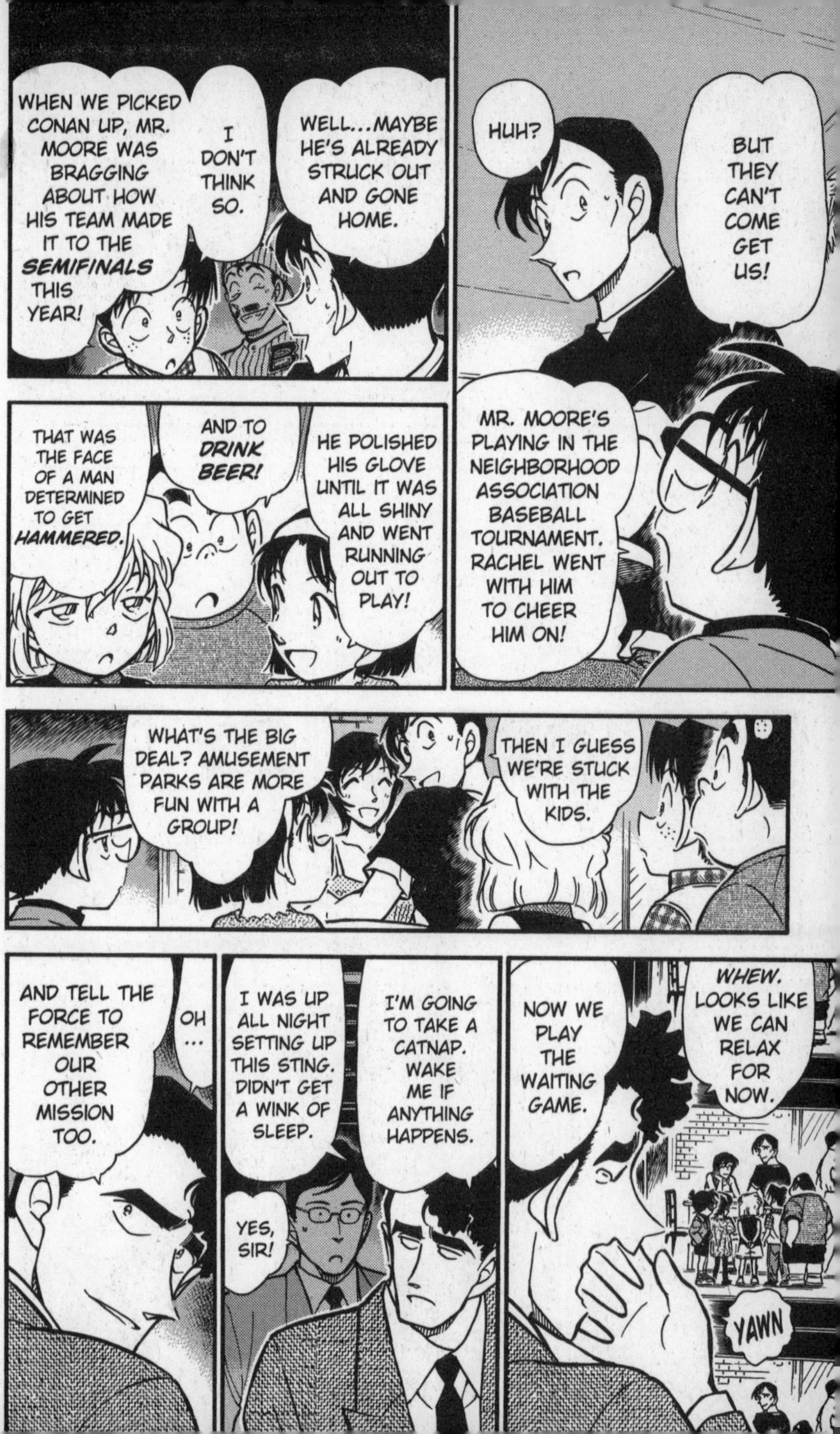
BUT THEY CAN'T COME GET US!
HUH?
WELL...MAYBE HE'S ALREADY STRUCK OUT AND GONE HOME.
I DON'T THINK SO.
WHEN WE PICKED CONAN UP, MR. MOORE WAS BRAGGING ABOUT HOW HIS TEAM MADE IT TO THE SEMIFINALS THIS YEAR!
MR. MOORE'S PLAYING IN THE NEIGHBORHOOD ASSOCIATION BASEBALL TOURNAMENT. RACHEL WENT WITH HIM TO CHEER HIM ON!
HE POLISHED HIS GLOVE UNTIL IT WAS ALL SHINY AND WENT RUNNING OUT TO PLAY!
AND TO DRINK BEER!
THAT WAS THE FACE OF A MAN DETERMINED TO GET HAMMERED.
THEN I GUESS WE'RE STUCK WITH THE KIDS.
WHAT'S THE BIG DEAL? AMUSEMENT PARKS ARE MORE FUN WITH A GROUP!
WHEW. LOOKS LIKE WE CAN RELAX FOR NOW.
NOW WE PLAY THE WAITING GAME.
YAWN
I'M GOING TO TAKE A CATNAP. WAKE ME IF ANYTHING HAPPENS.
I WAS UP ALL NIGHT SETTING UP THIS STING. DIDN'T GET A WINK OF SLEEP.
YES, SIR!
OH...
AND TELL THE FORCE TO REMEMBER OUR OTHER MISSION TOO.

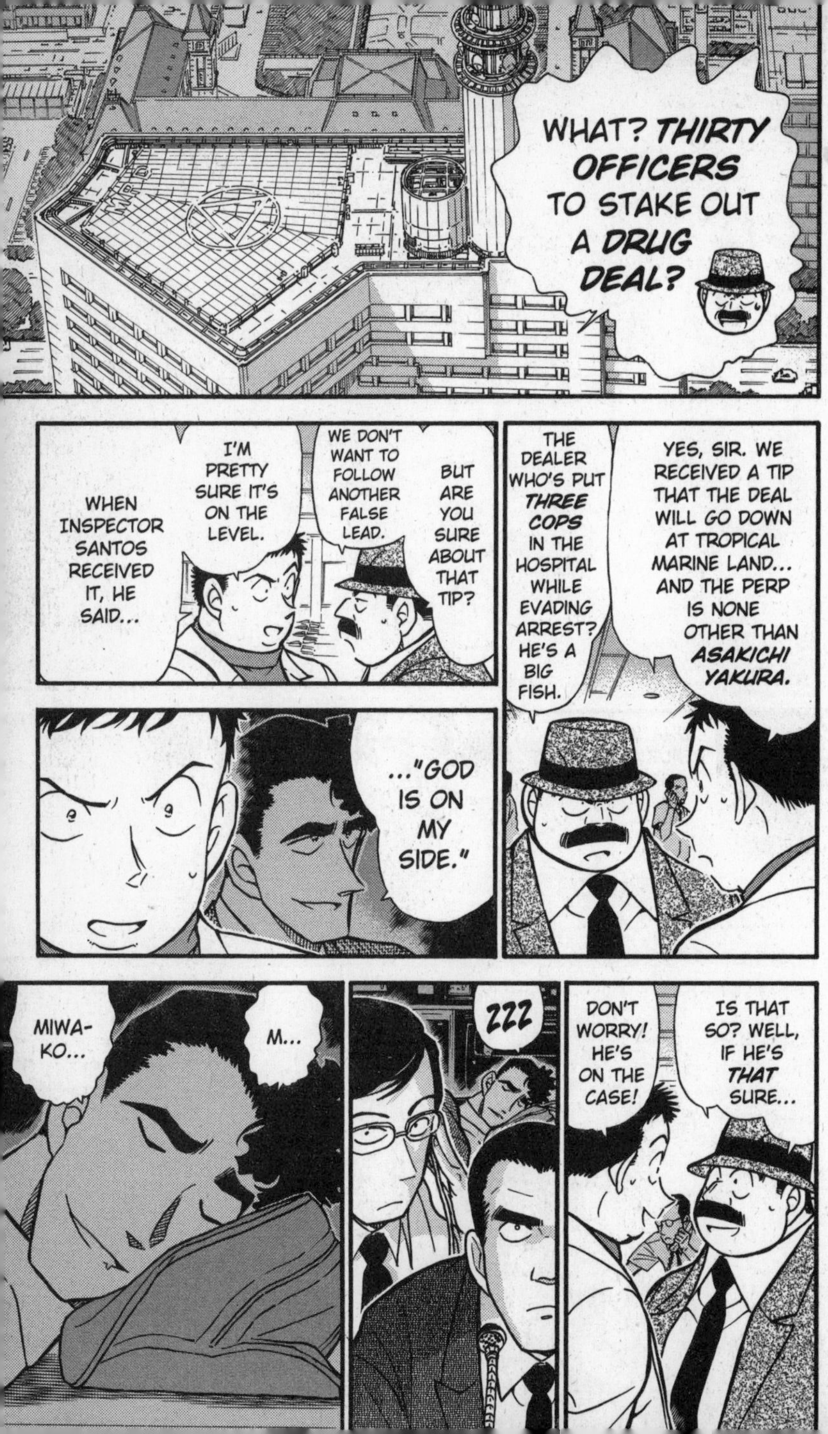
WHAT? THIRTY OFFICERS TO STAKE OUT A DRUG DEAL?
YES, SIR. WE RECEIVED A TIP THAT THE DEAL WILL GO DOWN AT TROPICAL MARINE LAND... AND THE PERP IS NONE OTHER THAN ASAKICHI YAKURA.
THE DEALER WHO'S PUT THREE COPS IN THE HOSPITAL WHILE EVADING ARREST? HE'S A BIG FISH.
BUT ARE YOU SURE ABOUT THAT TIP?
WE DON'T WANT TO FOLLOW ANOTHER FALSE LEAD.
I'M PRETTY SURE IT'S ON THE LEVEL.
WHEN INSPECTOR SANTOS RECEIVED IT, HE SAID...
..."GOD IS ON MY SIDE."
IS THAT SO? WELL, IF HE'S THAT SURE...
DON'T WORRY! HE'S ON THE CASE!
ZZZ
M...
MIWAKO...

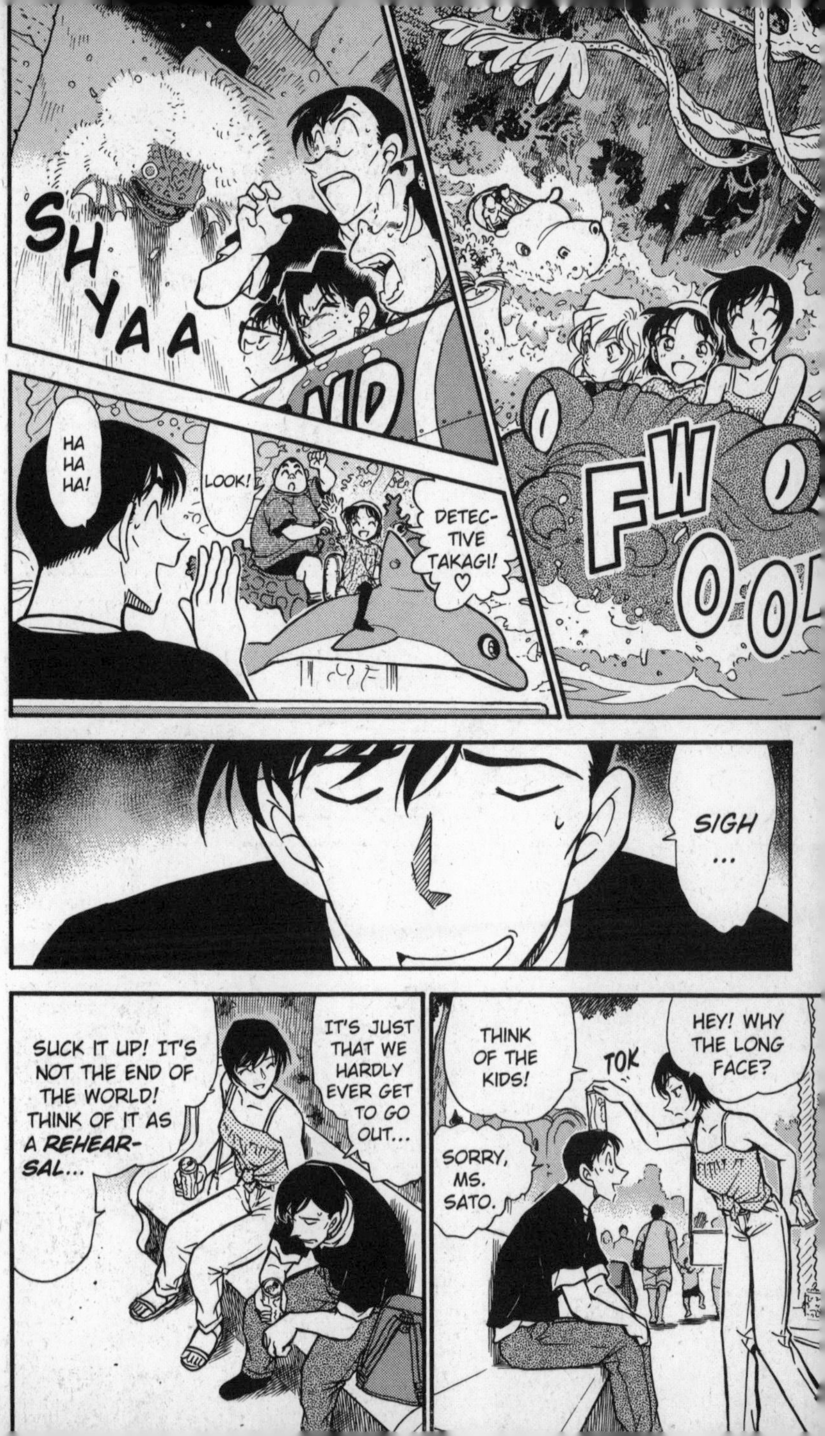
FWOOOO
SHYAA
DETEC-TIVE TAKAGI! ♡
LOOK!
HA HA HA!
SIGH...
HEY! WHY THE LONG FACE?
TOK
THINK OF THE KIDS!
SORRY, MS. SATO.
IT'S JUST THAT WE HARDLY EVER GET TO GO OUT...
SUCK IT UP! IT'S NOT THE END OF THE WORLD! THINK OF IT AS A *REHEAR-SAL*...

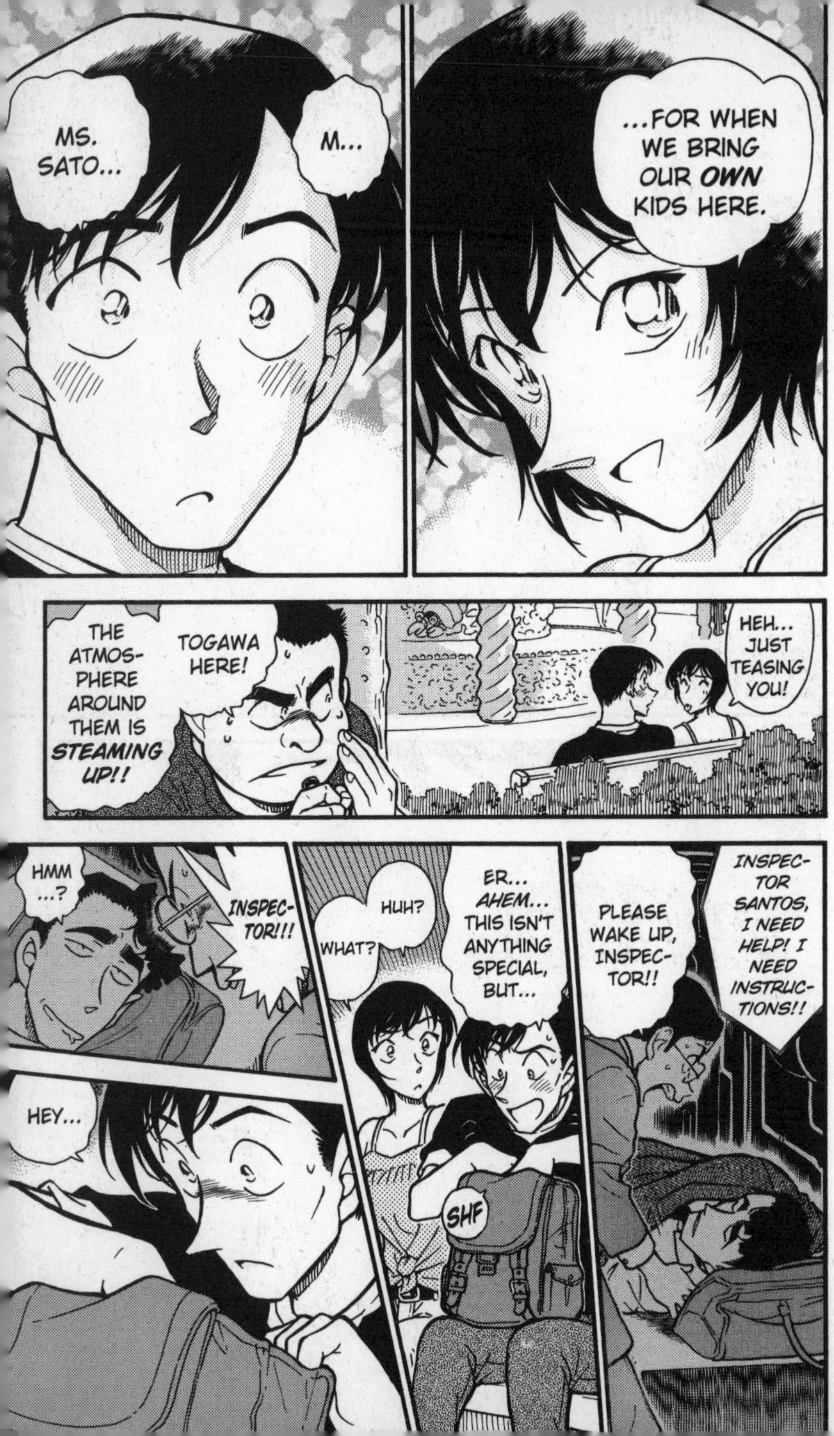
...FOR WHEN WE BRING OUR *OWN* KIDS HERE.
M...
MS. SATO...
HEH... JUST TEASING YOU!
TOGAWA HERE!
THE ATMOS-PHERE AROUND THEM IS *STEAMING UP!!*
INSPEC-TOR SANTOS, I NEED HELP! I NEED INSTRUC-TIONS!!
PLEASE WAKE UP, INSPEC-TOR!!
ER... *AHEM...* THIS ISN'T ANYTHING SPECIAL, BUT...
HUH?
WHAT?
SHF
INSPEC-TOR!!!
HMM ...?
HEY...

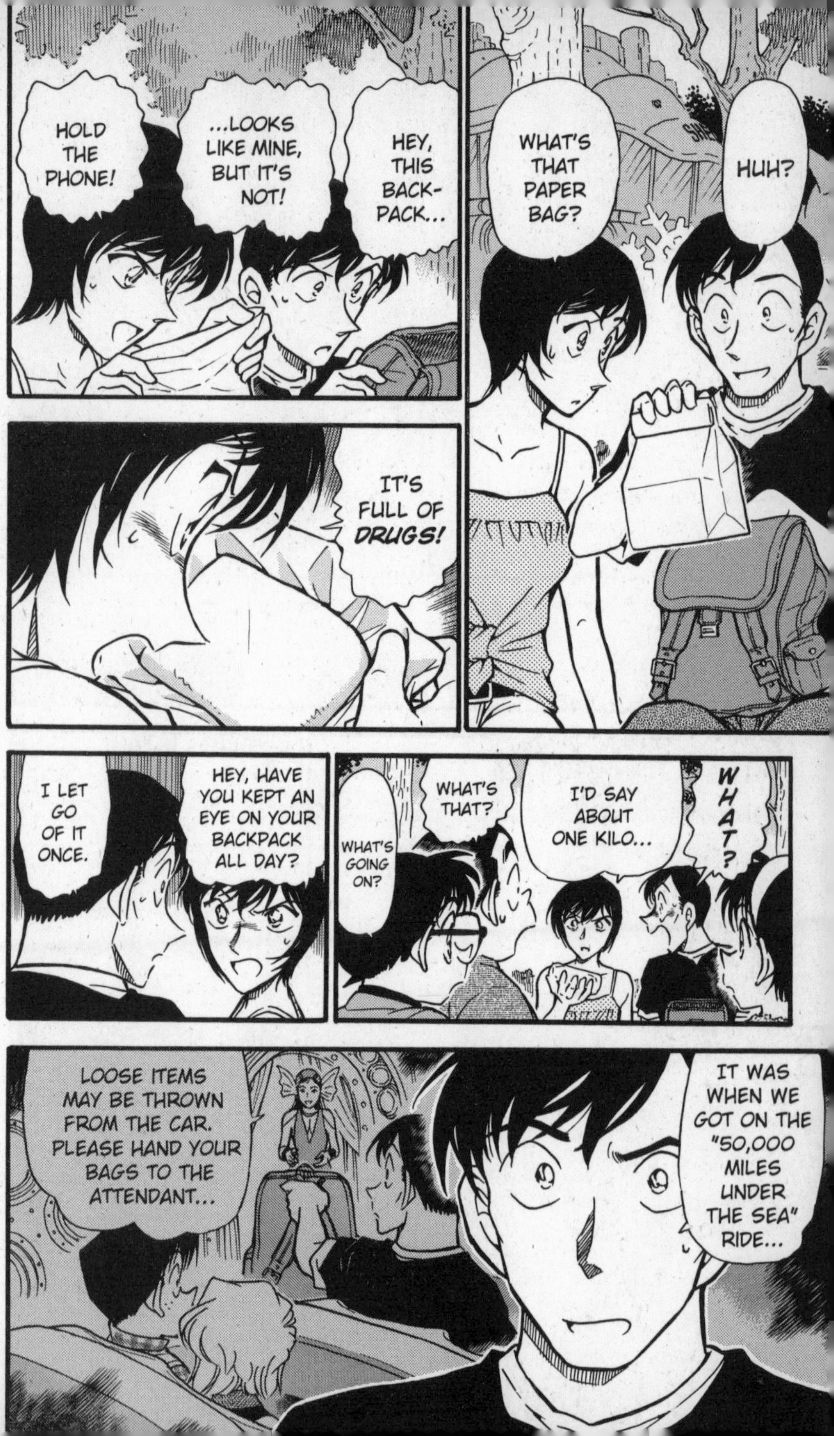
HUH?
WHAT'S THAT PAPER BAG?
HEY, THIS BACK-PACK...
...LOOKS LIKE MINE, BUT IT'S NOT!
HOLD THE PHONE!
IT'S FULL OF DRUGS!
WHAT?
I'D SAY ABOUT ONE KILO...
WHAT'S THAT?
WHAT'S GOING ON?
HEY, HAVE YOU KEPT AN EYE ON YOUR BACKPACK ALL DAY?
I LET GO OF IT ONCE.
IT WAS WHEN WE GOT ON THE "50,000 MILES UNDER THE SEA" RIDE...
LOOSE ITEMS MAY BE THROWN FROM THE CAR. PLEASE HAND YOUR BAGS TO THE ATTENDANT...

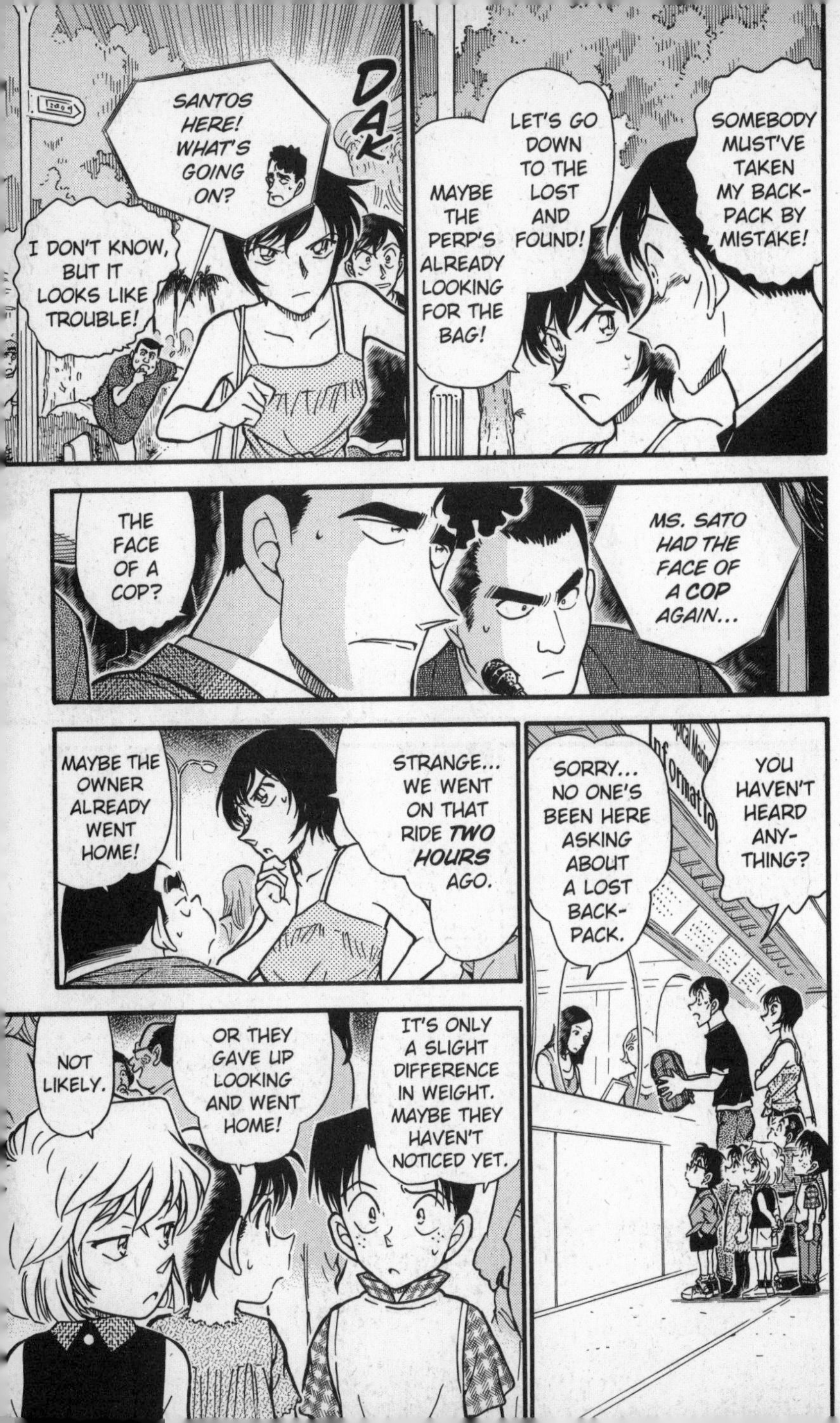
SOMEBODY MUST'VE TAKEN MY BACK-PACK BY MISTAKE!
LET'S GO DOWN TO THE LOST AND FOUND!
MAYBE THE PERP'S ALREADY LOOKING FOR THE BAG!
DAK
SANTOS HERE! WHAT'S GOING ON?
I DON'T KNOW, BUT IT LOOKS LIKE TROUBLE!
MS. SATO HAD THE FACE OF A COP AGAIN...
THE FACE OF A COP?
YOU HAVEN'T HEARD ANY-THING?
SORRY... NO ONE'S BEEN HERE ASKING ABOUT A LOST BACK-PACK.
STRANGE... WE WENT ON THAT RIDE TWO HOURS AGO.
MAYBE THE OWNER ALREADY WENT HOME!
IT'S ONLY A SLIGHT DIFFERENCE IN WEIGHT. MAYBE THEY HAVEN'T NOTICED YET.
OR THEY GAVE UP LOOKING AND WENT HOME!
NOT LIKELY.

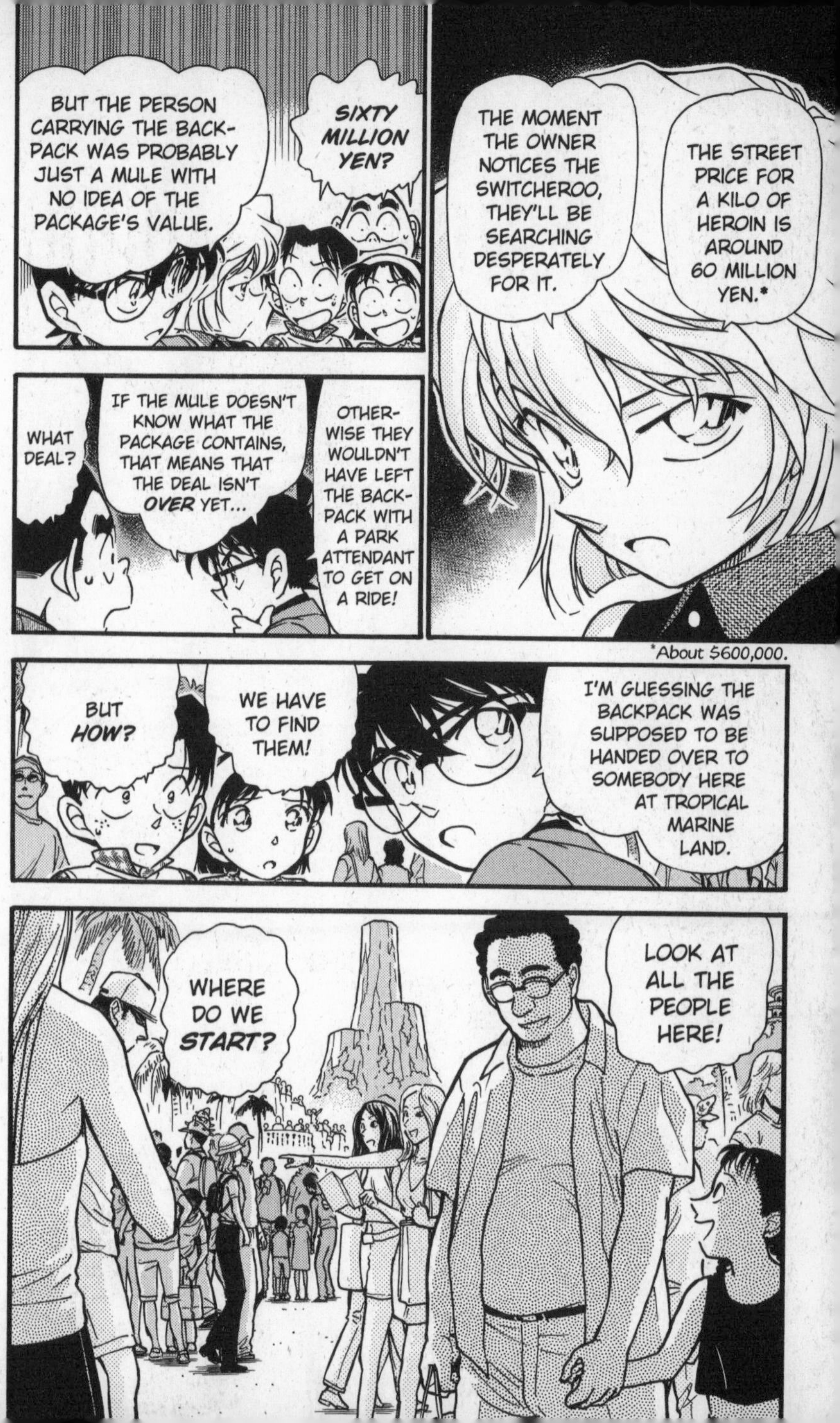
THE STREET PRICE FOR A KILO OF HEROIN IS AROUND 60 MILLION YEN.*
THE MOMENT THE OWNER NOTICES THE SWITCHEROO, THEY'LL BE SEARCHING DESPERATELY FOR IT.
SIXTY MILLION YEN?
BUT THE PERSON CARRYING THE BACK-PACK WAS PROBABLY JUST A MULE WITH NO IDEA OF THE PACKAGE'S VALUE.
OTHER-WISE THEY WOULDN'T HAVE LEFT THE BACK-PACK WITH A PARK ATTENDANT TO GET ON A RIDE!
IF THE MULE DOESN'T KNOW WHAT THE PACKAGE CONTAINS, THAT MEANS THAT THE DEAL ISN'T OVER YET...
WHAT DEAL?
*About $600,000.
I'M GUESSING THE BACKPACK WAS SUPPOSED TO BE HANDED OVER TO SOMEBODY HERE AT TROPICAL MARINE LAND.
WE HAVE TO FIND THEM!
BUT HOW?
LOOK AT ALL THE PEOPLE HERE!
WHERE DO WE START?

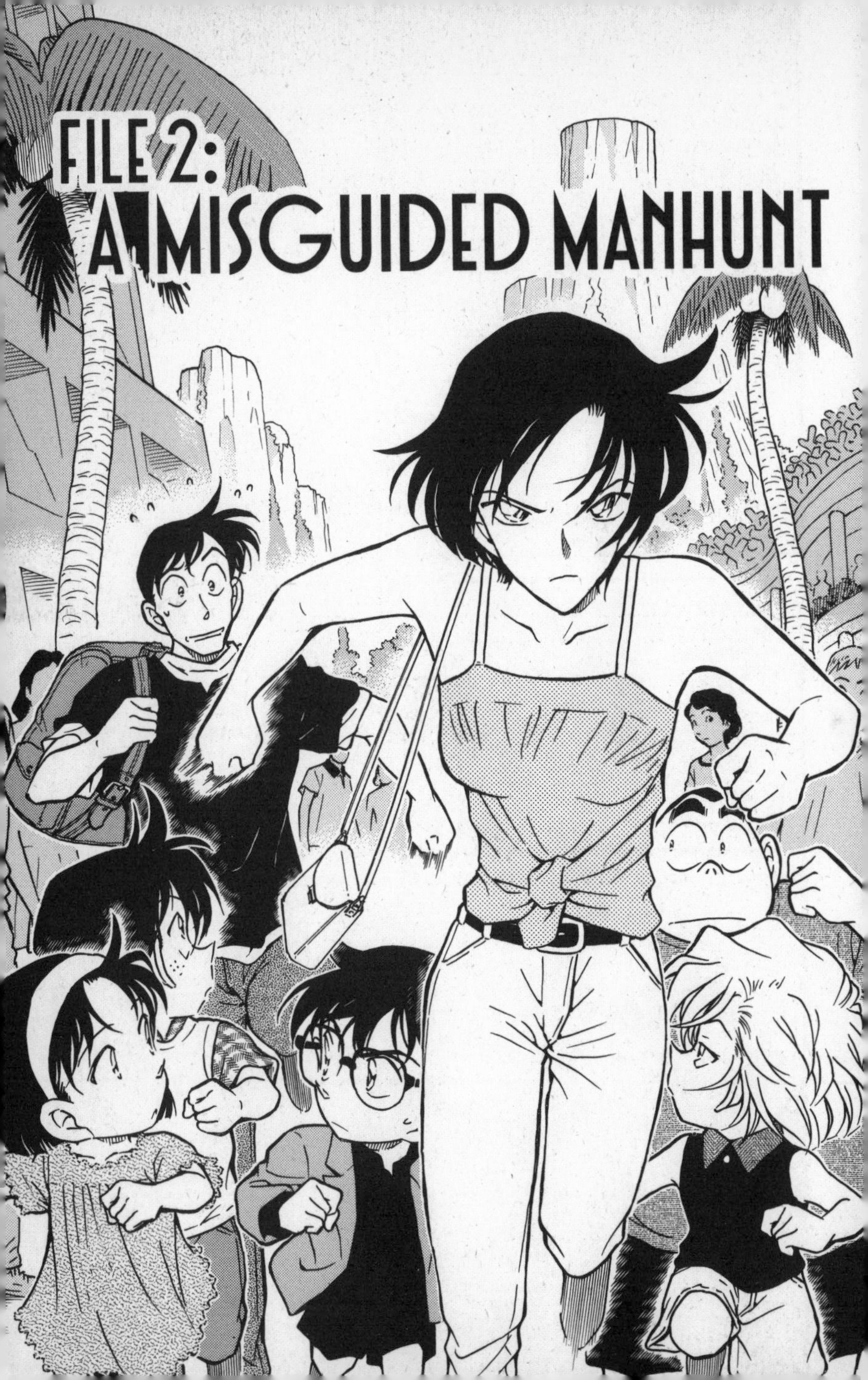
FILE 2:
A MISGUIDED MANHUNT

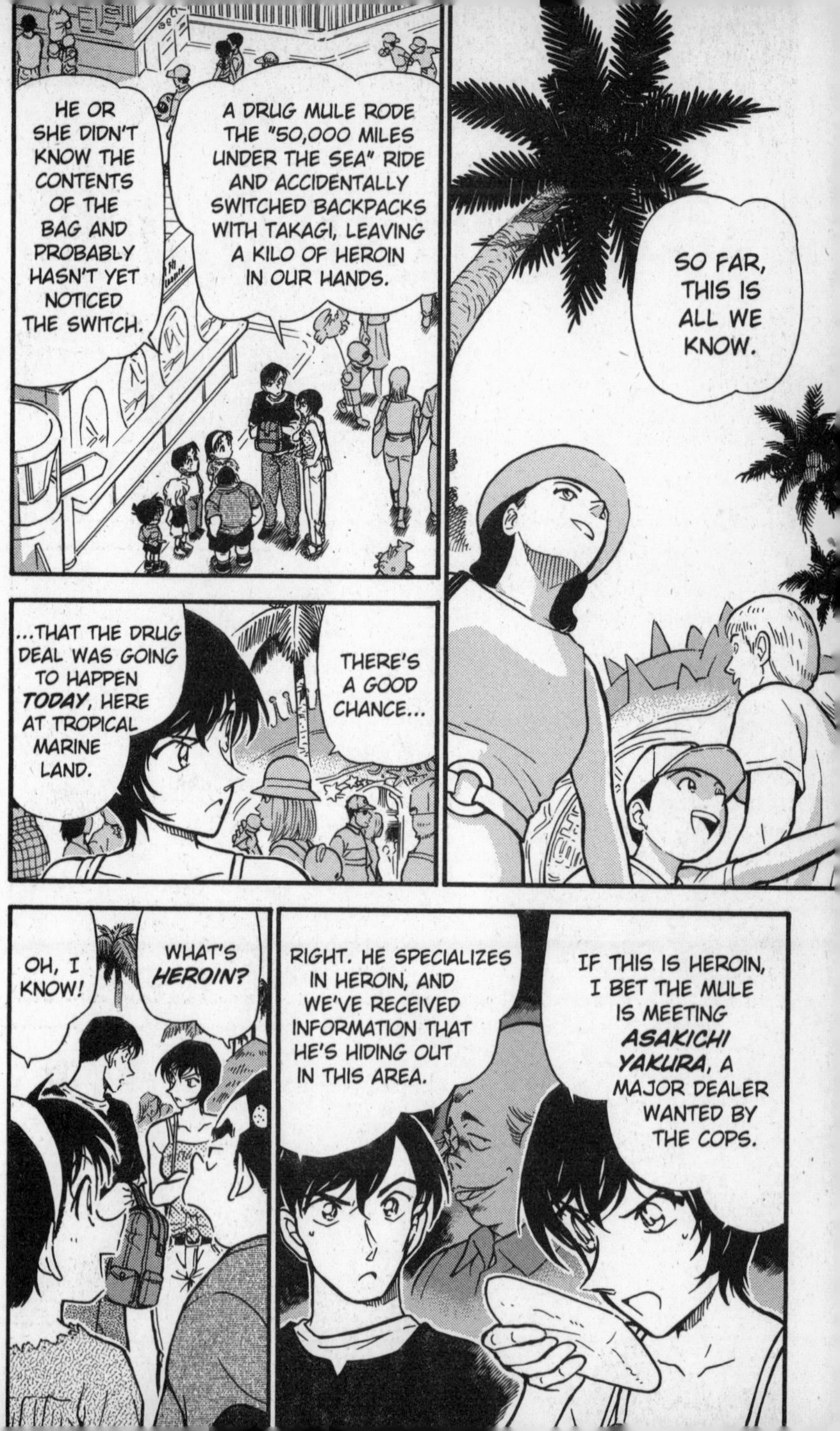
SO FAR, THIS IS ALL WE KNOW.
A DRUG MULE RODE THE "50,000 MILES UNDER THE SEA" RIDE AND ACCIDENTALLY SWITCHED BACKPACKS WITH TAKAGI, LEAVING A KILO OF HEROIN IN OUR HANDS.
HE OR SHE DIDN'T KNOW THE CONTENTS OF THE BAG AND PROBABLY HASN'T YET NOTICED THE SWITCH.
THERE'S A GOOD CHANCE...
...THAT THE DRUG DEAL WAS GOING TO HAPPEN *TODAY*, HERE AT TROPICAL MARINE LAND.
IF THIS IS HEROIN, I BET THE MULE IS MEETING ***ASAKICHI YAKURA***, A MAJOR DEALER WANTED BY THE COPS.
RIGHT. HE SPECIALIZES IN HEROIN, AND WE'VE RECEIVED INFORMATION THAT HE'S HIDING OUT IN THIS AREA.
WHAT'S ***HEROIN?***
OH, I KNOW!

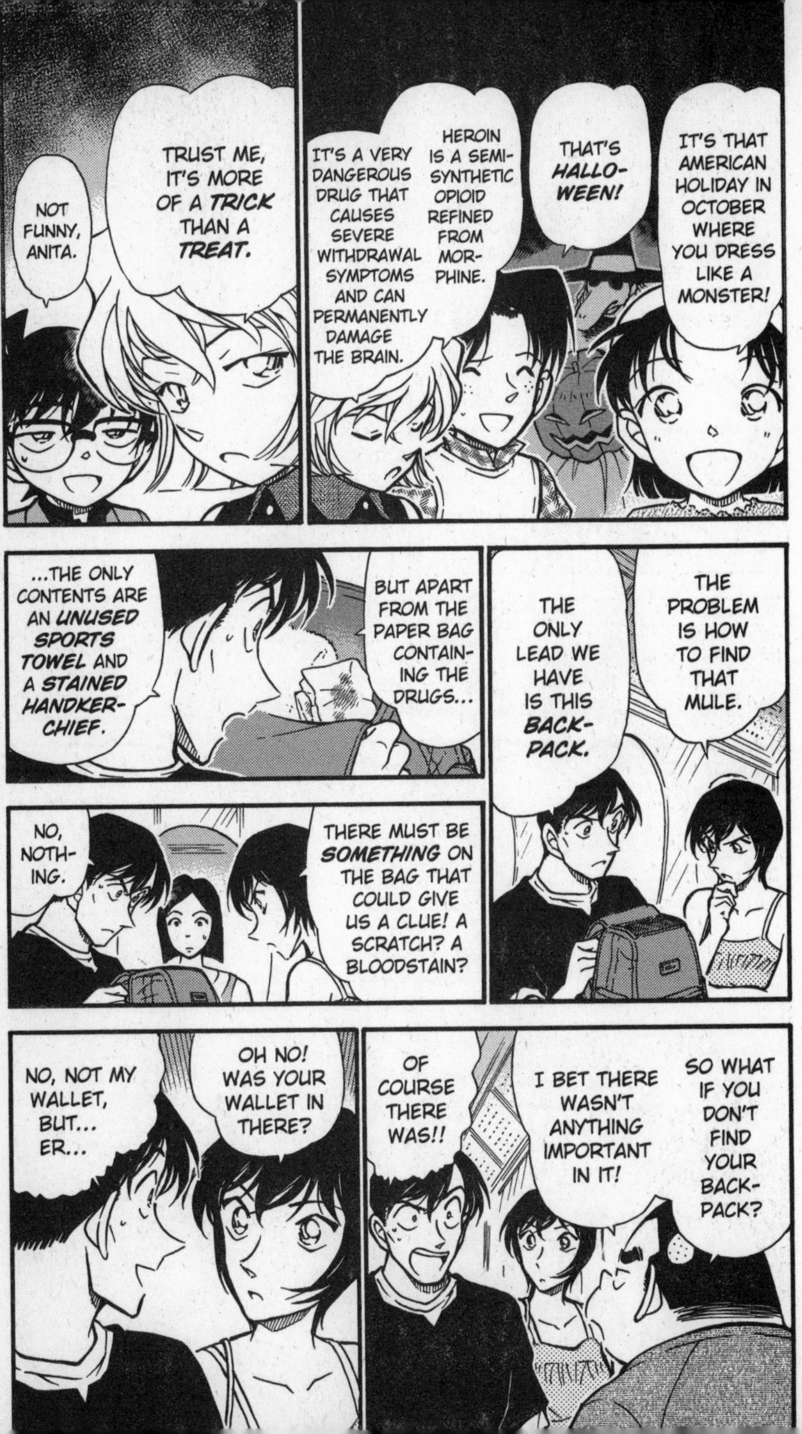
IT'S THAT AMERICAN HOLIDAY IN OCTOBER WHERE YOU DRESS LIKE A MONSTER!
THAT'S HALLOWEEN!
HEROIN IS A SEMI-SYNTHETIC OPIOID REFINED FROM MORPHINE.
IT'S A VERY DANGEROUS DRUG THAT CAUSES SEVERE WITHDRAWAL SYMPTOMS AND CAN PERMANENTLY DAMAGE THE BRAIN.
TRUST ME, IT'S MORE OF A TRICK THAN A TREAT.
NOT FUNNY, ANITA.
THE PROBLEM IS HOW TO FIND THAT MULE.
THE ONLY LEAD WE HAVE IS THIS BACKPACK.
BUT APART FROM THE PAPER BAG CONTAINING THE DRUGS...
...THE ONLY CONTENTS ARE AN UNUSED SPORTS TOWEL AND A STAINED HANDKERCHIEF.
THERE MUST BE SOMETHING ON THE BAG THAT COULD GIVE US A CLUE! A SCRATCH? A BLOODSTAIN?
NO, NOTHING.
SO WHAT IF YOU DON'T FIND YOUR BACKPACK?
I BET THERE WASN'T ANYTHING IMPORTANT IN IT!
OF COURSE THERE WAS!!
OH NO! WAS YOUR WALLET IN THERE?
NO, NOT MY WALLET, BUT... ER...

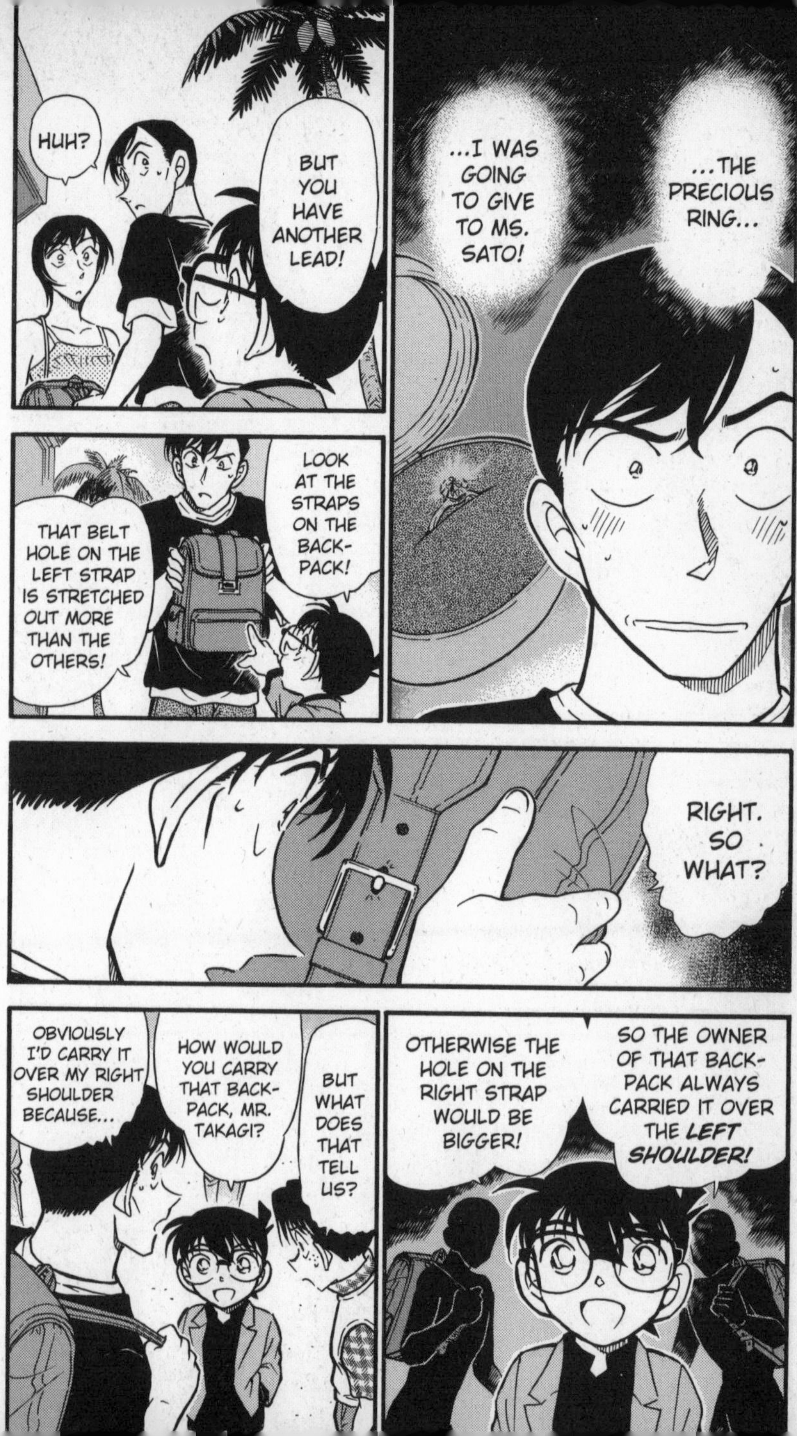
...THE PRECIOUS RING...
...I WAS GOING TO GIVE TO MS. SATO!
BUT YOU HAVE ANOTHER LEAD!
HUH?
LOOK AT THE STRAPS ON THE BACK-PACK!
THAT BELT HOLE ON THE LEFT STRAP IS STRETCHED OUT MORE THAN THE OTHERS!
RIGHT. SO WHAT?
SO THE OWNER OF THAT BACK-PACK ALWAYS CARRIED IT OVER THE *LEFT SHOULDER!*
OTHERWISE THE HOLE ON THE RIGHT STRAP WOULD BE BIGGER!
BUT WHAT DOES THAT TELL US?
HOW WOULD YOU CARRY THAT BACK-PACK, MR. TAKAGI?
OBVIOUSLY I'D CARRY IT OVER MY RIGHT SHOULDER BECAUSE...

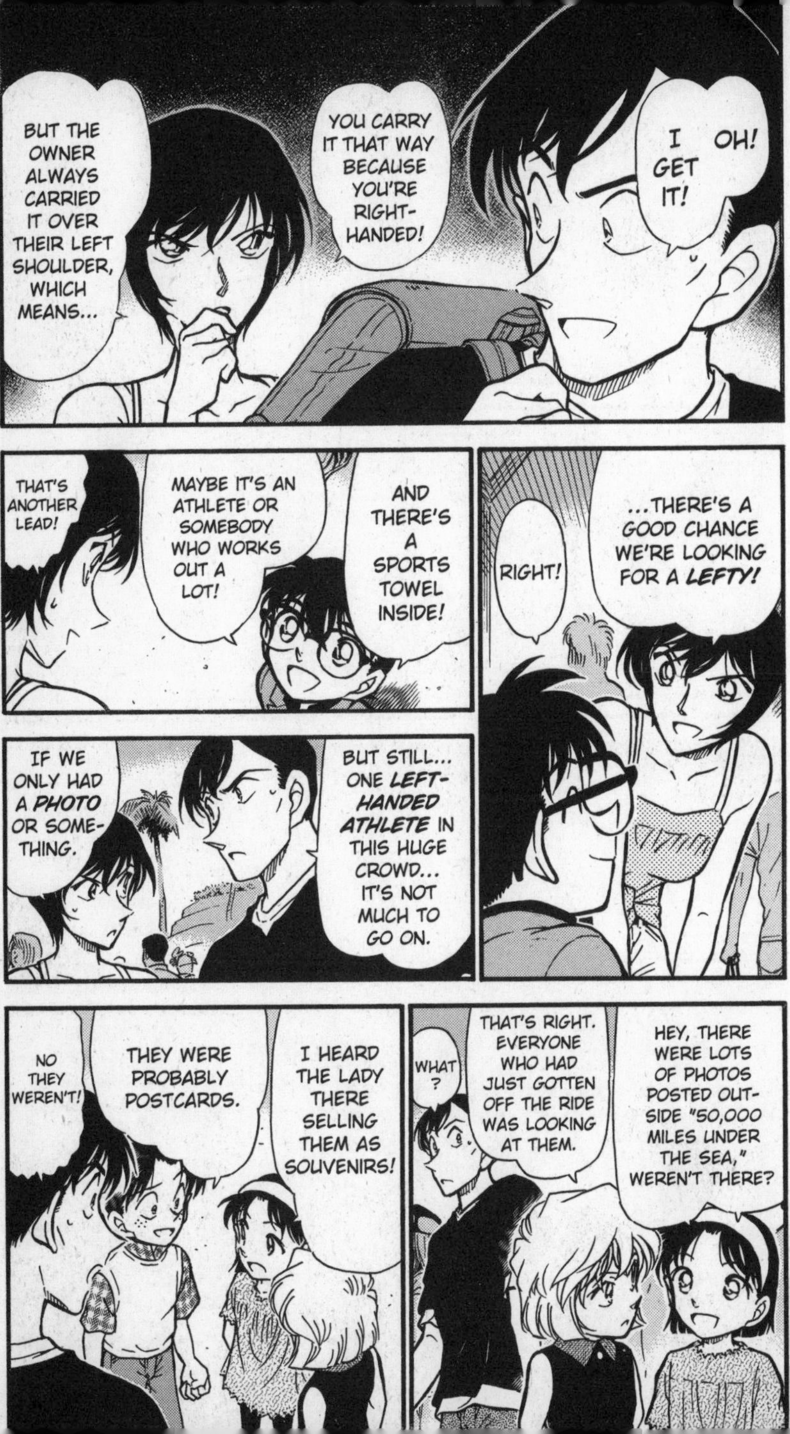
OH! I GET IT!
YOU CARRY IT THAT WAY BECAUSE YOU'RE RIGHT-HANDED!
BUT THE OWNER ALWAYS CARRIED IT OVER THEIR LEFT SHOULDER, WHICH MEANS...
...THERE'S A GOOD CHANCE WE'RE LOOKING FOR A *LEFTY!*
RIGHT!
AND THERE'S A SPORTS TOWEL INSIDE!
MAYBE IT'S AN ATHLETE OR SOMEBODY WHO WORKS OUT A LOT!
THAT'S ANOTHER LEAD!
BUT STILL... ONE *LEFT-HANDED ATHLETE* IN THIS HUGE CROWD... IT'S NOT MUCH TO GO ON.
IF WE ONLY HAD A *PHOTO* OR SOME-THING.
HEY, THERE WERE LOTS OF PHOTOS POSTED OUT-SIDE "50,000 MILES UNDER THE SEA," WEREN'T THERE?
THAT'S RIGHT. EVERYONE WHO HAD JUST GOTTEN OFF THE RIDE WAS LOOKING AT THEM.
WHAT?
I HEARD THE LADY THERE SELLING THEM AS SOUVENIRS!
THEY WERE PROBABLY POSTCARDS.
NO THEY WEREN'T!

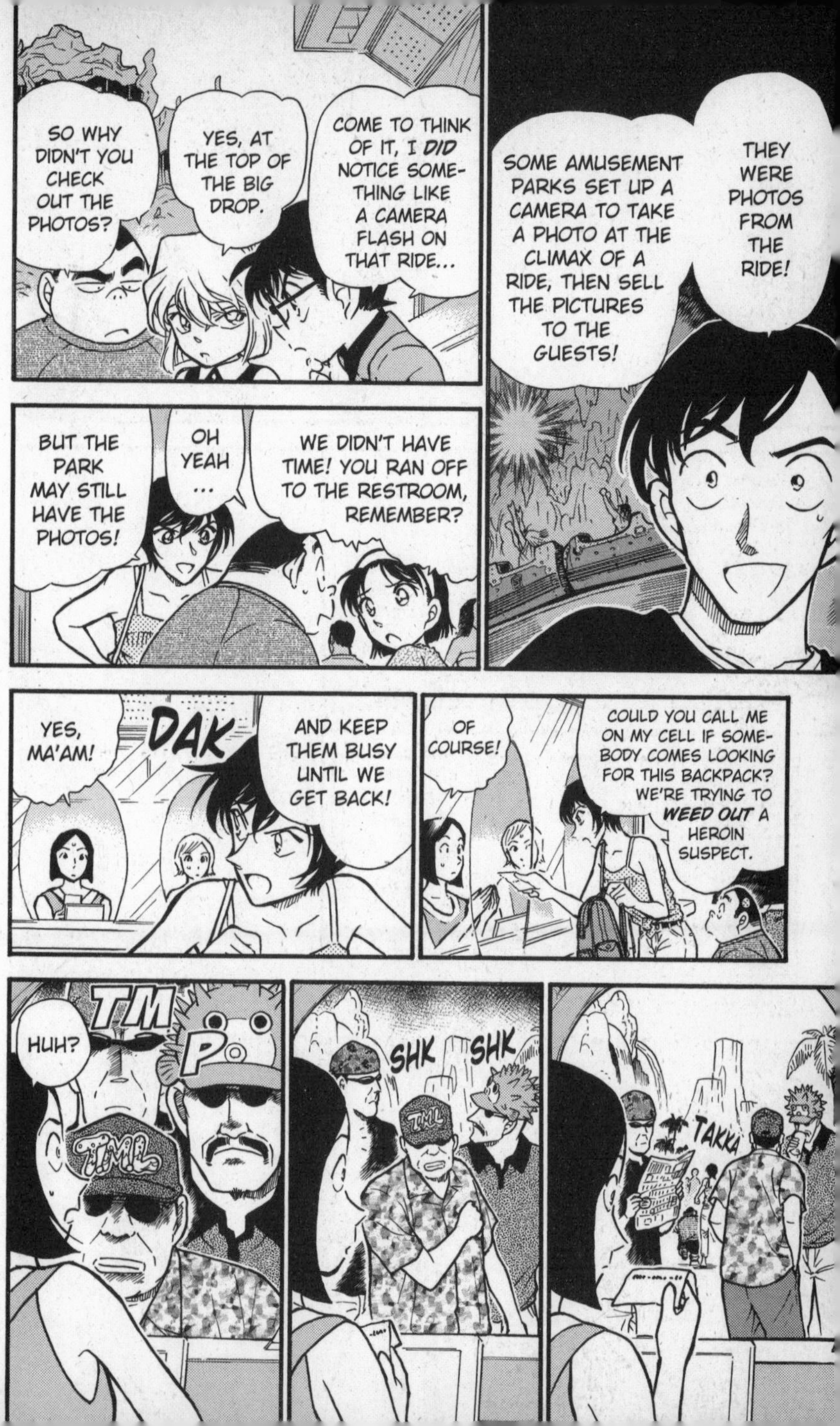
THEY WERE PHOTOS FROM THE RIDE!
SOME AMUSEMENT PARKS SET UP A CAMERA TO TAKE A PHOTO AT THE CLIMAX OF A RIDE, THEN SELL THE PICTURES TO THE GUESTS!
COME TO THINK OF IT, I *DID* NOTICE SOME-THING LIKE A CAMERA FLASH ON THAT RIDE...
YES, AT THE TOP OF THE BIG DROP.
SO WHY DIDN'T YOU CHECK OUT THE PHOTOS?
WE DIDN'T HAVE TIME! YOU RAN OFF TO THE RESTROOM, REMEMBER?
OH YEAH ...
BUT THE PARK MAY STILL HAVE THE PHOTOS!
COULD YOU CALL ME ON MY CELL IF SOME-BODY COMES LOOKING FOR THIS BACKPACK? WE'RE TRYING TO ***WEED OUT*** A HEROIN SUSPECT.
OF COURSE!
AND KEEP THEM BUSY UNTIL WE GET BACK!
DAK
YES, MA'AM!
TAKKA
SHK SHK
HUH?

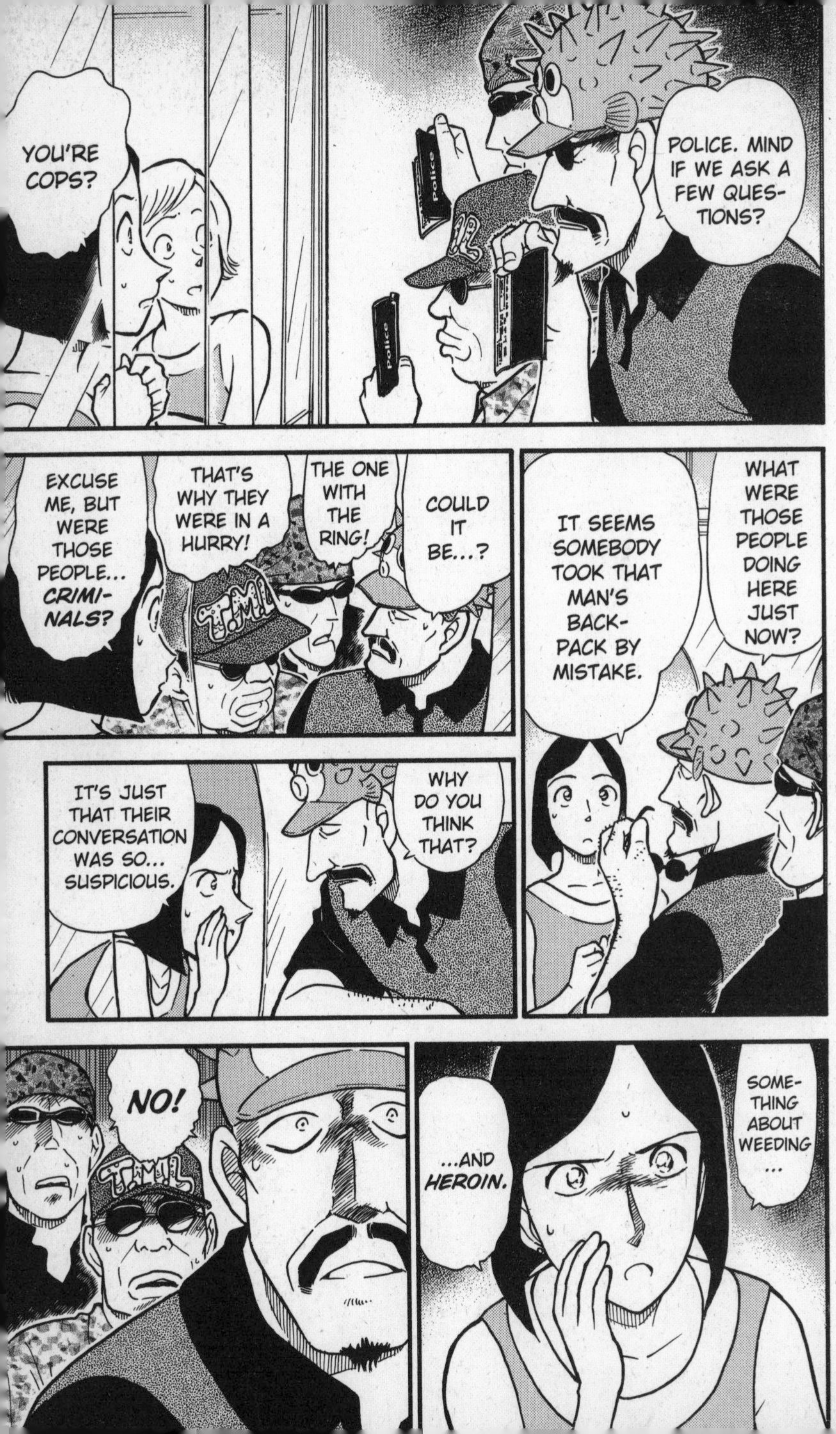
POLICE. MIND IF WE ASK A FEW QUESTIONS?
YOU'RE COPS?
WHAT WERE THOSE PEOPLE DOING HERE JUST NOW?
IT SEEMS SOMEBODY TOOK THAT MAN'S BACKPACK BY MISTAKE.
COULD IT BE...?
THE ONE WITH THE RING!
THAT'S WHY THEY WERE IN A HURRY!
EXCUSE ME, BUT WERE THOSE PEOPLE... *CRIMINALS?*
WHY DO YOU THINK THAT?
IT'S JUST THAT THEIR CONVERSATION WAS SO... SUSPICIOUS.
SOMETHING ABOUT WEEDING...
...AND *HEROIN.*
NO!

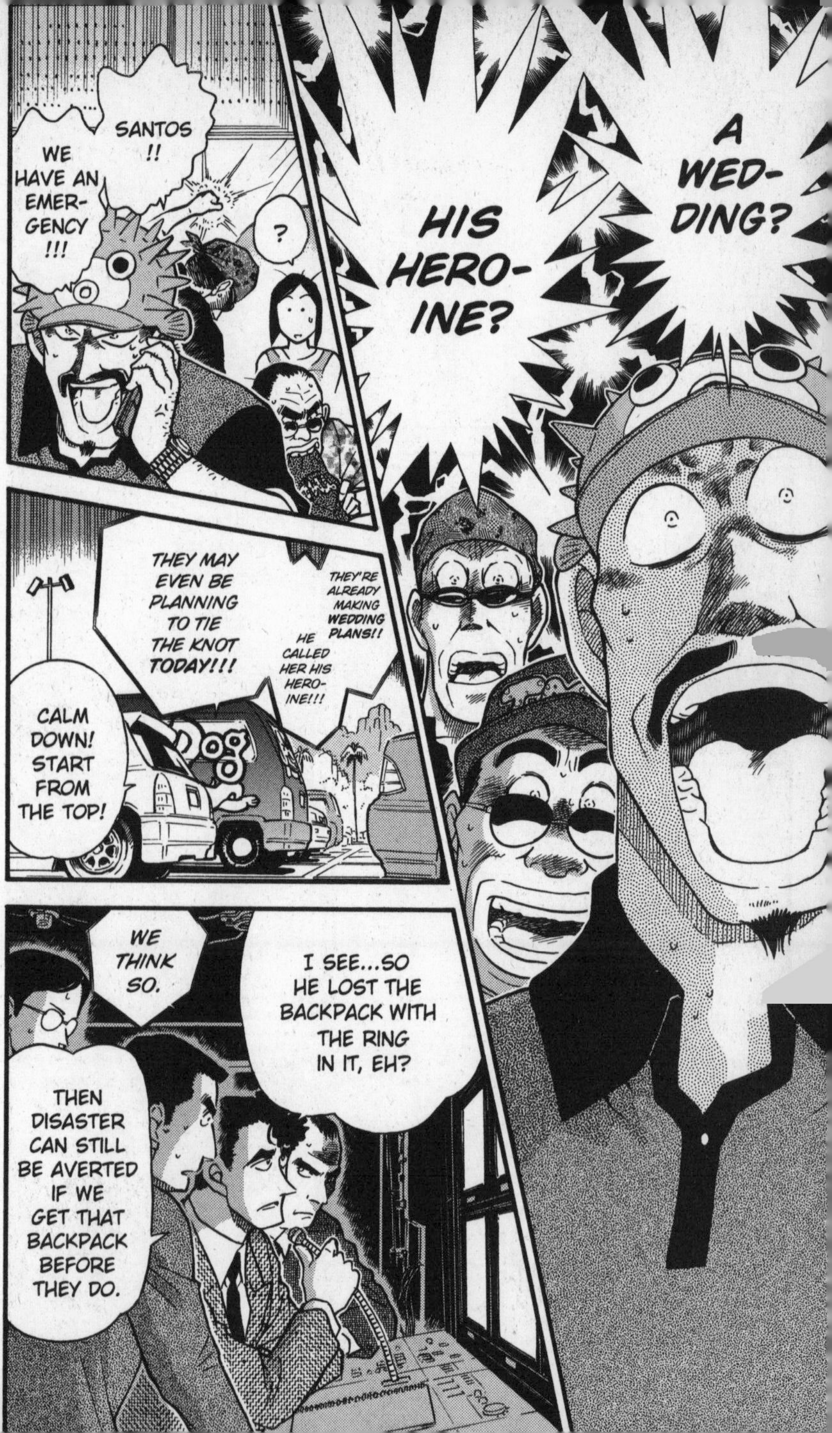
A WEDDING?
HIS HEROINE?
SANTOS!!
WE HAVE AN EMERGENCY!!!
?
THEY'RE ALREADY MAKING WEDDING PLANS!!
HE CALLED HER HIS HEROINE!!!
THEY MAY EVEN BE PLANNING TO TIE THE KNOT TODAY!!!
CALM DOWN! START FROM THE TOP!
I SEE...SO HE LOST THE BACKPACK WITH THE RING IN IT, EH?
WE THINK SO.
THEN DISASTER CAN STILL BE AVERTED IF WE GET THAT BACKPACK BEFORE THEY DO.

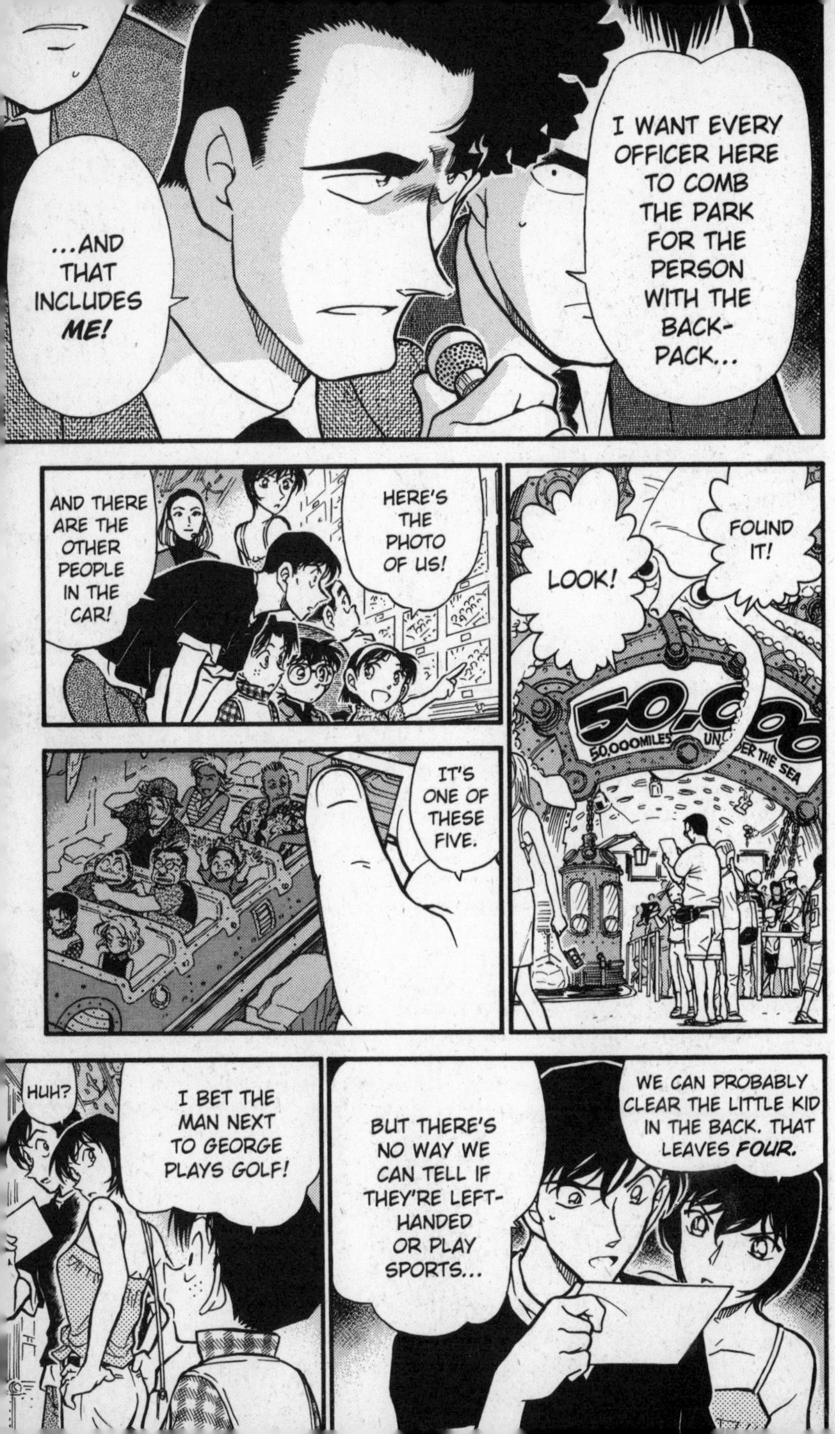
I WANT EVERY OFFICER HERE TO COMB THE PARK FOR THE PERSON WITH THE BACK-PACK...
...AND THAT INCLUDES *ME!*
FOUND IT!
LOOK!
50,000MILES
HERE'S THE PHOTO OF US!
AND THERE ARE THE OTHER PEOPLE IN THE CAR!
IT'S ONE OF THESE FIVE.
WE CAN PROBABLY CLEAR THE LITTLE KID IN THE BACK. THAT LEAVES *FOUR.*
BUT THERE'S NO WAY WE CAN TELL IF THEY'RE LEFT-HANDED OR PLAY SPORTS...
I BET THE MAN NEXT TO GEORGE PLAYS GOLF!
HUH?

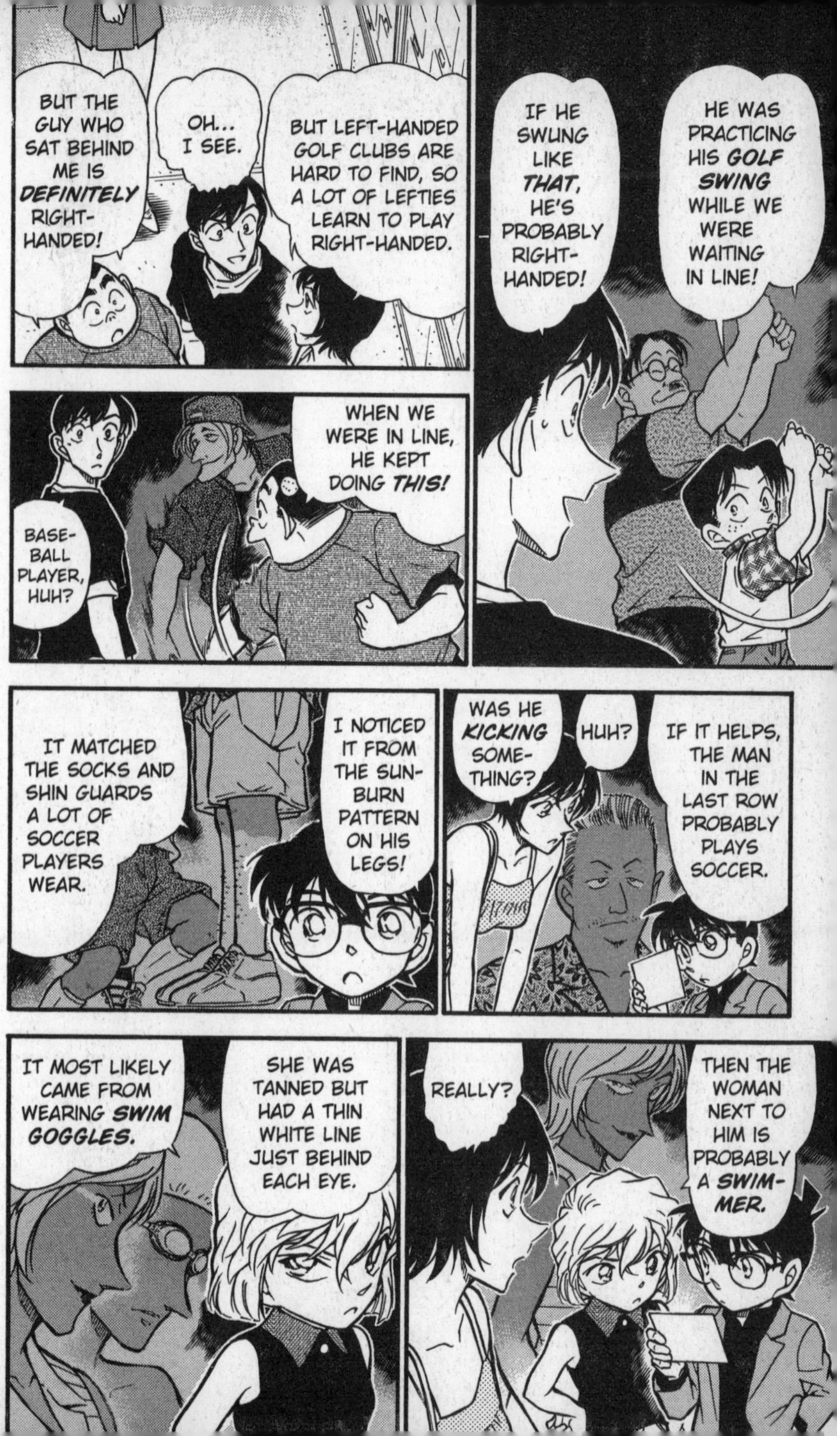
HE WAS PRACTICING HIS GOLF SWING WHILE WE WERE WAITING IN LINE!
IF HE SWUNG LIKE THAT, HE'S PROBABLY RIGHT-HANDED!
BUT LEFT-HANDED GOLF CLUBS ARE HARD TO FIND, SO A LOT OF LEFTIES LEARN TO PLAY RIGHT-HANDED.
OH... I SEE.
BUT THE GUY WHO SAT BEHIND ME IS DEFINITELY RIGHT-HANDED!
WHEN WE WERE IN LINE, HE KEPT DOING THIS!
BASE-BALL PLAYER, HUH?
IF IT HELPS, THE MAN IN THE LAST ROW PROBABLY PLAYS SOCCER.
HUH?
WAS HE KICKING SOME-THING?
I NOTICED IT FROM THE SUN-BURN PATTERN ON HIS LEGS!
IT MATCHED THE SOCKS AND SHIN GUARDS A LOT OF SOCCER PLAYERS WEAR.
THEN THE WOMAN NEXT TO HIM IS PROBABLY A SWIM-MER.
REALLY?
SHE WAS TANNED BUT HAD A THIN WHITE LINE JUST BEHIND EACH EYE.
IT MOST LIKELY CAME FROM WEARING SWIM GOGGLES.

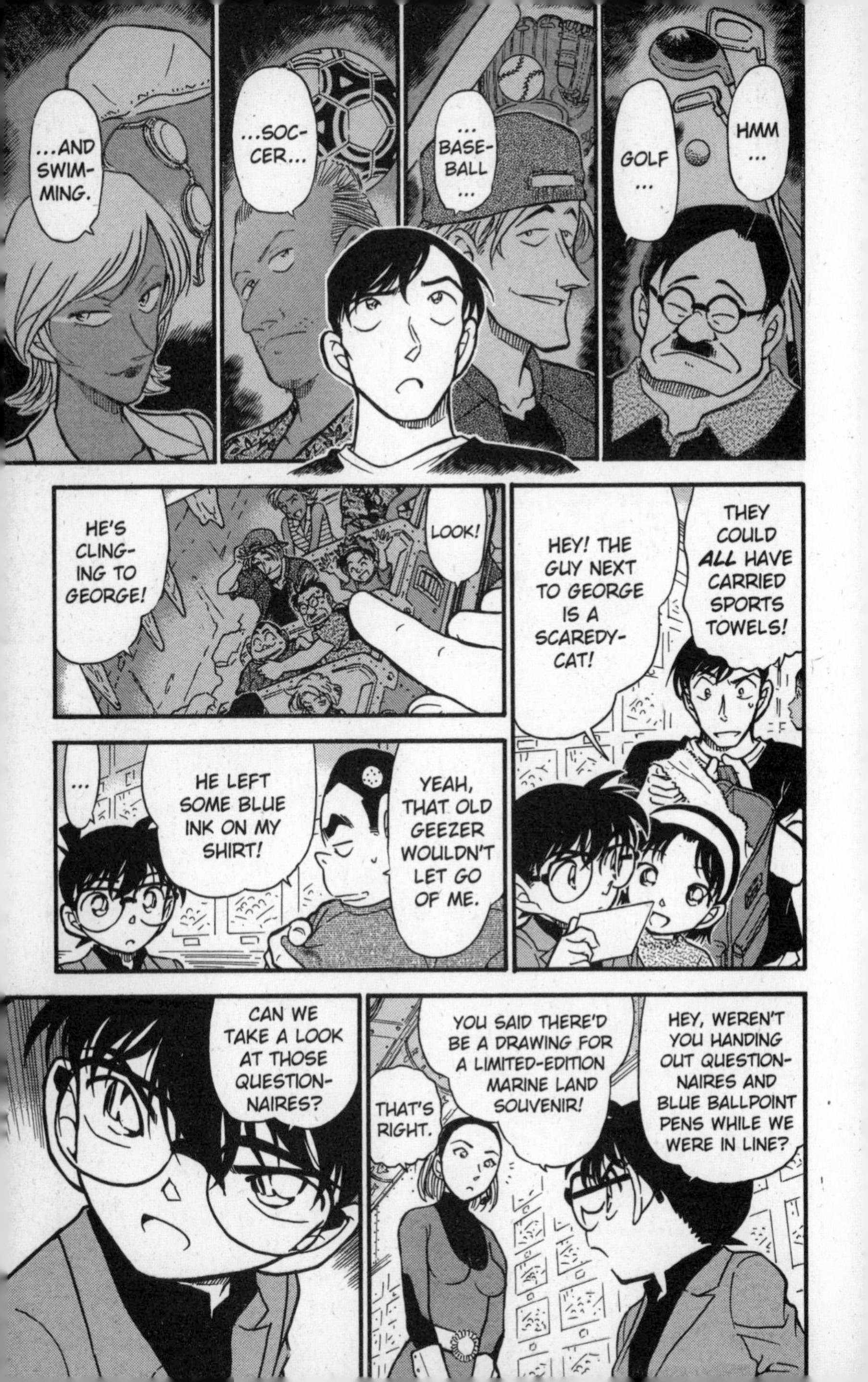
HMM ...
GOLF ...
... BASE-BALL ...
...SOC-CER...
...AND SWIM-MING.
THEY COULD **ALL** HAVE CARRIED SPORTS TOWELS!
HEY! THE GUY NEXT TO GEORGE IS A SCAREDY-CAT!
LOOK!
HE'S CLING-ING TO GEORGE!
YEAH, THAT OLD GEEZER WOULDN'T LET GO OF ME.
HE LEFT SOME BLUE INK ON MY SHIRT!
...
HEY, WEREN'T YOU HANDING OUT QUESTION-NAIRES AND BLUE BALLPOINT PENS WHILE WE WERE IN LINE?
YOU SAID THERE'D BE A DRAWING FOR A LIMITED-EDITION MARINE LAND SOUVENIR!
THAT'S RIGHT.
CAN WE TAKE A LOOK AT THOSE QUESTION-NAIRES?

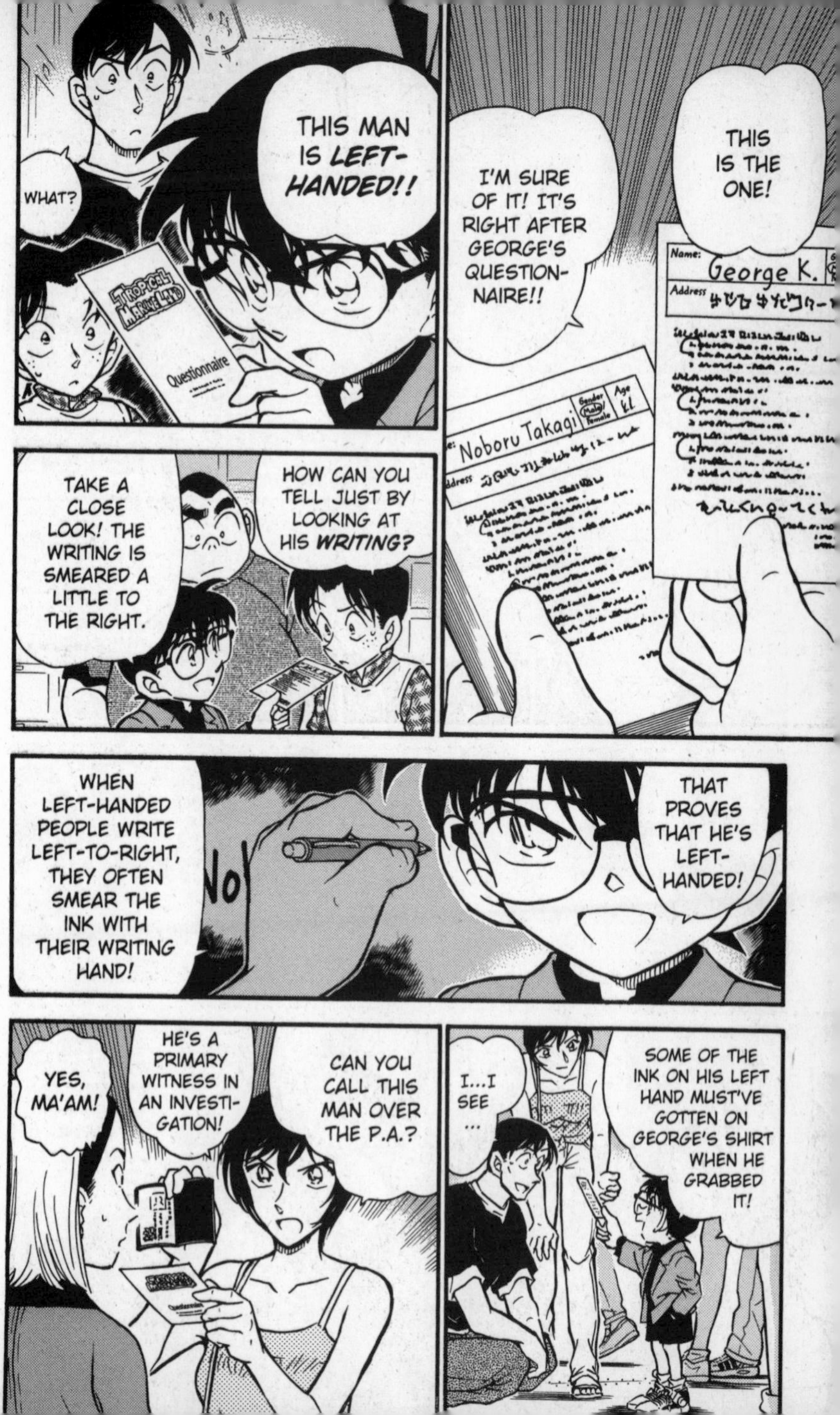
THIS IS THE ONE!
Name: George K.
Address
I'M SURE OF IT! IT'S RIGHT AFTER GEORGE'S QUESTION-NAIRE!!
Noboru Takagi
Gender Male/Female
Age
Address
THIS MAN IS *LEFT-HANDED!!*
WHAT?
TROPICAL MARINE LAND
Questionnaire
HOW CAN YOU TELL JUST BY LOOKING AT HIS *WRITING?*
TAKE A CLOSE LOOK! THE WRITING IS SMEARED A LITTLE TO THE RIGHT.
THAT PROVES THAT HE'S LEFT-HANDED!
No
WHEN LEFT-HANDED PEOPLE WRITE LEFT-TO-RIGHT, THEY OFTEN SMEAR THE INK WITH THEIR WRITING HAND!
SOME OF THE INK ON HIS LEFT HAND MUST'VE GOTTEN ON GEORGE'S SHIRT WHEN HE GRABBED IT!
I...I SEE ...
CAN YOU CALL THIS MAN OVER THE P.A.?
HE'S A PRIMARY WITNESS IN AN INVESTI-GATION!
YES, MA'AM!

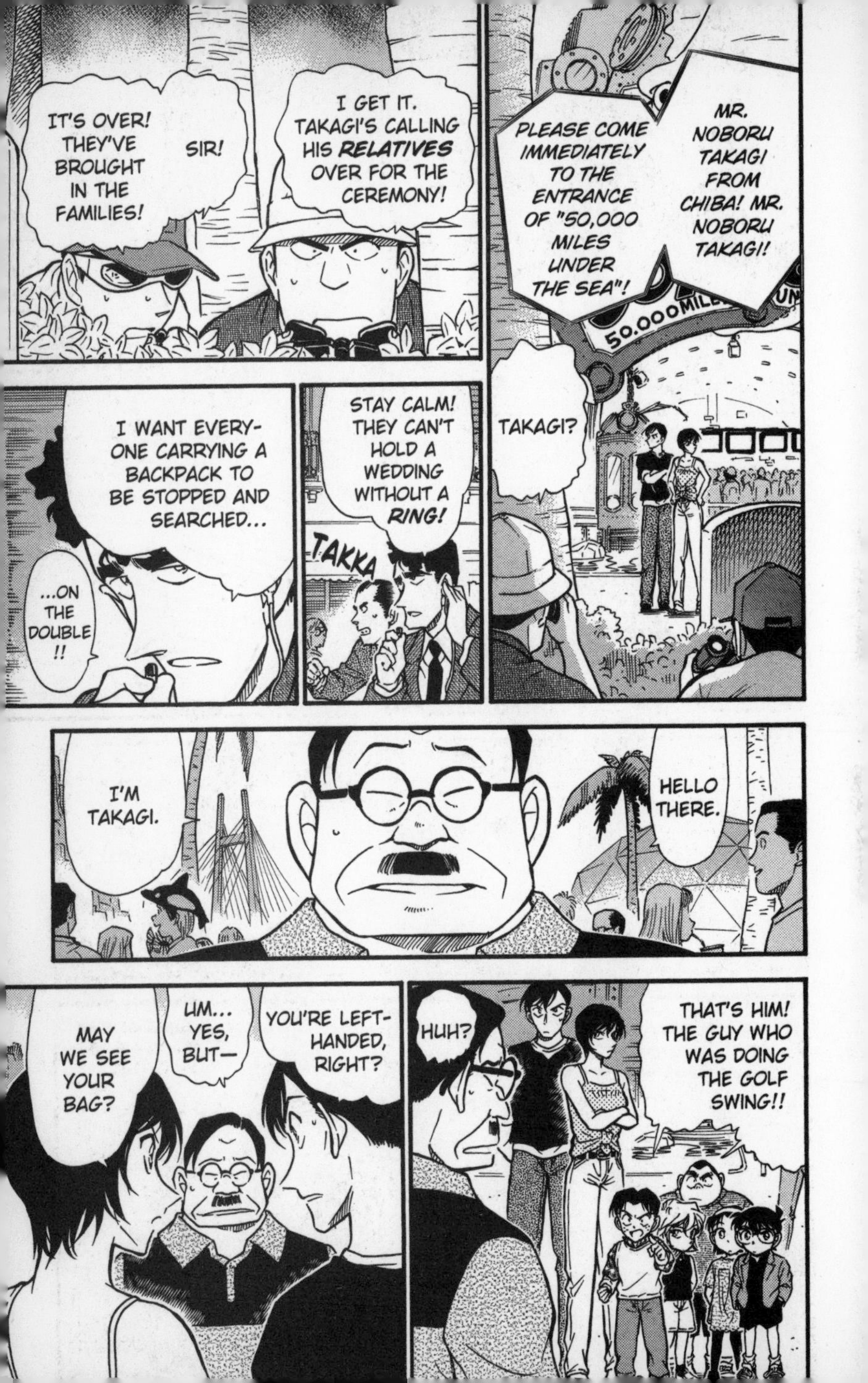
MR. NOBORU TAKAGI FROM CHIBA! MR. NOBORU TAKAGI!
PLEASE COME IMMEDIATELY TO THE ENTRANCE OF "50,000 MILES UNDER THE SEA"!
TAKAGI?
I GET IT. TAKAGI'S CALLING HIS **RELATIVES** OVER FOR THE CEREMONY!
SIR!
IT'S OVER! THEY'VE BROUGHT IN THE FAMILIES!
STAY CALM! THEY CAN'T HOLD A WEDDING WITHOUT A **RING!**
TAKKA
I WANT EVERY-ONE CARRYING A BACKPACK TO BE STOPPED AND SEARCHED...
...ON THE DOUBLE!!
HELLO THERE.
I'M TAKAGI.
THAT'S HIM! THE GUY WHO WAS DOING THE GOLF SWING!!
HUH?
YOU'RE LEFT-HANDED, RIGHT?
UM... YES, BUT—
MAY WE SEE YOUR BAG?

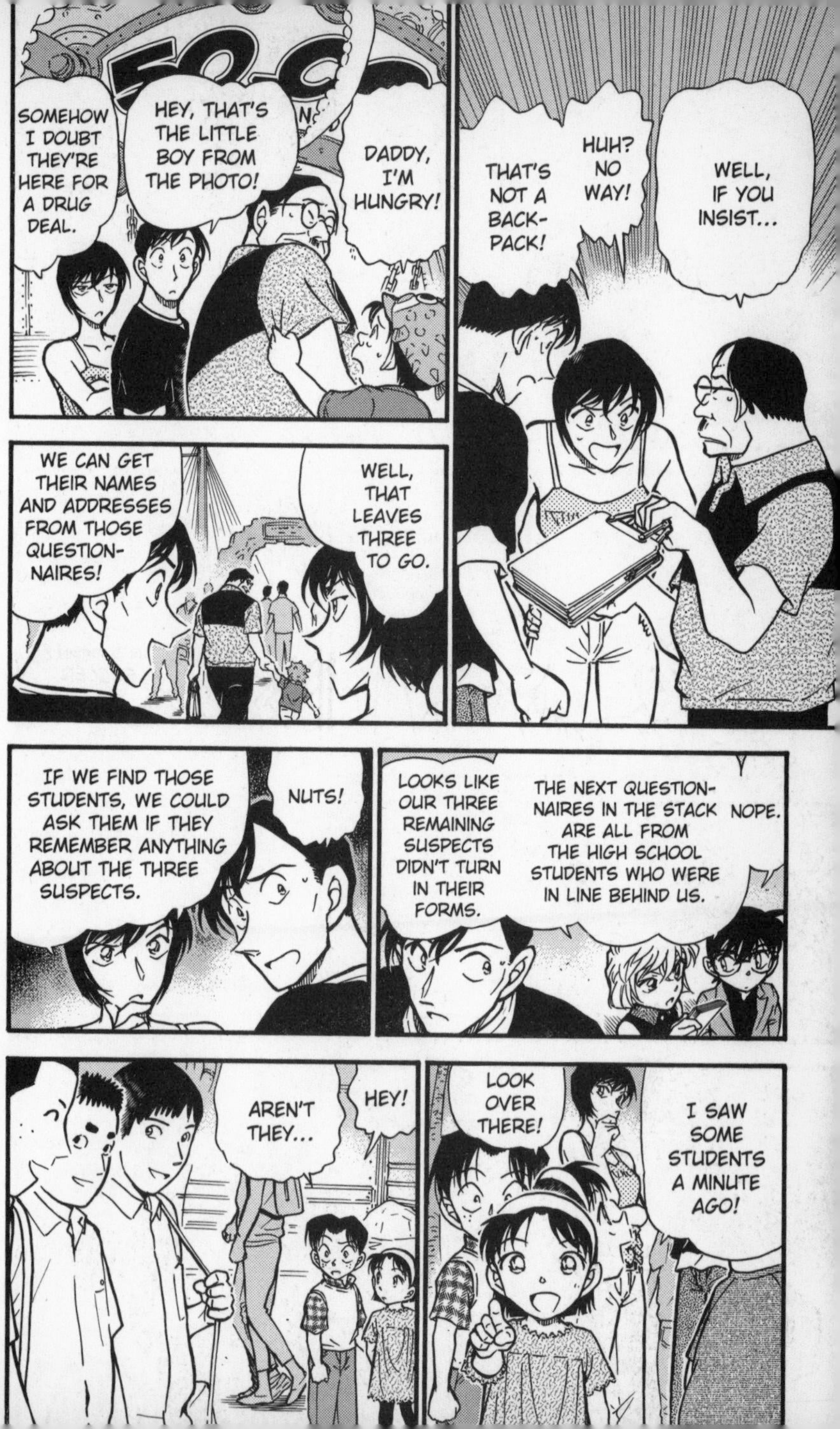
WELL, IF YOU INSIST...
HUH? NO WAY!
THAT'S NOT A BACKPACK!
DADDY, I'M HUNGRY!
HEY, THAT'S THE LITTLE BOY FROM THE PHOTO!
SOMEHOW I DOUBT THEY'RE HERE FOR A DRUG DEAL.
WELL, THAT LEAVES THREE TO GO.
WE CAN GET THEIR NAMES AND ADDRESSES FROM THOSE QUESTIONNAIRES!
NOPE.
THE NEXT QUESTIONNAIRES IN THE STACK ARE ALL FROM THE HIGH SCHOOL STUDENTS WHO WERE IN LINE BEHIND US.
LOOKS LIKE OUR THREE REMAINING SUSPECTS DIDN'T TURN IN THEIR FORMS.
NUTS!
IF WE FIND THOSE STUDENTS, WE COULD ASK THEM IF THEY REMEMBER ANYTHING ABOUT THE THREE SUSPECTS.
I SAW SOME STUDENTS A MINUTE AGO!
LOOK OVER THERE!
HEY!
AREN'T THEY...

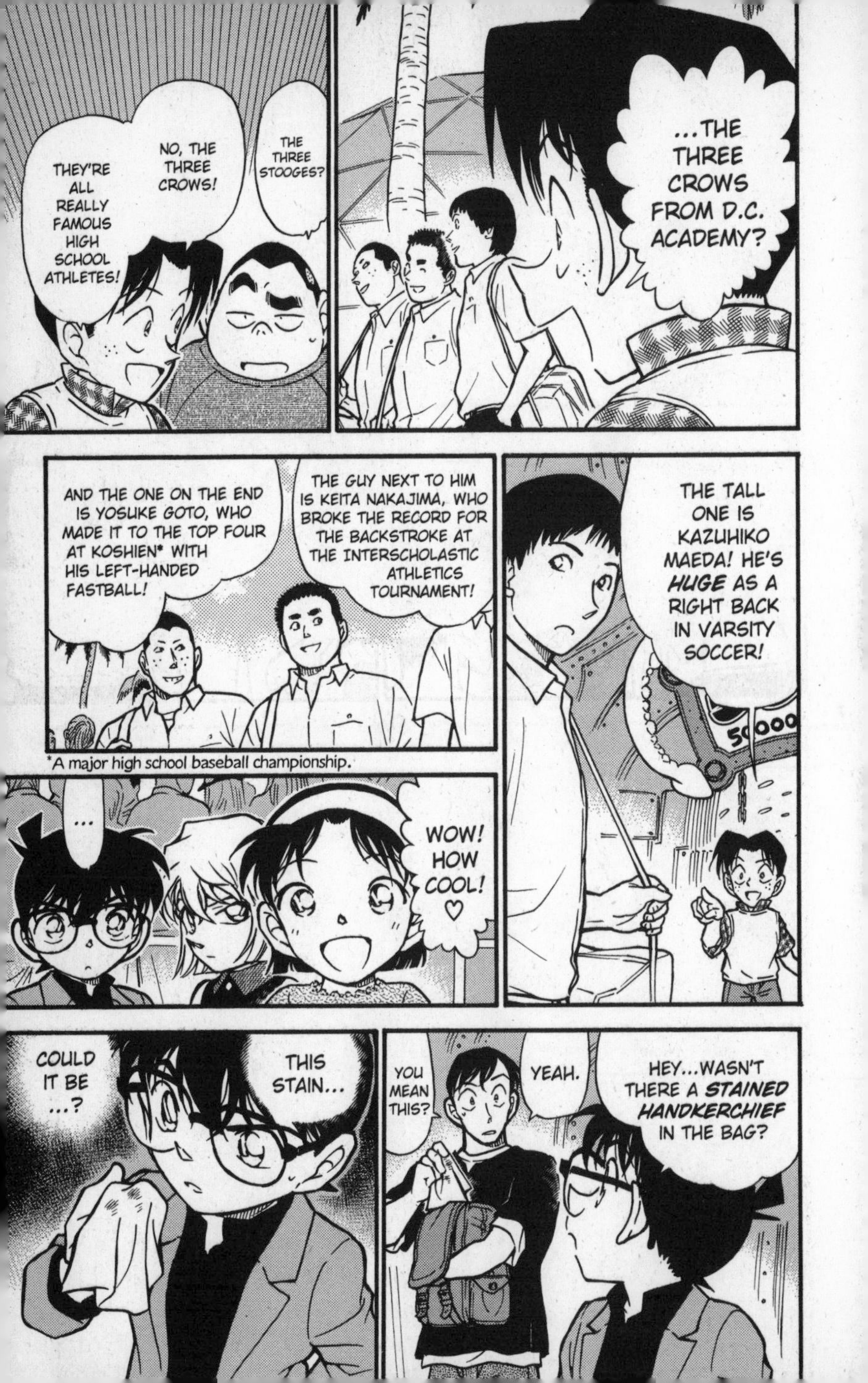
...THE THREE CROWS FROM D.C. ACADEMY?
THE THREE STOOGES?
NO, THE THREE CROWS!
THEY'RE ALL REALLY FAMOUS HIGH SCHOOL ATHLETES!
THE TALL ONE IS KAZUHIKO MAEDA! HE'S *HUGE* AS A RIGHT BACK IN VARSITY SOCCER!
THE GUY NEXT TO HIM IS KEITA NAKAJIMA, WHO BROKE THE RECORD FOR THE BACKSTROKE AT THE INTERSCHOLASTIC ATHLETICS TOURNAMENT!
AND THE ONE ON THE END IS YOSUKE GOTO, WHO MADE IT TO THE TOP FOUR AT KOSHIEN* WITH HIS LEFT-HANDED FASTBALL!
WOW! HOW COOL! ♡
...
HEY...WASN'T THERE A *STAINED HANDKERCHIEF* IN THE BAG?
YEAH.
YOU MEAN THIS?
THIS STAIN...
COULD IT BE ...?

*A major high school baseball championship.

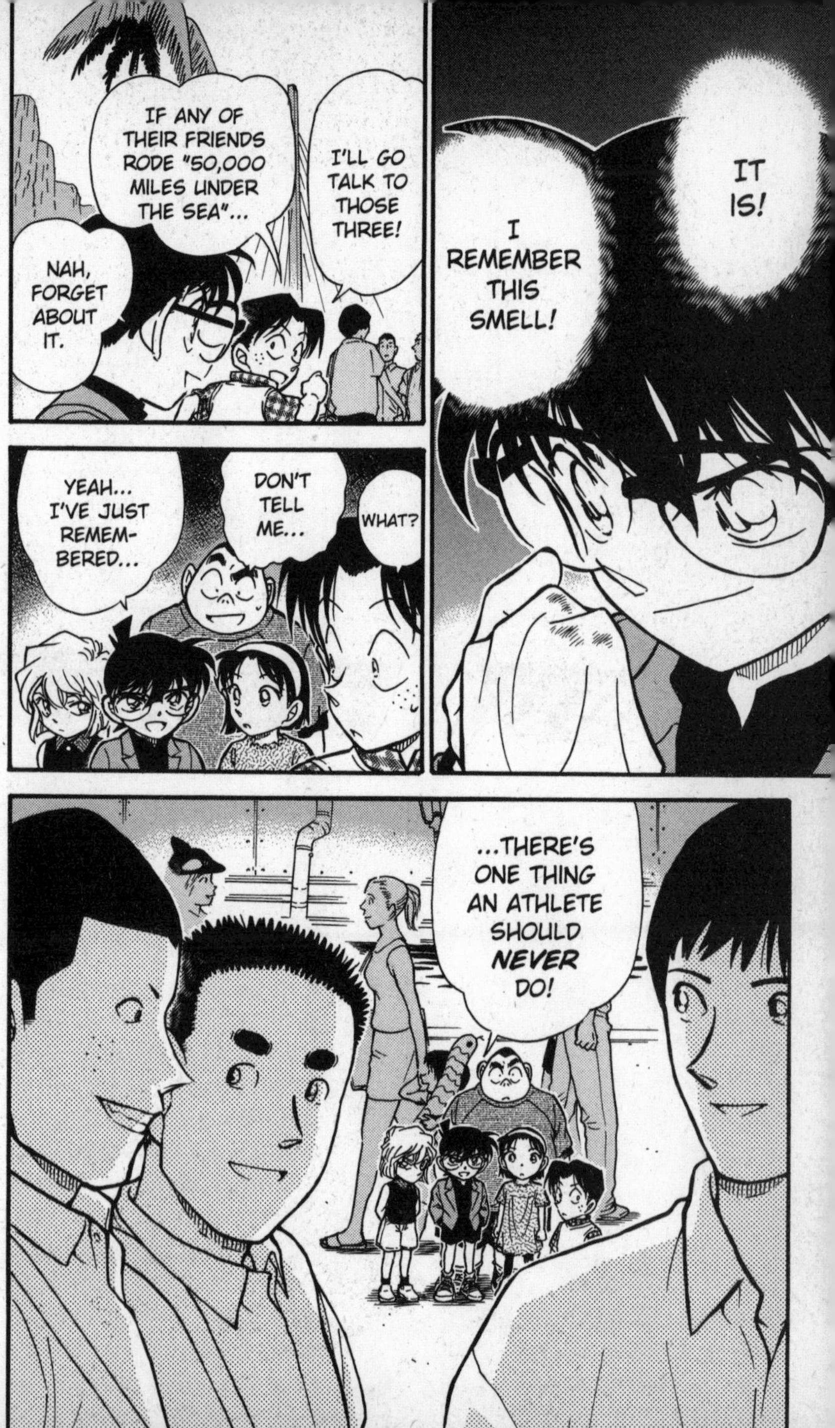
IT IS!
I REMEMBER THIS SMELL!
I'LL GO TALK TO THOSE THREE!
IF ANY OF THEIR FRIENDS RODE "50,000 MILES UNDER THE SEA"...
NAH, FORGET ABOUT IT.
WHAT?
DON'T TELL ME...
YEAH... I'VE JUST REMEMBERED...
...THERE'S ONE THING AN ATHLETE SHOULD *NEVER* DO!

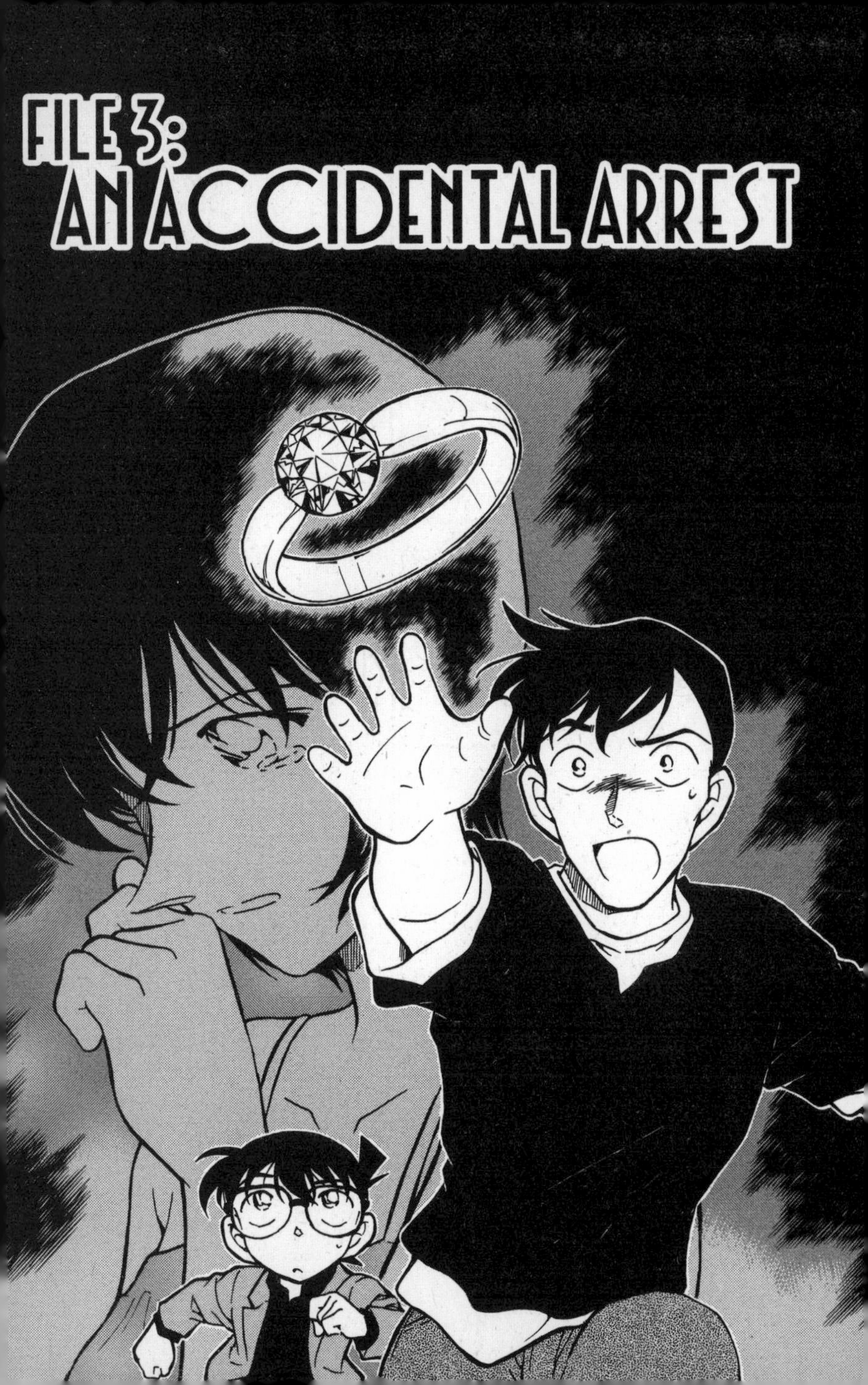
FILE 3:
AN ACCIDENTAL ARREST

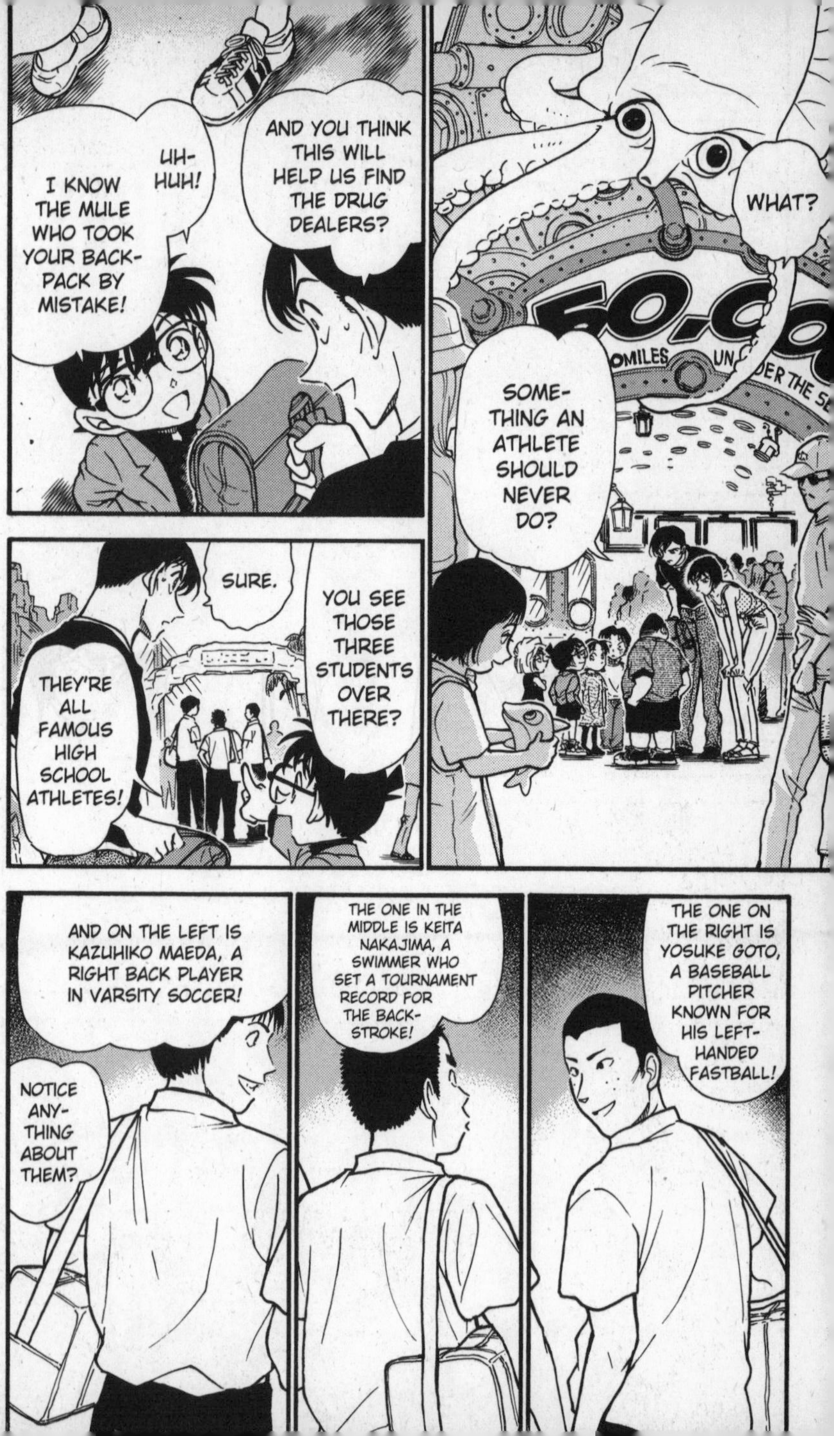
WHAT?
SOME-THING AN ATHLETE SHOULD NEVER DO?
AND YOU THINK THIS WILL HELP US FIND THE DRUG DEALERS?
UH-HUH!
I KNOW THE MULE WHO TOOK YOUR BACK-PACK BY MISTAKE!
SURE.
YOU SEE THOSE THREE STUDENTS OVER THERE?
THEY'RE ALL FAMOUS HIGH SCHOOL ATHLETES!
THE ONE ON THE RIGHT IS YOSUKE GOTO, A BASEBALL PITCHER KNOWN FOR HIS LEFT-HANDED FASTBALL!
THE ONE IN THE MIDDLE IS KEITA NAKAJIMA, A SWIMMER WHO SET A TOURNAMENT RECORD FOR THE BACK-STROKE!
AND ON THE LEFT IS KAZUHIKO MAEDA, A RIGHT BACK PLAYER IN VARSITY SOCCER!
NOTICE ANY-THING ABOUT THEM?

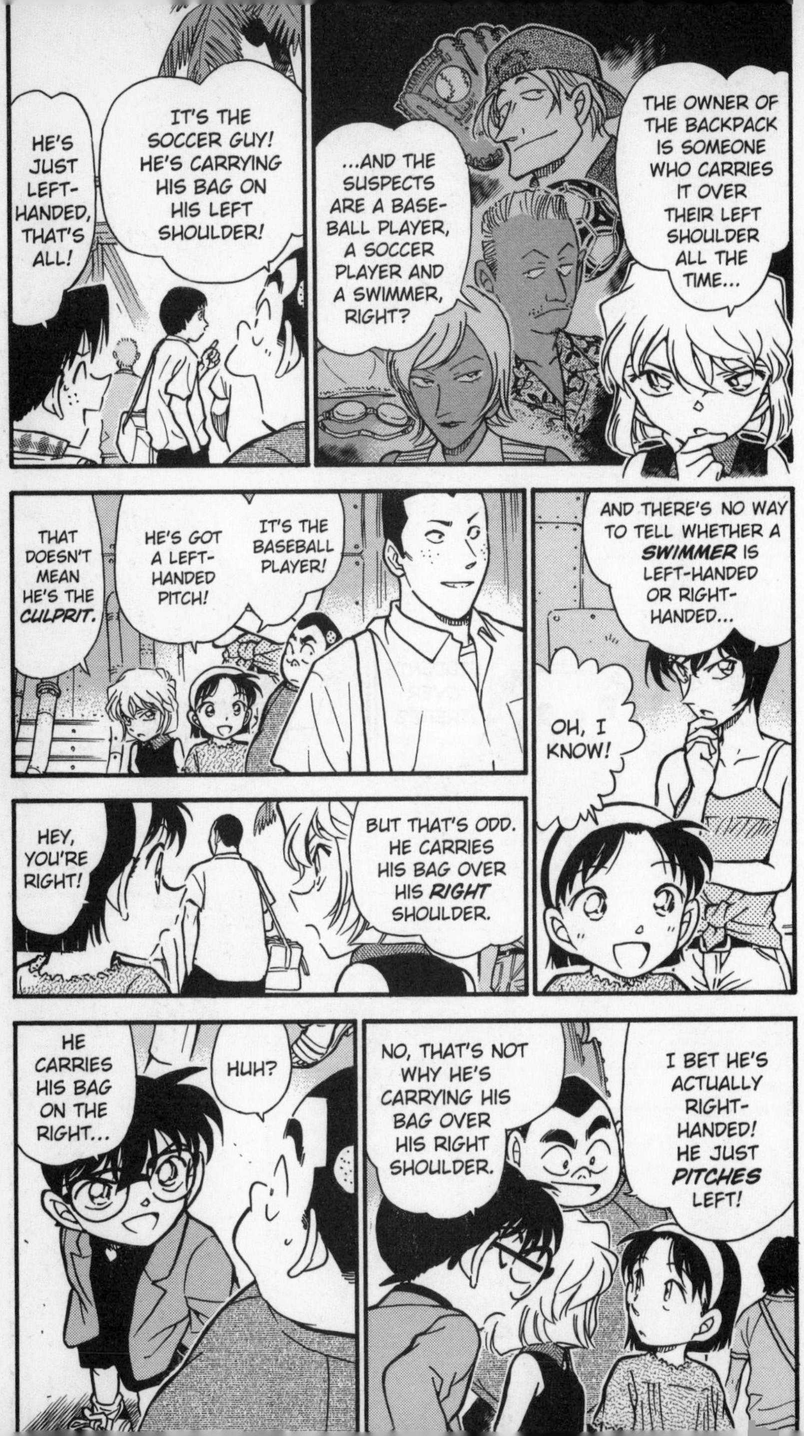
THE OWNER OF THE BACKPACK IS SOMEONE WHO CARRIES IT OVER THEIR LEFT SHOULDER ALL THE TIME...
...AND THE SUSPECTS ARE A BASEBALL PLAYER, A SOCCER PLAYER AND A SWIMMER, RIGHT?
IT'S THE SOCCER GUY! HE'S CARRYING HIS BAG ON HIS LEFT SHOULDER!
HE'S JUST LEFT-HANDED, THAT'S ALL!
AND THERE'S NO WAY TO TELL WHETHER A ***SWIMMER*** IS LEFT-HANDED OR RIGHT-HANDED...
OH, I KNOW!
IT'S THE BASEBALL PLAYER!
HE'S GOT A LEFT-HANDED PITCH!
THAT DOESN'T MEAN HE'S THE ***CULPRIT.***
BUT THAT'S ODD. HE CARRIES HIS BAG OVER HIS ***RIGHT*** SHOULDER.
HEY, YOU'RE RIGHT!
I BET HE'S ACTUALLY RIGHT-HANDED! HE JUST ***PITCHES*** LEFT!
NO, THAT'S NOT WHY HE'S CARRYING HIS BAG OVER HIS RIGHT SHOULDER.
HUH?
HE CARRIES HIS BAG ON THE RIGHT...

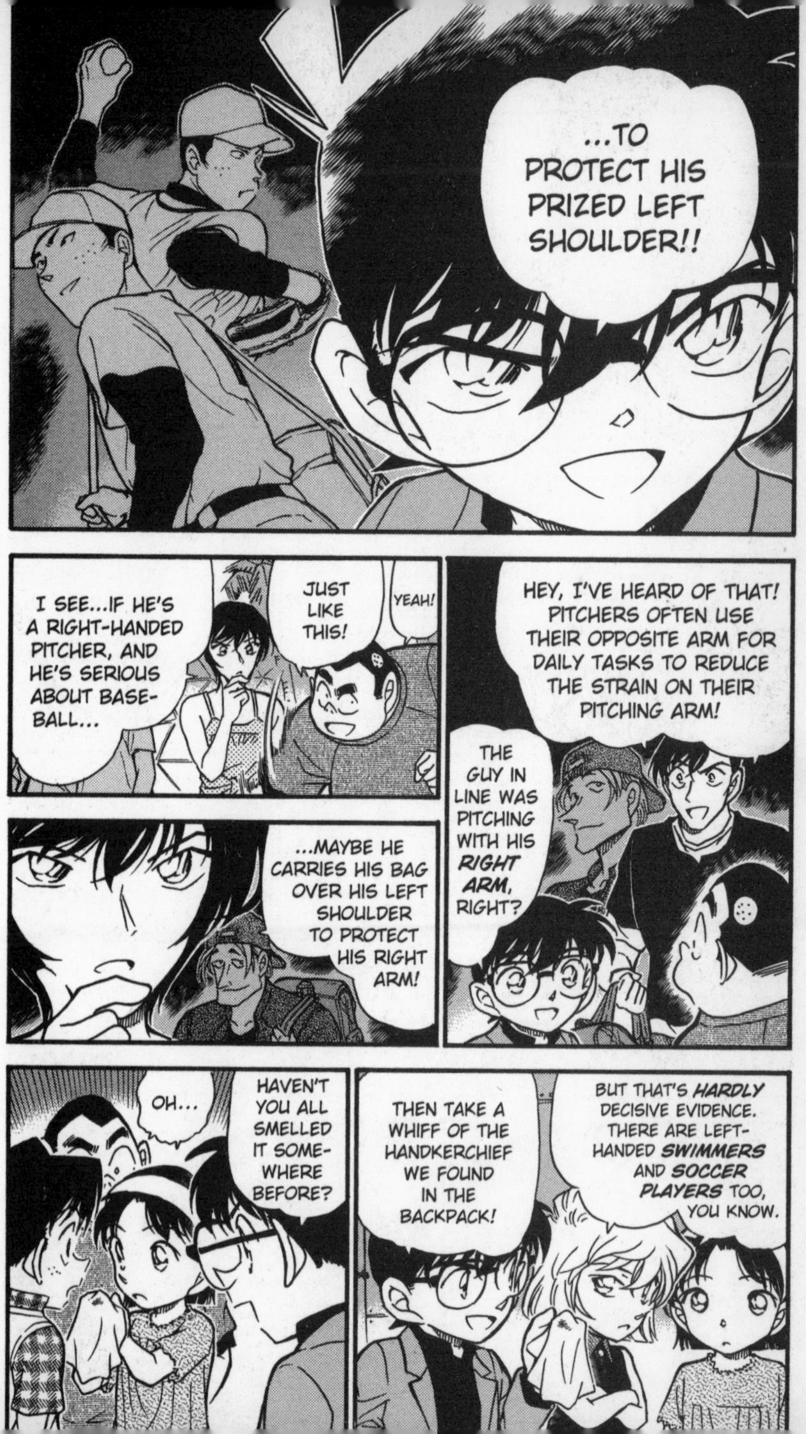
...TO PROTECT HIS PRIZED LEFT SHOULDER!!
HEY, I'VE HEARD OF THAT! PITCHERS OFTEN USE THEIR OPPOSITE ARM FOR DAILY TASKS TO REDUCE THE STRAIN ON THEIR PITCHING ARM!
THE GUY IN LINE WAS PITCHING WITH HIS *RIGHT ARM*, RIGHT?
YEAH!
JUST LIKE THIS!
I SEE...IF HE'S A RIGHT-HANDED PITCHER, AND HE'S SERIOUS ABOUT BASE-BALL...
...MAYBE HE CARRIES HIS BAG OVER HIS LEFT SHOULDER TO PROTECT HIS RIGHT ARM!
BUT THAT'S *HARDLY* DECISIVE EVIDENCE. THERE ARE LEFT-HANDED *SWIMMERS* AND *SOCCER PLAYERS* TOO, YOU KNOW.
THEN TAKE A WHIFF OF THE HANDKERCHIEF WE FOUND IN THE BACKPACK!
HAVEN'T YOU ALL SMELLED IT SOME-WHERE BEFORE?
OH...

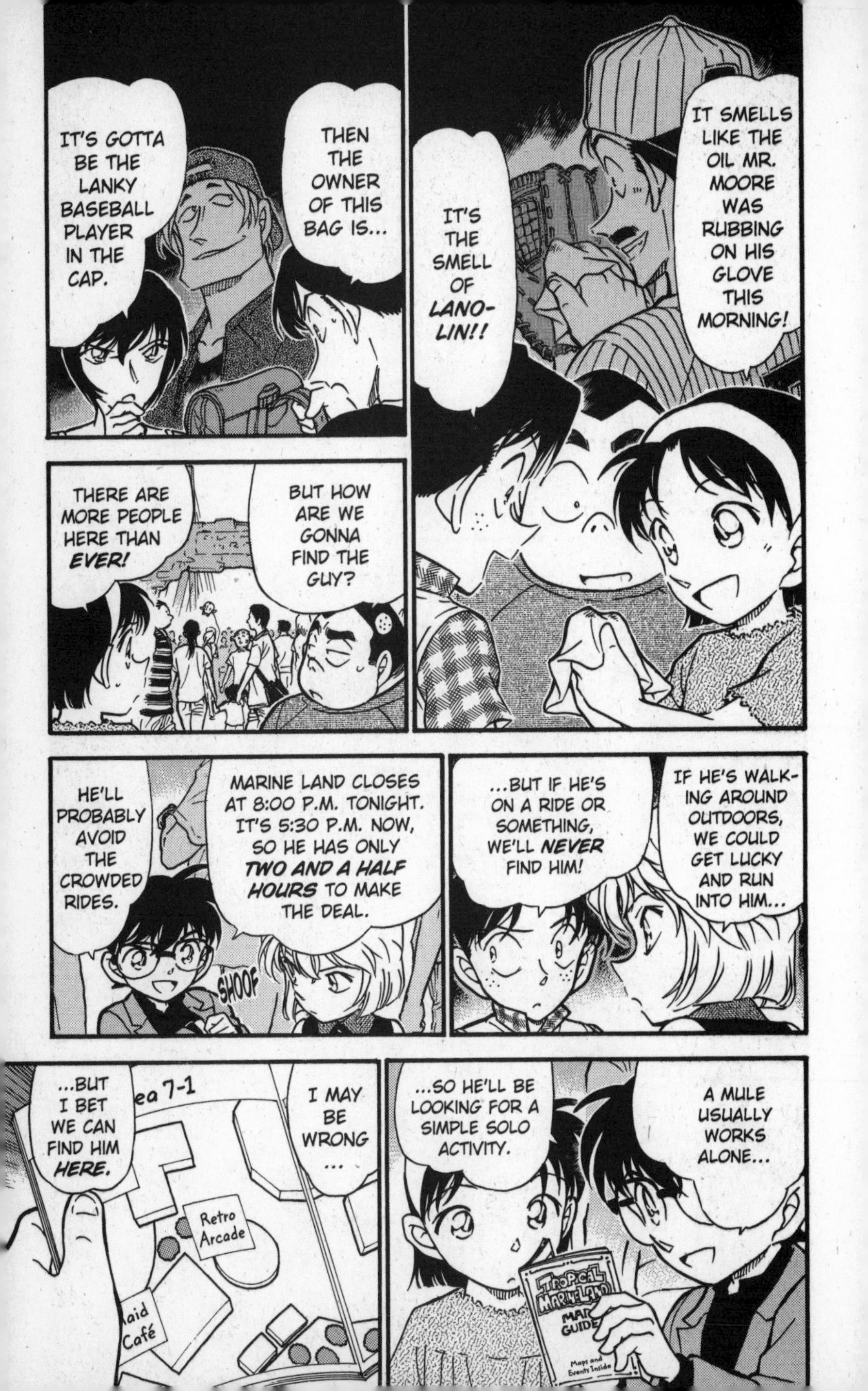
IT SMELLS LIKE THE OIL MR. MOORE WAS RUBBING ON HIS GLOVE THIS MORNING!
IT'S THE SMELL OF *LANO-LIN!!*
THEN THE OWNER OF THIS BAG IS...
IT'S GOTTA BE THE LANKY BASEBALL PLAYER IN THE CAP.
BUT HOW ARE WE GONNA FIND THE GUY?
THERE ARE MORE PEOPLE HERE THAN ***EVER!***
IF HE'S WALK-ING AROUND OUTDOORS, WE COULD GET LUCKY AND RUN INTO HIM...
...BUT IF HE'S ON A RIDE OR SOMETHING, WE'LL ***NEVER*** FIND HIM!
MARINE LAND CLOSES AT 8:00 P.M. TONIGHT. IT'S 5:30 P.M. NOW, SO HE HAS ONLY ***TWO AND A HALF HOURS*** TO MAKE THE DEAL.
SHOOF
HE'LL PROBABLY AVOID THE CROWDED RIDES.
A MULE USUALLY WORKS ALONE...
...SO HE'LL BE LOOKING FOR A SIMPLE SOLO ACTIVITY.
TROPICAL MARINE LAND
MAP GUIDE
Maps and Events Inside
I MAY BE WRONG...
...BUT I BET WE CAN FIND HIM ***HERE.***
ea 7-1
Retro Arcade
aid Café

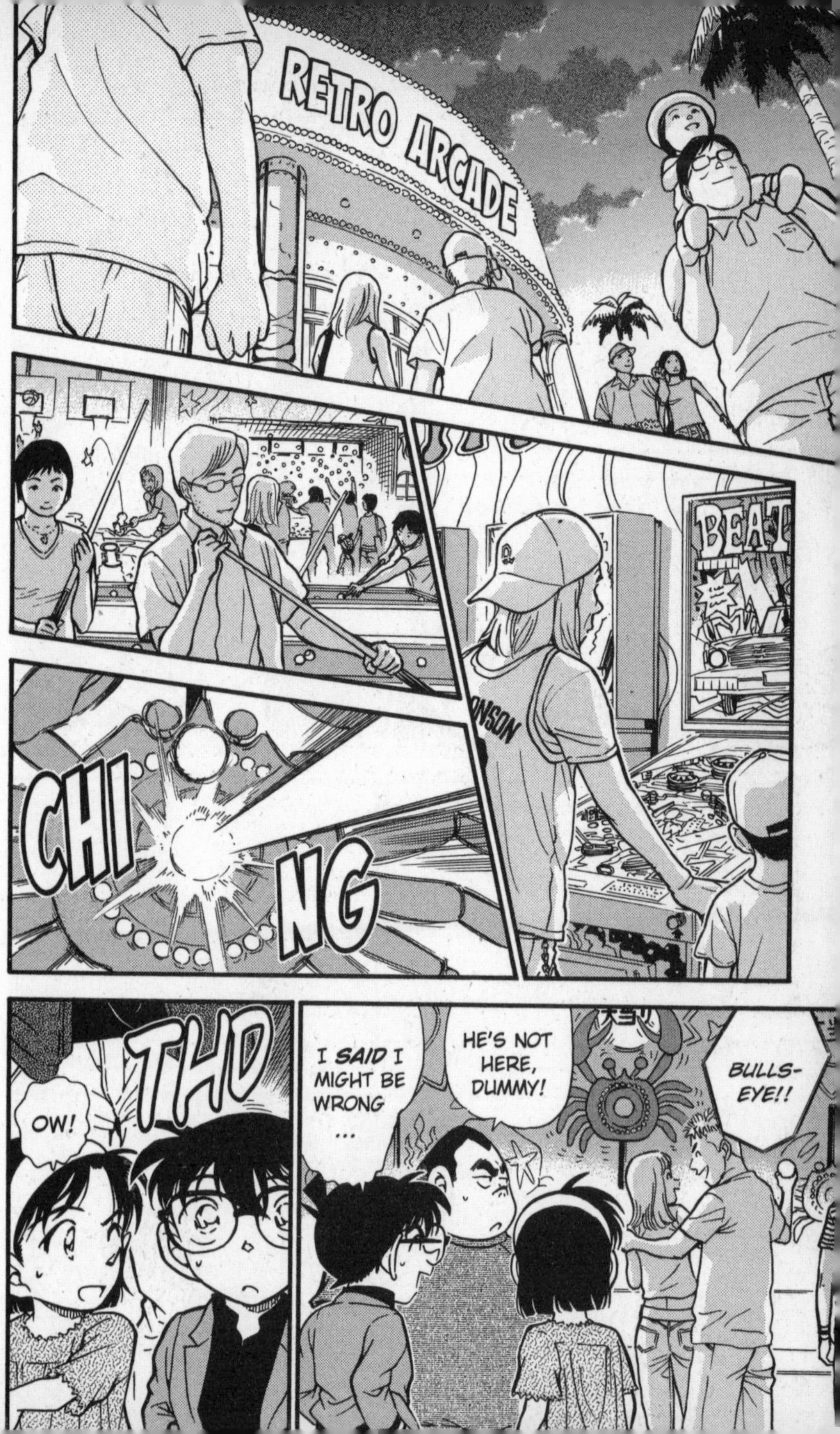
RETRO ARCADE
BEAT
CHI
NG
BULLS-EYE!!
HE'S NOT HERE, DUMMY!
I *SAID* I MIGHT BE WRONG ...
THD
OW!

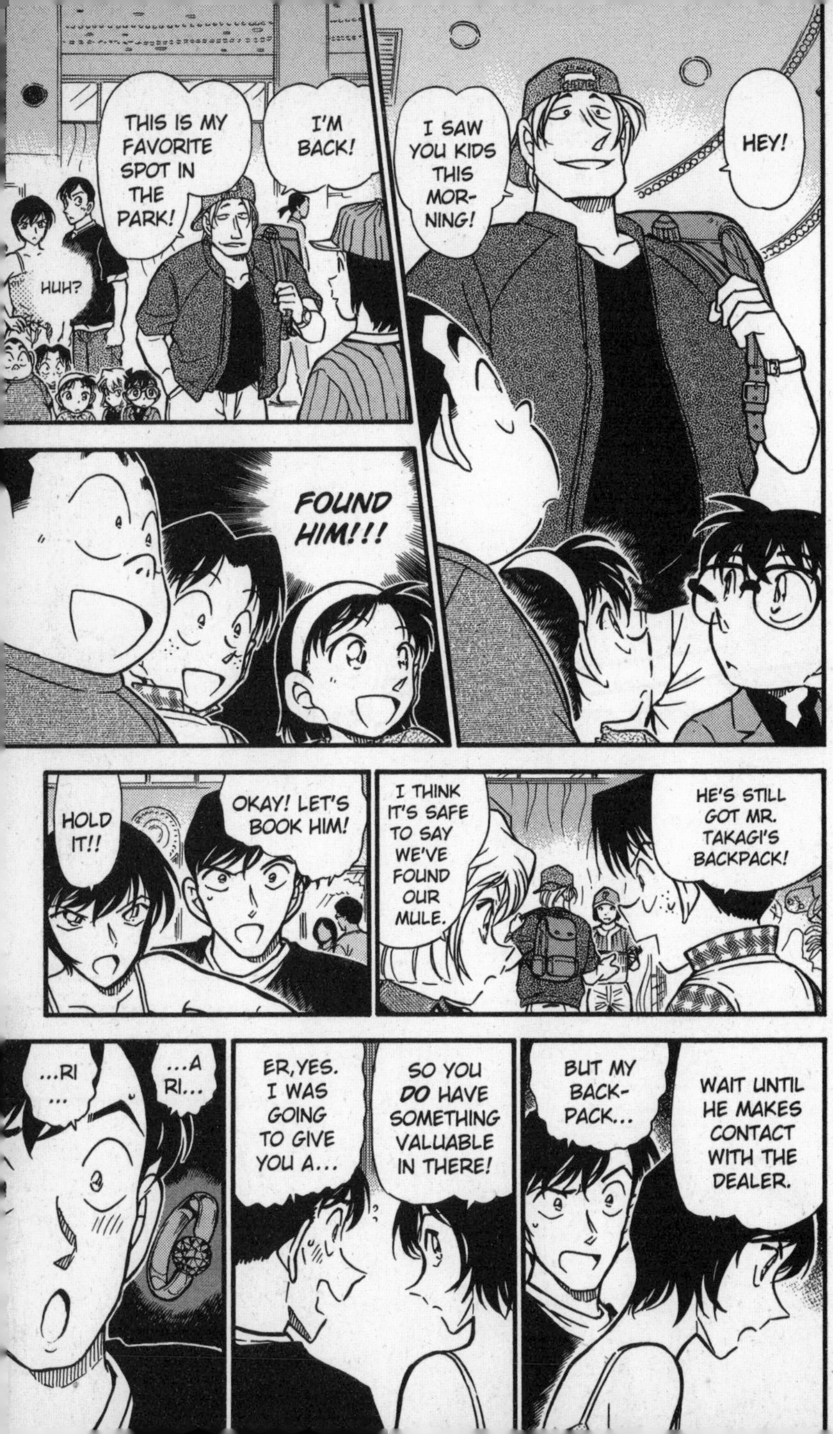
HEY!
I SAW YOU KIDS THIS MORNING!
I'M BACK!
THIS IS MY FAVORITE SPOT IN THE PARK!
HUH?
FOUND HIM!!!
HE'S STILL GOT MR. TAKAGI'S BACKPACK!
I THINK IT'S SAFE TO SAY WE'VE FOUND OUR MULE.
OKAY! LET'S BOOK HIM!
HOLD IT!!
WAIT UNTIL HE MAKES CONTACT WITH THE DEALER.
BUT MY BACKPACK...
SO YOU DO HAVE SOMETHING VALUABLE IN THERE!
ER, YES. I WAS GOING TO GIVE YOU A...
...A RI...
...RI ...

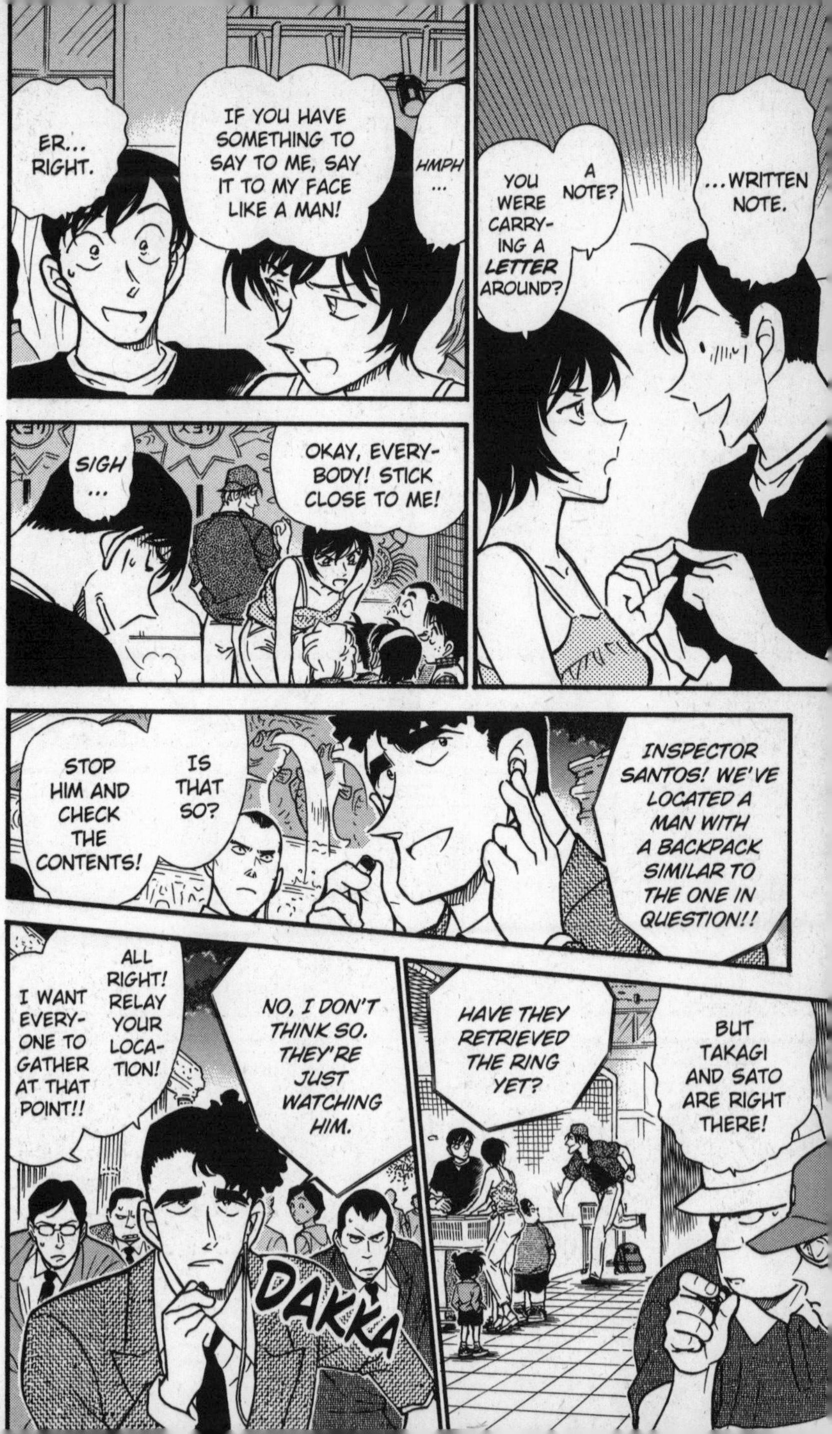
...WRITTEN NOTE.
A NOTE?
YOU WERE CARRY-ING A LETTER AROUND?
HMPH...
IF YOU HAVE SOMETHING TO SAY TO ME, SAY IT TO MY FACE LIKE A MAN!
ER... RIGHT.
OKAY, EVERY-BODY! STICK CLOSE TO ME!
SIGH...
INSPECTOR SANTOS! WE'VE LOCATED A MAN WITH A BACKPACK SIMILAR TO THE ONE IN QUESTION!!
IS THAT SO?
STOP HIM AND CHECK THE CONTENTS!
BUT TAKAGI AND SATO ARE RIGHT THERE!
HAVE THEY RETRIEVED THE RING YET?
NO, I DON'T THINK SO. THEY'RE JUST WATCHING HIM.
ALL RIGHT! RELAY YOUR LOCA-TION!
I WANT EVERY-ONE TO GATHER AT THAT POINT!!
DAKKA

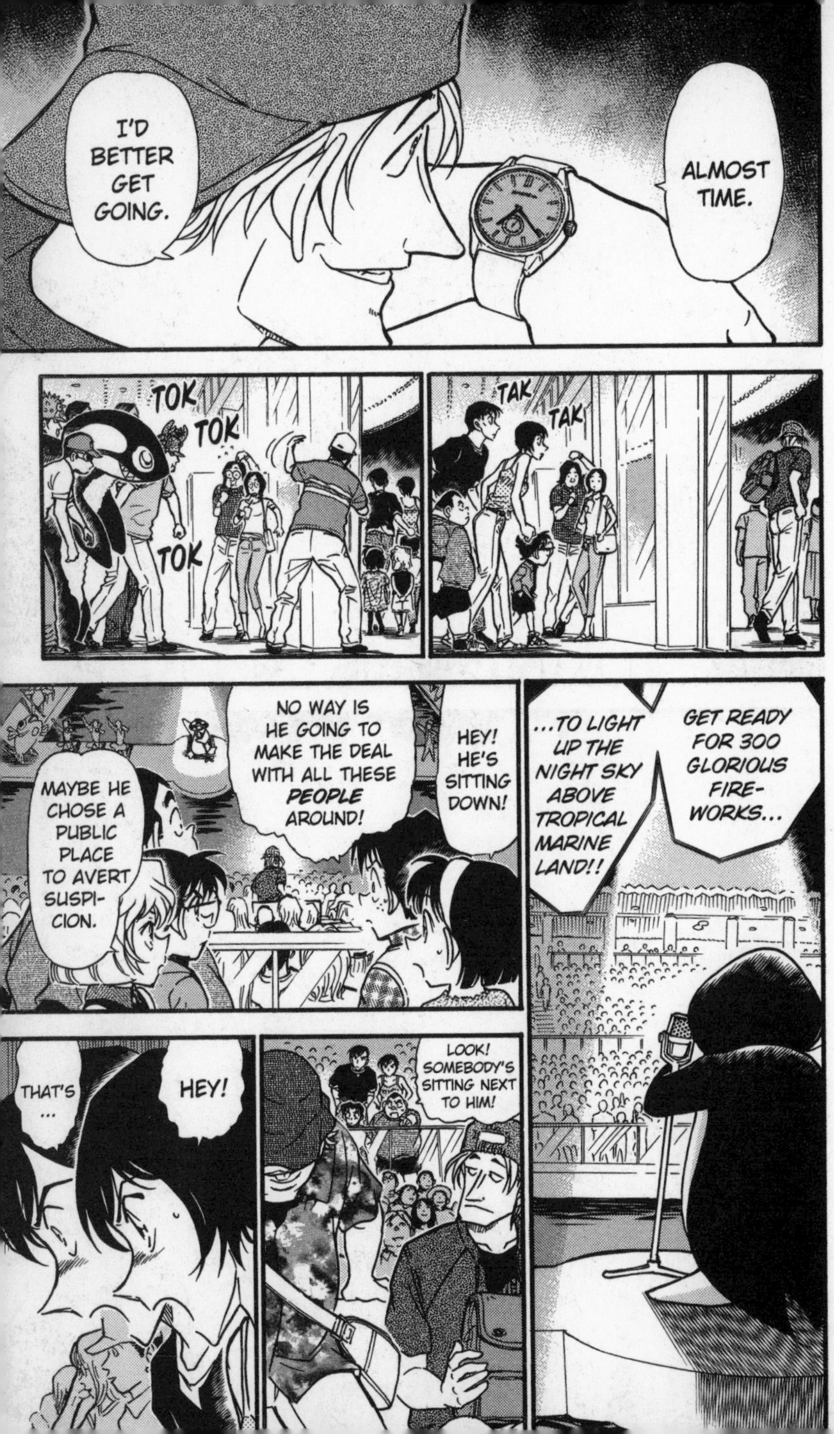
ALMOST TIME.
I'D BETTER GET GOING.
TAK
TAK
TOK
TOK
TOK
GET READY FOR 300 GLORIOUS FIRE-WORKS...
...TO LIGHT UP THE NIGHT SKY ABOVE TROPICAL MARINE LAND!!
HEY! HE'S SITTING DOWN!
NO WAY IS HE GOING TO MAKE THE DEAL WITH ALL THESE PEOPLE AROUND!
MAYBE HE CHOSE A PUBLIC PLACE TO AVERT SUSPI-CION.
LOOK! SOMEBODY'S SITTING NEXT TO HIM!
HEY!
THAT'S ...

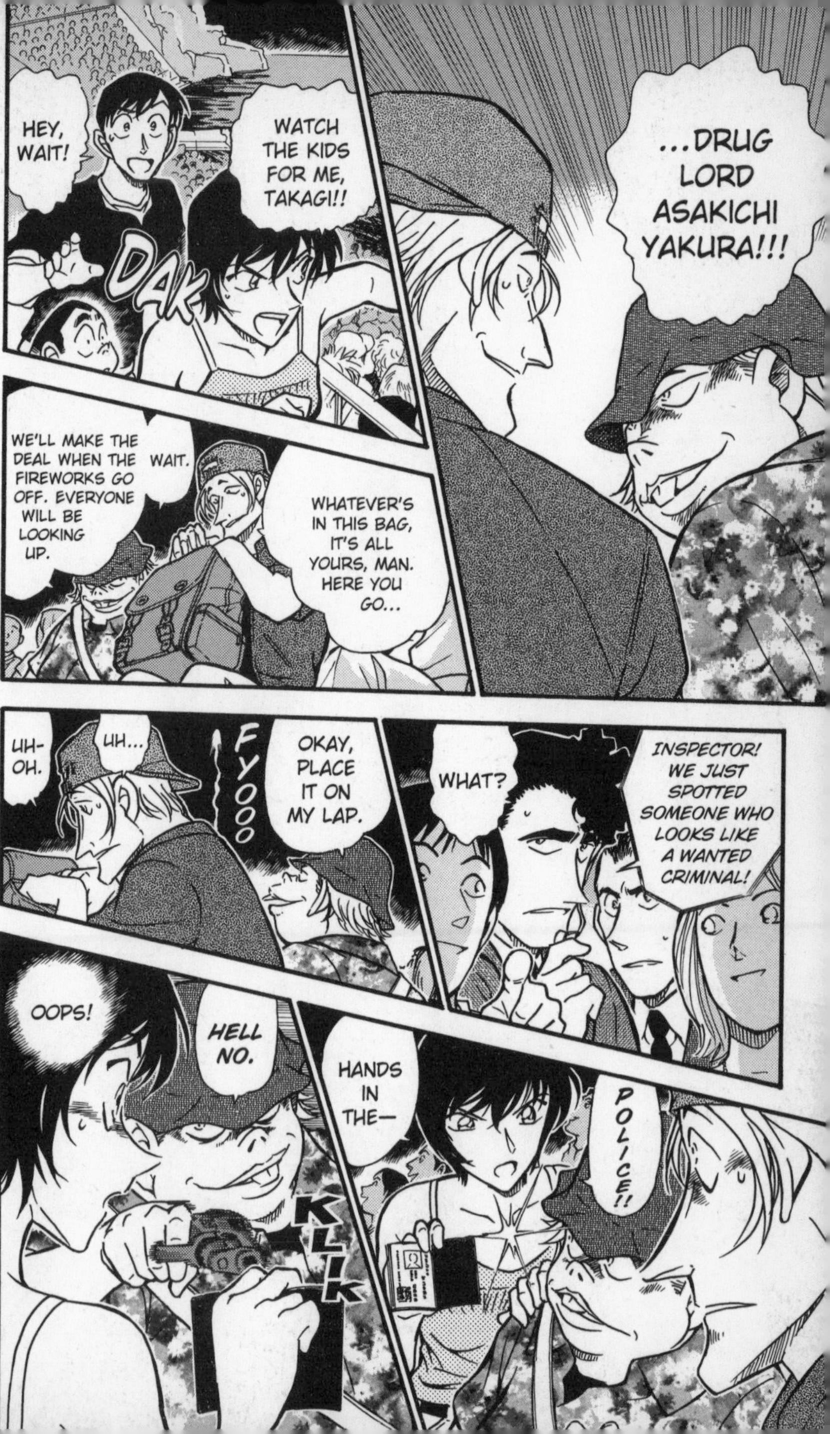
...DRUG LORD ASAKICHI YAKURA!!!
WATCH THE KIDS FOR ME, TAKAGI!!
HEY, WAIT!
DAK
WHATEVER'S IN THIS BAG, IT'S ALL YOURS, MAN. HERE YOU GO...
WAIT.
WE'LL MAKE THE DEAL WHEN THE FIREWORKS GO OFF. EVERYONE WILL BE LOOKING UP.
INSPECTOR! WE JUST SPOTTED SOMEONE WHO LOOKS LIKE A WANTED CRIMINAL!
WHAT?
OKAY, PLACE IT ON MY LAP.
FYOOO
UH...
UH-OH.
POLICE!!
HANDS IN THE—
HELL NO.
OOPS!
KLIK

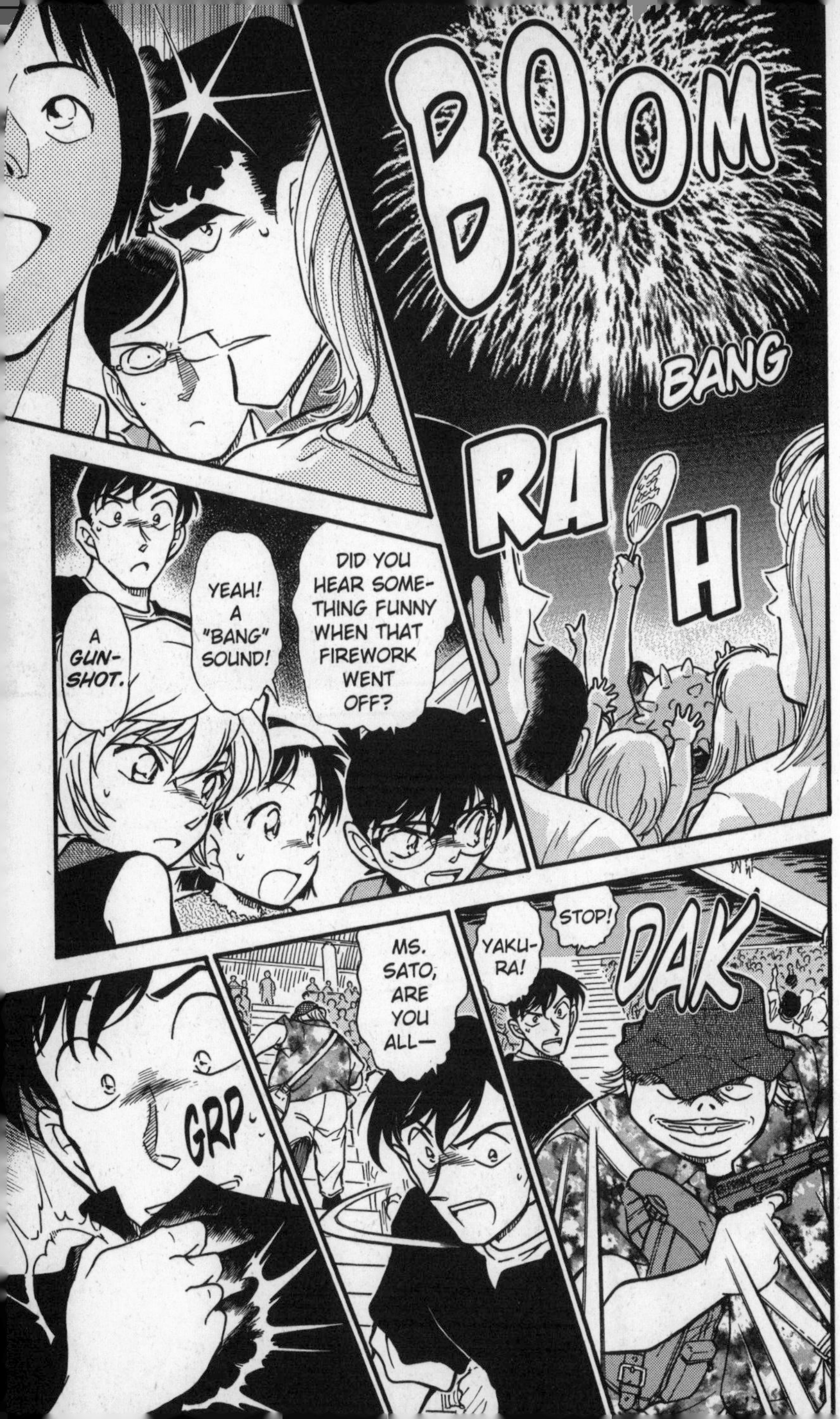
BOOM
BANG
RAH
DID YOU HEAR SOMETHING FUNNY WHEN THAT FIREWORK WENT OFF?
YEAH! A "BANG" SOUND!
A GUN-SHOT.
STOP!
DAK
YAKU-RA!
MS. SATO, ARE YOU ALL—
GRP

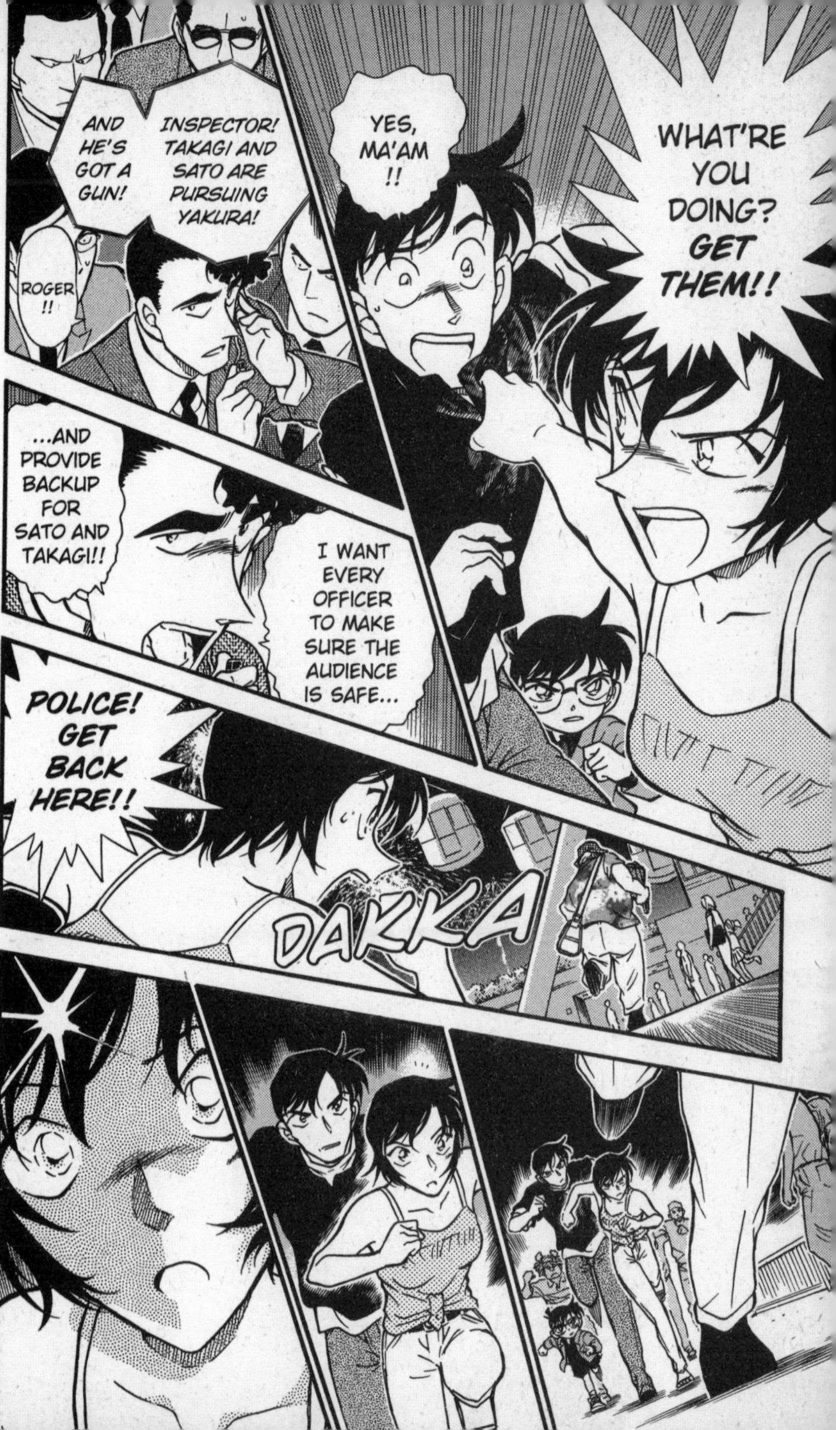
WHAT'RE YOU DOING? GET THEM!!
YES, MA'AM!!
INSPECTOR! TAKAGI AND SATO ARE PURSUING YAKURA!
AND HE'S GOT A GUN!
ROGER!!
I WANT EVERY OFFICER TO MAKE SURE THE AUDIENCE IS SAFE...
...AND PROVIDE BACKUP FOR SATO AND TAKAGI!!
POLICE! GET BACK HERE!!
DAKKA

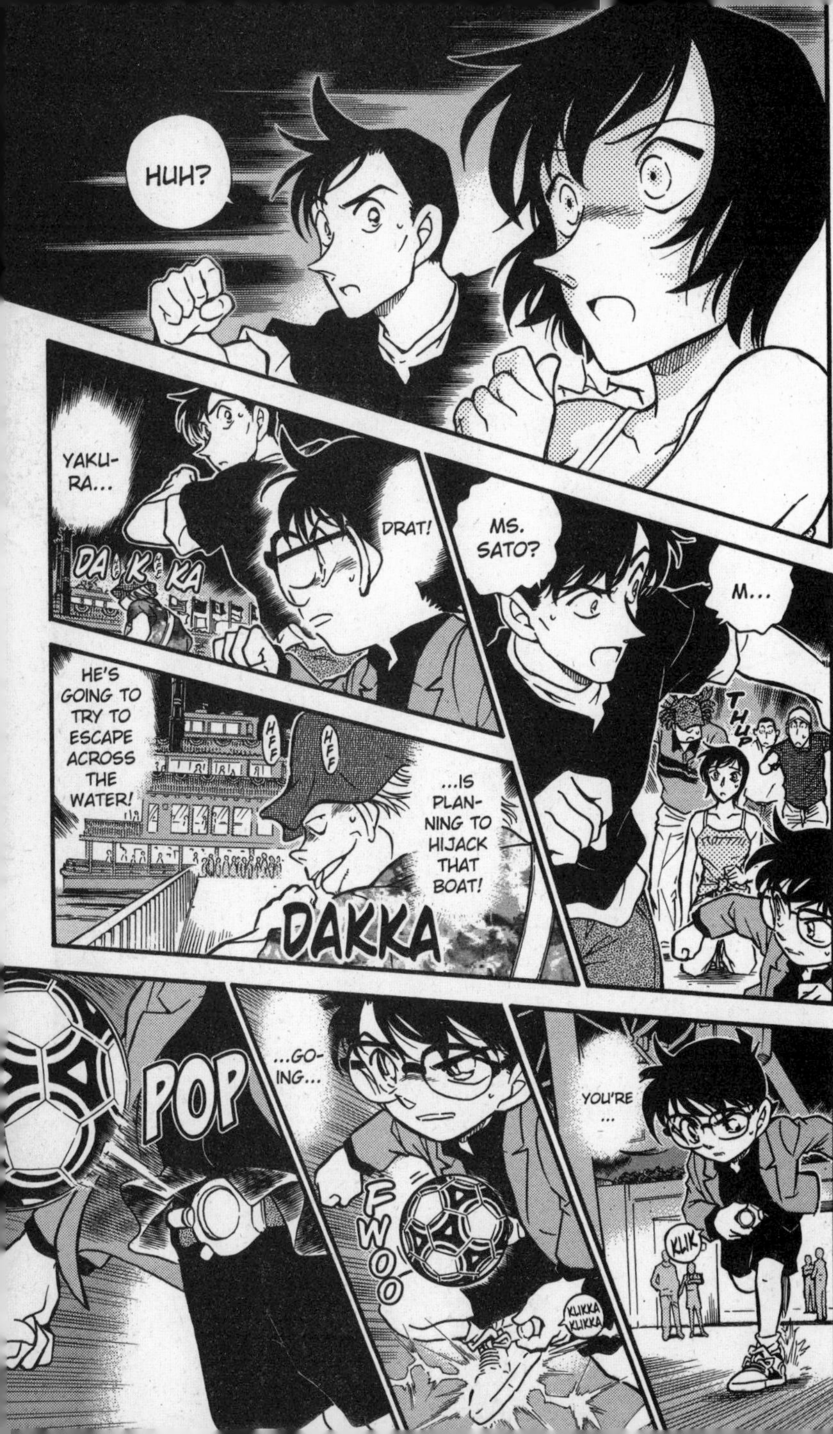
HUH?
MS. SATO?
M...
THUP
DRAT!
YAKU-RA...
DA K KA
HFF
HFF
...IS PLAN-NING TO HIJACK THAT BOAT!
HE'S GOING TO TRY TO ESCAPE ACROSS THE WATER!
DAKKA
YOU'RE ...
KLIK
...GO-ING...
FWOO
KLIKKA KLIKKA
POP

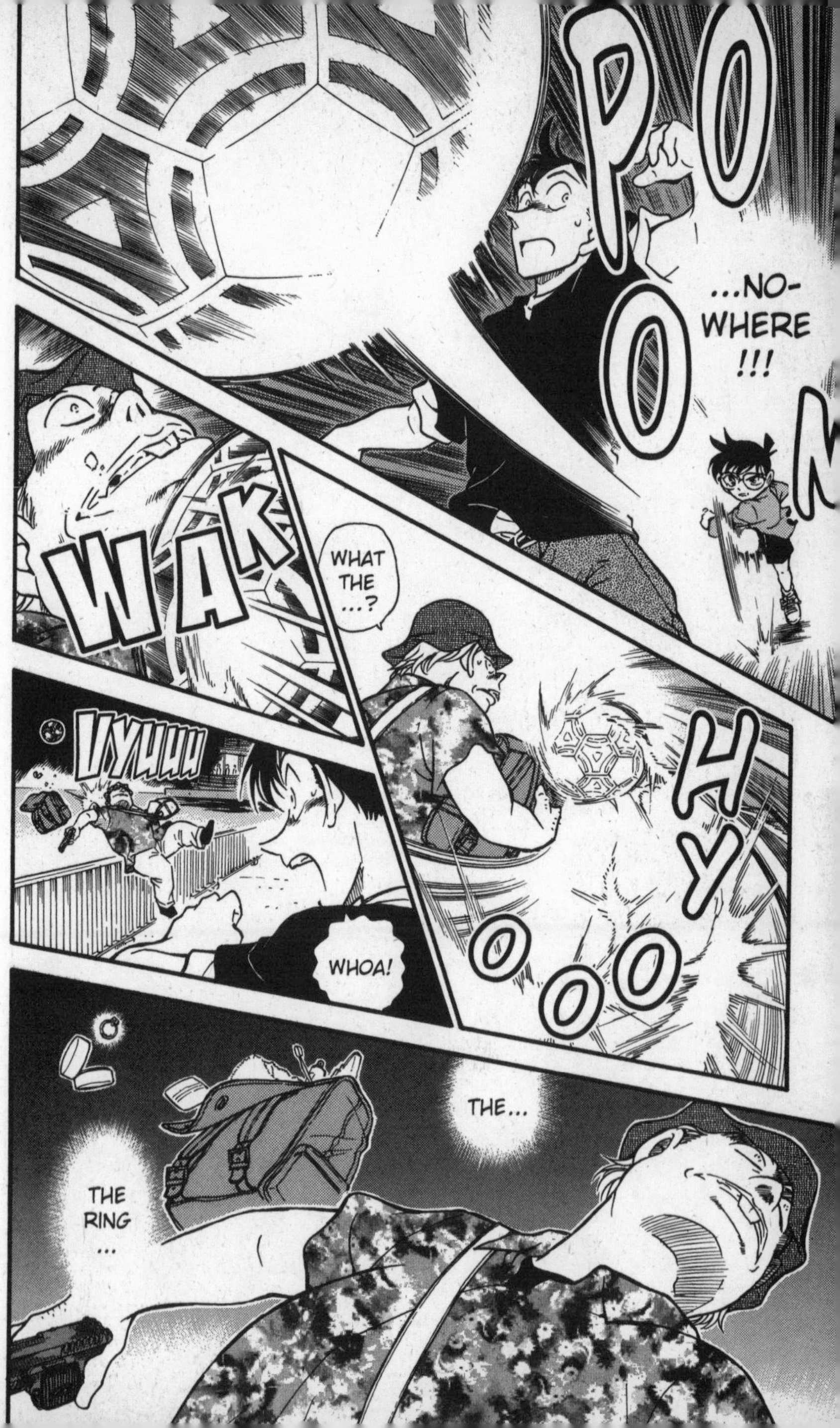

POOM
...NO-
WHERE
!!!
HYOOO
WHAT THE ...?
WAK
VYUUU
WHOA!
THE...
THE RING ...

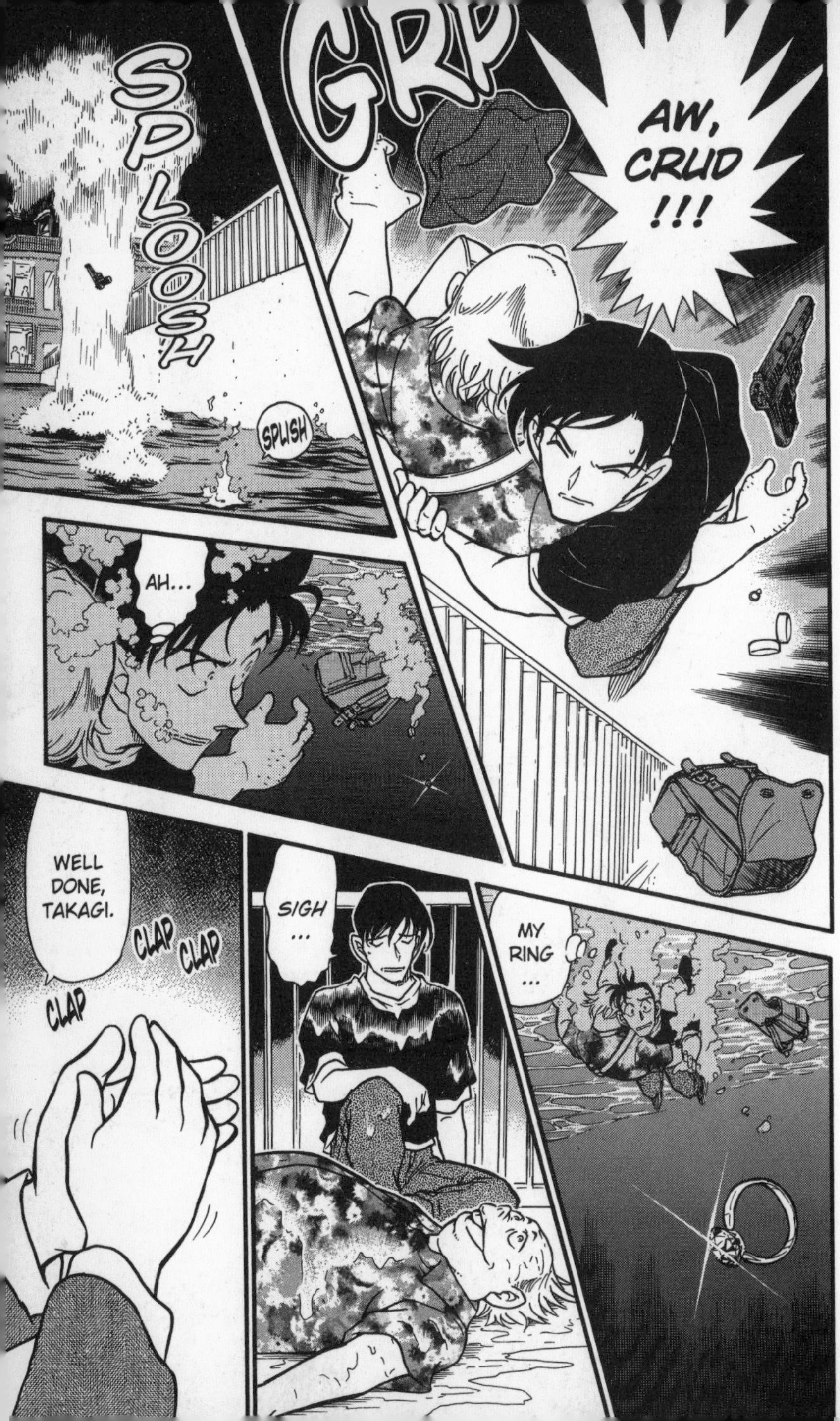
GRIP
AW, CRUD !!!
SPLOOSH
SPLISH
AH...
MY RING ...
SIGH ...
WELL DONE, TAKAGI.
CLAP
CLAP
CLAP

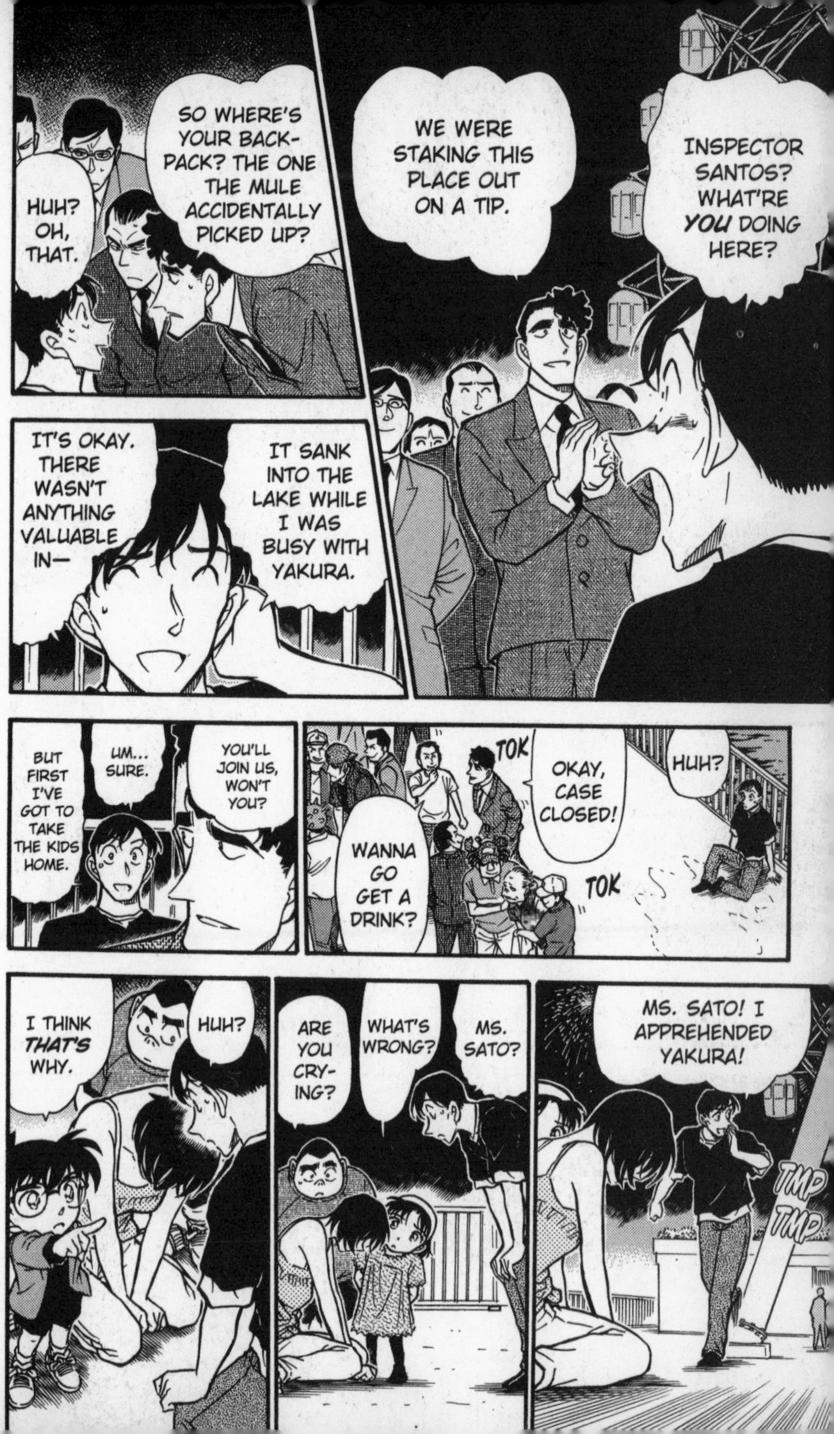
INSPECTOR SANTOS? WHAT'RE *YOU* DOING HERE?
WE WERE STAKING THIS PLACE OUT ON A TIP.
SO WHERE'S YOUR BACK-PACK? THE ONE THE MULE ACCIDENTALLY PICKED UP?
HUH? OH, THAT.
IT SANK INTO THE LAKE WHILE I WAS BUSY WITH YAKURA.
IT'S OKAY. THERE WASN'T ANYTHING VALUABLE IN—
HUH?
OKAY, CASE CLOSED!
TOK
WANNA GO GET A DRINK?
TOK
YOU'LL JOIN US, WON'T YOU?
UM... SURE.
BUT FIRST I'VE GOT TO TAKE THE KIDS HOME.
MS. SATO! I APPREHENDED YAKURA!
TMP TMP
MS. SATO?
WHAT'S WRONG?
ARE YOU CRY-ING?
HUH?
I THINK *THAT'S* WHY.

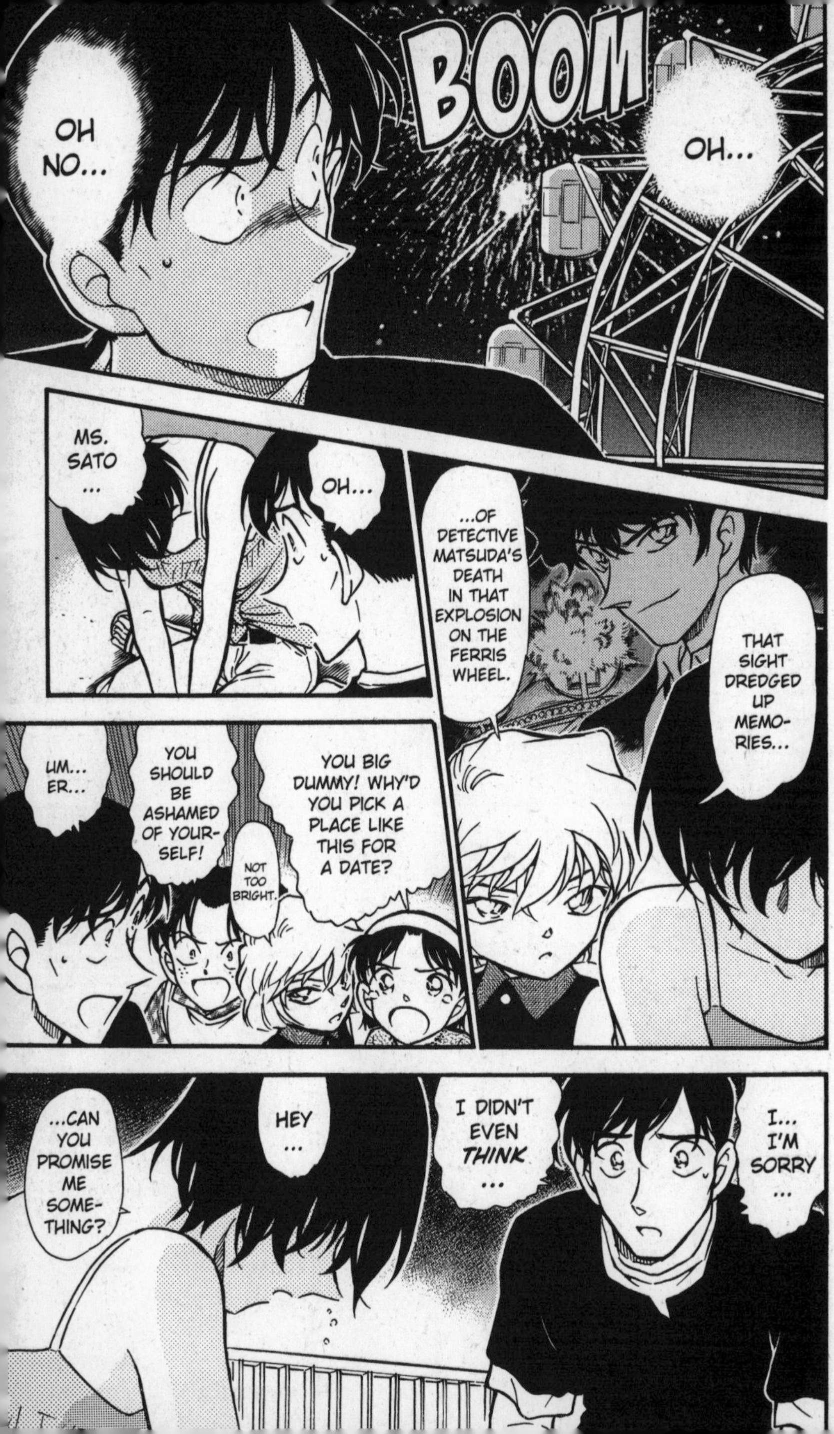
BOOM
OH...
OH NO...
THAT SIGHT DREDGED UP MEMO-RIES...
...OF DETECTIVE MATSUDA'S DEATH IN THAT EXPLOSION ON THE FERRIS WHEEL.
OH...
MS. SATO ...
YOU BIG DUMMY! WHY'D YOU PICK A PLACE LIKE THIS FOR A DATE?
NOT TOO BRIGHT.
YOU SHOULD BE ASHAMED OF YOUR-SELF!
UM... ER...
I... I'M SORRY ...
I DIDN'T EVEN *THINK* ...
HEY ...
...CAN YOU PROMISE ME SOME-THING?

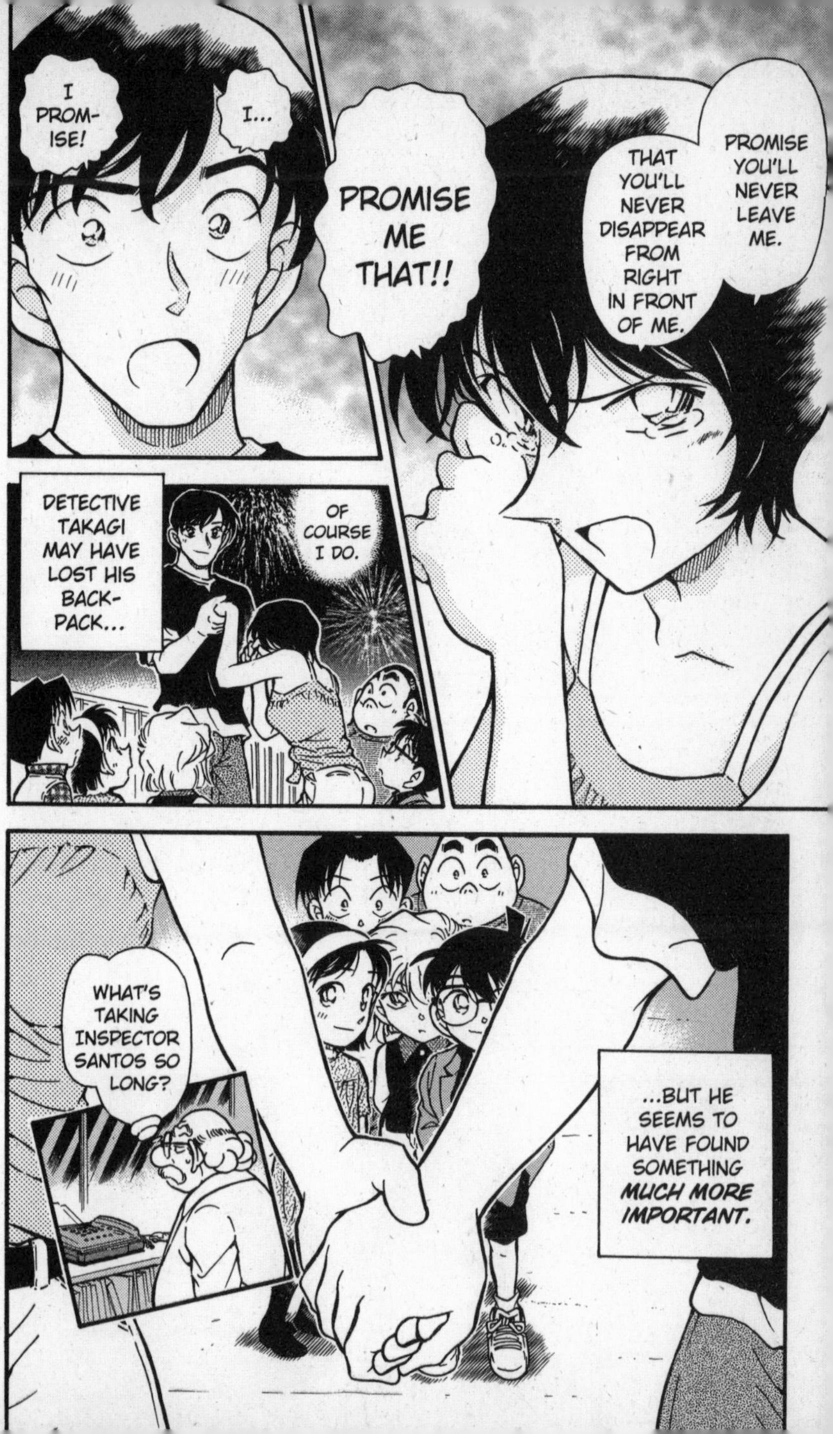
PROMISE YOU'LL NEVER LEAVE ME.
THAT YOU'LL NEVER DISAPPEAR FROM RIGHT IN FRONT OF ME.
PROMISE ME THAT!!
I...
I PROM-ISE!
OF COURSE I DO.
DETECTIVE TAKAGI MAY HAVE LOST HIS BACK-PACK...
...BUT HE SEEMS TO HAVE FOUND SOMETHING ***MUCH MORE IMPORTANT.***
WHAT'S TAKING INSPECTOR SANTOS SO LONG?

FILE 4: TENNIS COURT MEMORIES

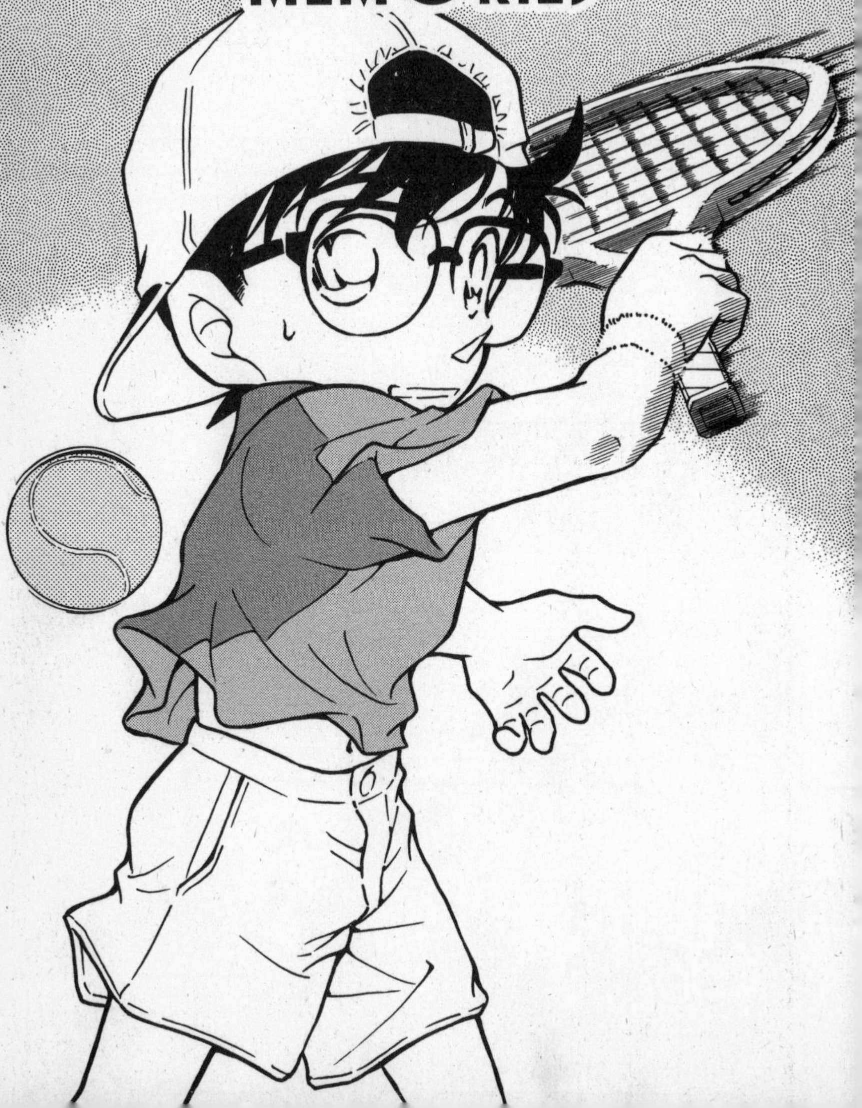

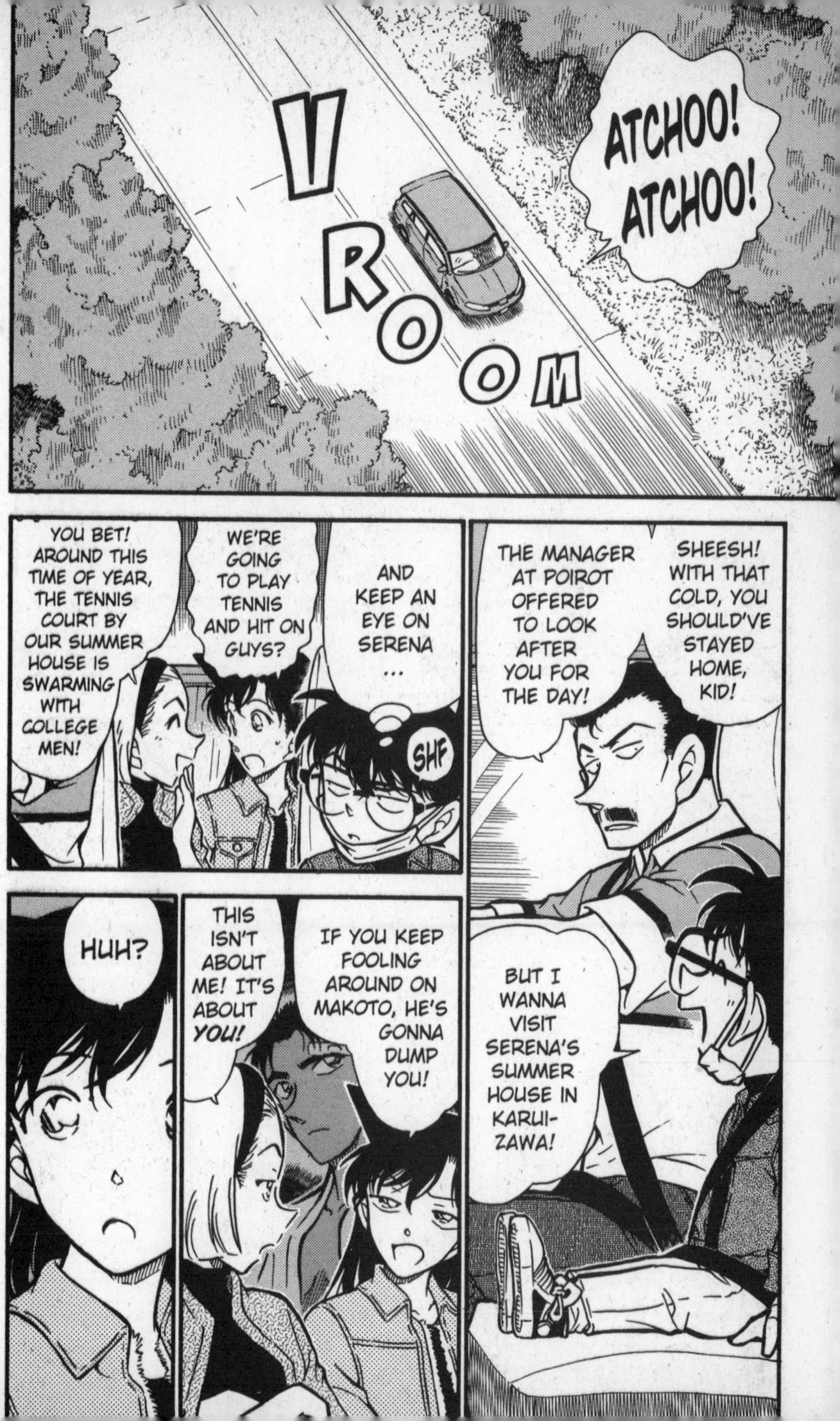
ATCHOO! ATCHOO!
VROOM
SHEESH! WITH THAT COLD, YOU SHOULD'VE STAYED HOME, KID!
THE MANAGER AT POIROT OFFERED TO LOOK AFTER YOU FOR THE DAY!
BUT I WANNA VISIT SERENA'S SUMMER HOUSE IN KARUI-ZAWA!
AND KEEP AN EYE ON SERENA...
SHF
WE'RE GOING TO PLAY TENNIS AND HIT ON GUYS?
YOU BET! AROUND THIS TIME OF YEAR, THE TENNIS COURT BY OUR SUMMER HOUSE IS SWARMING WITH COLLEGE MEN!
IF YOU KEEP FOOLING AROUND ON MAKOTO, HE'S GONNA DUMP YOU!
THIS ISN'T ABOUT ME! IT'S ABOUT *YOU!*
HUH?

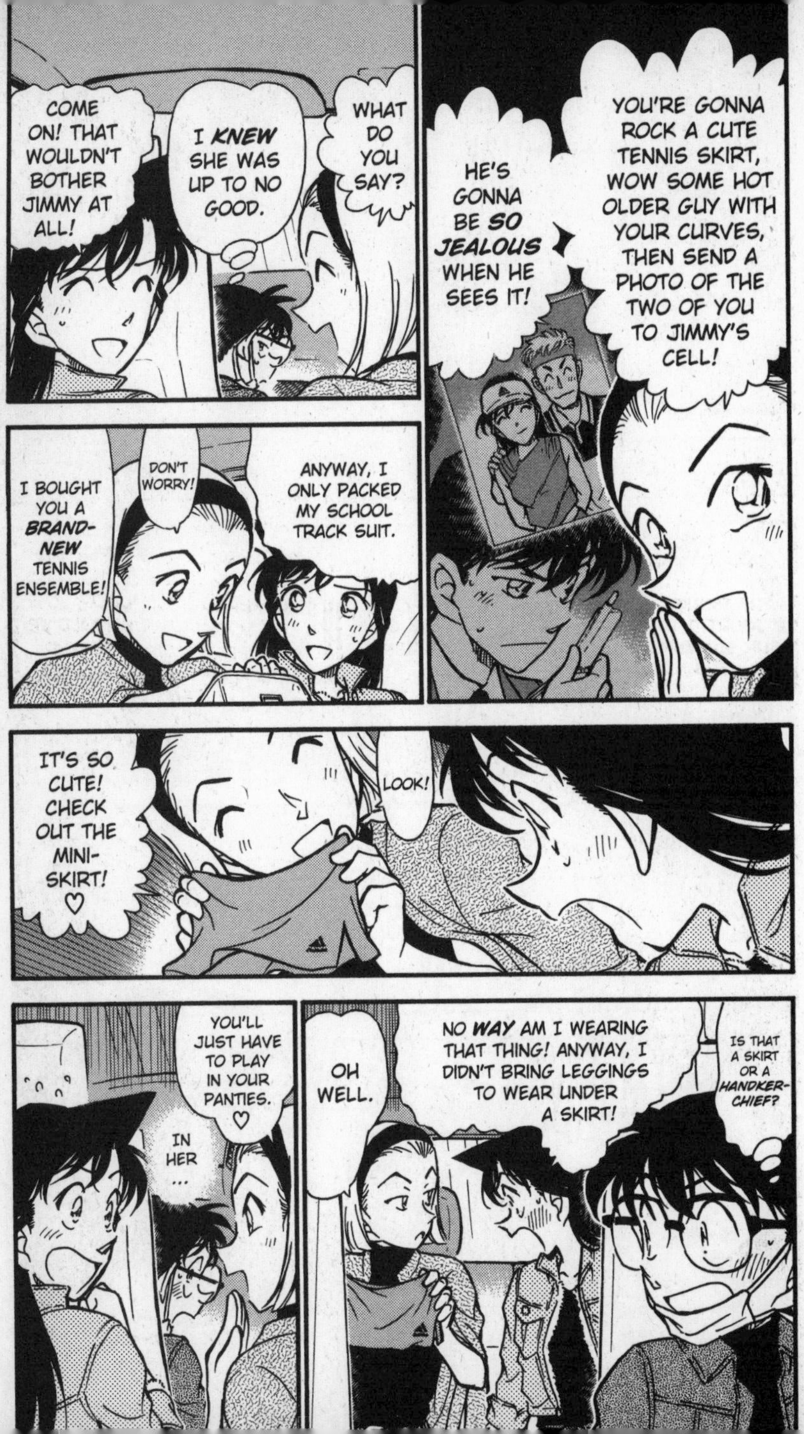
YOU'RE GONNA ROCK A CUTE TENNIS SKIRT, WOW SOME HOT OLDER GUY WITH YOUR CURVES, THEN SEND A PHOTO OF THE TWO OF YOU TO JIMMY'S CELL!
HE'S GONNA BE *SO JEALOUS* WHEN HE SEES IT!
WHAT DO YOU SAY?
I *KNEW* SHE WAS UP TO NO GOOD.
COME ON! THAT WOULDN'T BOTHER JIMMY AT ALL!
ANYWAY, I ONLY PACKED MY SCHOOL TRACK SUIT.
DON'T WORRY!
I BOUGHT YOU A *BRAND-NEW* TENNIS ENSEMBLE!
LOOK!
IT'S SO CUTE! CHECK OUT THE MINI-SKIRT! ♡
IS THAT A SKIRT OR A *HANDKER-CHIEF?*
NO *WAY* AM I WEARING THAT THING! ANYWAY, I DIDN'T BRING LEGGINGS TO WEAR UNDER A SKIRT!
OH WELL.
YOU'LL JUST HAVE TO PLAY IN YOUR PANTIES. ♡
IN HER ...

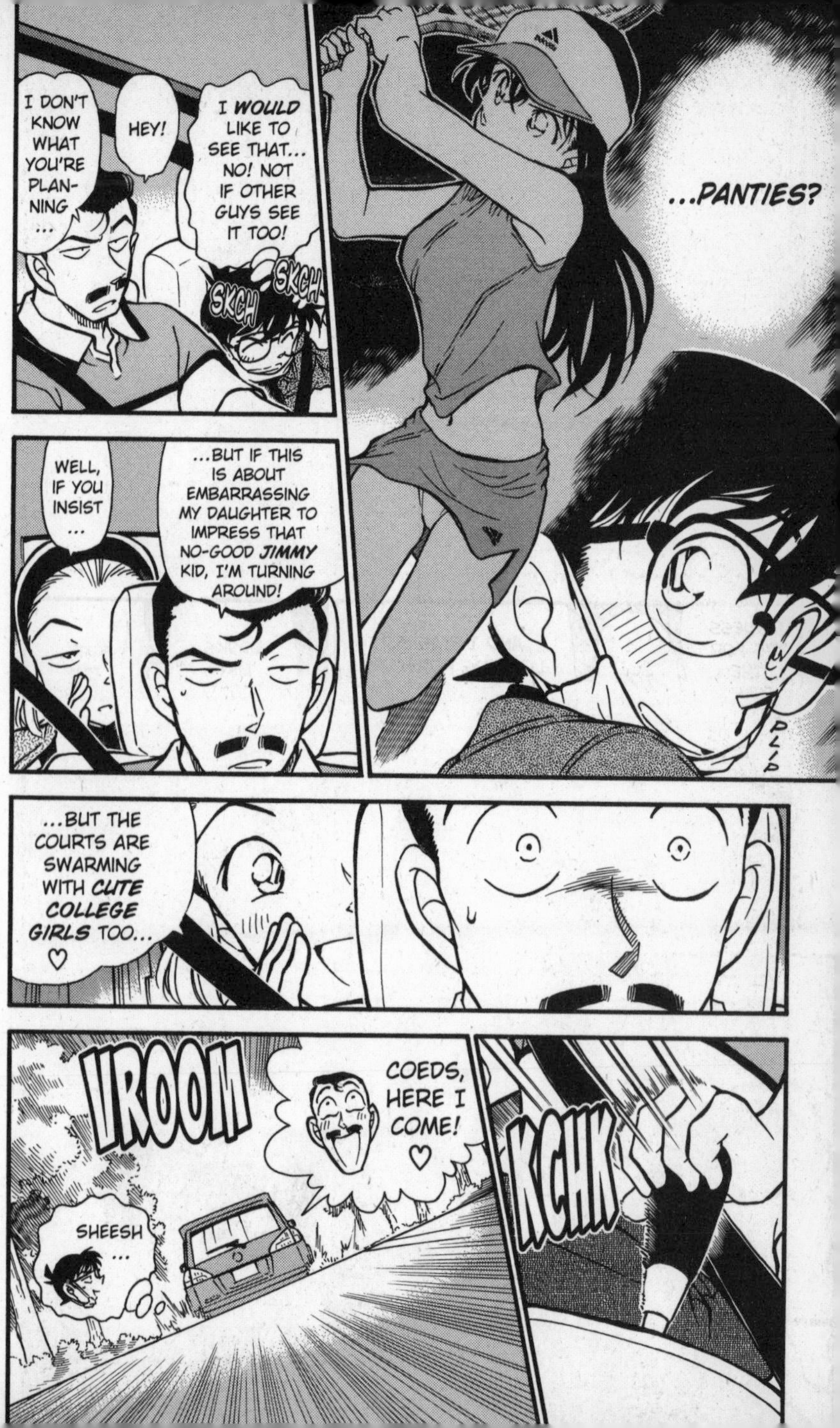
...PANTIES?
PLIP
I WOULD LIKE TO SEE THAT... NO! NOT IF OTHER GUYS SEE IT TOO!
HEY!
I DON'T KNOW WHAT YOU'RE PLAN-NING...
SKCH
SKCH
...BUT IF THIS IS ABOUT EMBARRASSING MY DAUGHTER TO IMPRESS THAT NO-GOOD JIMMY KID, I'M TURNING AROUND!
WELL, IF YOU INSIST...
...BUT THE COURTS ARE SWARMING WITH CUTE COLLEGE GIRLS TOO... ♡
KCHK
COEDS, HERE I COME! ♡
VROOM
SHEESH...

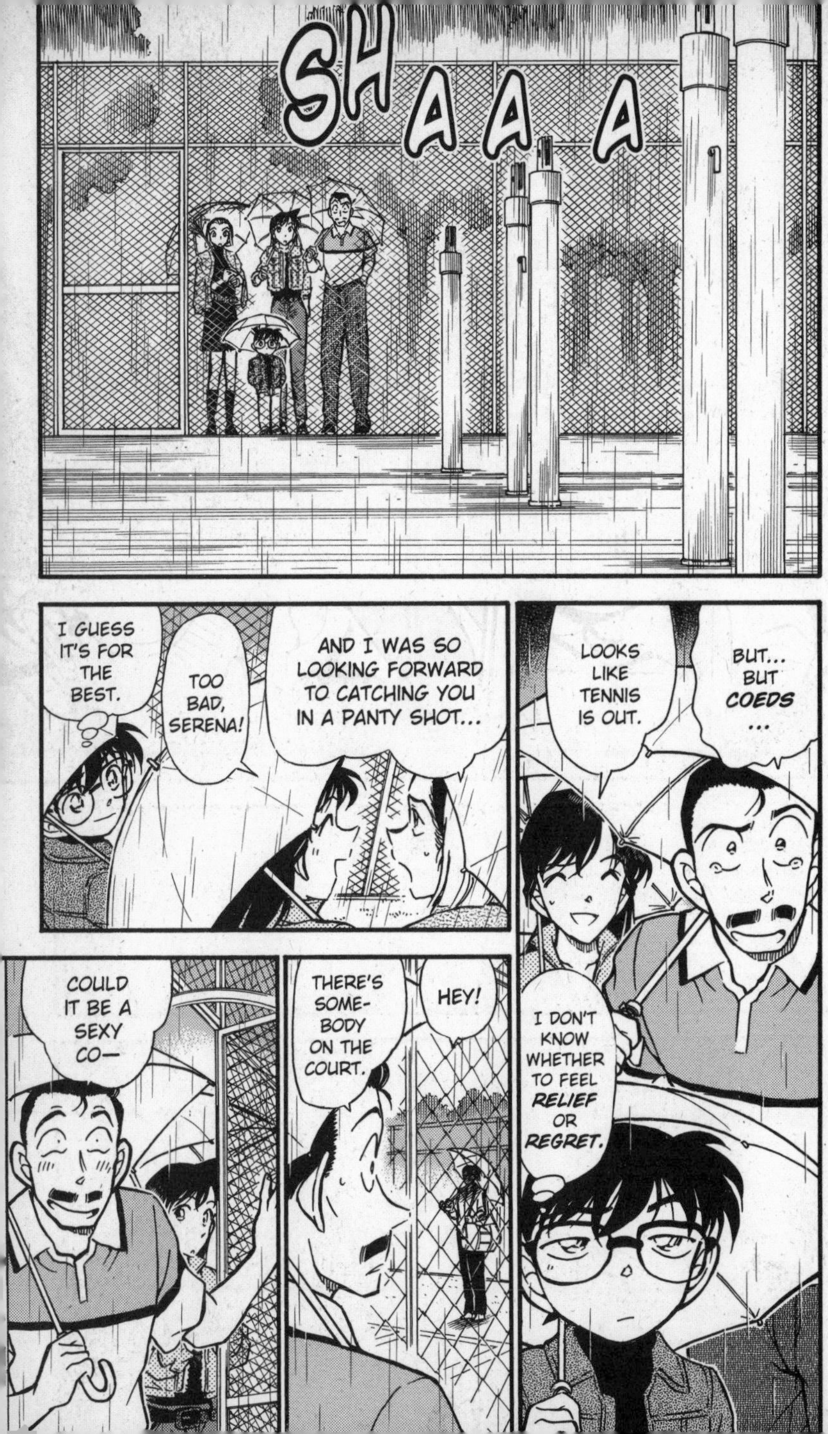
SHAAAA
LOOKS LIKE TENNIS IS OUT.
BUT... BUT **COEDS**...
I DON'T KNOW WHETHER TO FEEL **RELIEF** OR **REGRET.**
AND I WAS SO LOOKING FORWARD TO CATCHING YOU IN A PANTY SHOT...
TOO BAD, SERENA!
I GUESS IT'S FOR THE BEST.
HEY!
THERE'S SOME-BODY ON THE COURT.
COULD IT BE A SEXY CO—

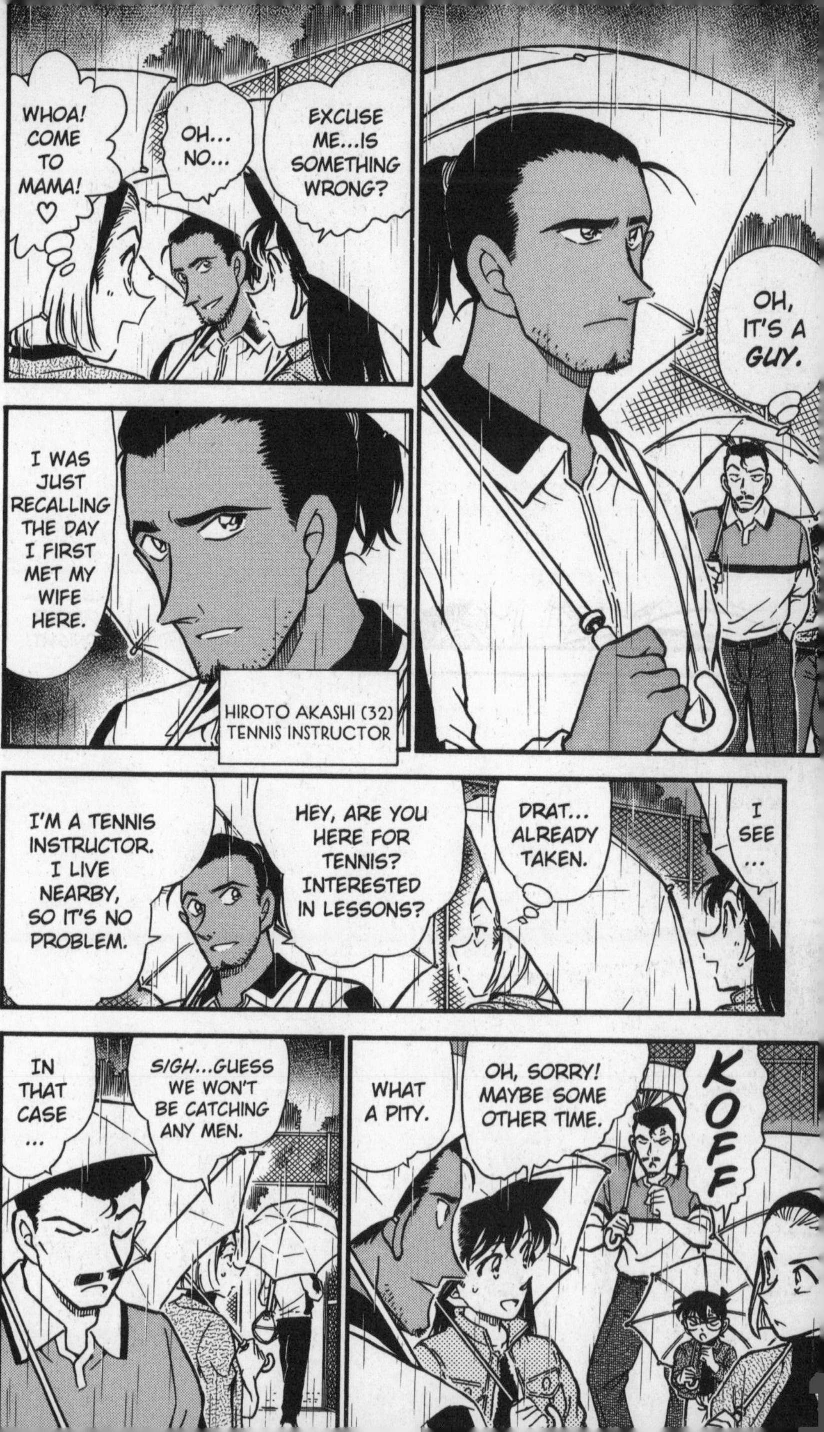

OH, IT'S A *GUY*.
EXCUSE ME...IS SOMETHING WRONG?
OH... NO...
WHOA! COME TO MAMA! ♡
I WAS JUST RECALLING THE DAY I FIRST MET MY WIFE HERE.
HIROTO AKASHI (32) TENNIS INSTRUCTOR
I SEE...
DRAT... ALREADY TAKEN.
HEY, ARE YOU HERE FOR TENNIS? INTERESTED IN LESSONS?
I'M A TENNIS INSTRUCTOR. I LIVE NEARBY, SO IT'S NO PROBLEM.
KOFF
OH, SORRY! MAYBE SOME OTHER TIME.
WHAT A PITY.
SIGH...GUESS WE WON'T BE CATCHING ANY MEN.
IN THAT CASE...

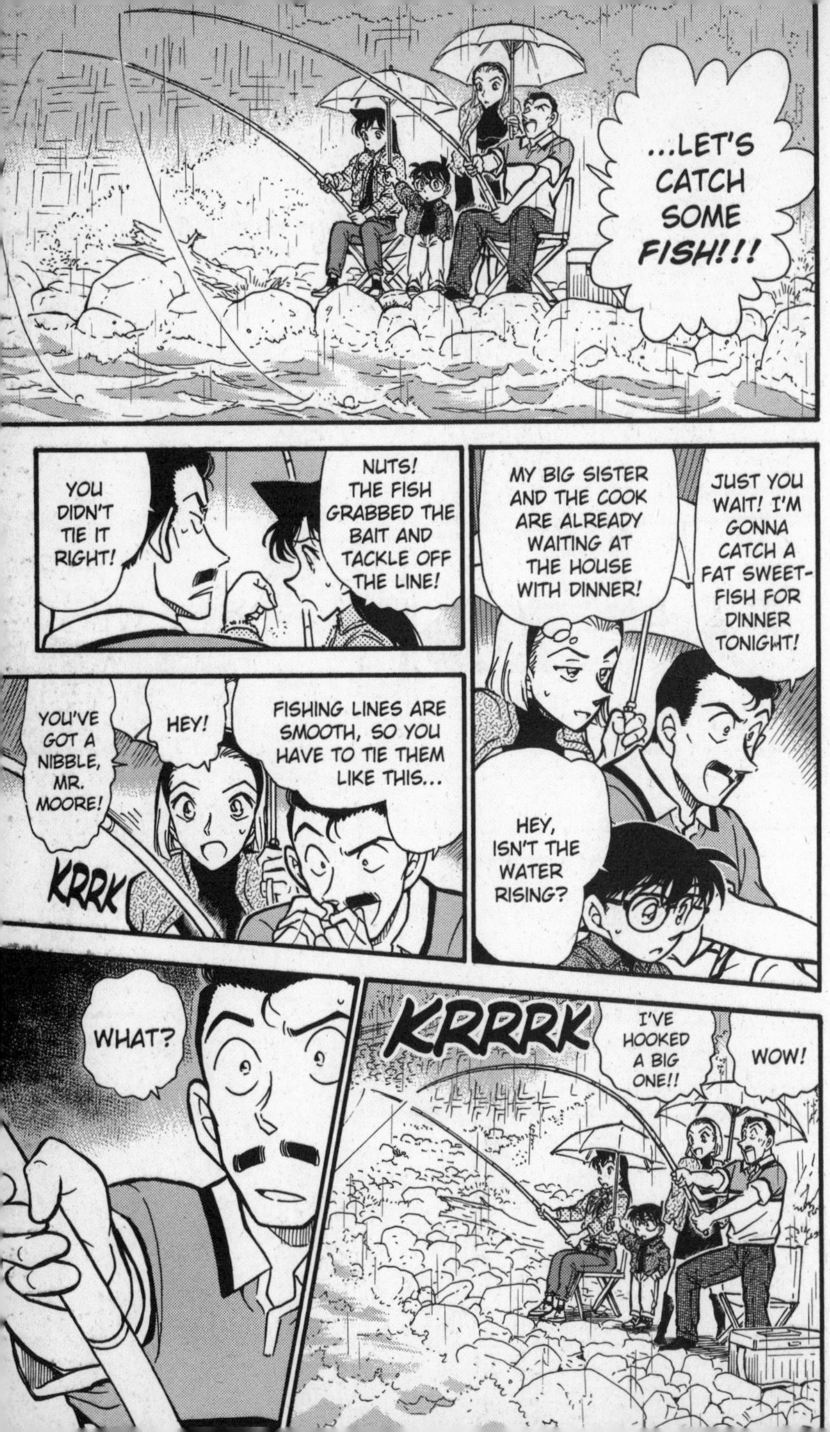
...LET'S CATCH SOME FISH!!!
JUST YOU WAIT! I'M GONNA CATCH A FAT SWEET-FISH FOR DINNER TONIGHT!
MY BIG SISTER AND THE COOK ARE ALREADY WAITING AT THE HOUSE WITH DINNER!
HEY, ISN'T THE WATER RISING?
NUTS! THE FISH GRABBED THE BAIT AND TACKLE OFF THE LINE!
YOU DIDN'T TIE IT RIGHT!
FISHING LINES ARE SMOOTH, SO YOU HAVE TO TIE THEM LIKE THIS...
HEY!
YOU'VE GOT A NIBBLE, MR. MOORE!
KRRK
WOW!
I'VE HOOKED A BIG ONE!!
KRRRK
WHAT?

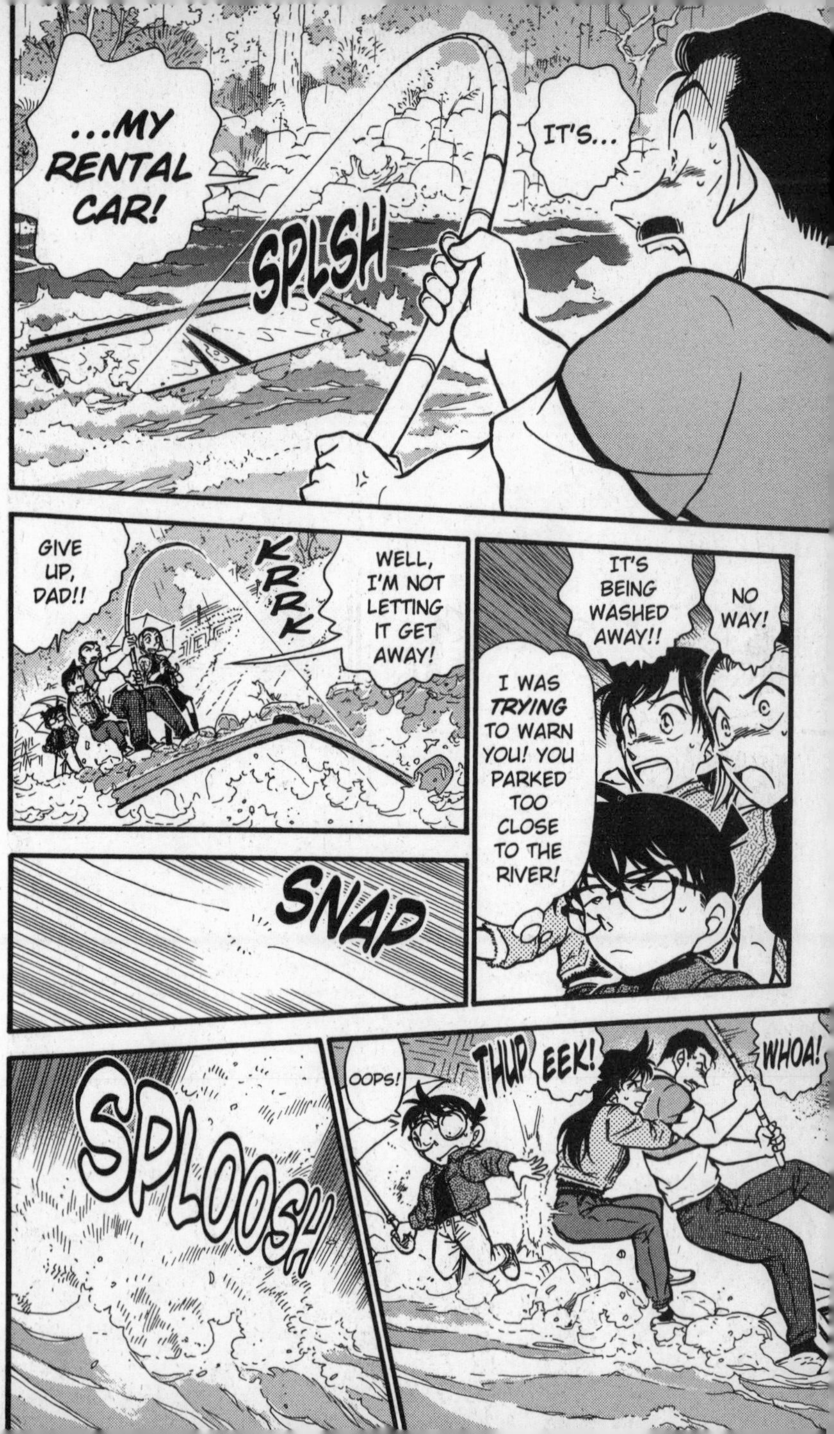
IT'S...
...MY RENTAL CAR!
SPLSH
NO WAY!
IT'S BEING WASHED AWAY!!
I WAS *TRYING* TO WARN YOU! YOU PARKED TOO CLOSE TO THE RIVER!
WELL, I'M NOT LETTING IT GET AWAY!
KRRK
GIVE UP, DAD!!
SNAP
WHOA!
EEK!
THUP
OOPS!
SPLOOSH

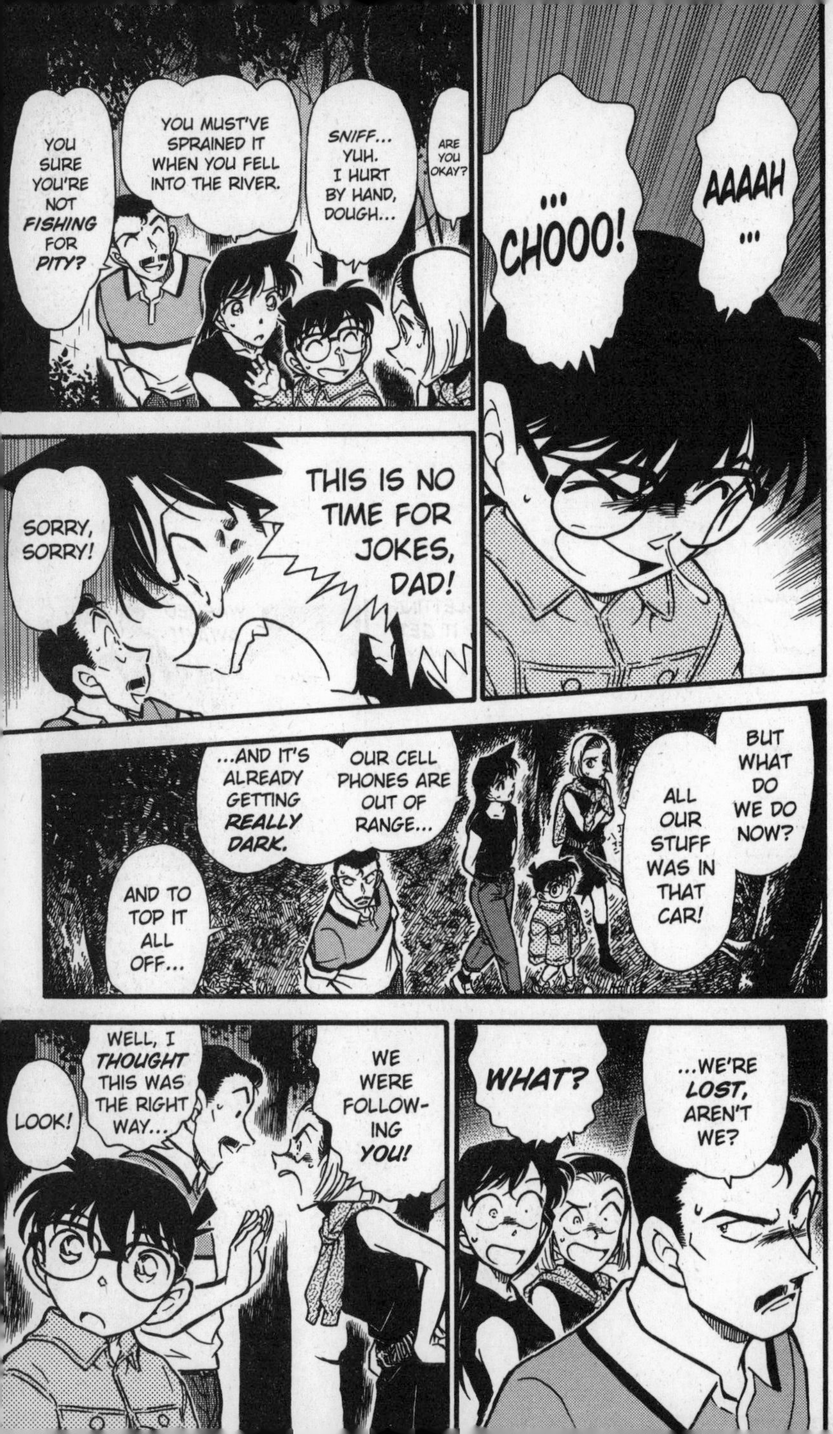
AAAAH ...
... CHOOO!
ARE YOU OKAY?
SNIFF... YUH. I HURT BY HAND, DOUGH...
YOU MUST'VE SPRAINED IT WHEN YOU FELL INTO THE RIVER.
YOU SURE YOU'RE NOT FISHING FOR PITY?
THIS IS NO TIME FOR JOKES, DAD!
SORRY, SORRY!
BUT WHAT DO WE DO NOW?
ALL OUR STUFF WAS IN THAT CAR!
OUR CELL PHONES ARE OUT OF RANGE...
...AND IT'S ALREADY GETTING REALLY DARK.
AND TO TOP IT ALL OFF...
...WE'RE LOST, AREN'T WE?
WHAT?
WE WERE FOLLOW-ING YOU!
WELL, I THOUGHT THIS WAS THE RIGHT WAY...
LOOK!

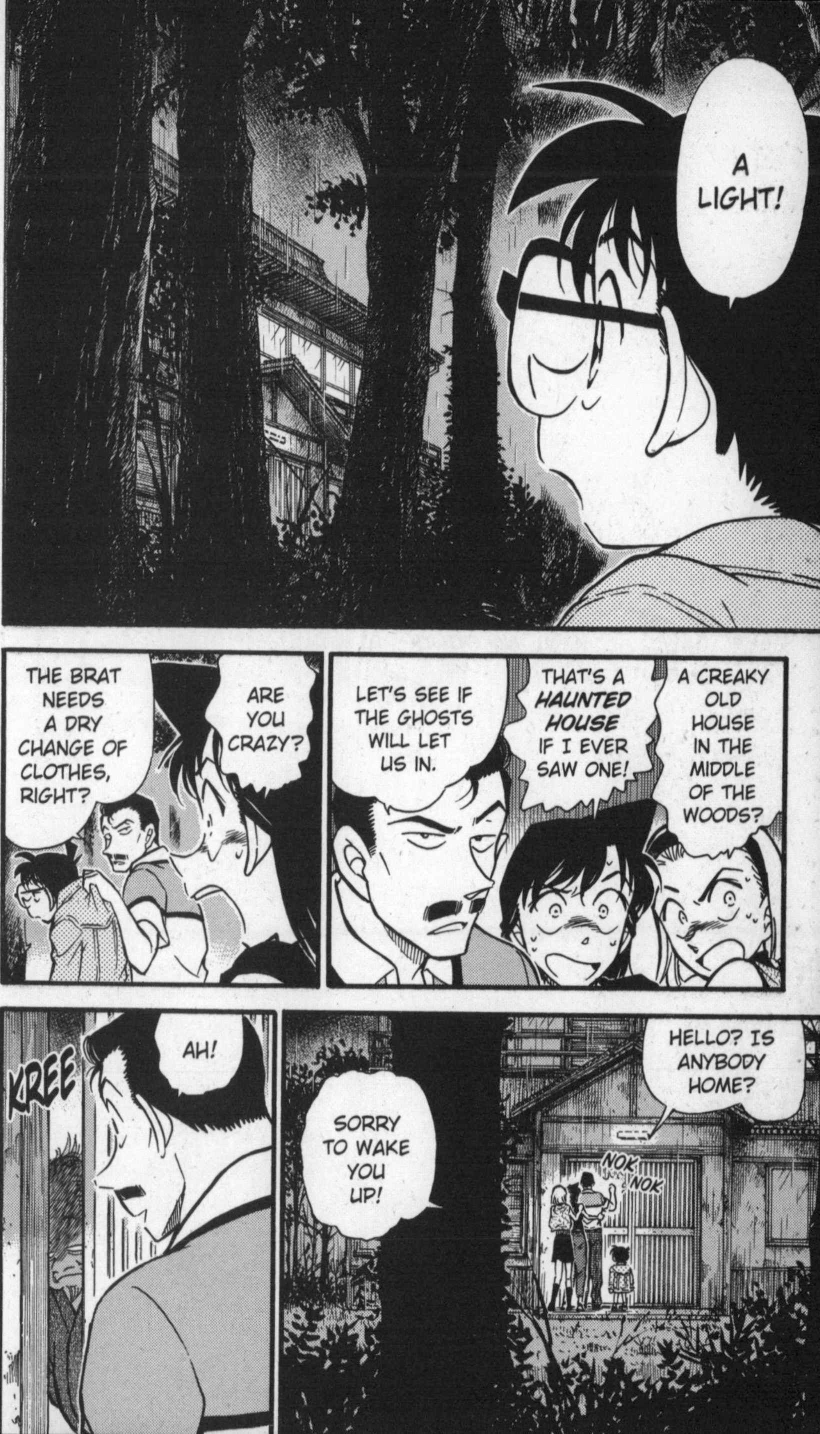
A LIGHT!
A CREAKY OLD HOUSE IN THE MIDDLE OF THE WOODS?
THAT'S A *HAUNTED HOUSE* IF I EVER SAW ONE!
LET'S SEE IF THE GHOSTS WILL LET US IN.
ARE YOU CRAZY?
THE BRAT NEEDS A DRY CHANGE OF CLOTHES, RIGHT?
HELLO? IS ANYBODY HOME?
NOK NOK
SORRY TO WAKE YOU UP!
AH!
KREE

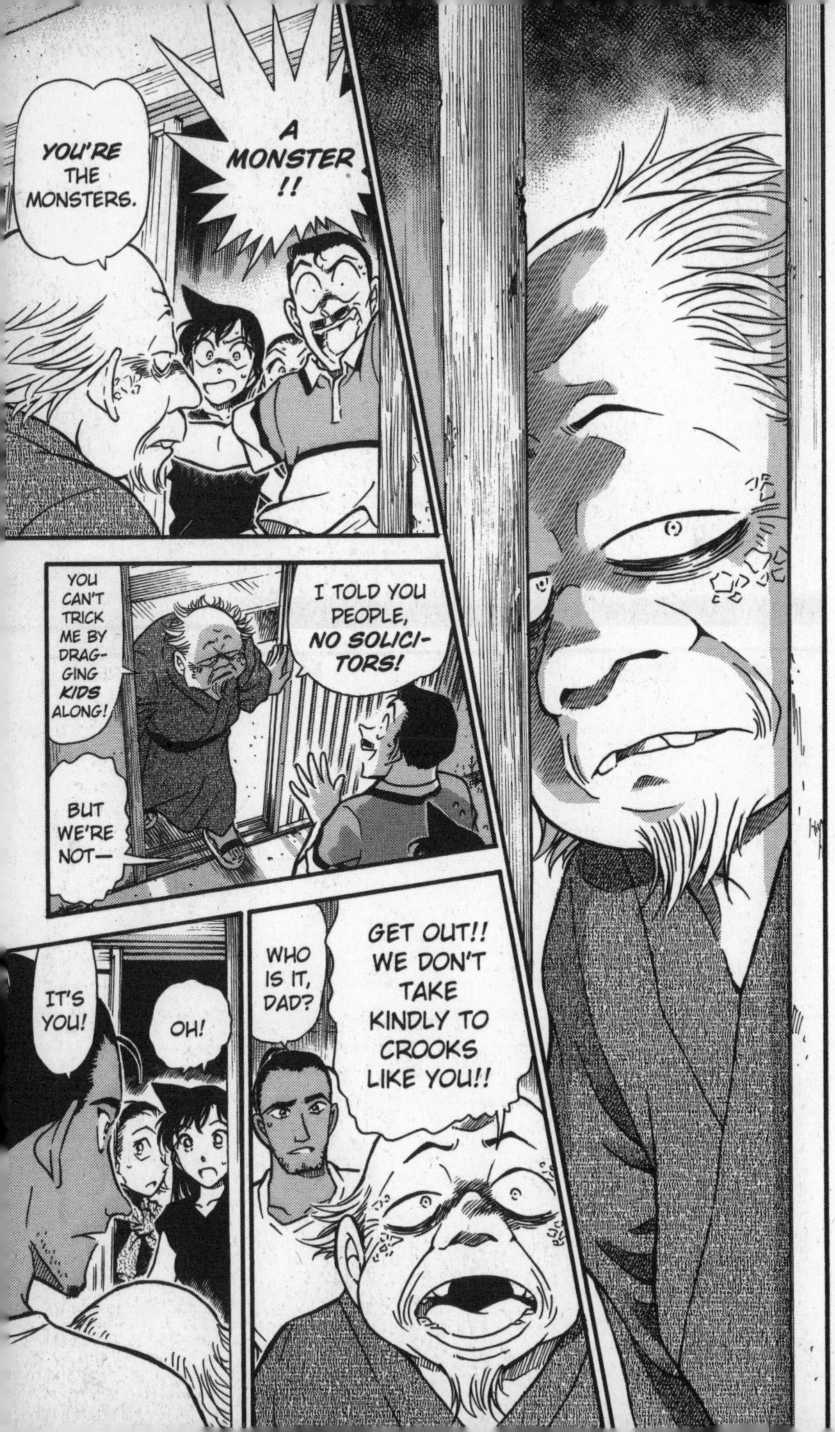

A MONSTER!!
YOU'RE THE MONSTERS.
I TOLD YOU PEOPLE, NO SOLICI-TORS!
YOU CAN'T TRICK ME BY DRAG-GING KIDS ALONG!
BUT WE'RE NOT—
GET OUT!! WE DON'T TAKE KINDLY TO CROOKS LIKE YOU!!
WHO IS IT, DAD?
OH!
IT'S YOU!

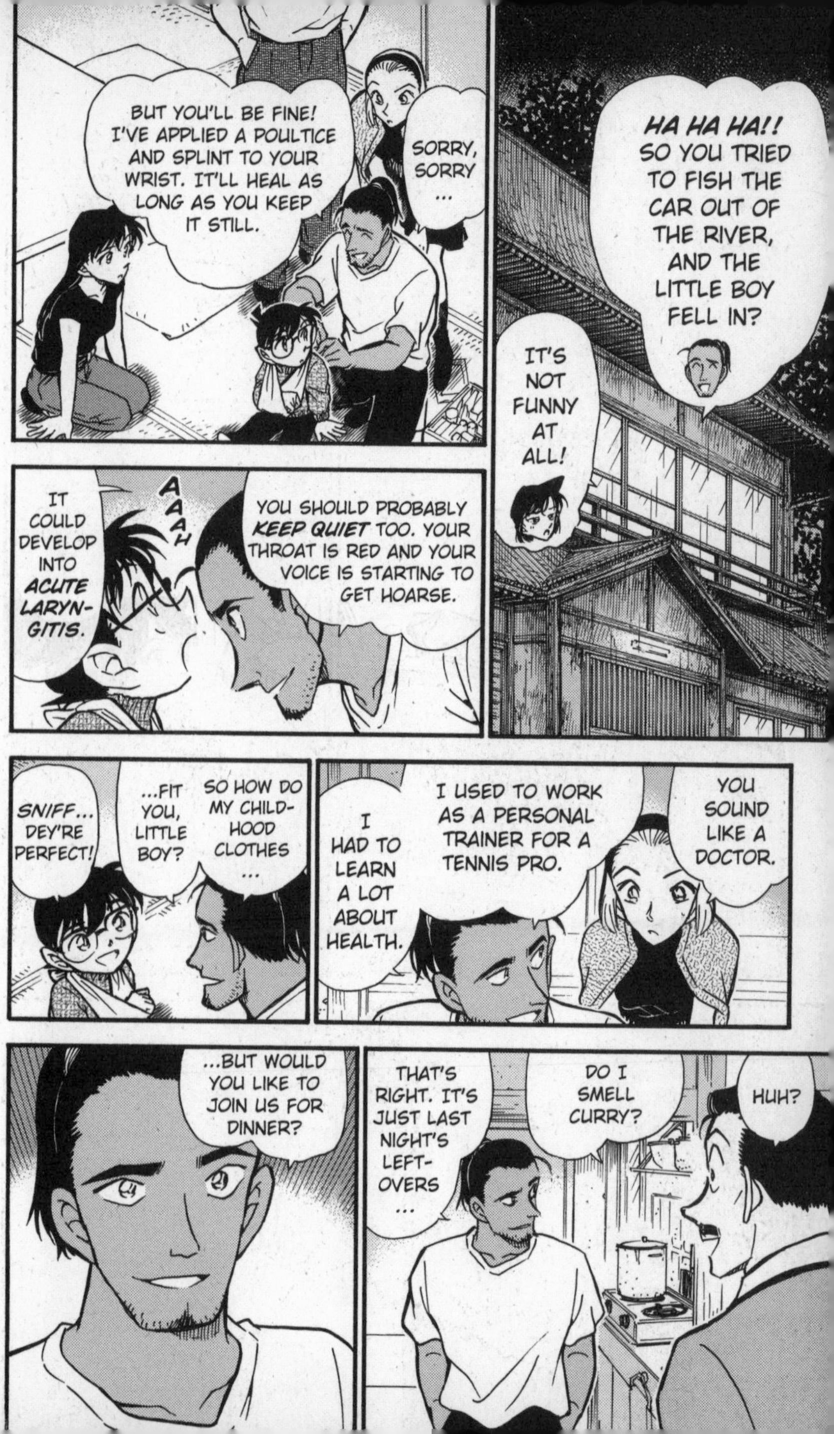
HA HA HA!! SO YOU TRIED TO FISH THE CAR OUT OF THE RIVER, AND THE LITTLE BOY FELL IN?
IT'S NOT FUNNY AT ALL!
SORRY, SORRY ...
BUT YOU'LL BE FINE! I'VE APPLIED A POULTICE AND SPLINT TO YOUR WRIST. IT'LL HEAL AS LONG AS YOU KEEP IT STILL.
YOU SHOULD PROBABLY KEEP QUIET TOO. YOUR THROAT IS RED AND YOUR VOICE IS STARTING TO GET HOARSE.
AAAH
IT COULD DEVELOP INTO ACUTE LARYNGITIS.
YOU SOUND LIKE A DOCTOR.
I USED TO WORK AS A PERSONAL TRAINER FOR A TENNIS PRO.
I HAD TO LEARN A LOT ABOUT HEALTH.
SO HOW DO MY CHILDHOOD CLOTHES ...
...FIT YOU, LITTLE BOY?
SNIFF... DEY'RE PERFECT!
HUH?
DO I SMELL CURRY?
THAT'S RIGHT. IT'S JUST LAST NIGHT'S LEFTOVERS ...
...BUT WOULD YOU LIKE TO JOIN US FOR DINNER?

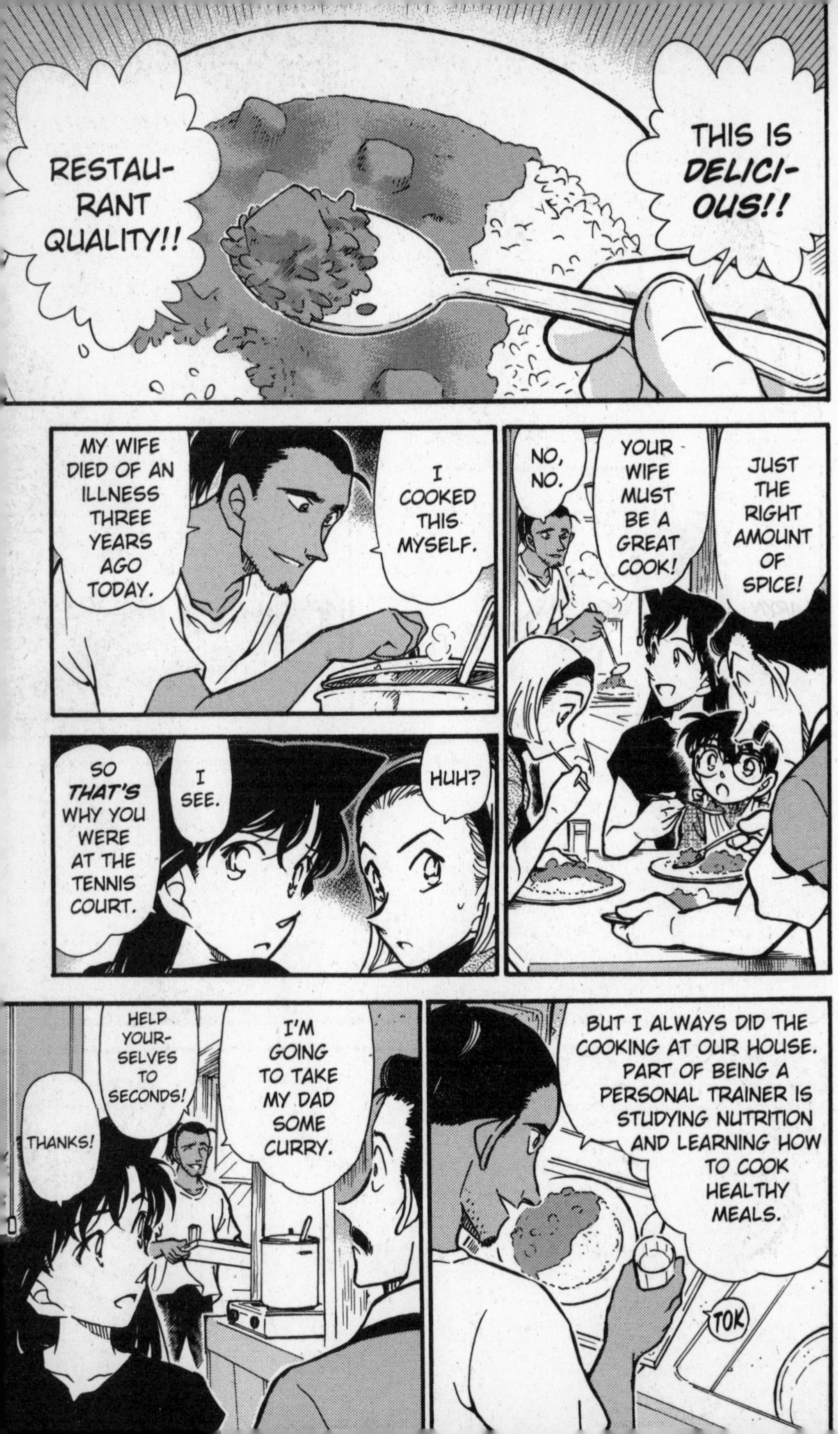
THIS IS DELICIOUS!!
RESTAURANT QUALITY!!
JUST THE RIGHT AMOUNT OF SPICE!
YOUR WIFE MUST BE A GREAT COOK!
NO, NO.
I COOKED THIS MYSELF.
MY WIFE DIED OF AN ILLNESS THREE YEARS AGO TODAY.
HUH?
I SEE.
SO THAT'S WHY YOU WERE AT THE TENNIS COURT.
BUT I ALWAYS DID THE COOKING AT OUR HOUSE. PART OF BEING A PERSONAL TRAINER IS STUDYING NUTRITION AND LEARNING HOW TO COOK HEALTHY MEALS.
TOK
I'M GOING TO TAKE MY DAD SOME CURRY.
HELP YOURSELVES TO SECONDS!
THANKS!

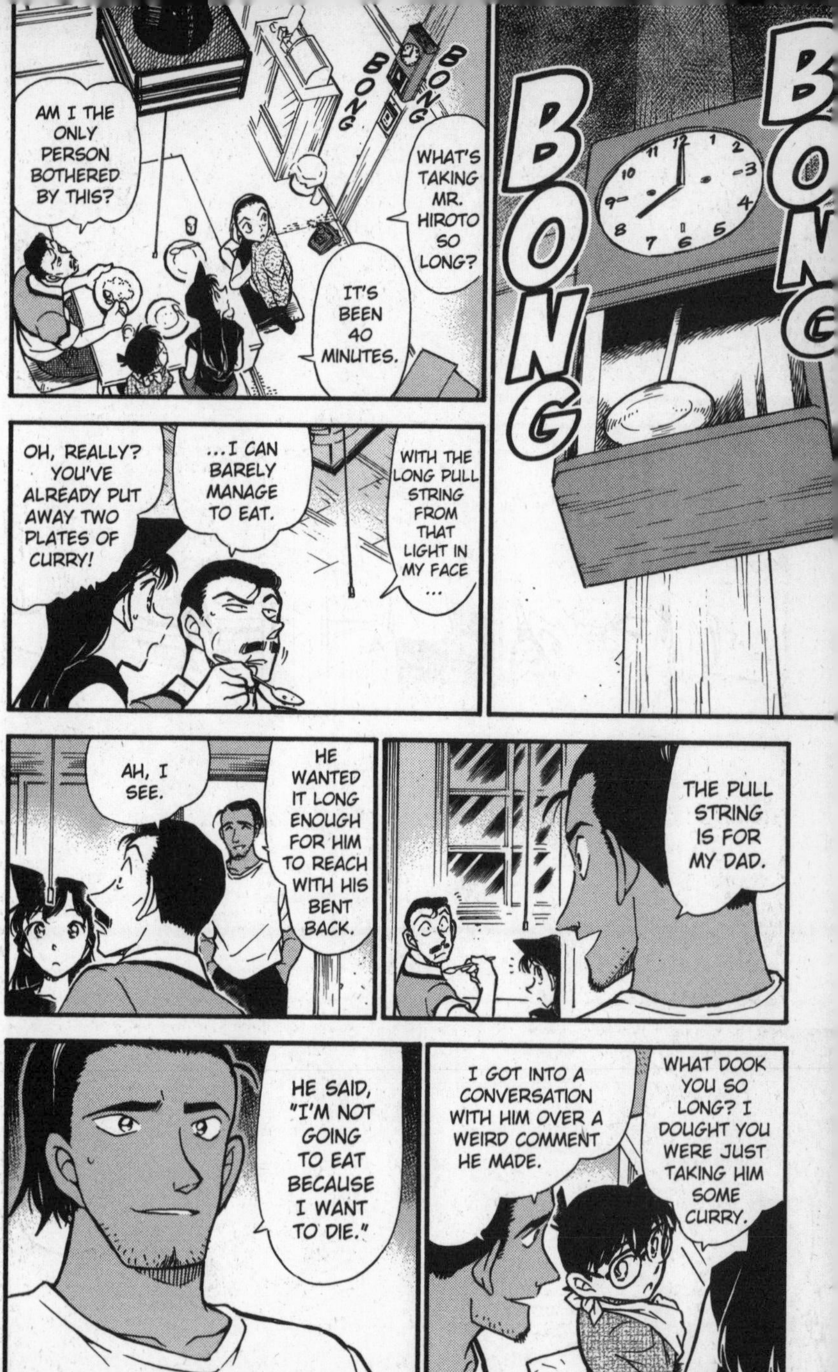
BONG
BONG
BONG
BONG
WHAT'S TAKING MR. HIROTO SO LONG?
IT'S BEEN 40 MINUTES.
AM I THE ONLY PERSON BOTHERED BY THIS?
WITH THE LONG PULL STRING FROM THAT LIGHT IN MY FACE ...
...I CAN BARELY MANAGE TO EAT.
OH, REALLY? YOU'VE ALREADY PUT AWAY TWO PLATES OF CURRY!
THE PULL STRING IS FOR MY DAD.
HE WANTED IT LONG ENOUGH FOR HIM TO REACH WITH HIS BENT BACK.
AH, I SEE.
WHAT DOOK YOU SO LONG? I DOUGHT YOU WERE JUST TAKING HIM SOME CURRY.
I GOT INTO A CONVERSATION WITH HIM OVER A WEIRD COMMENT HE MADE.
HE SAID, "I'M NOT GOING TO EAT BECAUSE I WANT TO DIE."

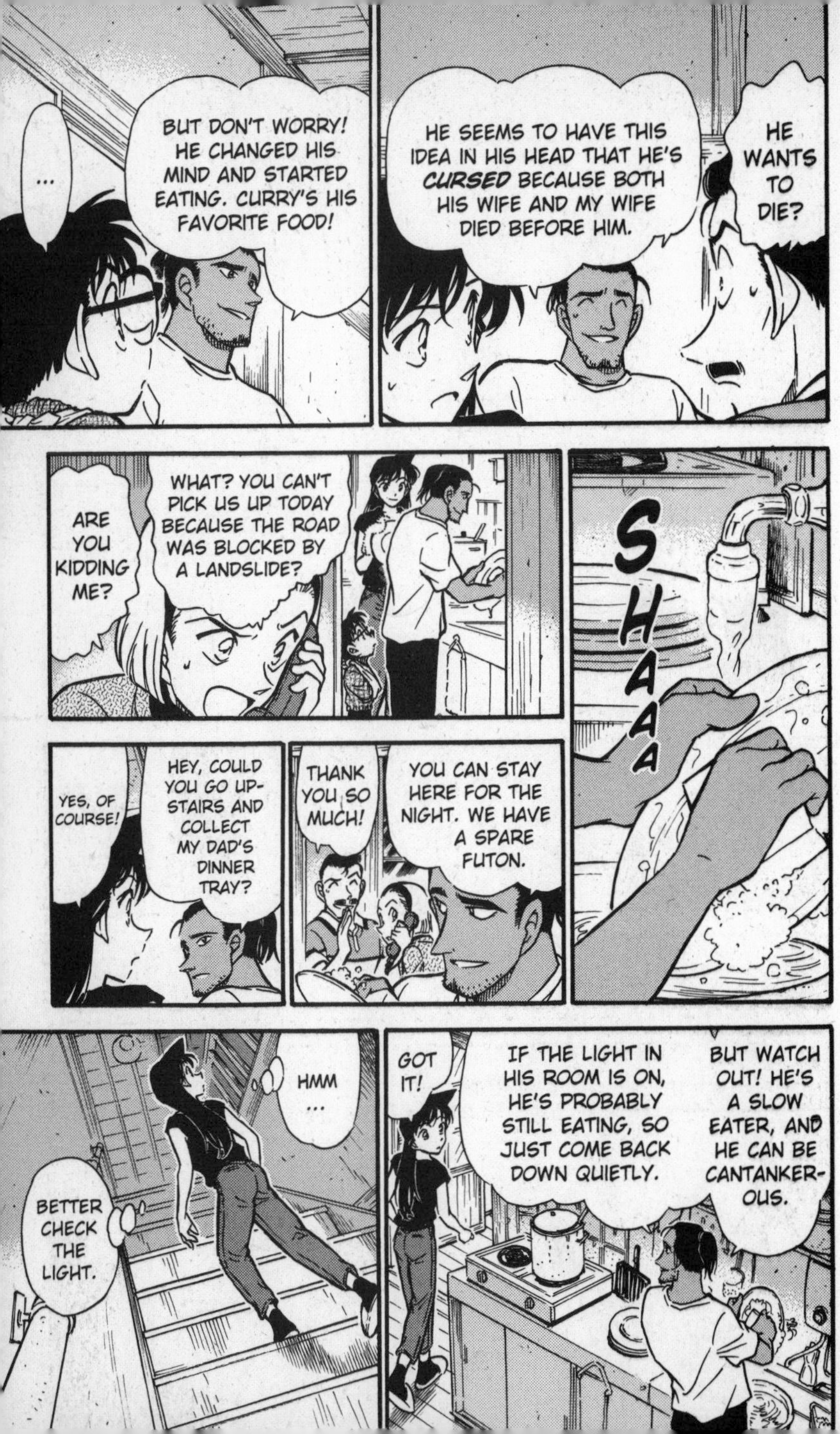
HE WANTS TO DIE?
HE SEEMS TO HAVE THIS IDEA IN HIS HEAD THAT HE'S *CURSED* BECAUSE BOTH HIS WIFE AND MY WIFE DIED BEFORE HIM.
BUT DON'T WORRY! HE CHANGED HIS MIND AND STARTED EATING. CURRY'S HIS FAVORITE FOOD!
...
SHAAAA
WHAT? YOU CAN'T PICK US UP TODAY BECAUSE THE ROAD WAS BLOCKED BY A LANDSLIDE?
ARE YOU KIDDING ME?
YOU CAN STAY HERE FOR THE NIGHT. WE HAVE A SPARE FUTON.
THANK YOU SO MUCH!
HEY, COULD YOU GO UP-STAIRS AND COLLECT MY DAD'S DINNER TRAY?
YES, OF COURSE!
BUT WATCH OUT! HE'S A SLOW EATER, AND HE CAN BE CANTANKER-OUS.
IF THE LIGHT IN HIS ROOM IS ON, HE'S PROBABLY STILL EATING, SO JUST COME BACK DOWN QUIETLY.
GOT IT!
HMM ...
BETTER CHECK THE LIGHT.

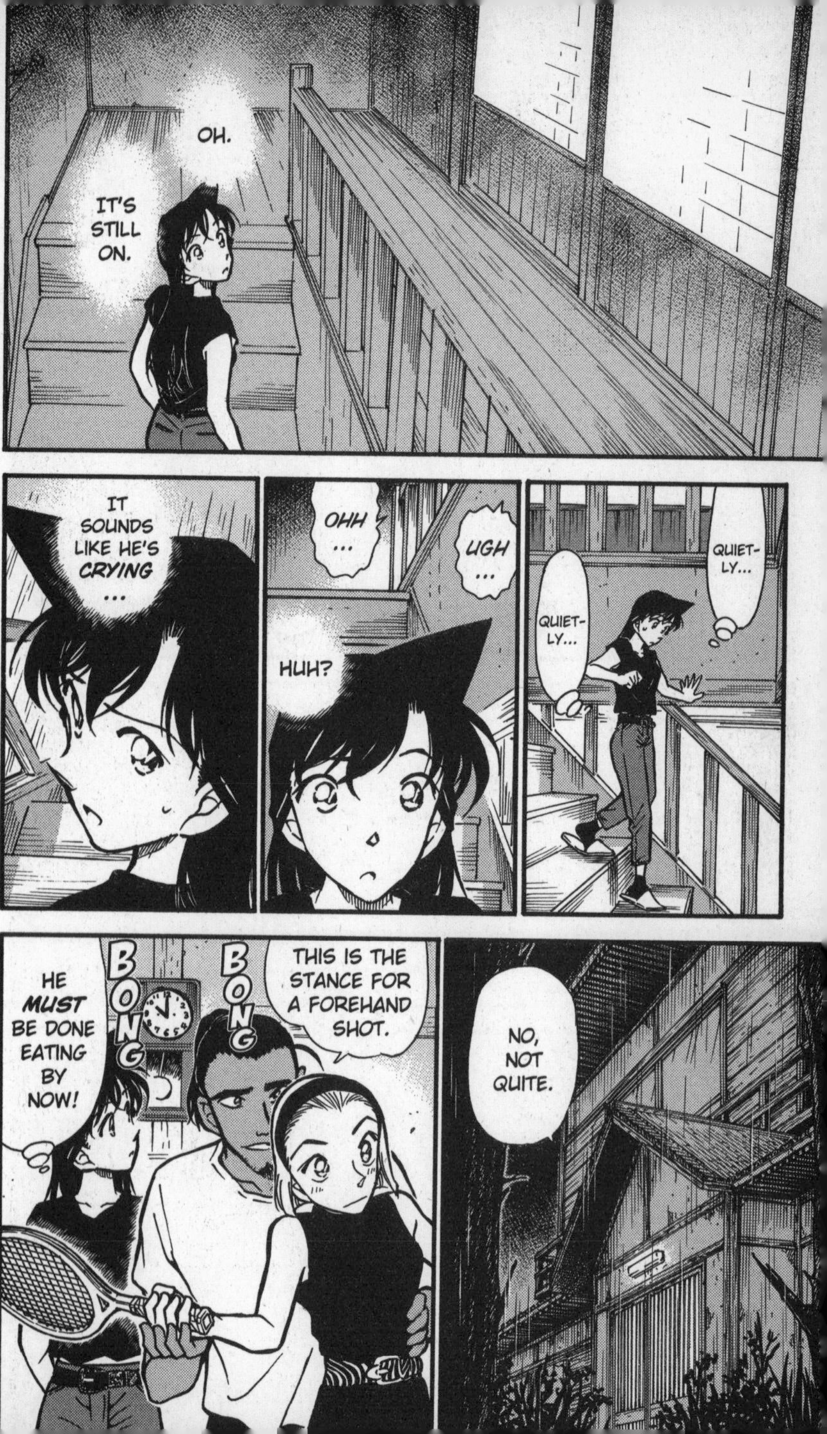
OH.
IT'S STILL ON.
QUIET-LY...
QUIET-LY...
UGH ...
OHH ...
HUH?
IT SOUNDS LIKE HE'S *CRYING* ...
NO, NOT QUITE.
THIS IS THE STANCE FOR A FOREHAND SHOT.
BONG
BONG
HE *MUST* BE DONE EATING BY NOW!

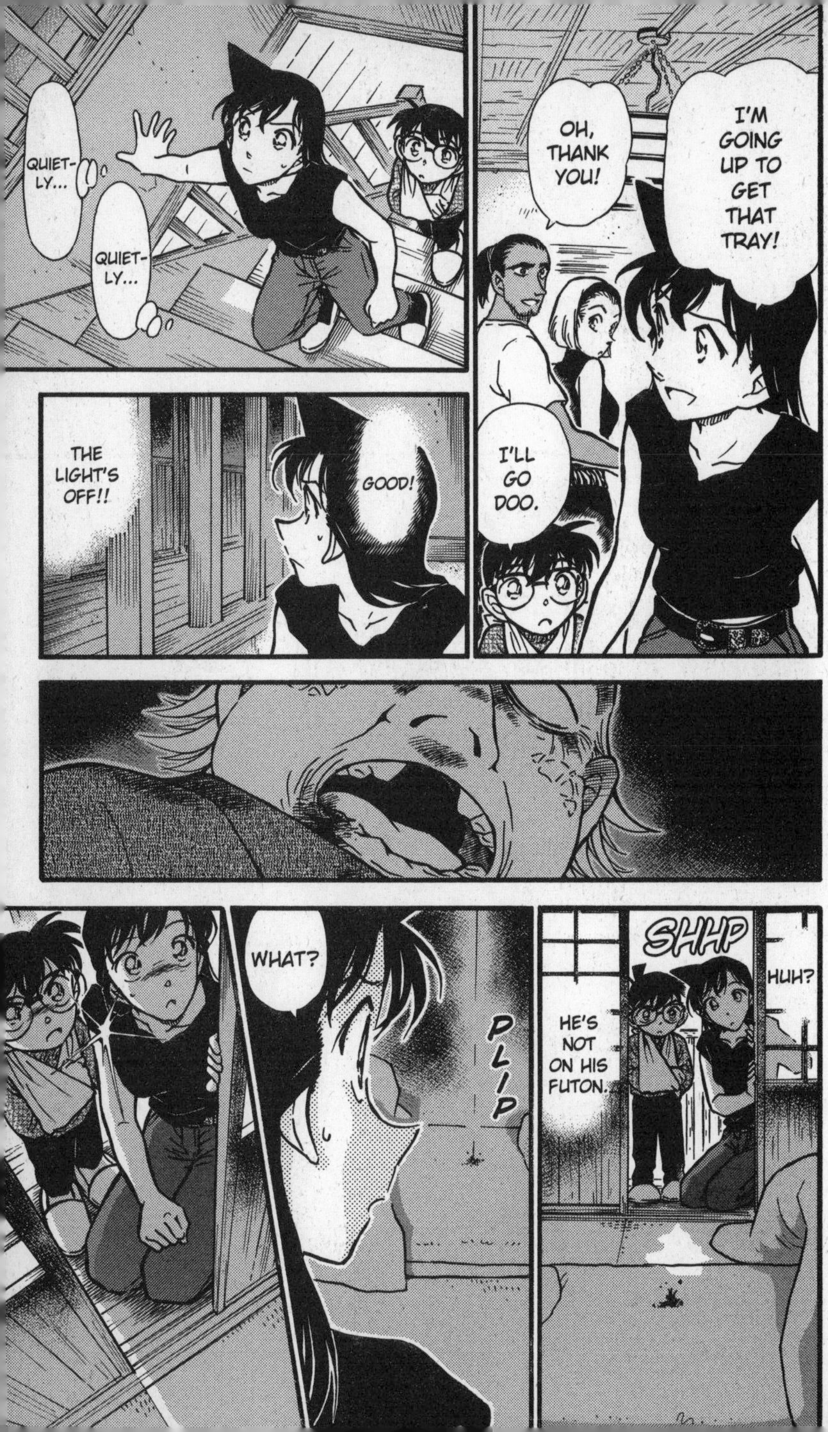
I'M GOING UP TO GET THAT TRAY!
OH, THANK YOU!
I'LL GO DOO.
QUIET-LY...
QUIET-LY...
GOOD!
THE LIGHT'S OFF!!
SHHP
HUH?
HE'S NOT ON HIS FUTON.
WHAT?
PLIP

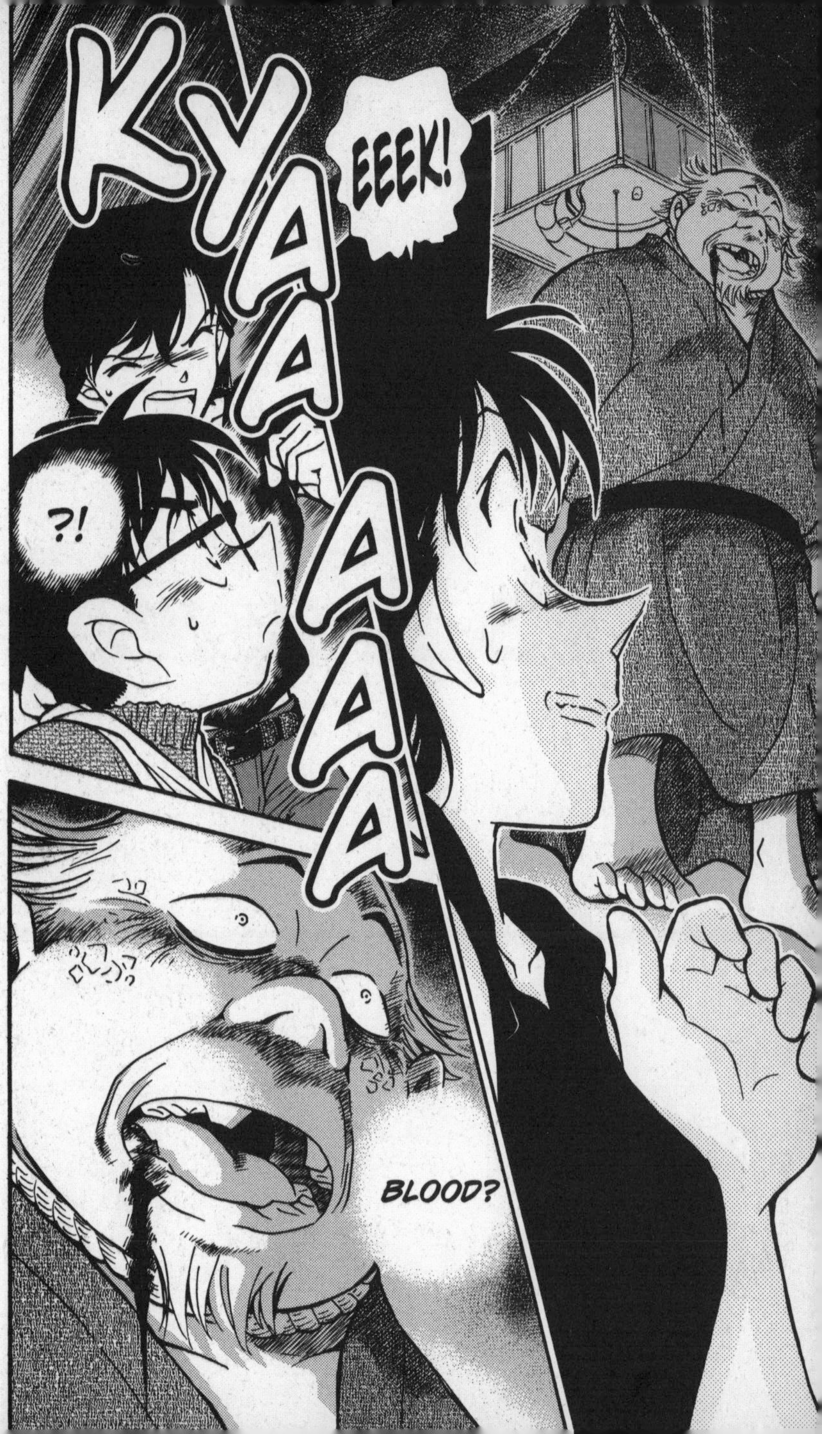
KYAAAAAAA
EEEK!
?!
BLOOD?

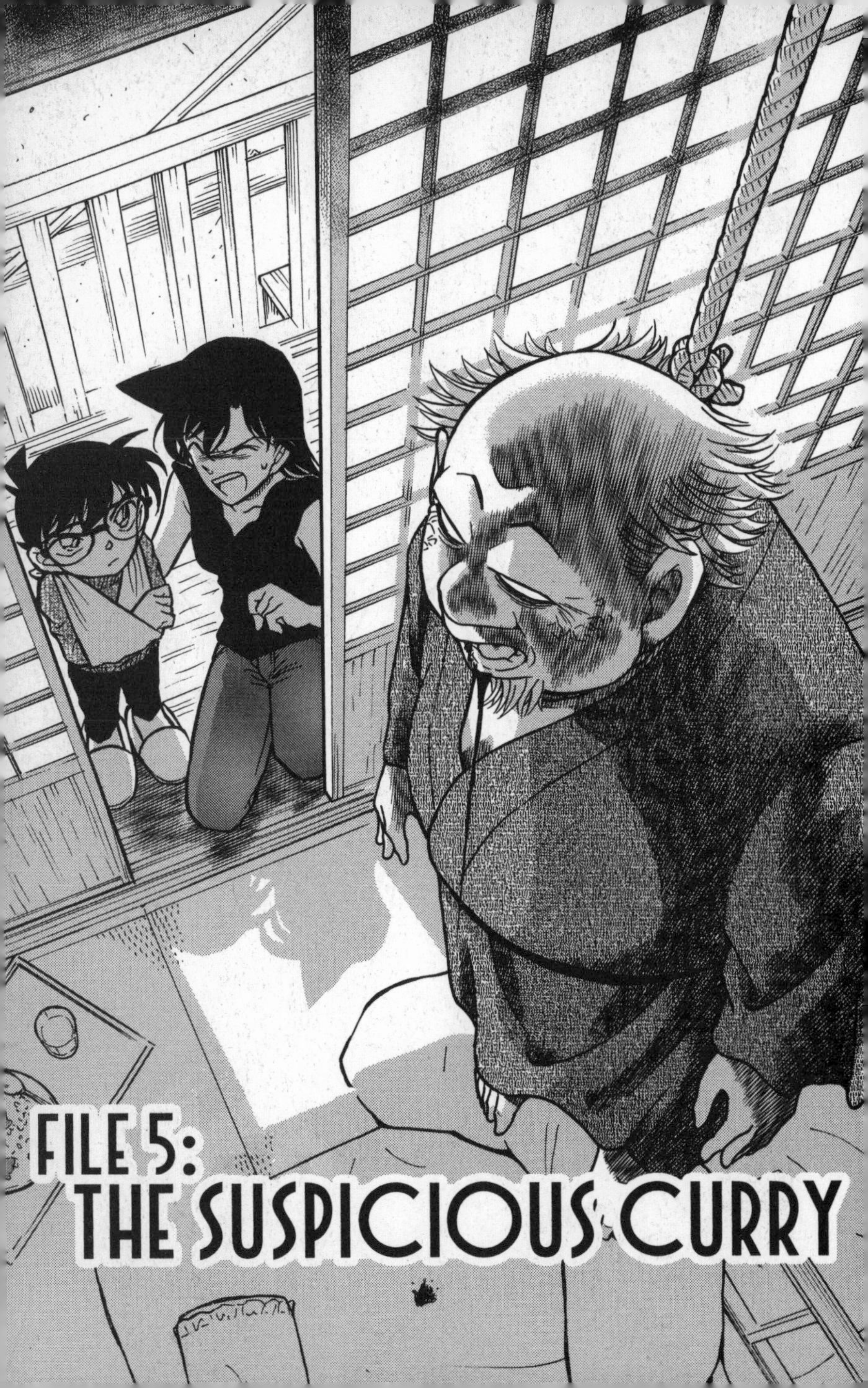
FILE 5:
THE SUSPICIOUS CURRY

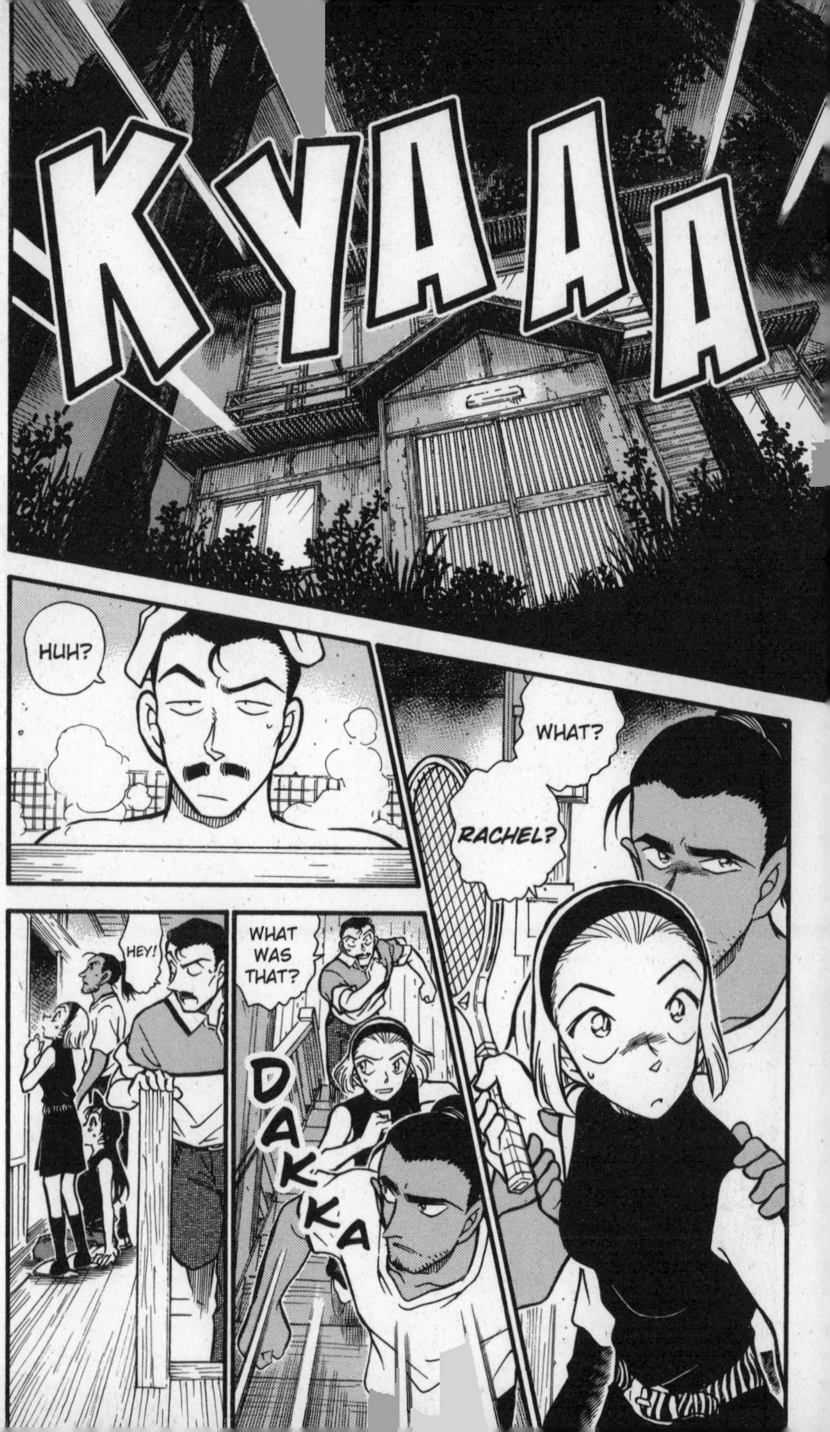
KYAAA
WHAT?
RACHEL?
HUH?
WHAT WAS THAT?
DAKKA
HEY!

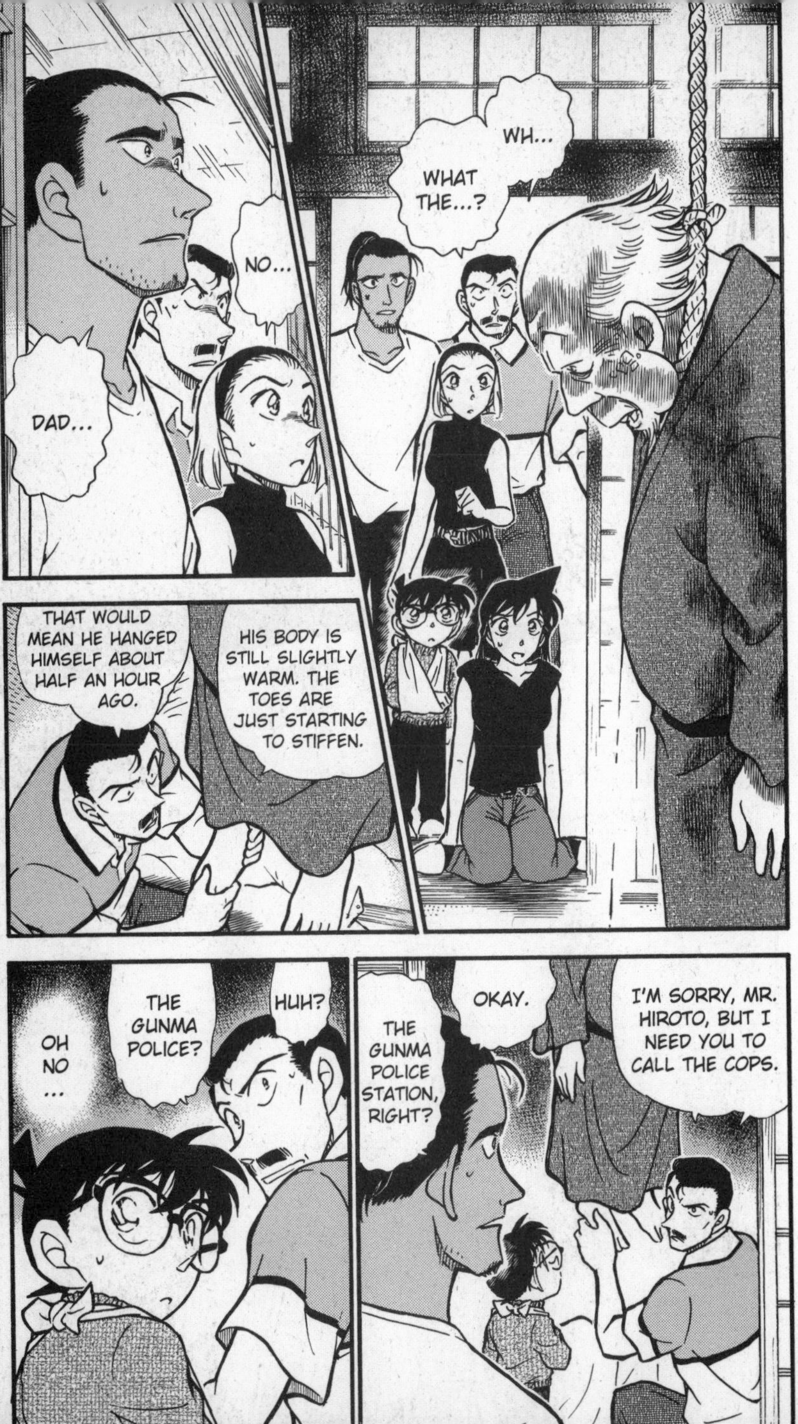
WH...
WHAT THE...?
NO...
DAD...
HIS BODY IS STILL SLIGHTLY WARM. THE TOES ARE JUST STARTING TO STIFFEN.
THAT WOULD MEAN HE HANGED HIMSELF ABOUT HALF AN HOUR AGO.
I'M SORRY, MR. HIROTO, BUT I NEED YOU TO CALL THE COPS.
OKAY.
THE GUNMA POLICE STATION, RIGHT?
HUH?
THE GUNMA POLICE?
OH NO ...

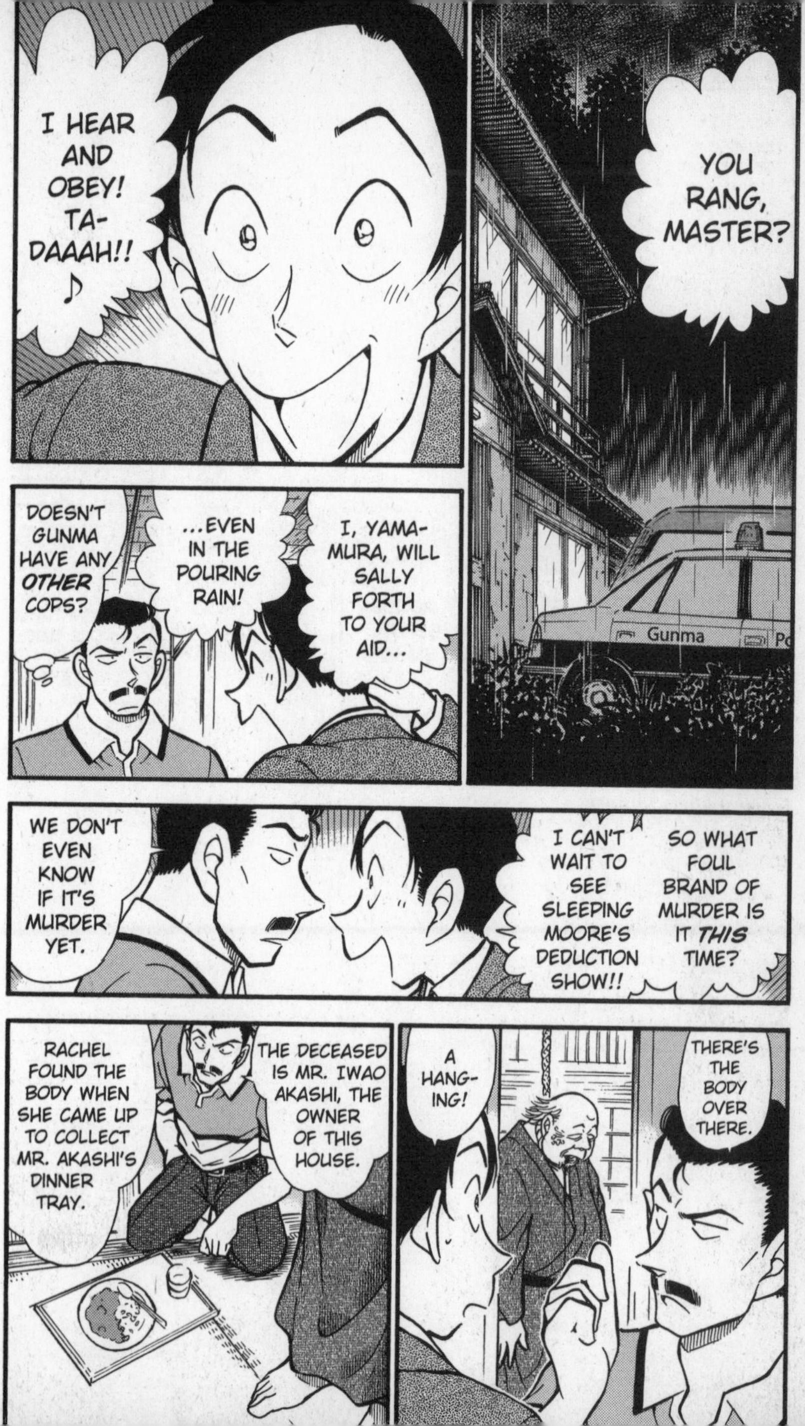
YOU RANG, MASTER?
Gunma
I HEAR AND OBEY! TA-DAAAH!! ♪
I, YAMAMURA, WILL SALLY FORTH TO YOUR AID...
...EVEN IN THE POURING RAIN!
DOESN'T GUNMA HAVE ANY *OTHER* COPS?
SO WHAT FOUL BRAND OF MURDER IS IT *THIS* TIME?
I CAN'T WAIT TO SEE SLEEPING MOORE'S DEDUCTION SHOW!!
WE DON'T EVEN KNOW IF IT'S MURDER YET.
THERE'S THE BODY OVER THERE.
A HANG-ING!
THE DECEASED IS MR. IWAO AKASHI, THE OWNER OF THIS HOUSE.
RACHEL FOUND THE BODY WHEN SHE CAME UP TO COLLECT MR. AKASHI'S DINNER TRAY.

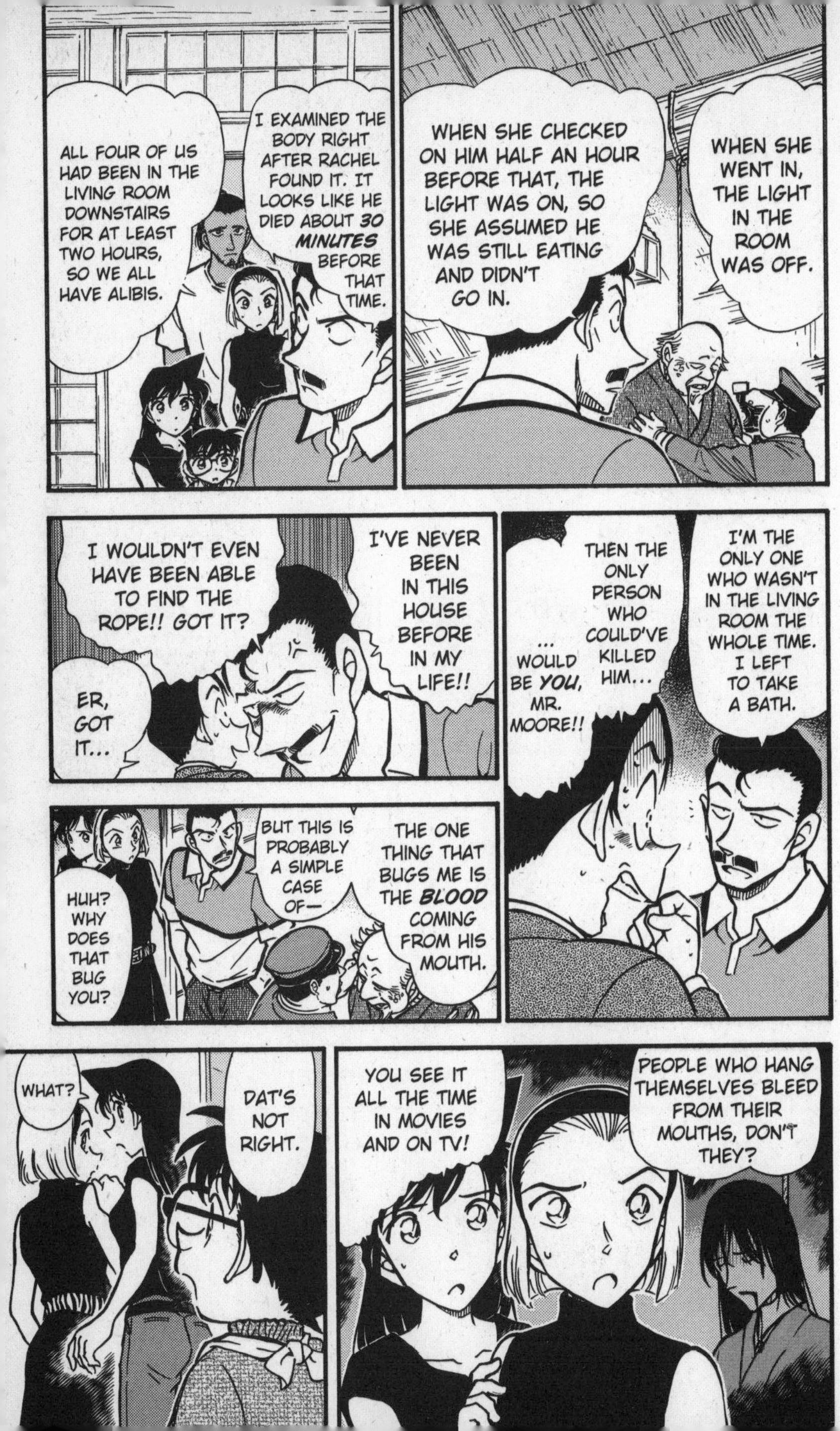
WHEN SHE WENT IN, THE LIGHT IN THE ROOM WAS OFF.
WHEN SHE CHECKED ON HIM HALF AN HOUR BEFORE THAT, THE LIGHT WAS ON, SO SHE ASSUMED HE WAS STILL EATING AND DIDN'T GO IN.
I EXAMINED THE BODY RIGHT AFTER RACHEL FOUND IT. IT LOOKS LIKE HE DIED ABOUT *30 MINUTES* BEFORE THAT TIME.
ALL FOUR OF US HAD BEEN IN THE LIVING ROOM DOWNSTAIRS FOR AT LEAST TWO HOURS, SO WE ALL HAVE ALIBIS.
I'M THE ONLY ONE WHO WASN'T IN THE LIVING ROOM THE WHOLE TIME. I LEFT TO TAKE A BATH.
THEN THE ONLY PERSON WHO COULD'VE KILLED HIM...
...WOULD BE *YOU*, MR. MOORE!!
I'VE NEVER BEEN IN THIS HOUSE BEFORE IN MY LIFE!!
I WOULDN'T EVEN HAVE BEEN ABLE TO FIND THE ROPE!! GOT IT?
ER, GOT IT...
THE ONE THING THAT BUGS ME IS THE *BLOOD* COMING FROM HIS MOUTH.
BUT THIS IS PROBABLY A SIMPLE CASE OF—
HUH? WHY DOES THAT BUG YOU?
PEOPLE WHO HANG THEMSELVES BLEED FROM THEIR MOUTHS, DON'T THEY?
YOU SEE IT ALL THE TIME IN MOVIES AND ON TV!
DAT'S NOT RIGHT.
WHAT?

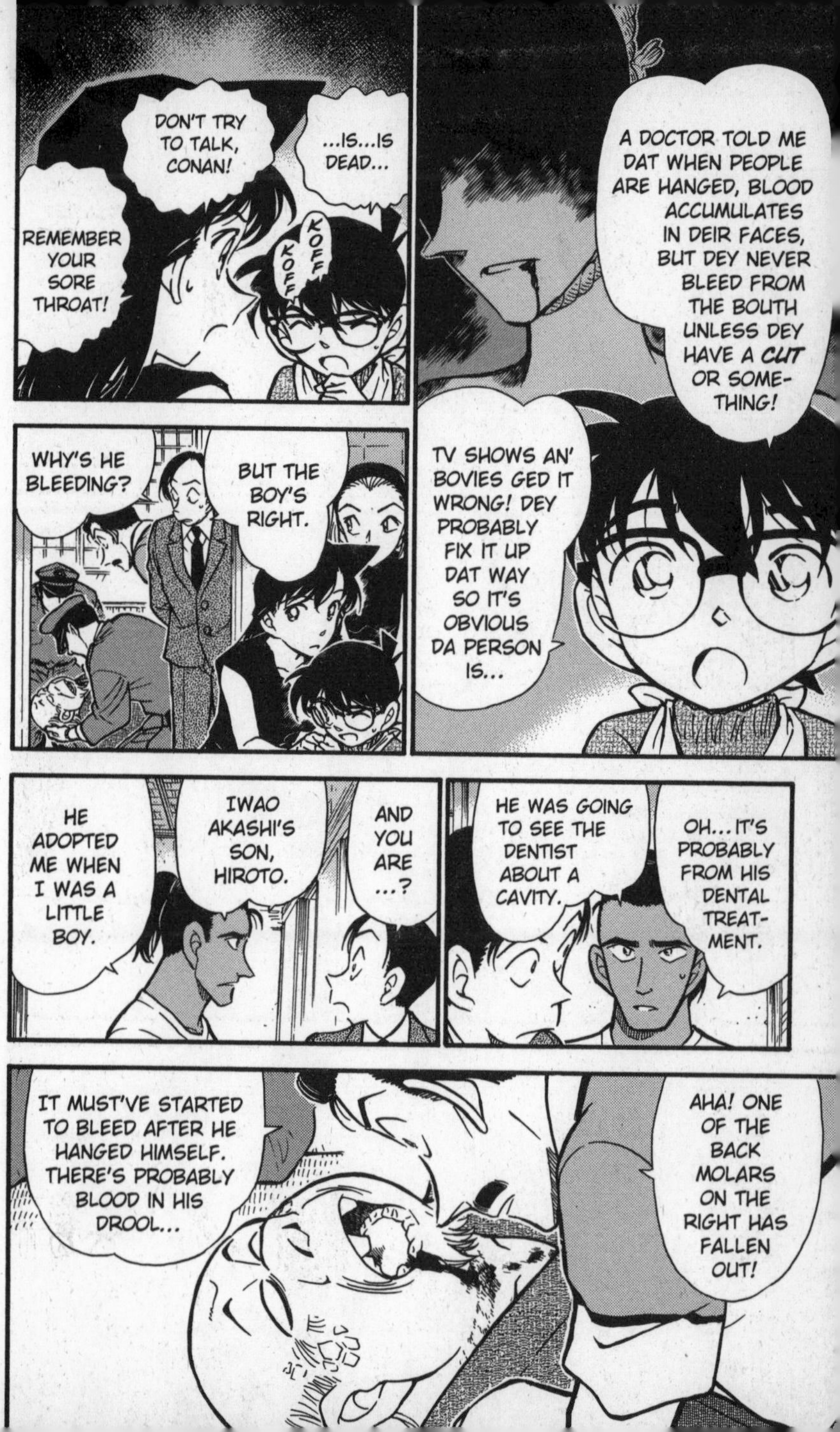
A DOCTOR TOLD ME DAT WHEN PEOPLE ARE HANGED, BLOOD ACCUMULATES IN DEIR FACES, BUT DEY NEVER BLEED FROM THE BOUTH UNLESS DEY HAVE A *CUT* OR SOME-THING!
TV SHOWS AN' BOVIES GED IT WRONG! DEY PROBABLY FIX IT UP DAT WAY SO IT'S OBVIOUS DA PERSON IS...
...IS...IS DEAD...
KOFF KOFF
DON'T TRY TO TALK, CONAN!
REMEMBER YOUR SORE THROAT!
BUT THE BOY'S RIGHT.
WHY'S HE BLEEDING?
OH... IT'S PROBABLY FROM HIS DENTAL TREAT-MENT.
HE WAS GOING TO SEE THE DENTIST ABOUT A CAVITY.
AND YOU ARE ...?
IWAO AKASHI'S SON, HIROTO.
HE ADOPTED ME WHEN I WAS A LITTLE BOY.
AHA! ONE OF THE BACK MOLARS ON THE RIGHT HAS FALLEN OUT!
IT MUST'VE STARTED TO BLEED AFTER HE HANGED HIMSELF. THERE'S PROBABLY BLOOD IN HIS DROOL...

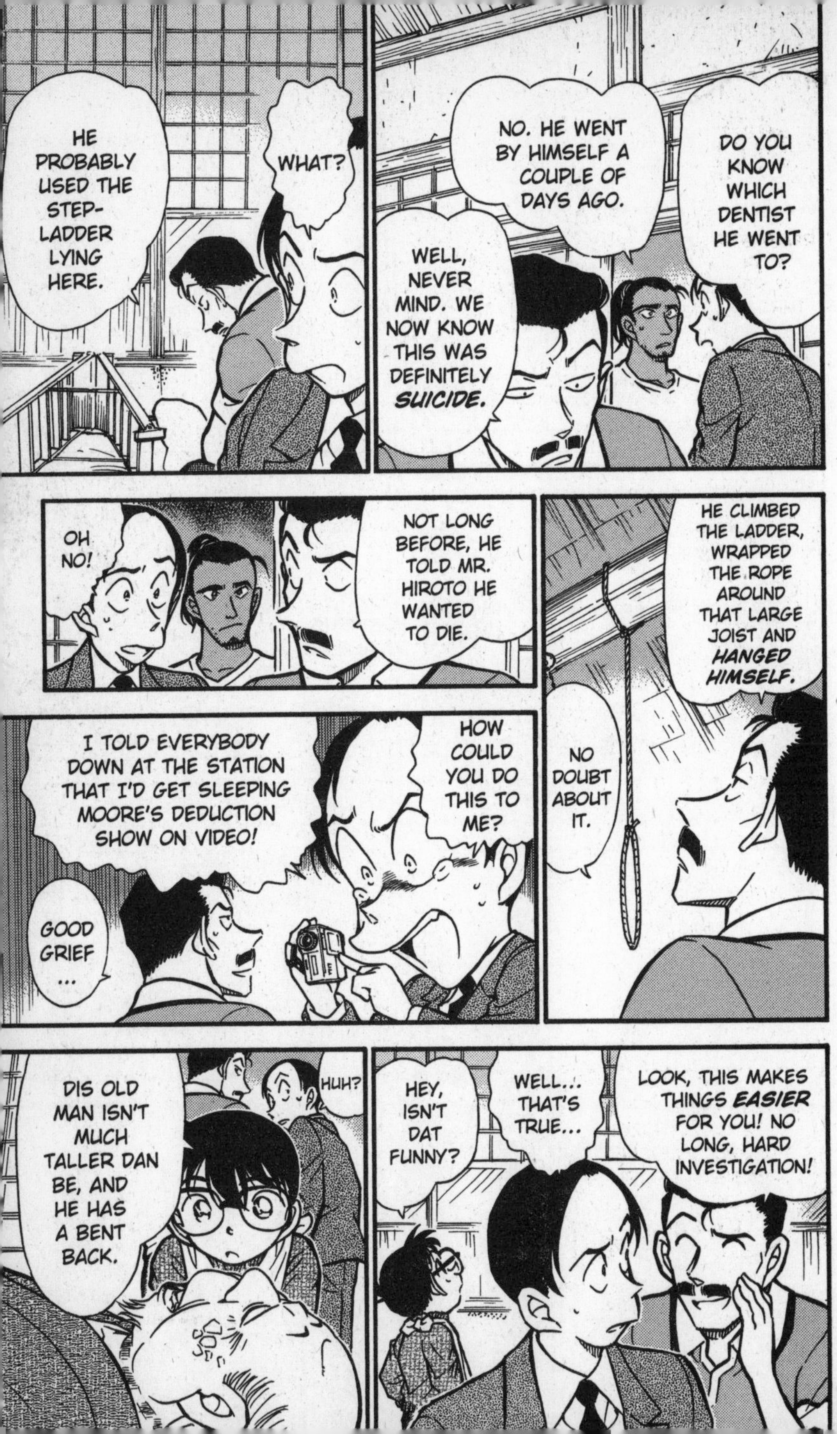
DO YOU KNOW WHICH DENTIST HE WENT TO?
NO. HE WENT BY HIMSELF A COUPLE OF DAYS AGO.
WELL, NEVER MIND. WE NOW KNOW THIS WAS DEFINITELY ***SUICIDE.***
WHAT?
HE PROBABLY USED THE STEP-LADDER LYING HERE.
HE CLIMBED THE LADDER, WRAPPED THE ROPE AROUND THAT LARGE JOIST AND ***HANGED HIMSELF.***
NO DOUBT ABOUT IT.
NOT LONG BEFORE, HE TOLD MR. HIROTO HE WANTED TO DIE.
OH NO!
HOW COULD YOU DO THIS TO ME?
I TOLD EVERYBODY DOWN AT THE STATION THAT I'D GET SLEEPING MOORE'S DEDUCTION SHOW ON VIDEO!
GOOD GRIEF ...
LOOK, THIS MAKES THINGS ***EASIER*** FOR YOU! NO LONG, HARD INVESTIGATION!
WELL... THAT'S TRUE...
HEY, ISN'T DAT FUNNY?
HUH?
DIS OLD MAN ISN'T MUCH TALLER DAN BE, AND HE HAS A BENT BACK.

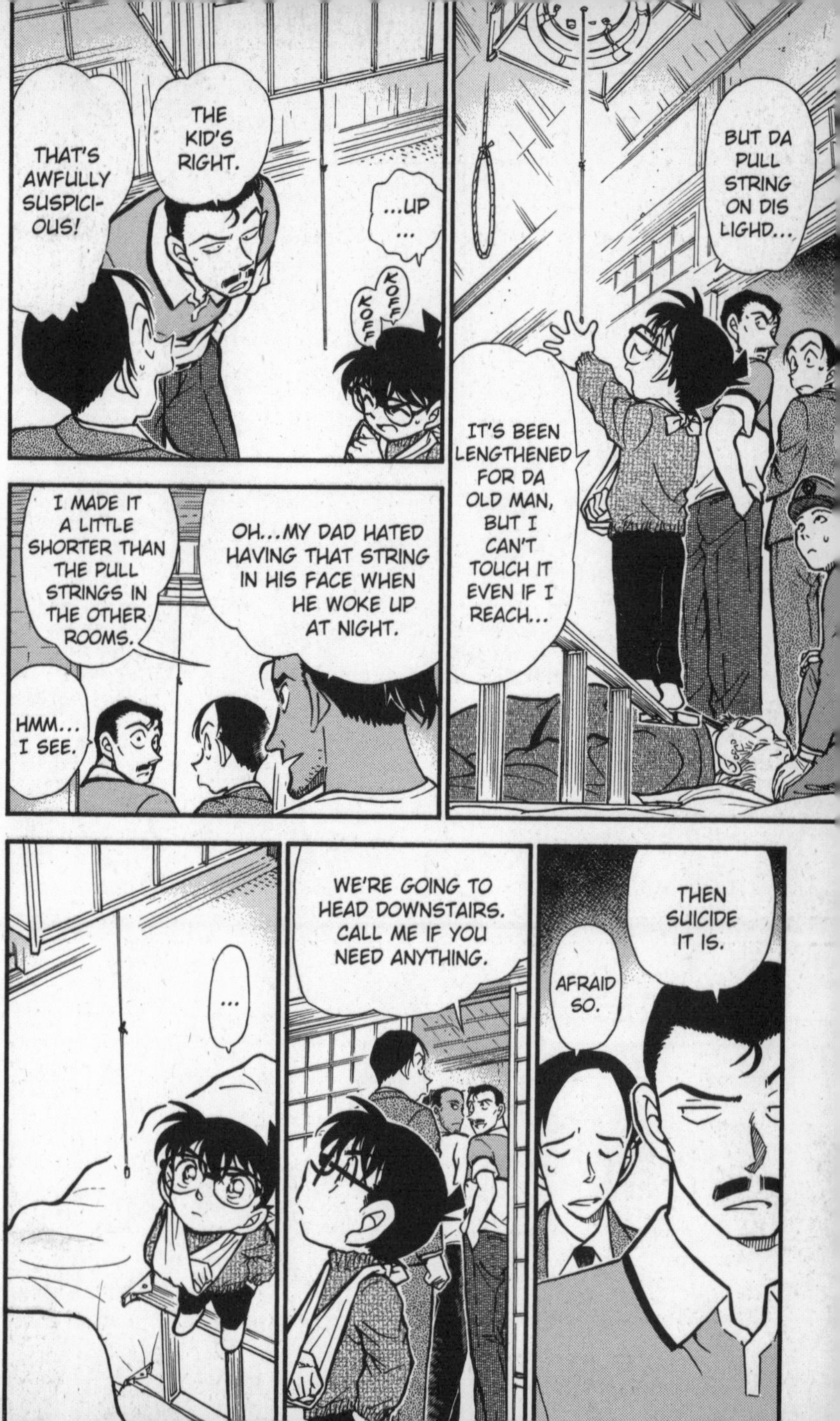
BUT DA PULL STRING ON DIS LIGHD...
IT'S BEEN LENGTHENED FOR DA OLD MAN, BUT I CAN'T TOUCH IT EVEN IF I REACH...
THE KID'S RIGHT.
THAT'S AWFULLY SUSPICIOUS!
...UP ...
KOFF KOFF
OH...MY DAD HATED HAVING THAT STRING IN HIS FACE WHEN HE WOKE UP AT NIGHT.
I MADE IT A LITTLE SHORTER THAN THE PULL STRINGS IN THE OTHER ROOMS.
HMM... I SEE.
THEN SUICIDE IT IS.
AFRAID SO.
WE'RE GOING TO HEAD DOWNSTAIRS. CALL ME IF YOU NEED ANYTHING.
...

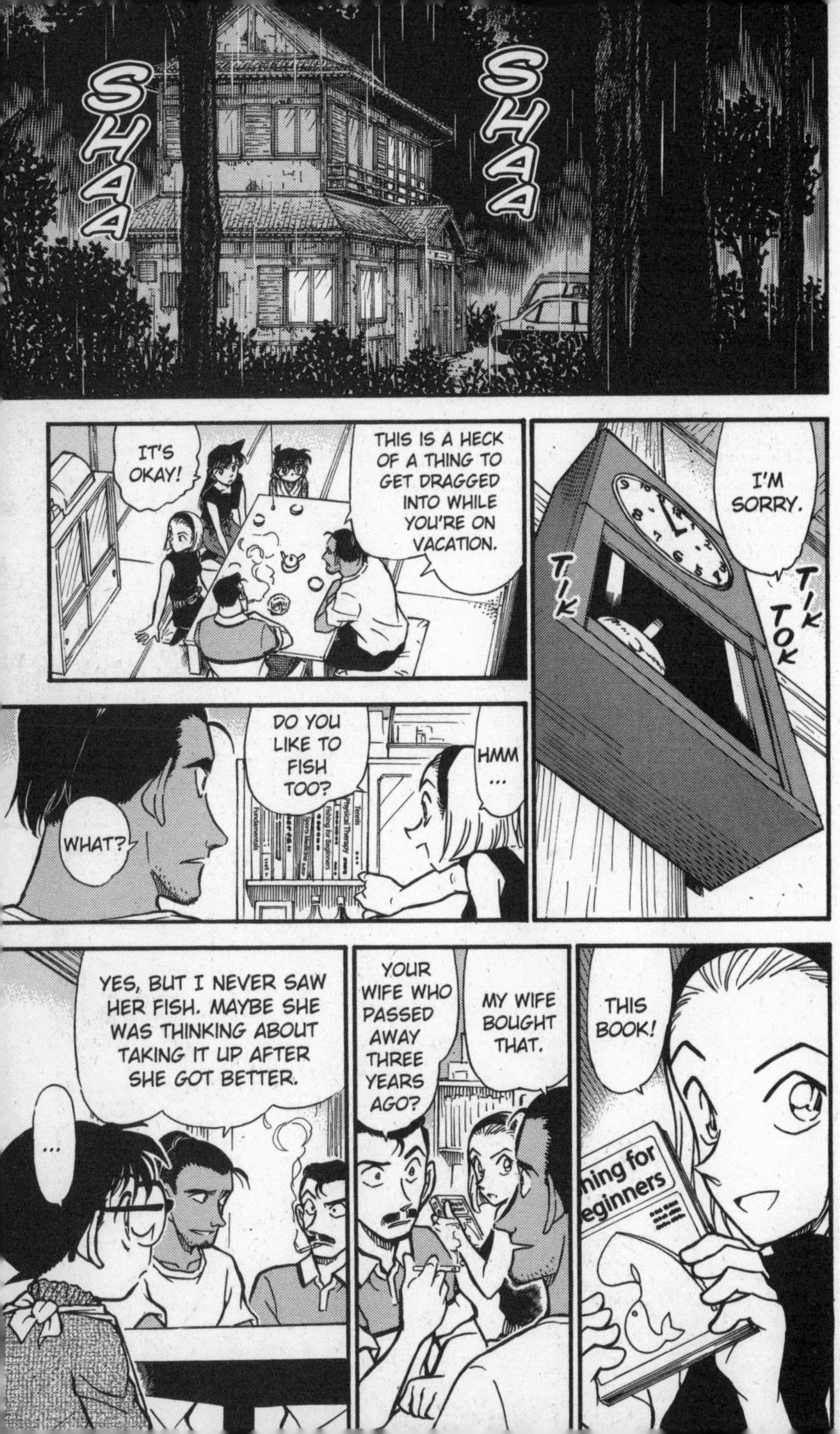
SHAA
SHAA
I'M SORRY.
TIK
TIK TOK
THIS IS A HECK OF A THING TO GET DRAGGED INTO WHILE YOU'RE ON VACATION.
IT'S OKAY!
HMM ...
DO YOU LIKE TO FISH TOO?
Tennis
Physical Therapy
Fishing for Beginners
Sports Medicine
Fundamentals
WHAT?
THIS BOOK!
hing for
eginners
MY WIFE BOUGHT THAT.
YOUR WIFE WHO PASSED AWAY THREE YEARS AGO?
YES, BUT I NEVER SAW HER FISH. MAYBE SHE WAS THINKING ABOUT TAKING IT UP AFTER SHE GOT BETTER.
...

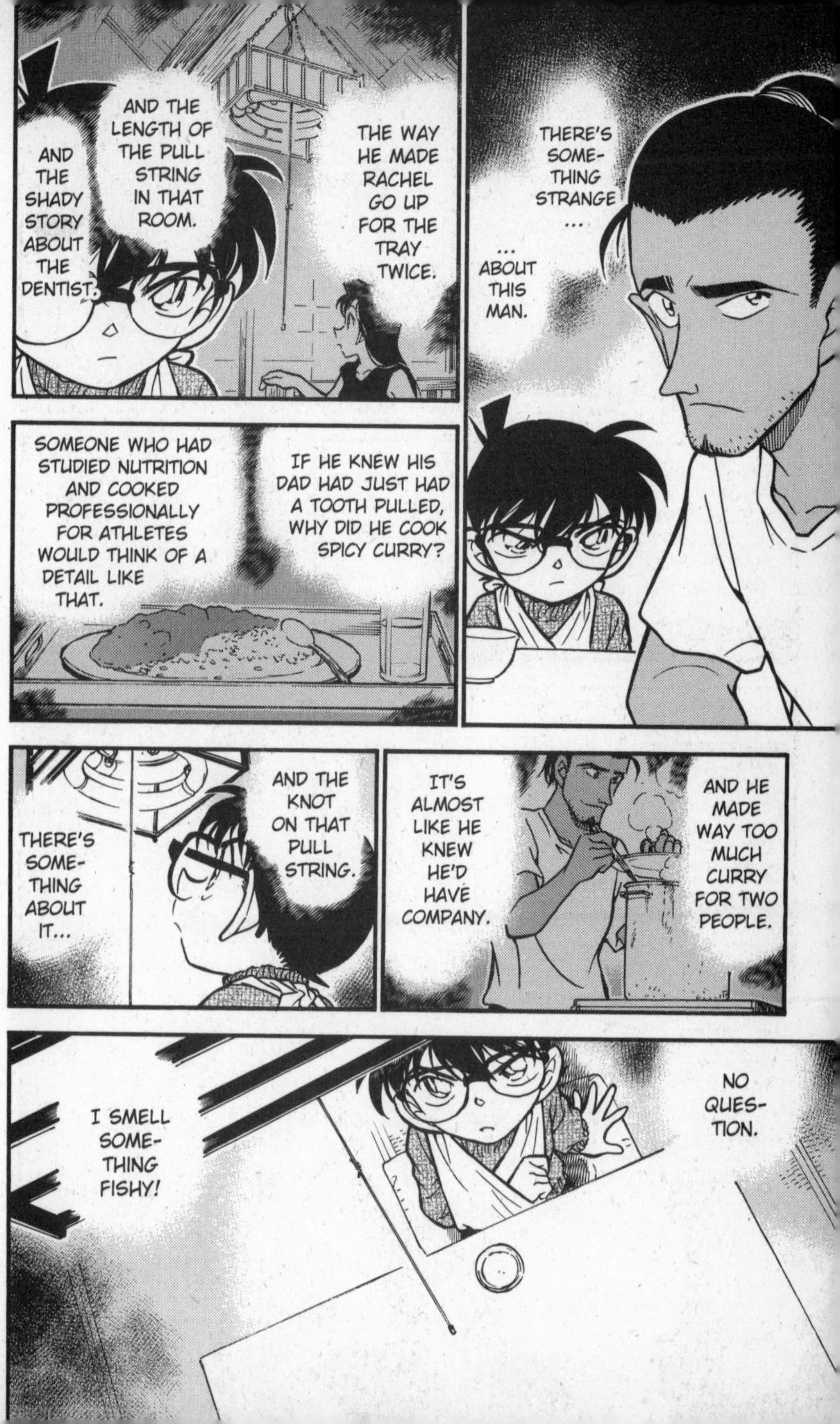
THERE'S SOMETHING STRANGE ...
... ABOUT THIS MAN.
THE WAY HE MADE RACHEL GO UP FOR THE TRAY TWICE.
AND THE LENGTH OF THE PULL STRING IN THAT ROOM.
AND THE SHADY STORY ABOUT THE DENTIST.
IF HE KNEW HIS DAD HAD JUST HAD A TOOTH PULLED, WHY DID HE COOK SPICY CURRY?
SOMEONE WHO HAD STUDIED NUTRITION AND COOKED PROFESSIONALLY FOR ATHLETES WOULD THINK OF A DETAIL LIKE THAT.
AND HE MADE WAY TOO MUCH CURRY FOR TWO PEOPLE.
IT'S ALMOST LIKE HE KNEW HE'D HAVE COMPANY.
AND THE KNOT ON THAT PULL STRING.
THERE'S SOMETHING ABOUT IT...
NO QUES-TION.
I SMELL SOME-THING FISHY!

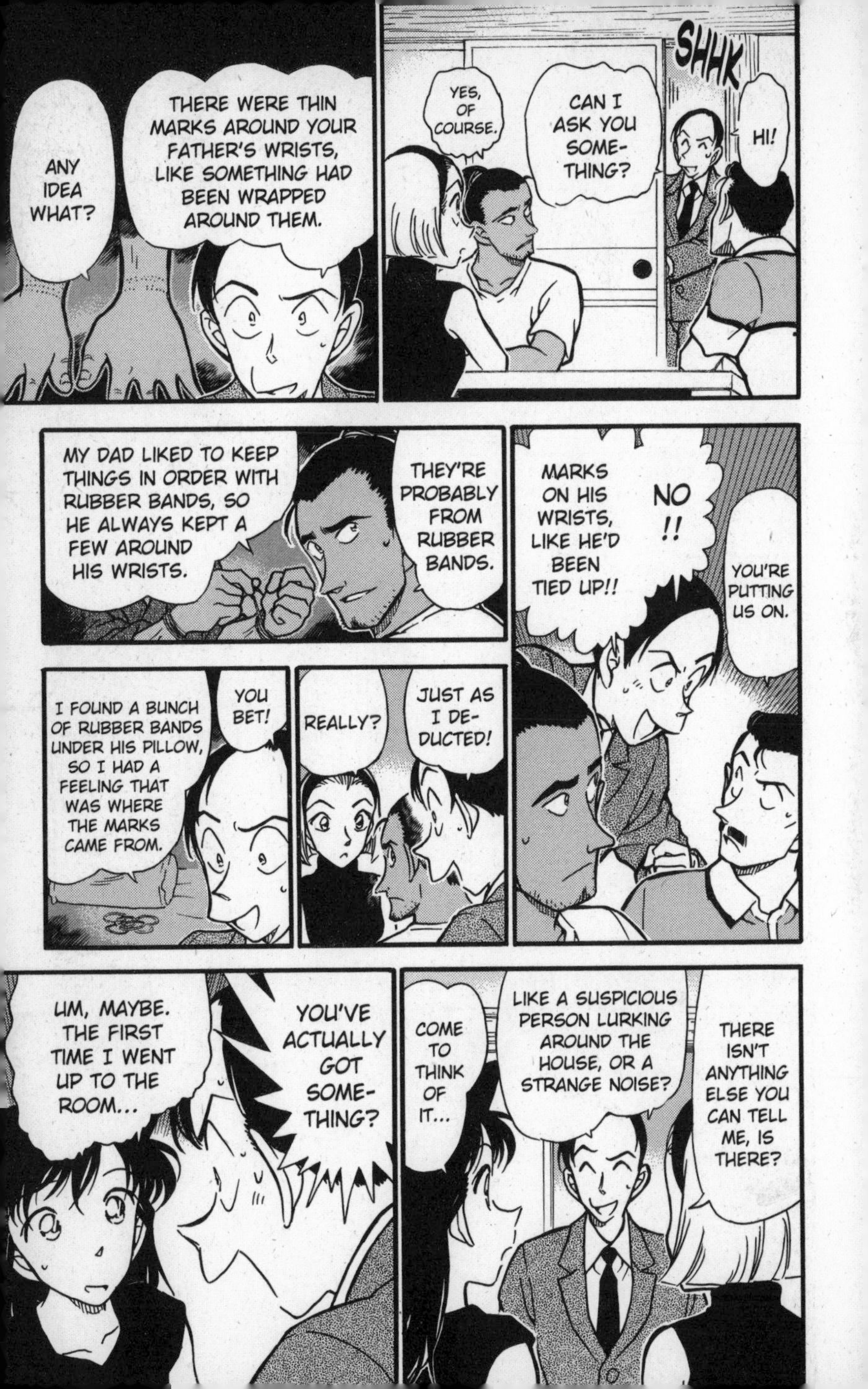
SHHK
HI!
CAN I ASK YOU SOME-THING?
YES, OF COURSE.
THERE WERE THIN MARKS AROUND YOUR FATHER'S WRISTS, LIKE SOMETHING HAD BEEN WRAPPED AROUND THEM.
ANY IDEA WHAT?
YOU'RE PUTTING US ON.
NO!! MARKS ON HIS WRISTS, LIKE HE'D BEEN TIED UP!!
THEY'RE PROBABLY FROM RUBBER BANDS.
MY DAD LIKED TO KEEP THINGS IN ORDER WITH RUBBER BANDS, SO HE ALWAYS KEPT A FEW AROUND HIS WRISTS.
JUST AS I DE-DUCTED!
REALLY?
YOU BET!
I FOUND A BUNCH OF RUBBER BANDS UNDER HIS PILLOW, SO I HAD A FEELING THAT WAS WHERE THE MARKS CAME FROM.
THERE ISN'T ANYTHING ELSE YOU CAN TELL ME, IS THERE?
LIKE A SUSPICIOUS PERSON LURKING AROUND THE HOUSE, OR A STRANGE NOISE?
COME TO THINK OF IT...
YOU'VE ACTUALLY GOT SOME-THING?
UM, MAYBE. THE FIRST TIME I WENT UP TO THE ROOM...

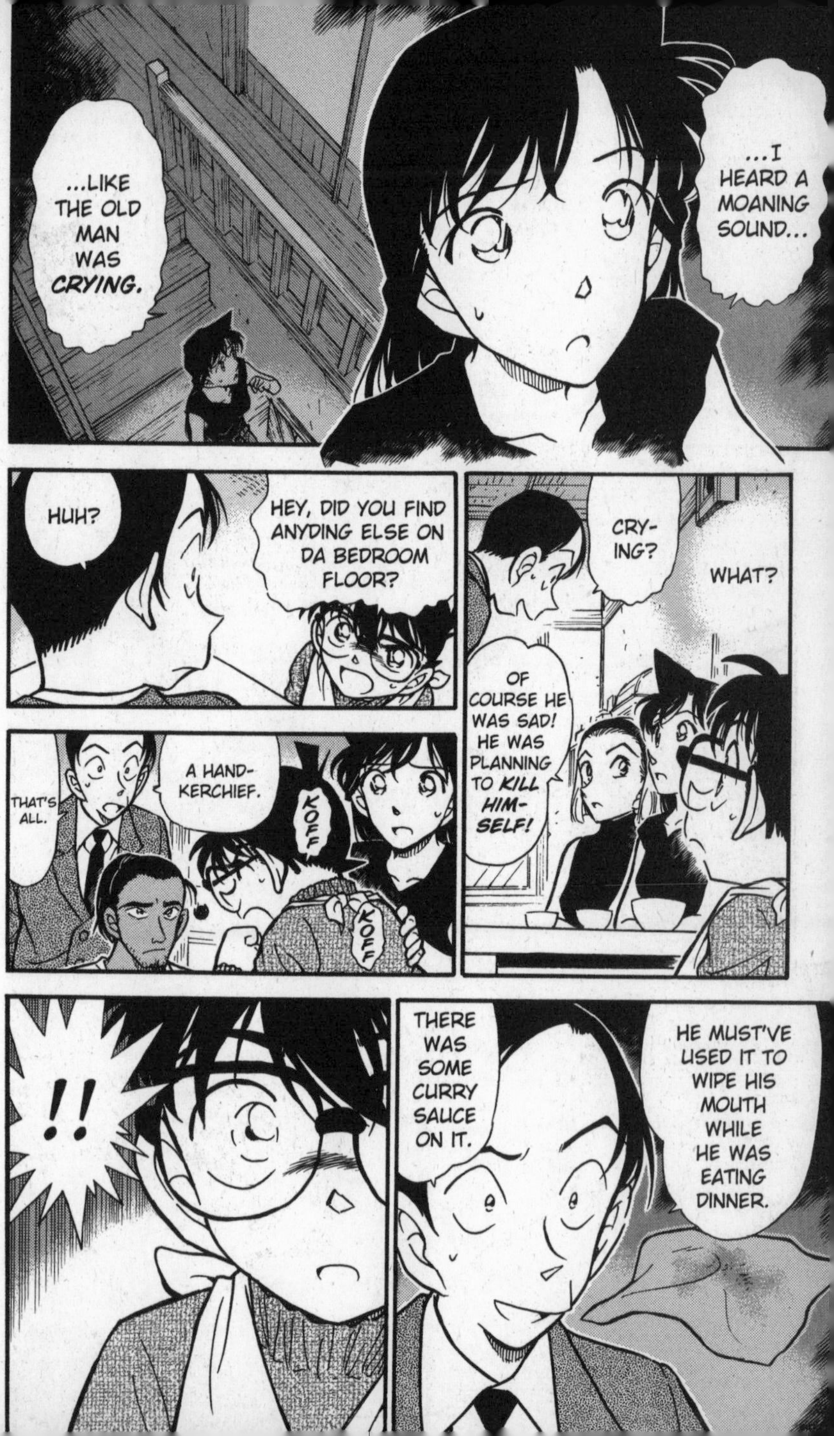

...I HEARD A MOANING SOUND...
...LIKE THE OLD MAN WAS CRYING.
CRY-ING?
WHAT?
OF COURSE HE WAS SAD! HE WAS PLANNING TO KILL HIM-SELF!
HEY, DID YOU FIND ANYDING ELSE ON DA BEDROOM FLOOR?
HUH?
KOFF
KOFF
A HAND-KERCHIEF.
THAT'S ALL.
HE MUST'VE USED IT TO WIPE HIS MOUTH WHILE HE WAS EATING DINNER.
THERE WAS SOME CURRY SAUCE ON IT.
!!

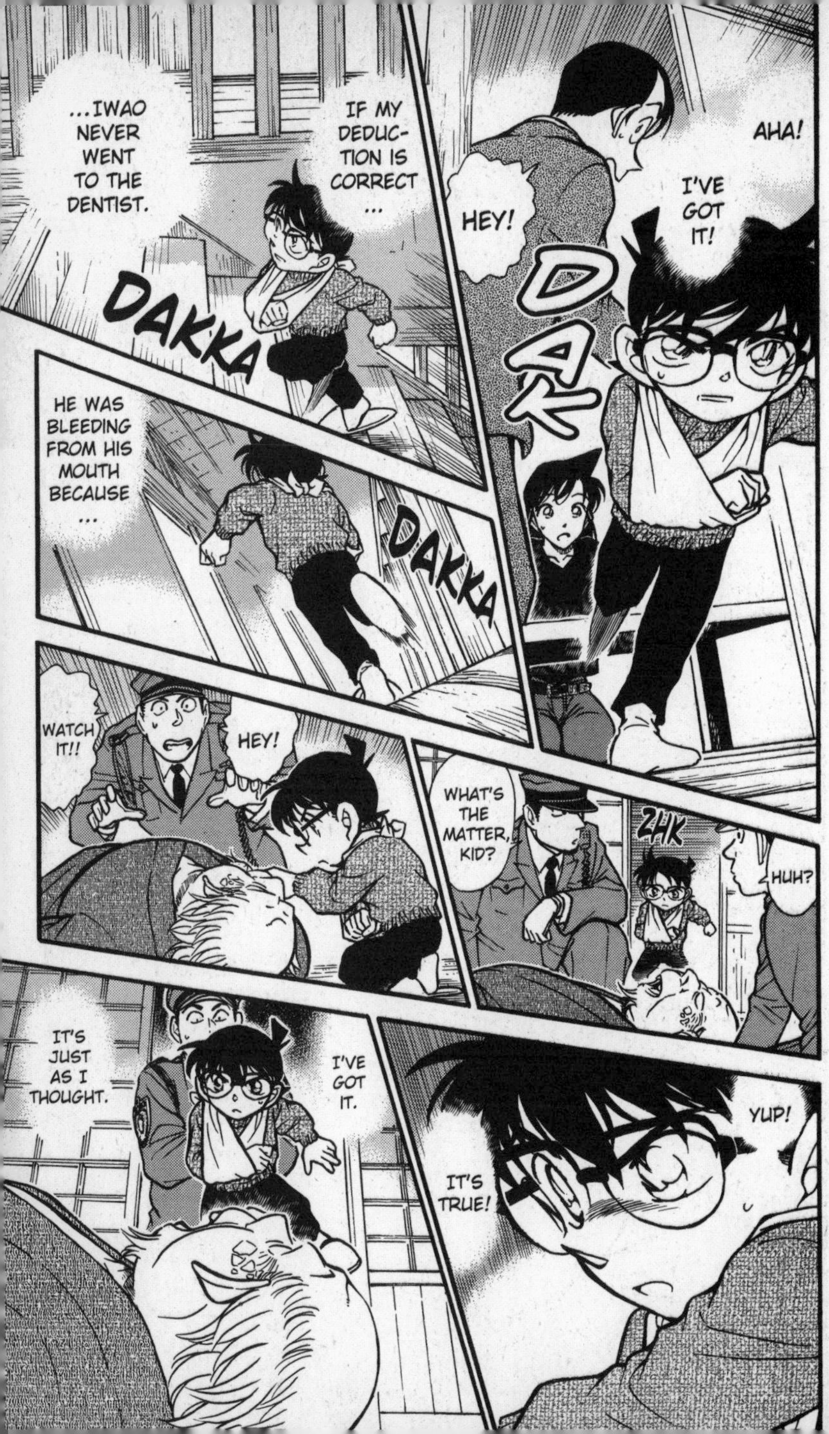
AHA!
I'VE GOT IT!
HEY!
DAK
IF MY DEDUCTION IS CORRECT ...
...IWAO NEVER WENT TO THE DENTIST.
DAKKA
HE WAS BLEEDING FROM HIS MOUTH BECAUSE ...
DAKKA
ZHK
HUH?
WHAT'S THE MATTER, KID?
HEY!
WATCH IT!!
YUP!
IT'S TRUE!
I'VE GOT IT.
IT'S JUST AS I THOUGHT.

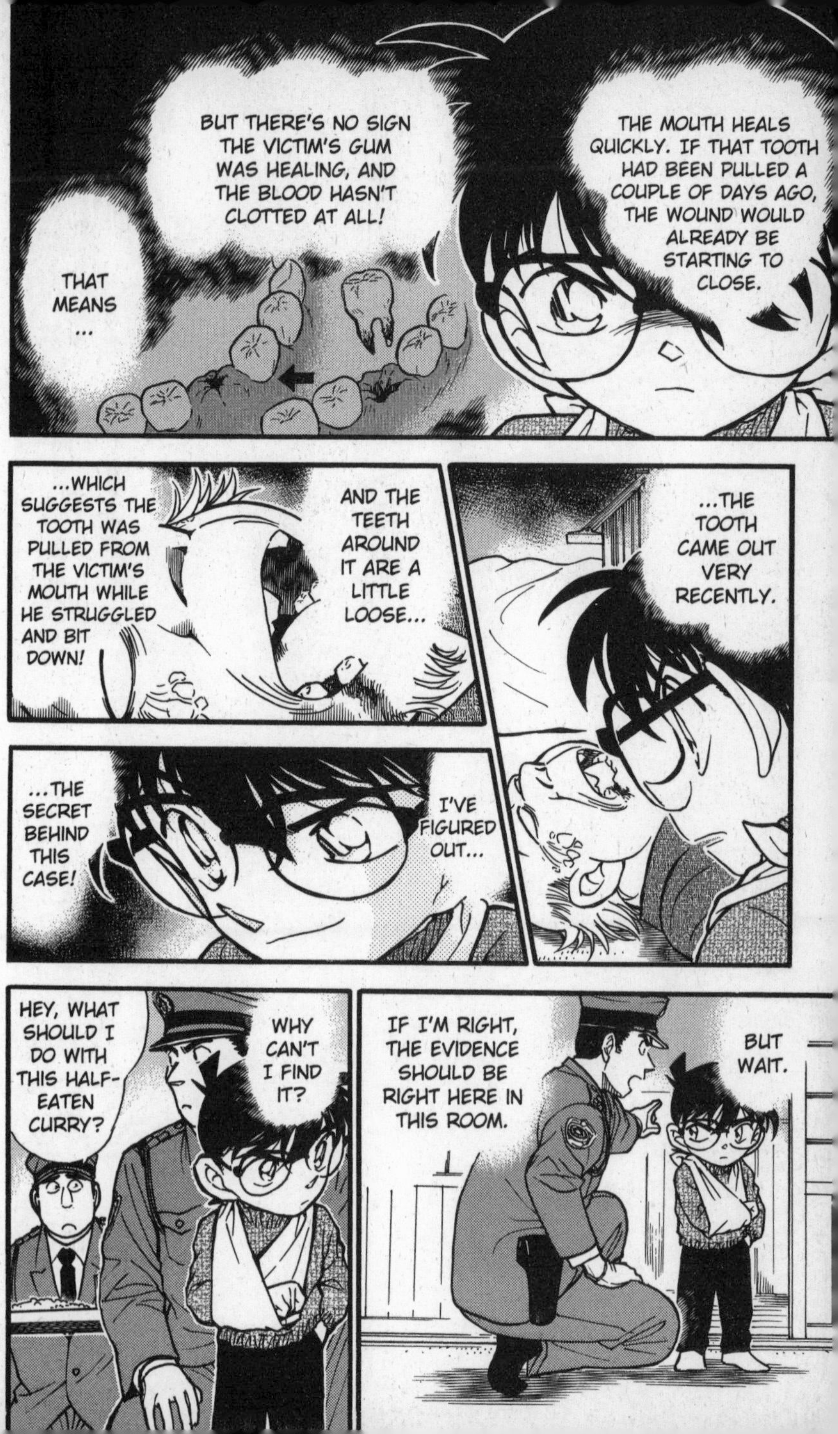
THE MOUTH HEALS QUICKLY. IF THAT TOOTH HAD BEEN PULLED A COUPLE OF DAYS AGO, THE WOUND WOULD ALREADY BE STARTING TO CLOSE.
BUT THERE'S NO SIGN THE VICTIM'S GUM WAS HEALING, AND THE BLOOD HASN'T CLOTTED AT ALL!
THAT MEANS ...
...THE TOOTH CAME OUT VERY RECENTLY.
AND THE TEETH AROUND IT ARE A LITTLE LOOSE...
...WHICH SUGGESTS THE TOOTH WAS PULLED FROM THE VICTIM'S MOUTH WHILE HE STRUGGLED AND BIT DOWN!
I'VE FIGURED OUT...
...THE SECRET BEHIND THIS CASE!
BUT WAIT.
IF I'M RIGHT, THE EVIDENCE SHOULD BE RIGHT HERE IN THIS ROOM.
WHY CAN'T I FIND IT?
HEY, WHAT SHOULD I DO WITH THIS HALF-EATEN CURRY?

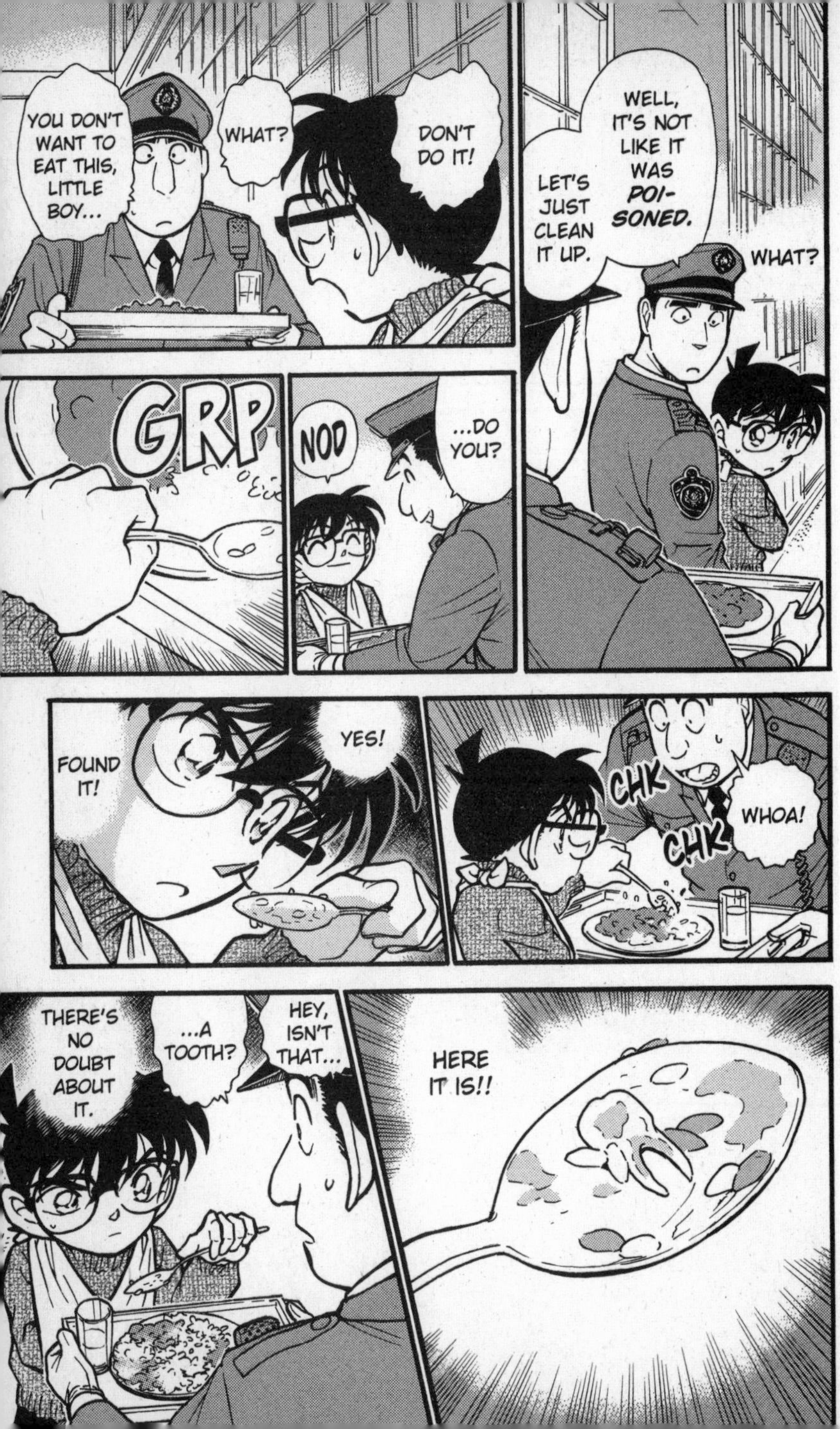
WELL, IT'S NOT LIKE IT WAS POI-SONED.
LET'S JUST CLEAN IT UP.
WHAT?
DON'T DO IT!
WHAT?
YOU DON'T WANT TO EAT THIS, LITTLE BOY...
...DO YOU?
NOD
GRP
WHOA!
CHK
CHK
YES!
FOUND IT!
HERE IT IS!!
HEY, ISN'T THAT...
...A TOOTH?
THERE'S NO DOUBT ABOUT IT.

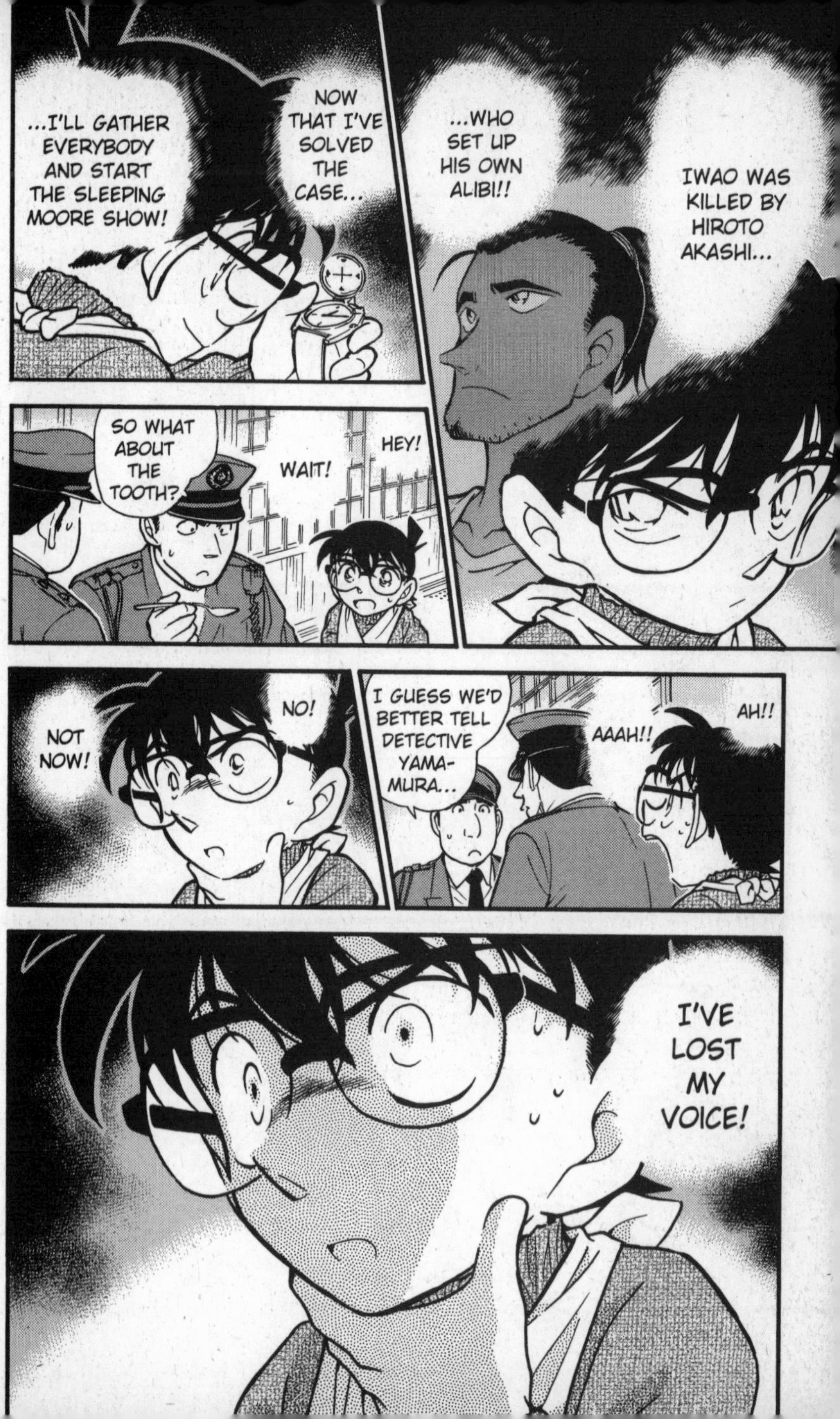
IWAO WAS KILLED BY HIROTO AKASHI...
...WHO SET UP HIS OWN ALIBI!!
NOW THAT I'VE SOLVED THE CASE...
...I'LL GATHER EVERYBODY AND START THE SLEEPING MOORE SHOW!
HEY!
WAIT!
SO WHAT ABOUT THE TOOTH?
AH!!
AAAH!!
I GUESS WE'D BETTER TELL DETECTIVE YAMA-MURA...
NO!
NOT NOW!
I'VE LOST MY VOICE!

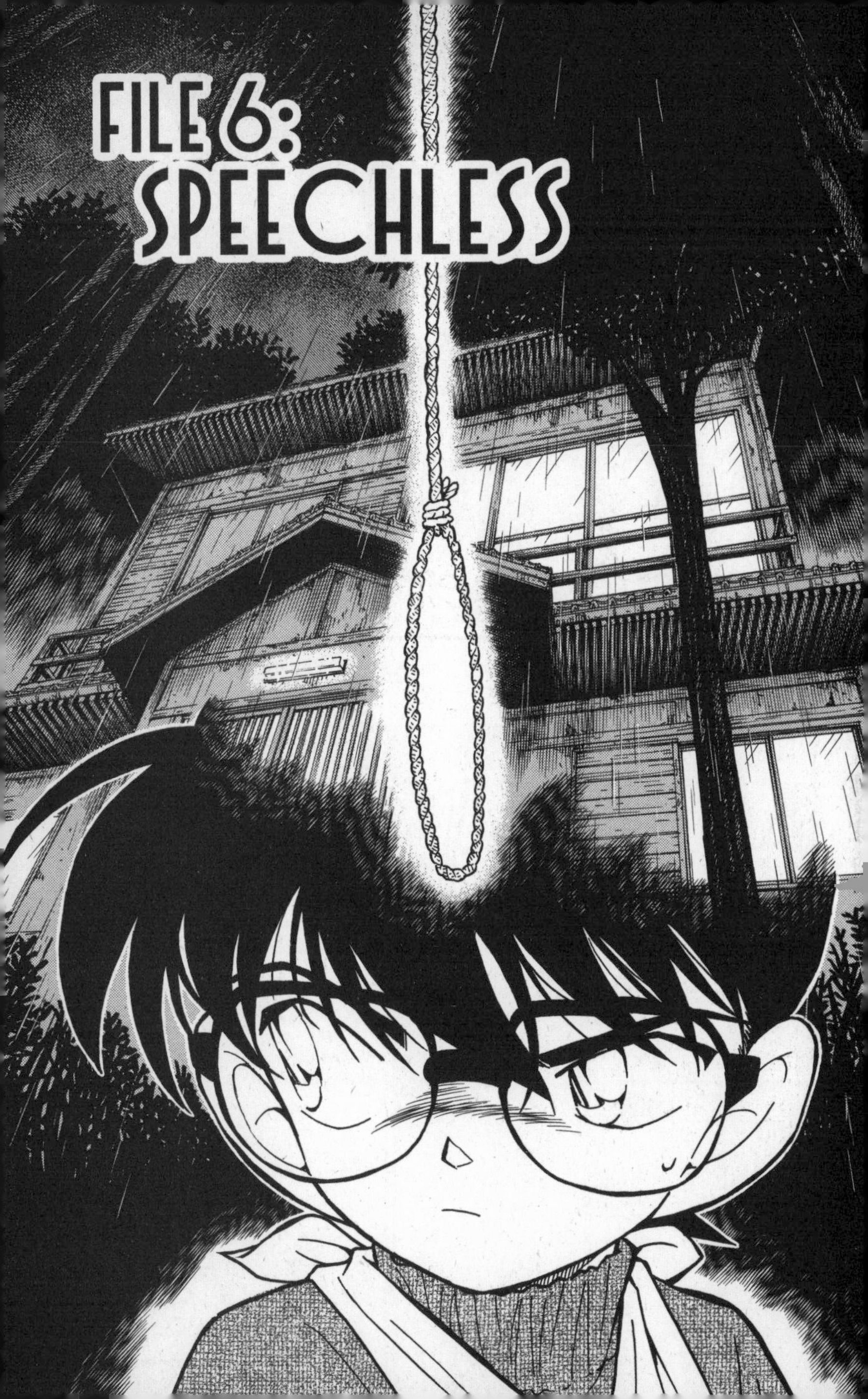
FILE 6:
SPEECHLESS

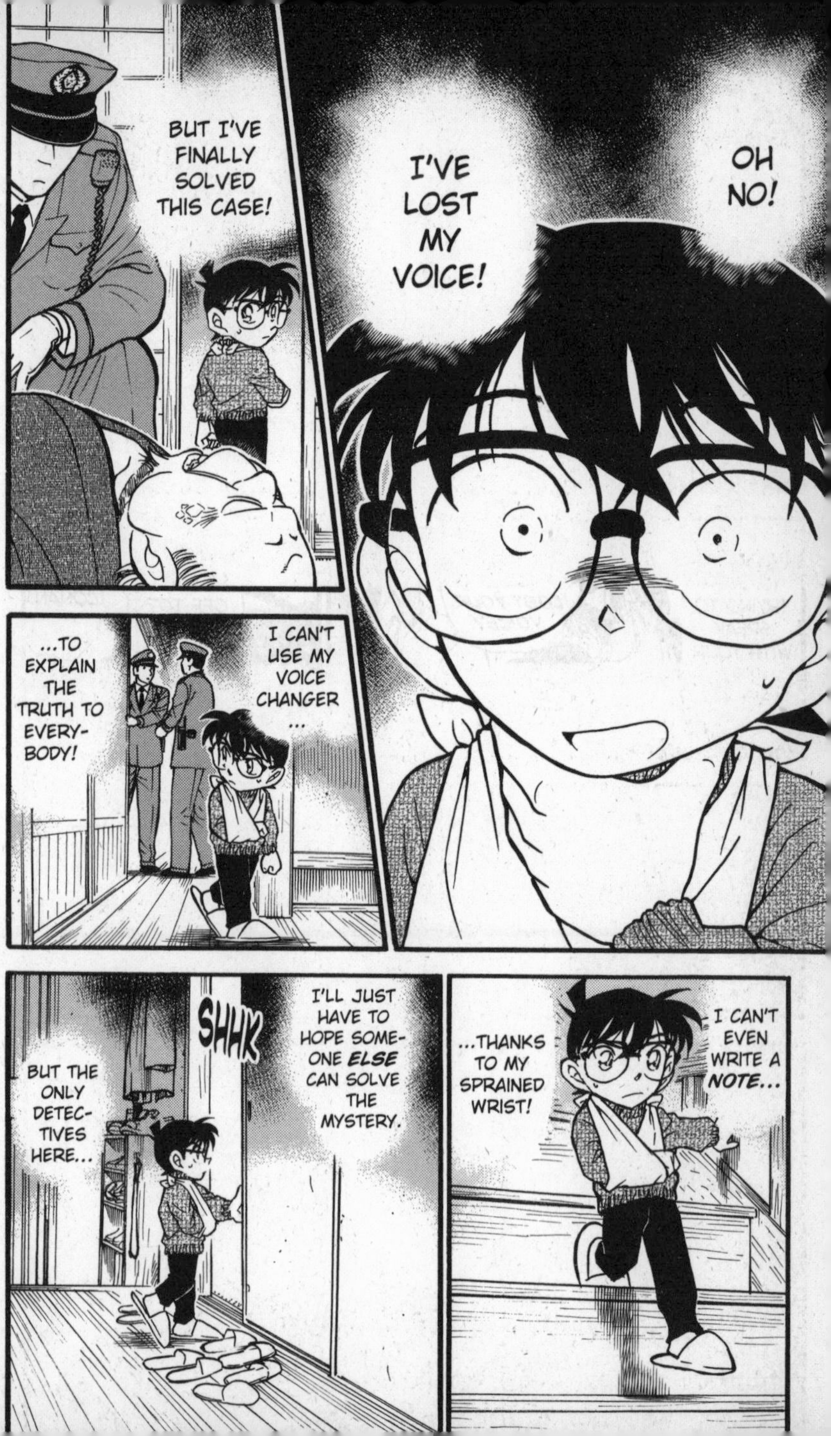
OH NO!
I'VE LOST MY VOICE!
BUT I'VE FINALLY SOLVED THIS CASE!
I CAN'T USE MY VOICE CHANGER...
...TO EXPLAIN THE TRUTH TO EVERYBODY!
I CAN'T EVEN WRITE A NOTE...
...THANKS TO MY SPRAINED WRIST!
I'LL JUST HAVE TO HOPE SOMEONE ELSE CAN SOLVE THE MYSTERY.
SHHK
BUT THE ONLY DETECTIVES HERE...

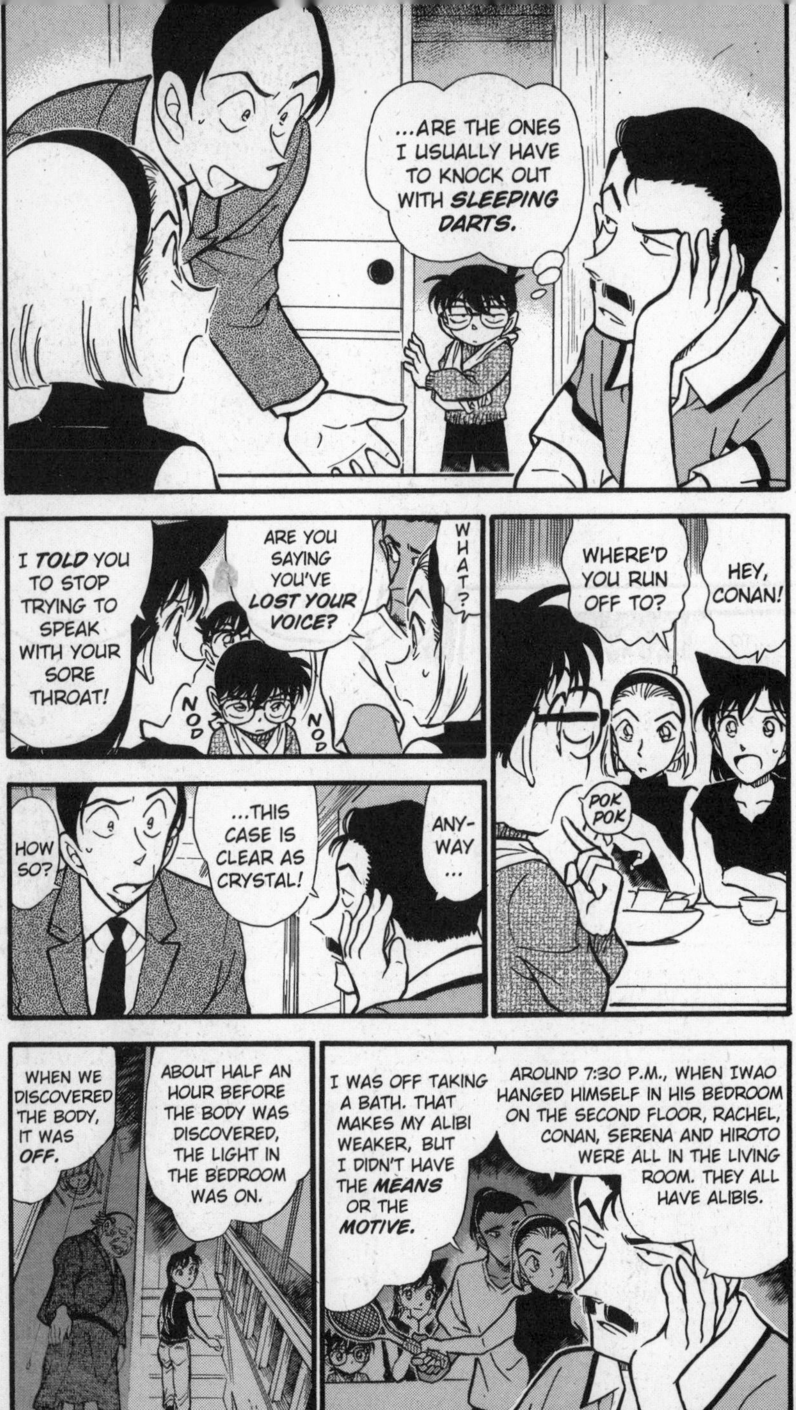
...ARE THE ONES I USUALLY HAVE TO KNOCK OUT WITH **SLEEPING DARTS.**
HEY, CONAN!
WHERE'D YOU RUN OFF TO?
POK POK
WHAT?
ARE YOU SAYING YOU'VE **LOST YOUR VOICE?**
NOD
NOD
I **TOLD** YOU TO STOP TRYING TO SPEAK WITH YOUR SORE THROAT!
ANY-WAY...
...THIS CASE IS CLEAR AS CRYSTAL!
HOW SO?
AROUND 7:30 P.M., WHEN IWAO HANGED HIMSELF IN HIS BEDROOM ON THE SECOND FLOOR, RACHEL, CONAN, SERENA AND HIROTO WERE ALL IN THE LIVING ROOM. THEY ALL HAVE ALIBIS.
I WAS OFF TAKING A BATH. THAT MAKES MY ALIBI WEAKER, BUT I DIDN'T HAVE THE **MEANS** OR THE **MOTIVE.**
ABOUT HALF AN HOUR BEFORE THE BODY WAS DISCOVERED, THE LIGHT IN THE BEDROOM WAS ON.
WHEN WE DISCOVERED THE BODY, IT WAS **OFF.**

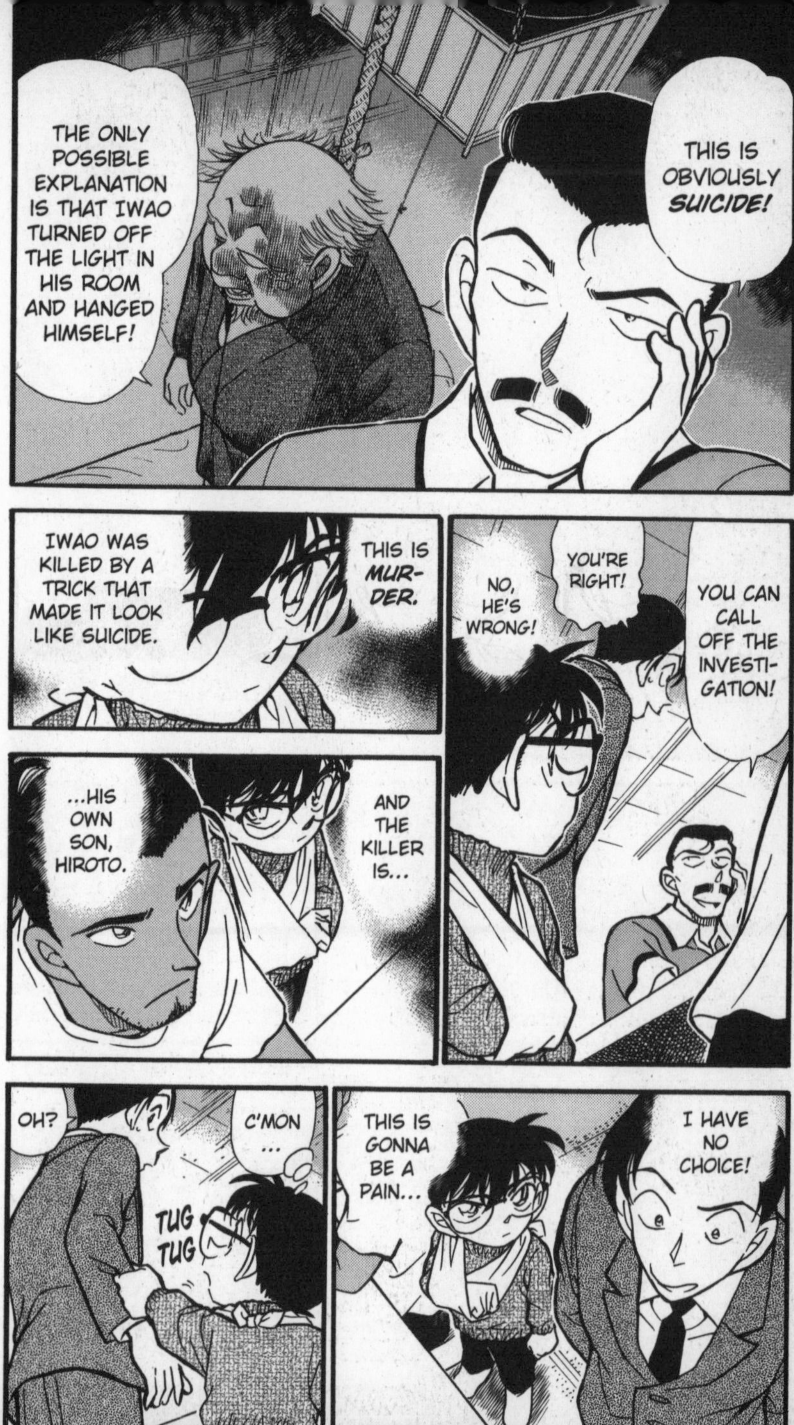
THIS IS OBVIOUSLY SUICIDE!
THE ONLY POSSIBLE EXPLANATION IS THAT IWAO TURNED OFF THE LIGHT IN HIS ROOM AND HANGED HIMSELF!
YOU CAN CALL OFF THE INVESTI-GATION!
YOU'RE RIGHT!
NO, HE'S WRONG!
THIS IS MUR-DER.
IWAO WAS KILLED BY A TRICK THAT MADE IT LOOK LIKE SUICIDE.
AND THE KILLER IS...
...HIS OWN SON, HIROTO.
I HAVE NO CHOICE!
THIS IS GONNA BE A PAIN...
C'MON ...
OH?
TUG TUG

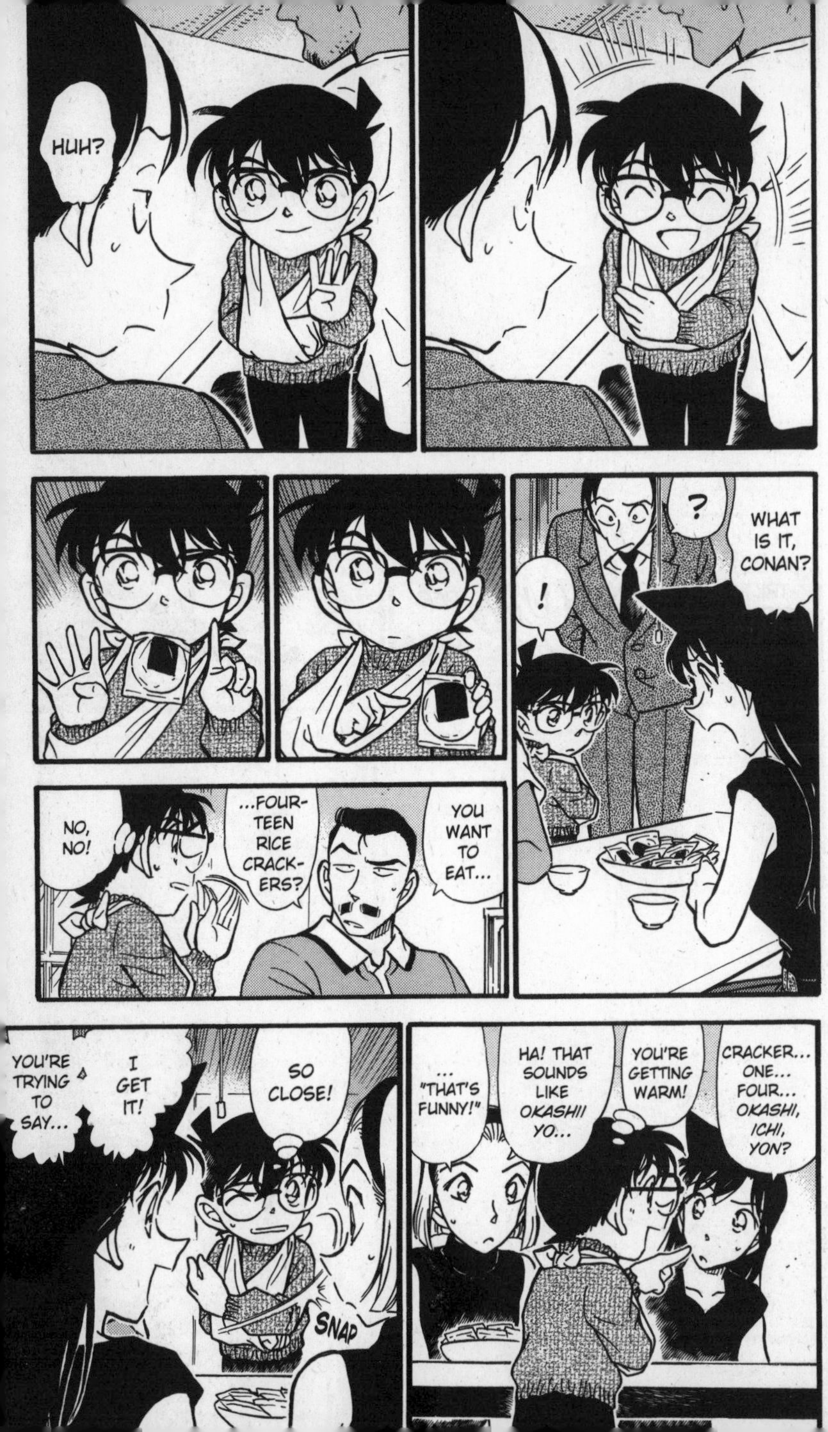
HUH?
WHAT IS IT, CONAN?
?
!
YOU WANT TO EAT...
...FOURTEEN RICE CRACKERS?
NO, NO!
CRACKER... ONE... FOUR... OKASHI, ICHI, YON?
YOU'RE GETTING WARM!
HA! THAT SOUNDS LIKE OKASHII YO...
... "THAT'S FUNNY!"
SO CLOSE!
I GET IT!
YOU'RE TRYING TO SAY...
SNAP

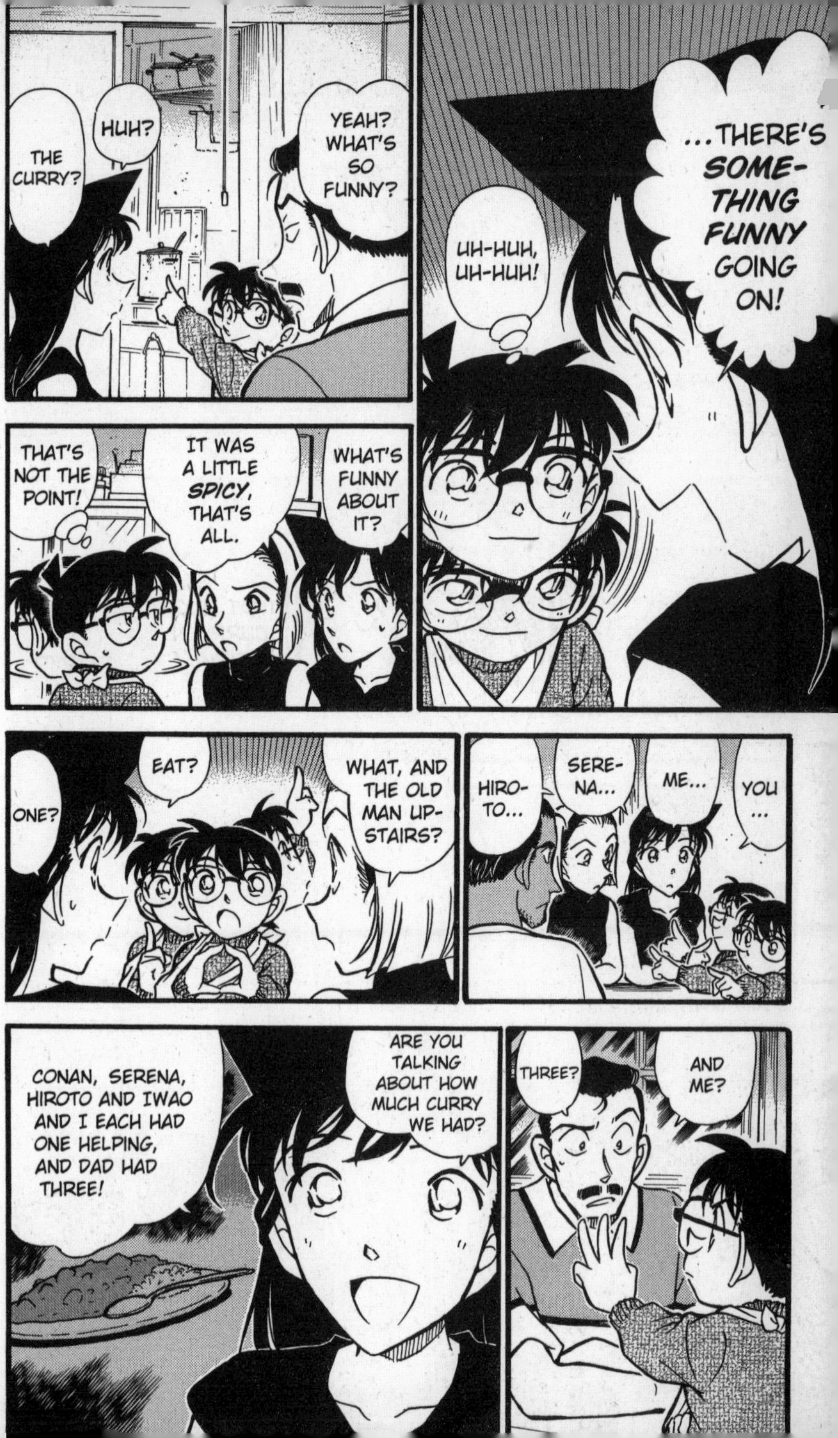
...THERE'S SOME-THING FUNNY GOING ON!
UH-HUH, UH-HUH!
YEAH? WHAT'S SO FUNNY?
HUH?
THE CURRY?
WHAT'S FUNNY ABOUT IT?
IT WAS A LITTLE SPICY, THAT'S ALL.
THAT'S NOT THE POINT!
YOU ...
ME...
SERE-NA...
HIRO-TO...
WHAT, AND THE OLD MAN UP-STAIRS?
EAT?
ONE?
AND ME?
THREE?
ARE YOU TALKING ABOUT HOW MUCH CURRY WE HAD?
CONAN, SERENA, HIROTO AND IWAO AND I EACH HAD ONE HELPING, AND DAD HAD THREE!

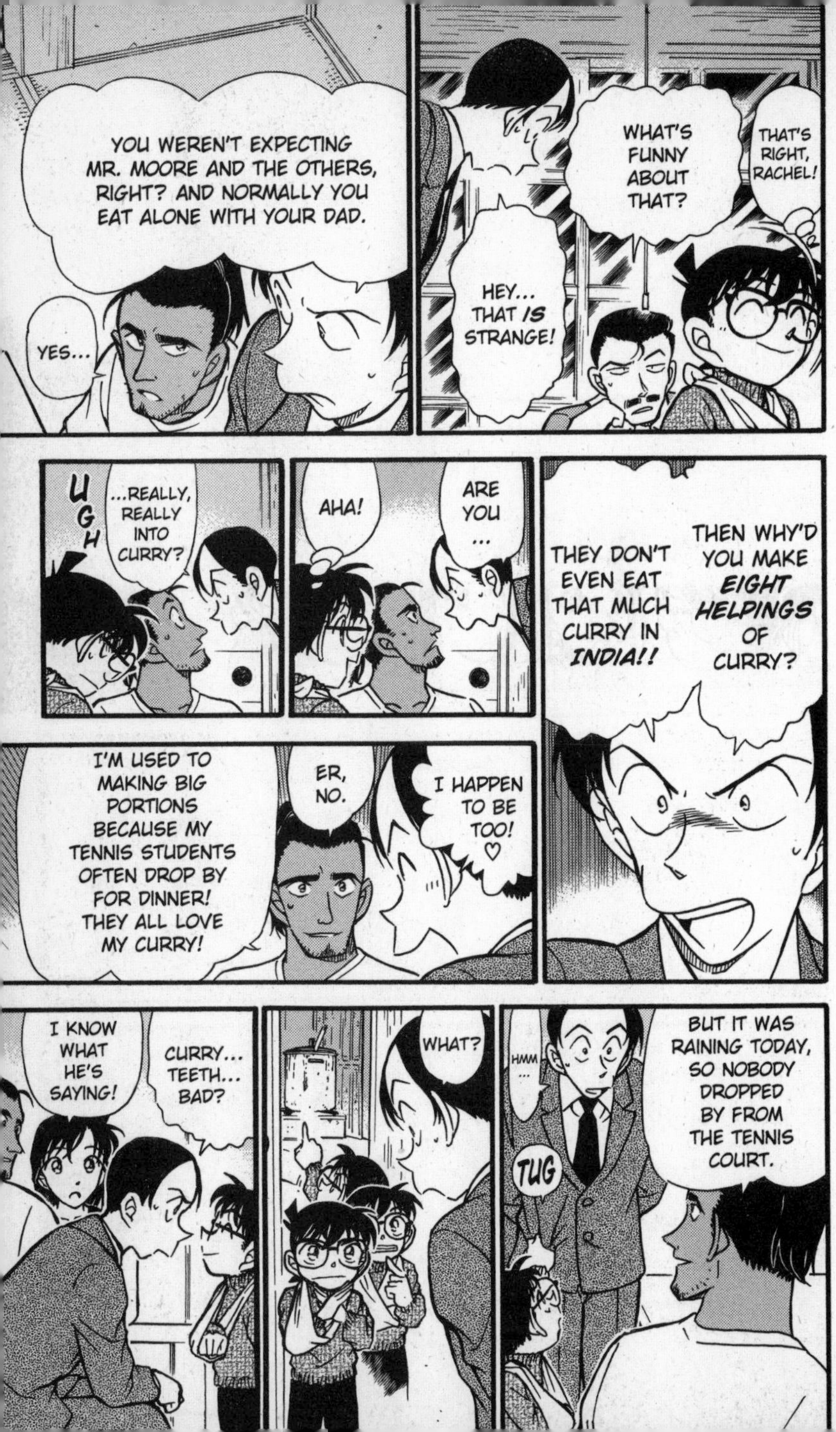
THAT'S RIGHT, RACHEL!
WHAT'S FUNNY ABOUT THAT?
HEY... THAT IS STRANGE!
YOU WEREN'T EXPECTING MR. MOORE AND THE OTHERS, RIGHT? AND NORMALLY YOU EAT ALONE WITH YOUR DAD.
YES...
THEN WHY'D YOU MAKE EIGHT HELPINGS OF CURRY?
THEY DON'T EVEN EAT THAT MUCH CURRY IN INDIA!!
ARE YOU ...
AHA!
...REALLY, REALLY INTO CURRY?
UGH
I HAPPEN TO BE TOO! ♡
ER, NO.
I'M USED TO MAKING BIG PORTIONS BECAUSE MY TENNIS STUDENTS OFTEN DROP BY FOR DINNER! THEY ALL LOVE MY CURRY!
BUT IT WAS RAINING TODAY, SO NOBODY DROPPED BY FROM THE TENNIS COURT.
HMM ...
TUG
WHAT?
CURRY... TEETH... BAD?
I KNOW WHAT HE'S SAYING!

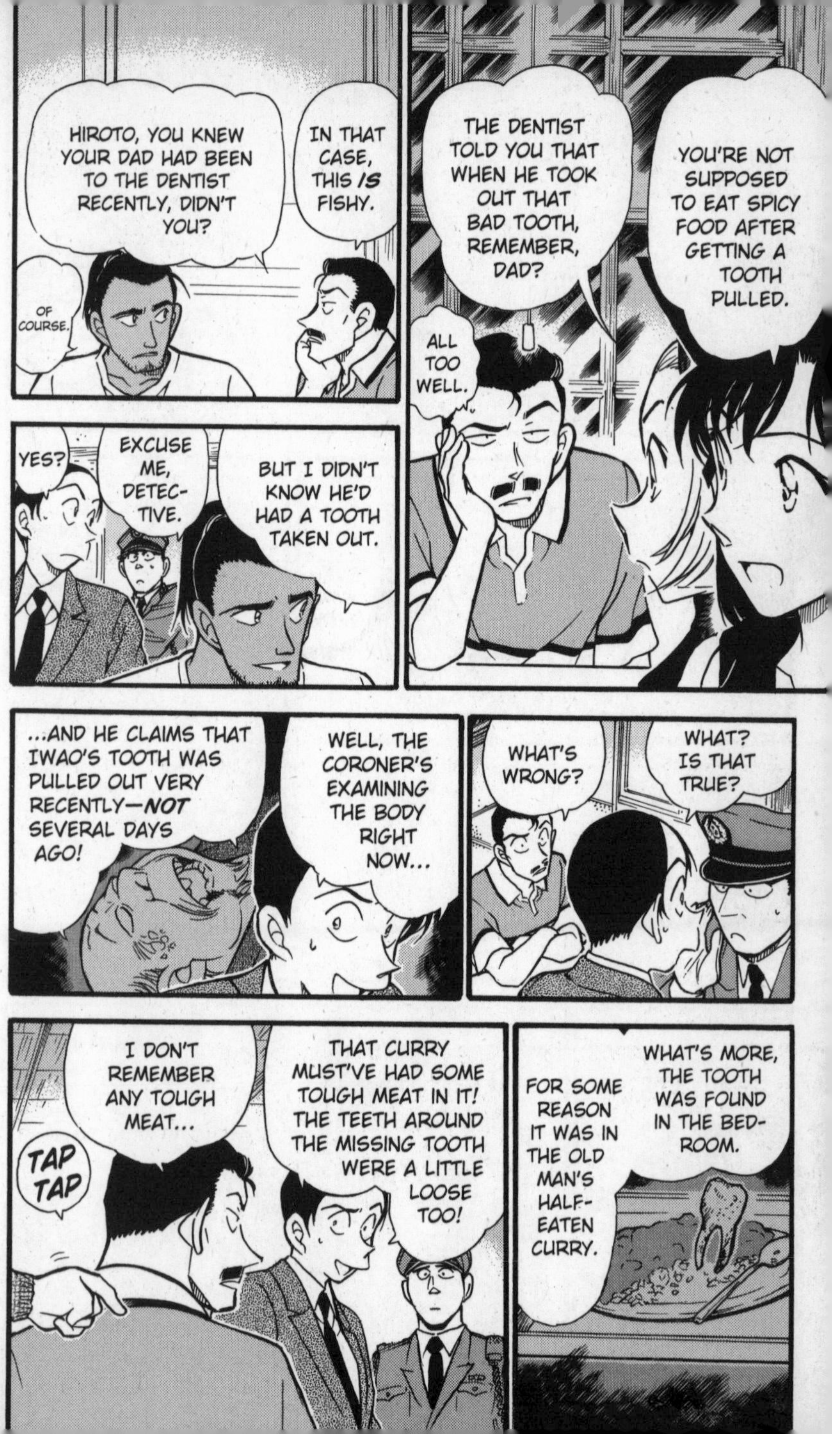
YOU'RE NOT SUPPOSED TO EAT SPICY FOOD AFTER GETTING A TOOTH PULLED.
THE DENTIST TOLD YOU THAT WHEN HE TOOK OUT THAT BAD TOOTH, REMEMBER, DAD?
ALL TOO WELL.
IN THAT CASE, THIS *IS* FISHY.
HIROTO, YOU KNEW YOUR DAD HAD BEEN TO THE DENTIST RECENTLY, DIDN'T YOU?
OF COURSE.
BUT I DIDN'T KNOW HE'D HAD A TOOTH TAKEN OUT.
EXCUSE ME, DETECTIVE.
YES?
WHAT? IS THAT TRUE?
WHAT'S WRONG?
WELL, THE CORONER'S EXAMINING THE BODY RIGHT NOW...
...AND HE CLAIMS THAT IWAO'S TOOTH WAS PULLED OUT VERY RECENTLY—**NOT** SEVERAL DAYS AGO!
WHAT'S MORE, THE TOOTH WAS FOUND IN THE BED-ROOM.
FOR SOME REASON IT WAS IN THE OLD MAN'S HALF-EATEN CURRY.
THAT CURRY MUST'VE HAD SOME TOUGH MEAT IN IT! THE TEETH AROUND THE MISSING TOOTH WERE A LITTLE LOOSE TOO!
I DON'T REMEMBER ANY TOUGH MEAT...
TAP TAP

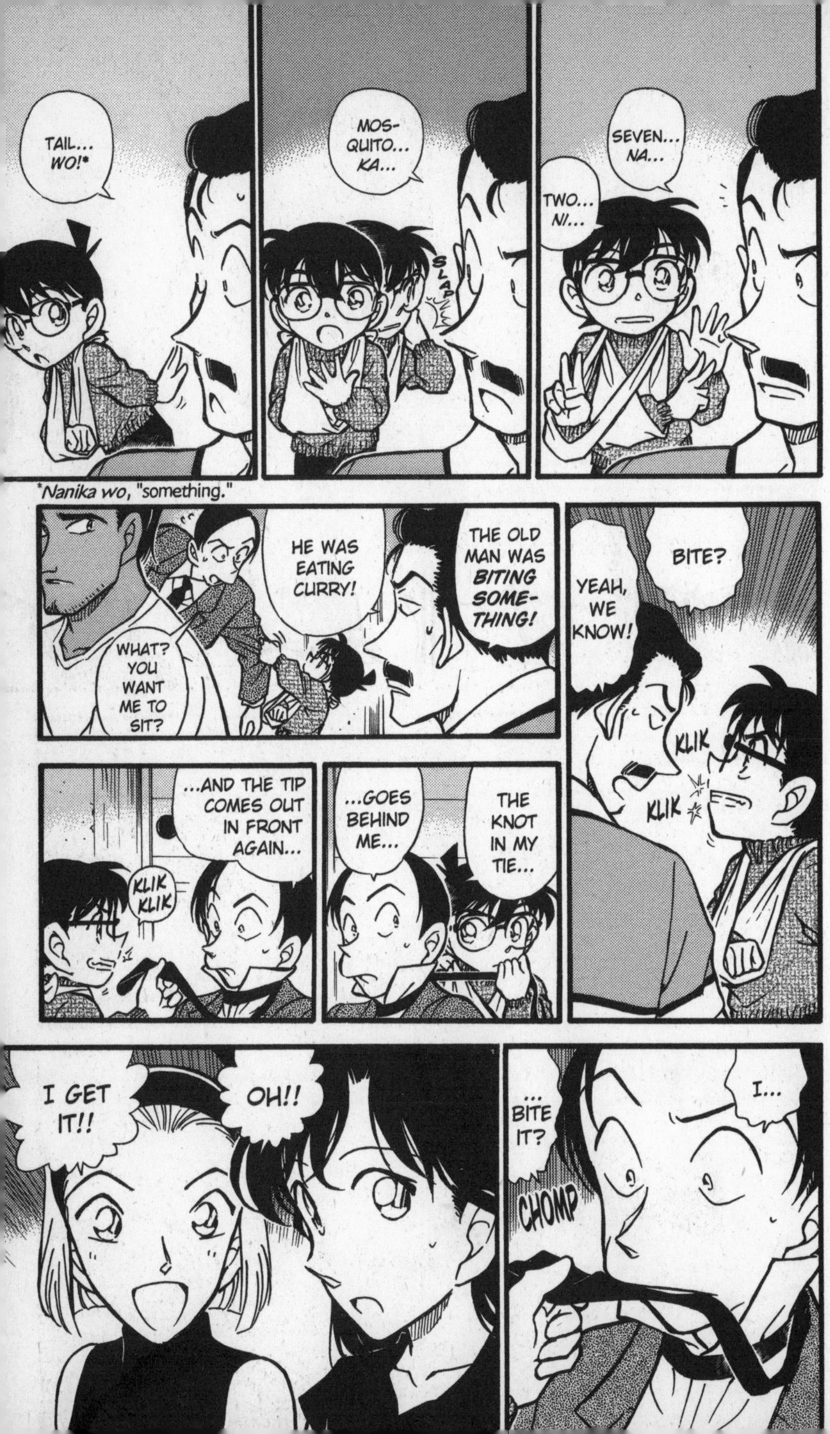
SEVEN... NA...
TWO... NI...
MOS-QUITO... KA...
SLAP
TAIL... WO!*
BITE?
YEAH, WE KNOW!
KLIK
KLIK
THE OLD MAN WAS BITING SOMETHING!
HE WAS EATING CURRY!
WHAT? YOU WANT ME TO SIT?
THE KNOT IN MY TIE...
...GOES BEHIND ME...
...AND THE TIP COMES OUT IN FRONT AGAIN...
KLIK KLIK
I...
...BITE IT?
CHOMP
OH!!
I GET IT!!

*Nanika wo, "something."

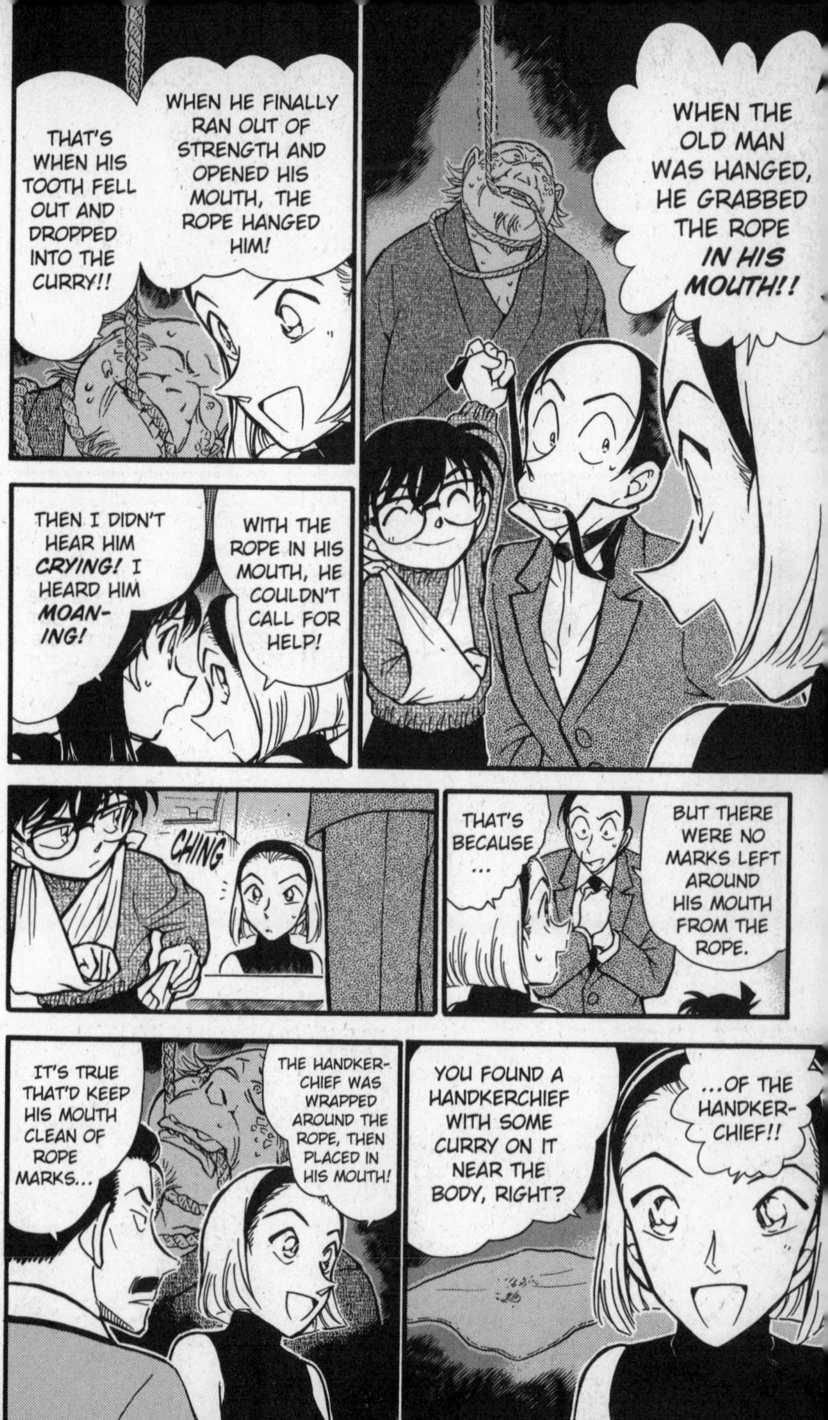
WHEN THE OLD MAN WAS HANGED, HE GRABBED THE ROPE *IN HIS MOUTH!!*
WHEN HE FINALLY RAN OUT OF STRENGTH AND OPENED HIS MOUTH, THE ROPE HANGED HIM!
THAT'S WHEN HIS TOOTH FELL OUT AND DROPPED INTO THE CURRY!!
WITH THE ROPE IN HIS MOUTH, HE COULDN'T CALL FOR HELP!
THEN I DIDN'T HEAR HIM *CRYING!* I HEARD HIM *MOAN-ING!*
BUT THERE WERE NO MARKS LEFT AROUND HIS MOUTH FROM THE ROPE.
THAT'S BECAUSE ...
CHING
...OF THE HANDKER-CHIEF!!
YOU FOUND A HANDKERCHIEF WITH SOME CURRY ON IT NEAR THE BODY, RIGHT?
THE HANDKER-CHIEF WAS WRAPPED AROUND THE ROPE, THEN PLACED IN HIS MOUTH!
IT'S TRUE THAT'D KEEP HIS MOUTH CLEAN OF ROPE MARKS...

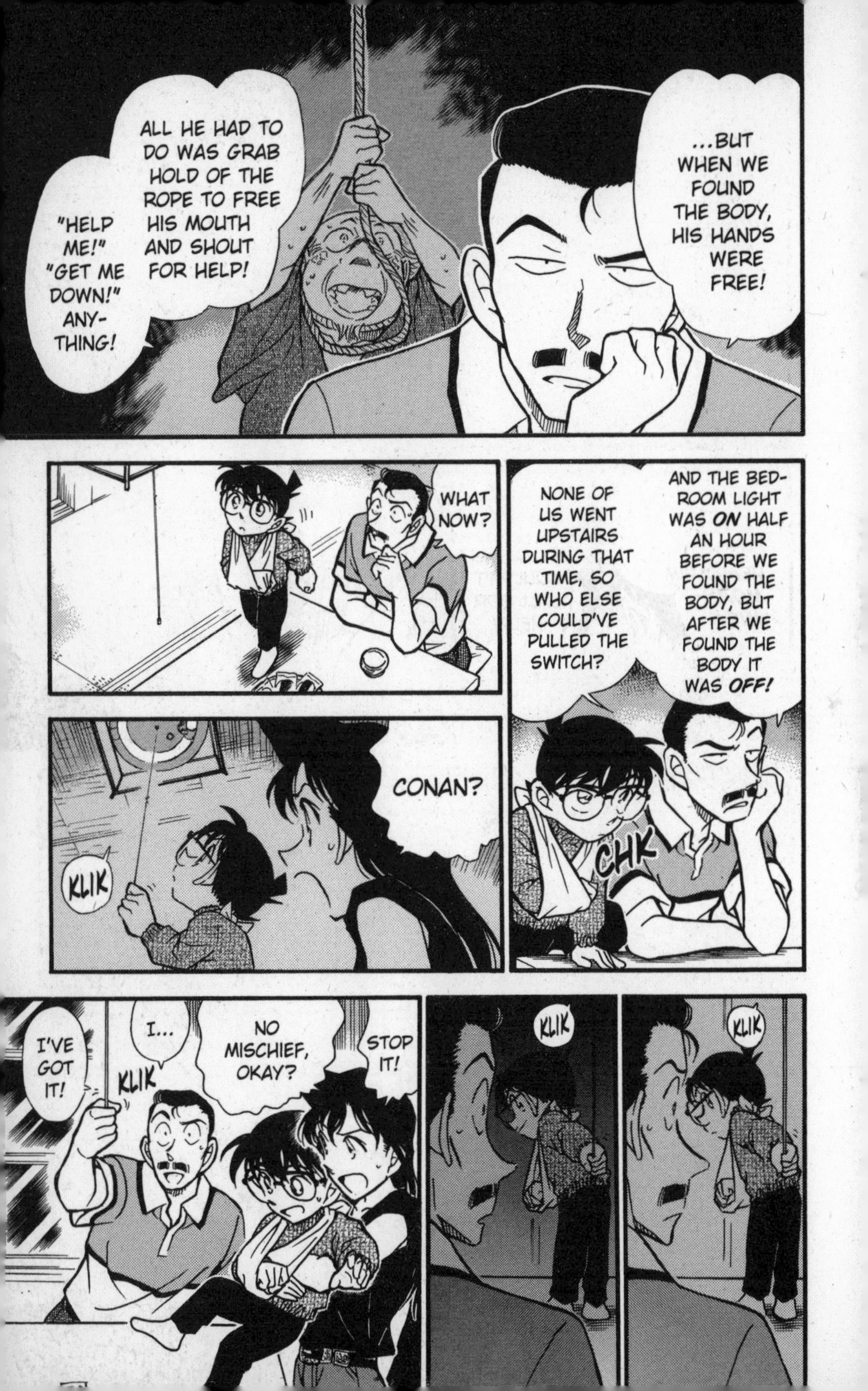
...BUT WHEN WE FOUND THE BODY, HIS HANDS WERE FREE!
ALL HE HAD TO DO WAS GRAB HOLD OF THE ROPE TO FREE HIS MOUTH AND SHOUT FOR HELP!
"HELP ME!" "GET ME DOWN!" ANY-THING!
AND THE BED-ROOM LIGHT WAS ON HALF AN HOUR BEFORE WE FOUND THE BODY, BUT AFTER WE FOUND THE BODY IT WAS OFF!
NONE OF US WENT UPSTAIRS DURING THAT TIME, SO WHO ELSE COULD'VE PULLED THE SWITCH?
CHK
WHAT NOW?
CONAN?
KLIK
KLIK
KLIK
STOP IT!
NO MISCHIEF, OKAY?
I...
KLIK
I'VE GOT IT!

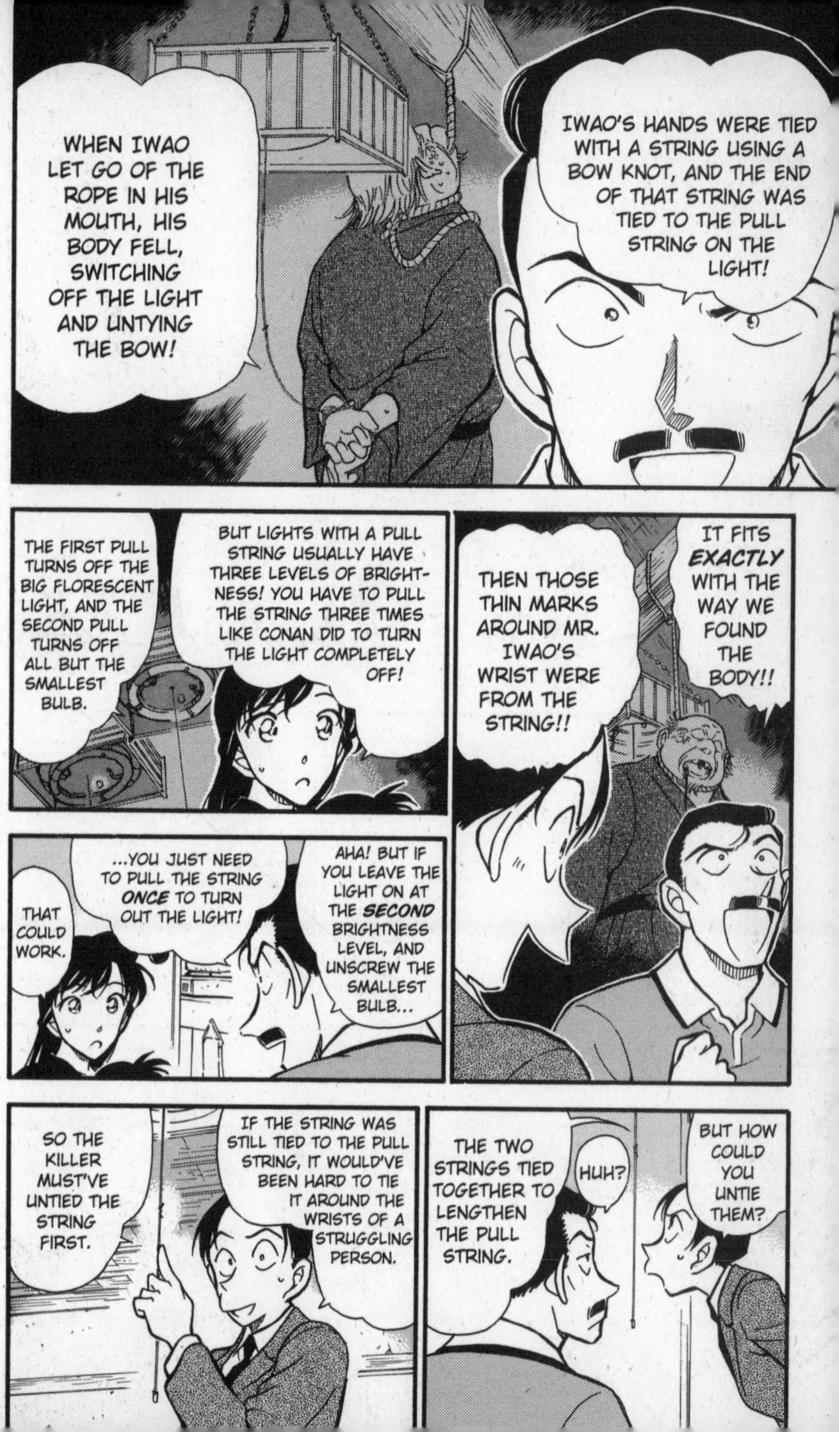
IWAO'S HANDS WERE TIED WITH A STRING USING A BOW KNOT, AND THE END OF THAT STRING WAS TIED TO THE PULL STRING ON THE LIGHT!
WHEN IWAO LET GO OF THE ROPE IN HIS MOUTH, HIS BODY FELL, SWITCHING OFF THE LIGHT AND UNTYING THE BOW!
IT FITS *EXACTLY* WITH THE WAY WE FOUND THE BODY!!
THEN THOSE THIN MARKS AROUND MR. IWAO'S WRIST WERE FROM THE STRING!!
BUT LIGHTS WITH A PULL STRING USUALLY HAVE THREE LEVELS OF BRIGHT-NESS! YOU HAVE TO PULL THE STRING THREE TIMES LIKE CONAN DID TO TURN THE LIGHT COMPLETELY OFF!
THE FIRST PULL TURNS OFF THE BIG FLORESCENT LIGHT, AND THE SECOND PULL TURNS OFF ALL BUT THE SMALLEST BULB.
AHA! BUT IF YOU LEAVE THE LIGHT ON AT THE *SECOND* BRIGHTNESS LEVEL, AND UNSCREW THE SMALLEST BULB...
...YOU JUST NEED TO PULL THE STRING *ONCE* TO TURN OUT THE LIGHT!
THAT COULD WORK.
BUT HOW COULD YOU UNTIE THEM?
HUH?
THE TWO STRINGS TIED TOGETHER TO LENGTHEN THE PULL STRING.
IF THE STRING WAS STILL TIED TO THE PULL STRING, IT WOULD'VE BEEN HARD TO TIE IT AROUND THE WRISTS OF A STRUGGLING PERSON.
SO THE KILLER MUST'VE UNTIED THE STRING FIRST.

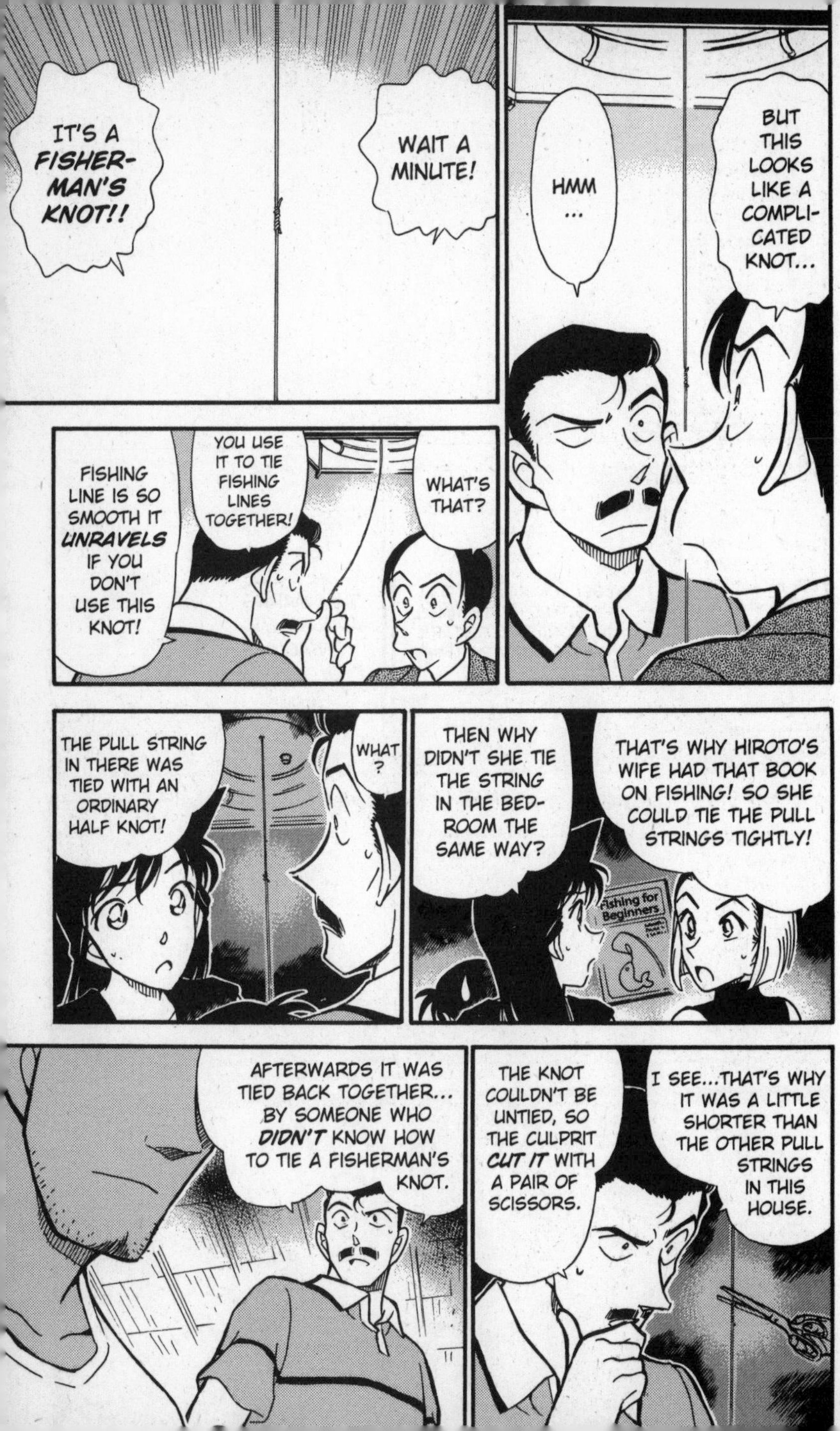
BUT THIS LOOKS LIKE A COMPLICATED KNOT...
HMM ...
WAIT A MINUTE!
IT'S A FISHERMAN'S KNOT!!
WHAT'S THAT?
YOU USE IT TO TIE FISHING LINES TOGETHER!
FISHING LINE IS SO SMOOTH IT UNRAVELS IF YOU DON'T USE THIS KNOT!
THAT'S WHY HIROTO'S WIFE HAD THAT BOOK ON FISHING! SO SHE COULD TIE THE PULL STRINGS TIGHTLY!
Fishing for Beginners
THEN WHY DIDN'T SHE TIE THE STRING IN THE BEDROOM THE SAME WAY?
WHAT ?
THE PULL STRING IN THERE WAS TIED WITH AN ORDINARY HALF KNOT!
I SEE...THAT'S WHY IT WAS A LITTLE SHORTER THAN THE OTHER PULL STRINGS IN THIS HOUSE.
THE KNOT COULDN'T BE UNTIED, SO THE CULPRIT CUT IT WITH A PAIR OF SCISSORS.
AFTERWARDS IT WAS TIED BACK TOGETHER... BY SOMEONE WHO DIDN'T KNOW HOW TO TIE A FISHERMAN'S KNOT.

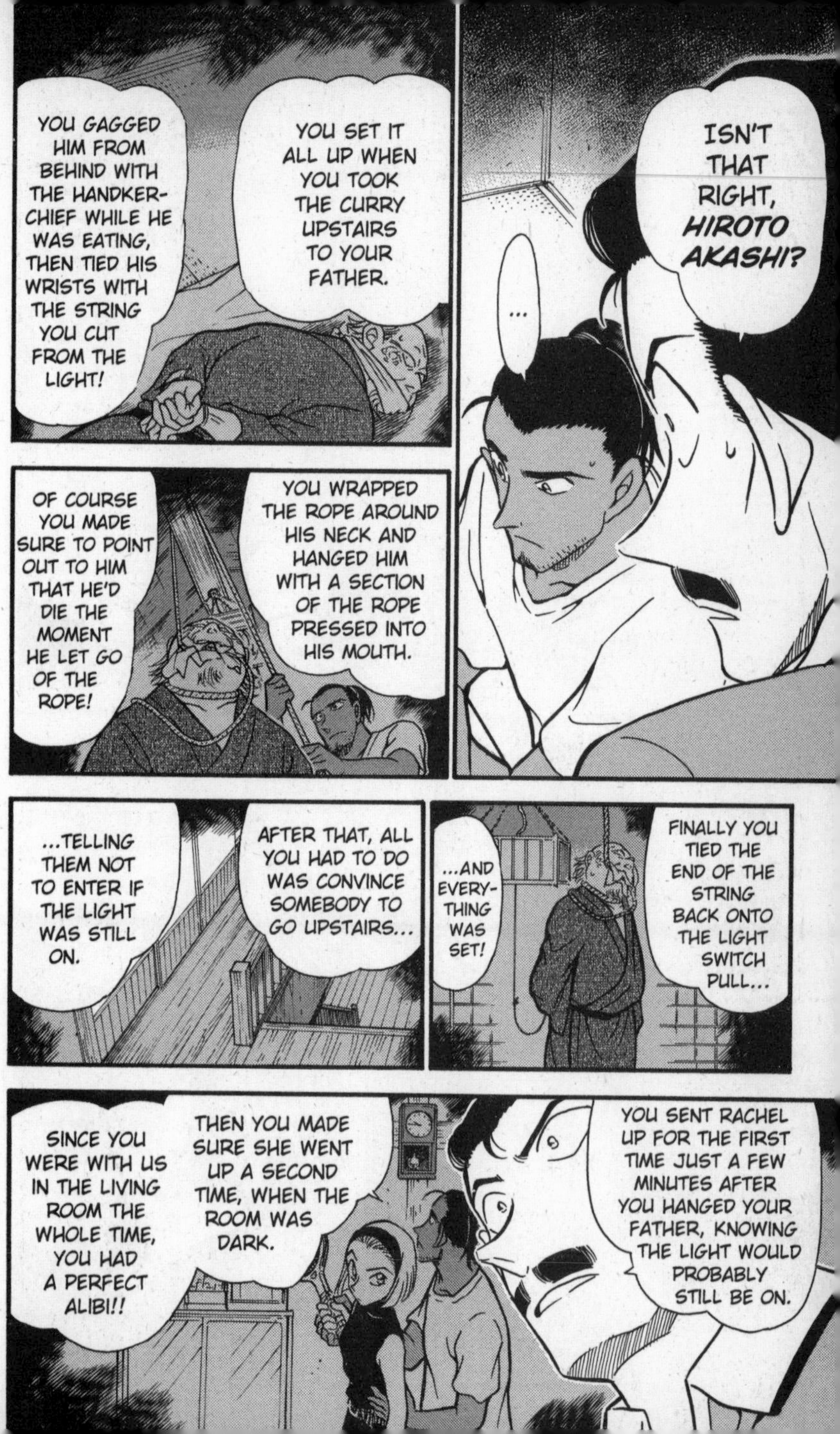
ISN'T THAT RIGHT, *HIROTO AKASHI?*
...
YOU SET IT ALL UP WHEN YOU TOOK THE CURRY UPSTAIRS TO YOUR FATHER.
YOU GAGGED HIM FROM BEHIND WITH THE HANDKERCHIEF WHILE HE WAS EATING, THEN TIED HIS WRISTS WITH THE STRING YOU CUT FROM THE LIGHT!
YOU WRAPPED THE ROPE AROUND HIS NECK AND HANGED HIM WITH A SECTION OF THE ROPE PRESSED INTO HIS MOUTH.
OF COURSE YOU MADE SURE TO POINT OUT TO HIM THAT HE'D DIE THE MOMENT HE LET GO OF THE ROPE!
FINALLY YOU TIED THE END OF THE STRING BACK ONTO THE LIGHT SWITCH PULL...
...AND EVERYTHING WAS SET!
AFTER THAT, ALL YOU HAD TO DO WAS CONVINCE SOMEBODY TO GO UPSTAIRS...
...TELLING THEM NOT TO ENTER IF THE LIGHT WAS STILL ON.
YOU SENT RACHEL UP FOR THE FIRST TIME JUST A FEW MINUTES AFTER YOU HANGED YOUR FATHER, KNOWING THE LIGHT WOULD PROBABLY STILL BE ON.
THEN YOU MADE SURE SHE WENT UP A SECOND TIME, WHEN THE ROOM WAS DARK.
SINCE YOU WERE WITH US IN THE LIVING ROOM THE WHOLE TIME, YOU HAD A PERFECT ALIBI!!

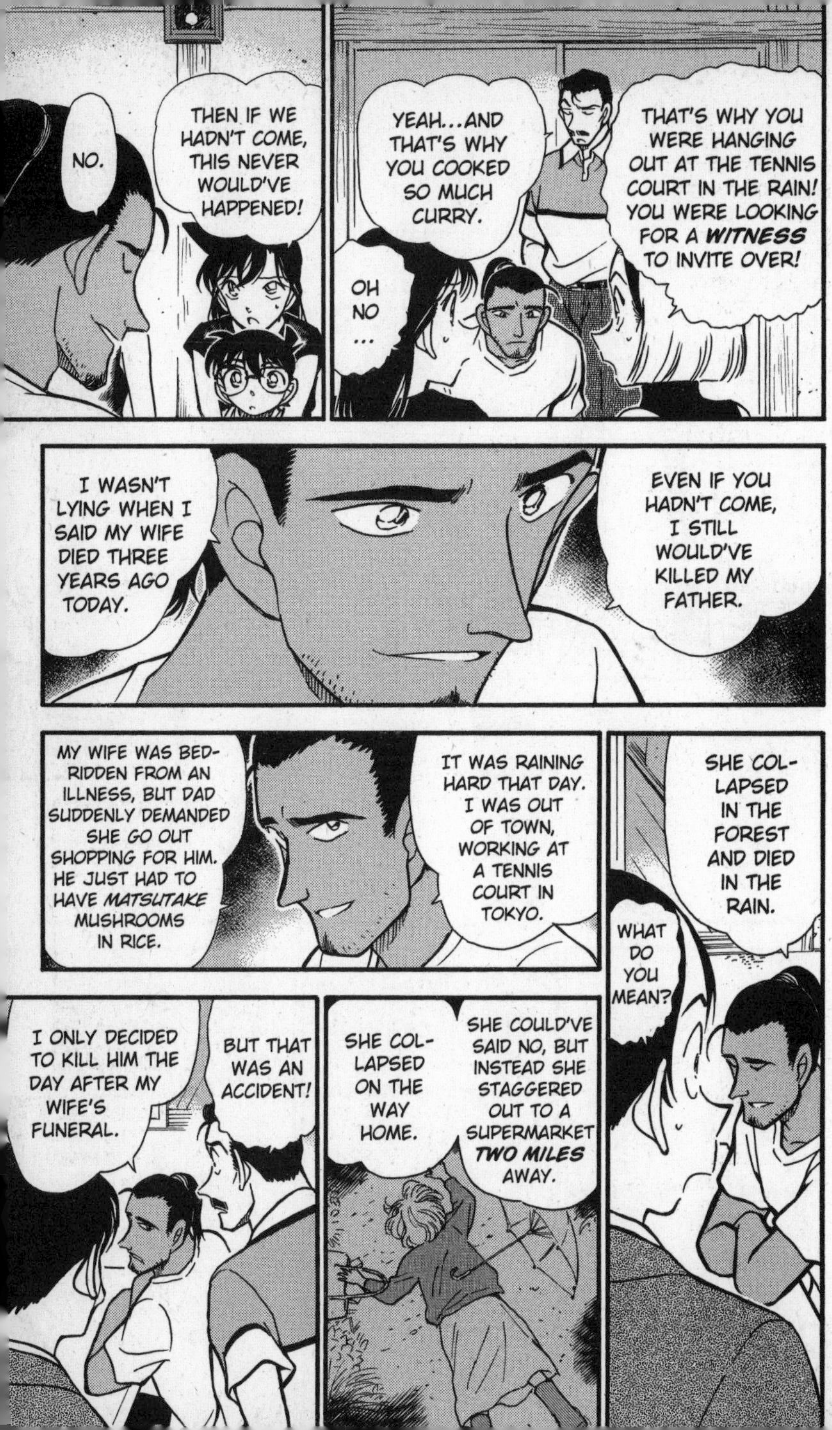

YEAH...AND THAT'S WHY YOU COOKED SO MUCH CURRY.
THAT'S WHY YOU WERE HANGING OUT AT THE TENNIS COURT IN THE RAIN! YOU WERE LOOKING FOR A **WITNESS** TO INVITE OVER!
OH NO ...
THEN IF WE HADN'T COME, THIS NEVER WOULD'VE HAPPENED!
NO.
EVEN IF YOU HADN'T COME, I STILL WOULD'VE KILLED MY FATHER.
I WASN'T LYING WHEN I SAID MY WIFE DIED THREE YEARS AGO TODAY.
SHE COLLAPSED IN THE FOREST AND DIED IN THE RAIN.
WHAT DO YOU MEAN?
IT WAS RAINING HARD THAT DAY. I WAS OUT OF TOWN, WORKING AT A TENNIS COURT IN TOKYO.
MY WIFE WAS BEDRIDDEN FROM AN ILLNESS, BUT DAD SUDDENLY DEMANDED SHE GO OUT SHOPPING FOR HIM. HE JUST HAD TO HAVE *MATSUTAKE* MUSHROOMS IN RICE.
SHE COULD'VE SAID NO, BUT INSTEAD SHE STAGGERED OUT TO A SUPERMARKET **TWO MILES** AWAY.
SHE COLLAPSED ON THE WAY HOME.
BUT THAT WAS AN ACCIDENT!
I ONLY DECIDED TO KILL HIM THE DAY AFTER MY WIFE'S FUNERAL.

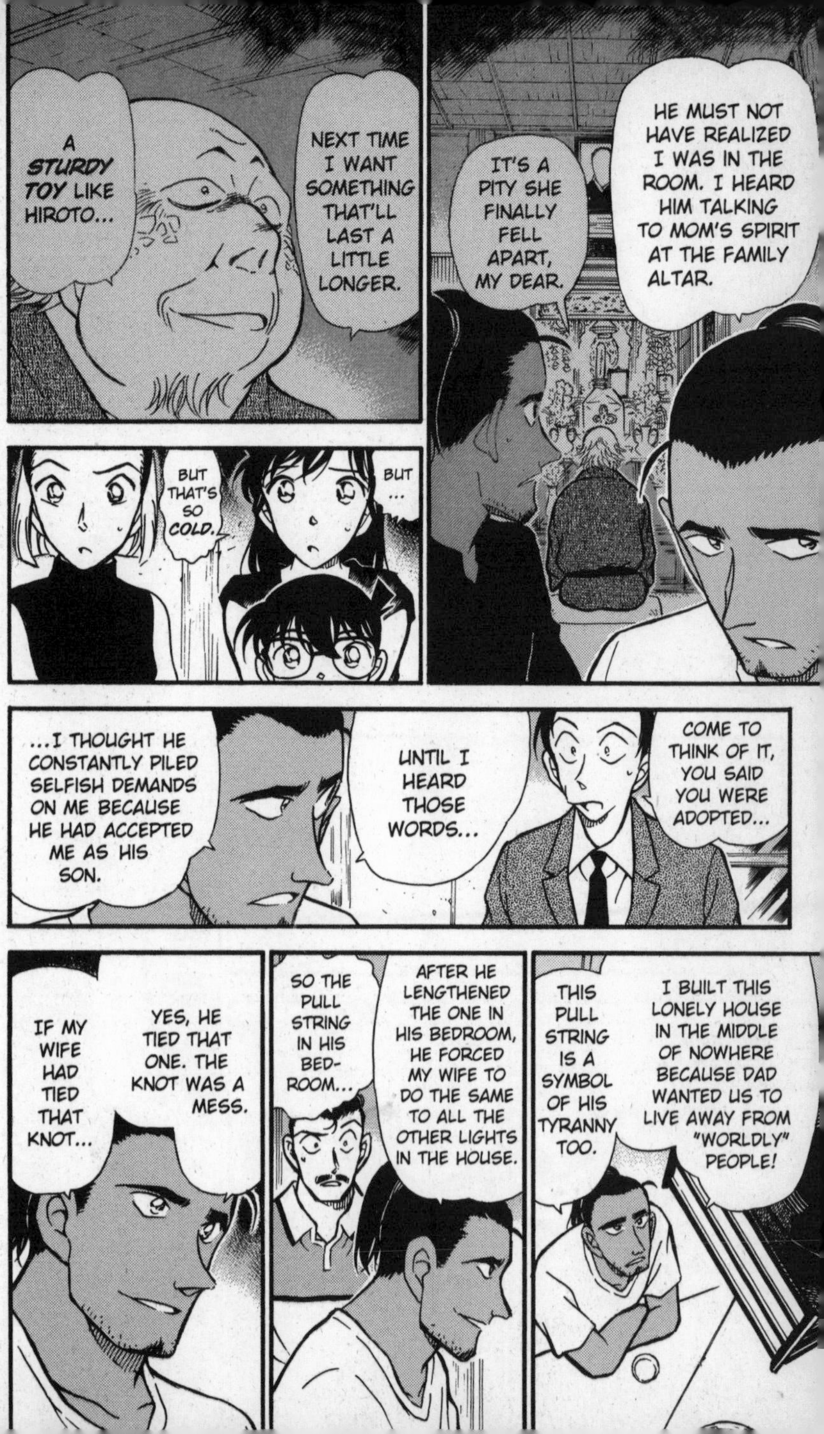
HE MUST NOT HAVE REALIZED I WAS IN THE ROOM. I HEARD HIM TALKING TO MOM'S SPIRIT AT THE FAMILY ALTAR.
IT'S A PITY SHE FINALLY FELL APART, MY DEAR.
NEXT TIME I WANT SOMETHING THAT'LL LAST A LITTLE LONGER.
A *STURDY TOY* LIKE HIROTO...
BUT ...
BUT THAT'S SO *COLD*.
COME TO THINK OF IT, YOU SAID YOU WERE ADOPTED...
UNTIL I HEARD THOSE WORDS...
...I THOUGHT HE CONSTANTLY PILED SELFISH DEMANDS ON ME BECAUSE HE HAD ACCEPTED ME AS HIS SON.
I BUILT THIS LONELY HOUSE IN THE MIDDLE OF NOWHERE BECAUSE DAD WANTED US TO LIVE AWAY FROM "WORLDLY" PEOPLE!
THIS PULL STRING IS A SYMBOL OF HIS TYRANNY TOO.
AFTER HE LENGTHENED THE ONE IN HIS BEDROOM, HE FORCED MY WIFE TO DO THE SAME TO ALL THE OTHER LIGHTS IN THE HOUSE.
SO THE PULL STRING IN HIS BED-ROOM...
YES, HE TIED THAT ONE. THE KNOT WAS A MESS.
IF MY WIFE HAD TIED THAT KNOT...

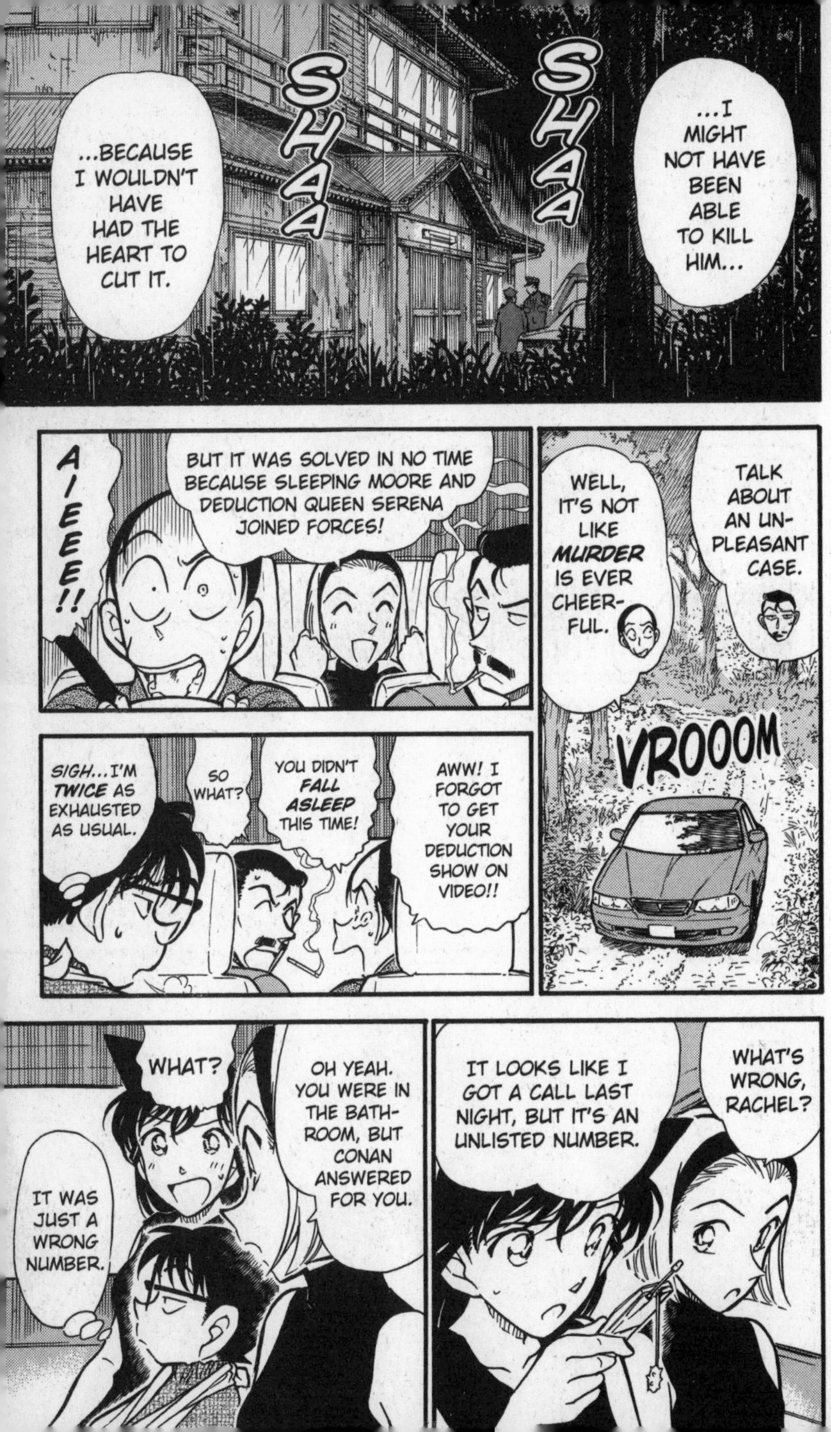
...I MIGHT NOT HAVE BEEN ABLE TO KILL HIM...
SHAA
SHAA
...BECAUSE I WOULDN'T HAVE HAD THE HEART TO CUT IT.
TALK ABOUT AN UN-PLEASANT CASE.
WELL, IT'S NOT LIKE *MURDER* IS EVER CHEER-FUL.
VROOOM
BUT IT WAS SOLVED IN NO TIME BECAUSE SLEEPING MOORE AND DEDUCTION QUEEN SERENA JOINED FORCES!
AIEEE!!
AWW! I FORGOT TO GET YOUR DEDUCTION SHOW ON VIDEO!!
YOU DIDN'T *FALL ASLEEP* THIS TIME!
SO WHAT?
SIGH...I'M *TWICE* AS EXHAUSTED AS USUAL.
WHAT'S WRONG, RACHEL?
IT LOOKS LIKE I GOT A CALL LAST NIGHT, BUT IT'S AN UNLISTED NUMBER.
OH YEAH. YOU WERE IN THE BATH-ROOM, BUT CONAN ANSWERED FOR YOU.
WHAT?
IT WAS JUST A WRONG NUMBER.

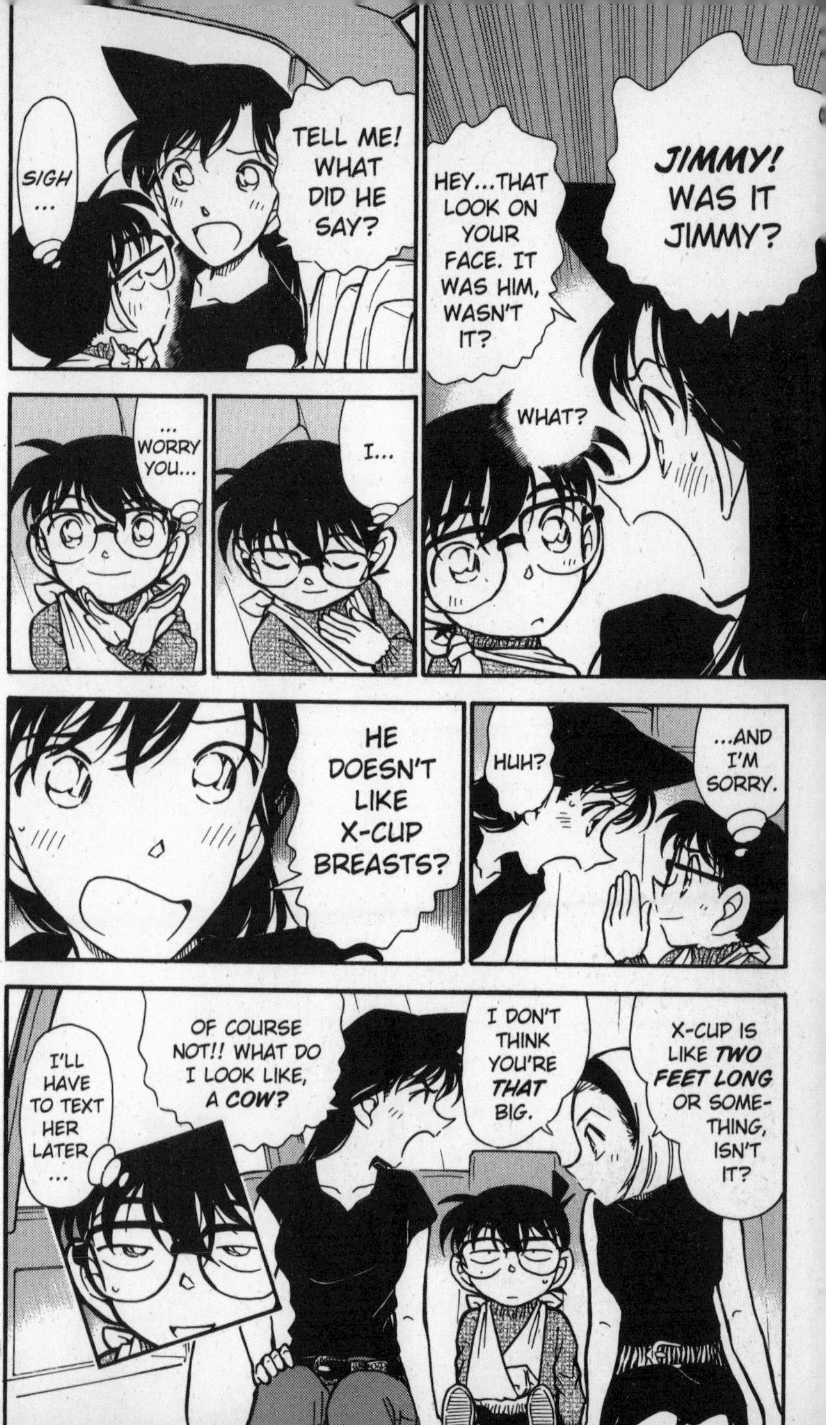
JIMMY! WAS IT JIMMY?
HEY...THAT LOOK ON YOUR FACE. IT WAS HIM, WASN'T IT?
WHAT?
TELL ME! WHAT DID HE SAY?
SIGH...
I...
...WORRY YOU...
...AND I'M SORRY.
HUH?
HE DOESN'T LIKE X-CUP BREASTS?
X-CUP IS LIKE TWO FEET LONG OR SOME-THING, ISN'T IT?
I DON'T THINK YOU'RE THAT BIG.
OF COURSE NOT!! WHAT DO I LOOK LIKE, A COW?
I'LL HAVE TO TEXT HER LATER...

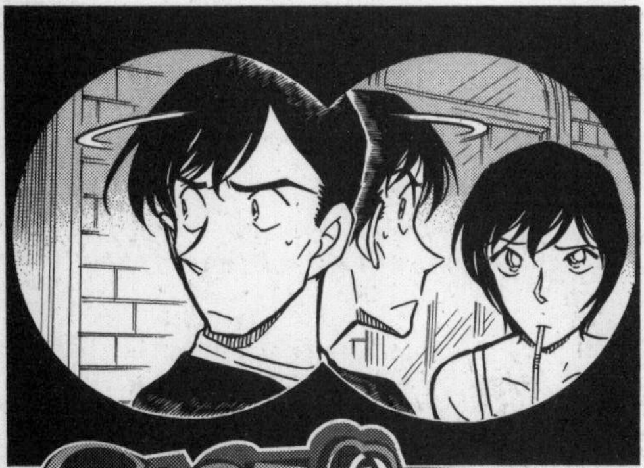

CASE CLOSED

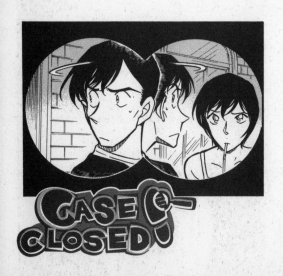

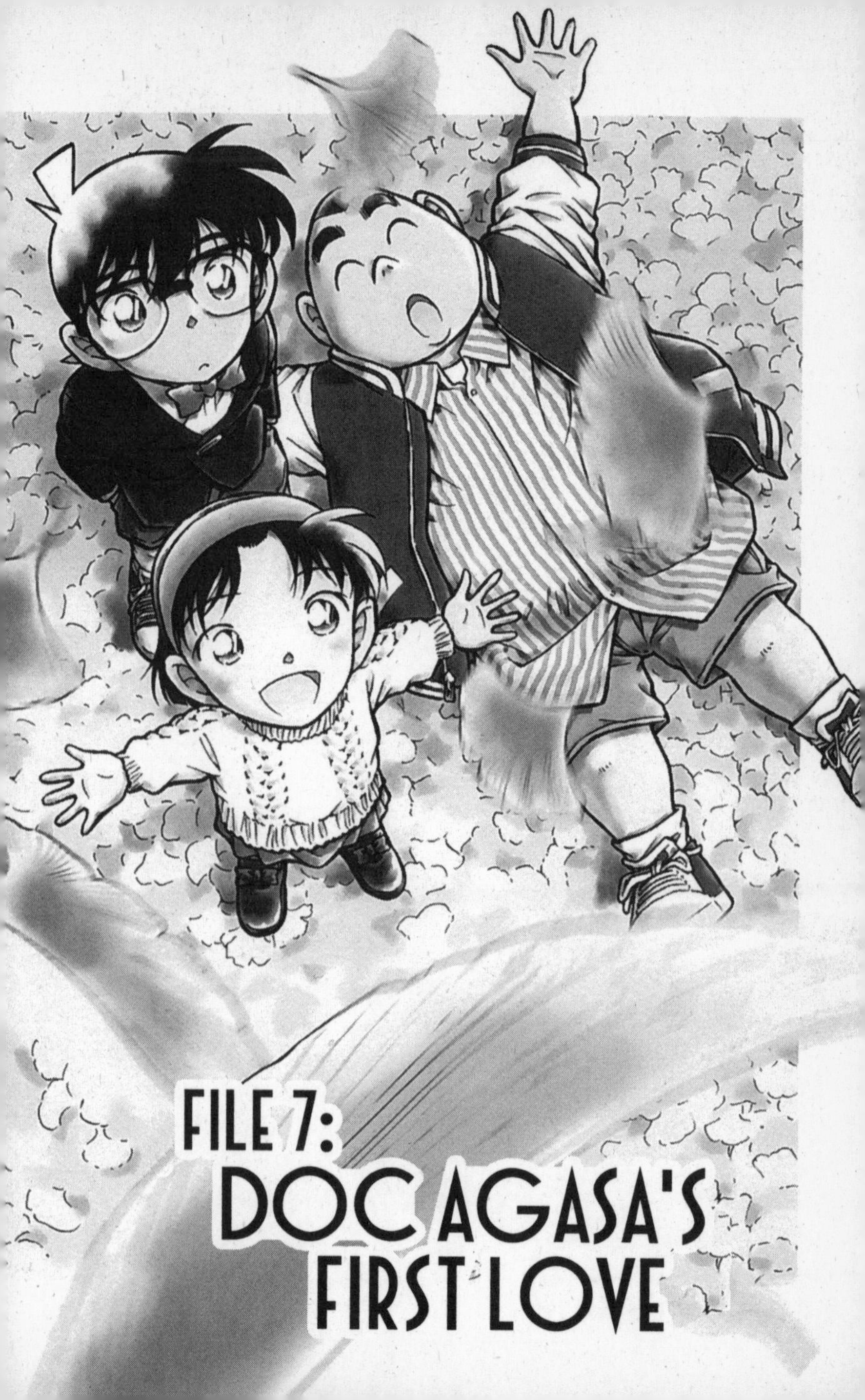

FILE 7: DOC AGASA'S FIRST LOVE

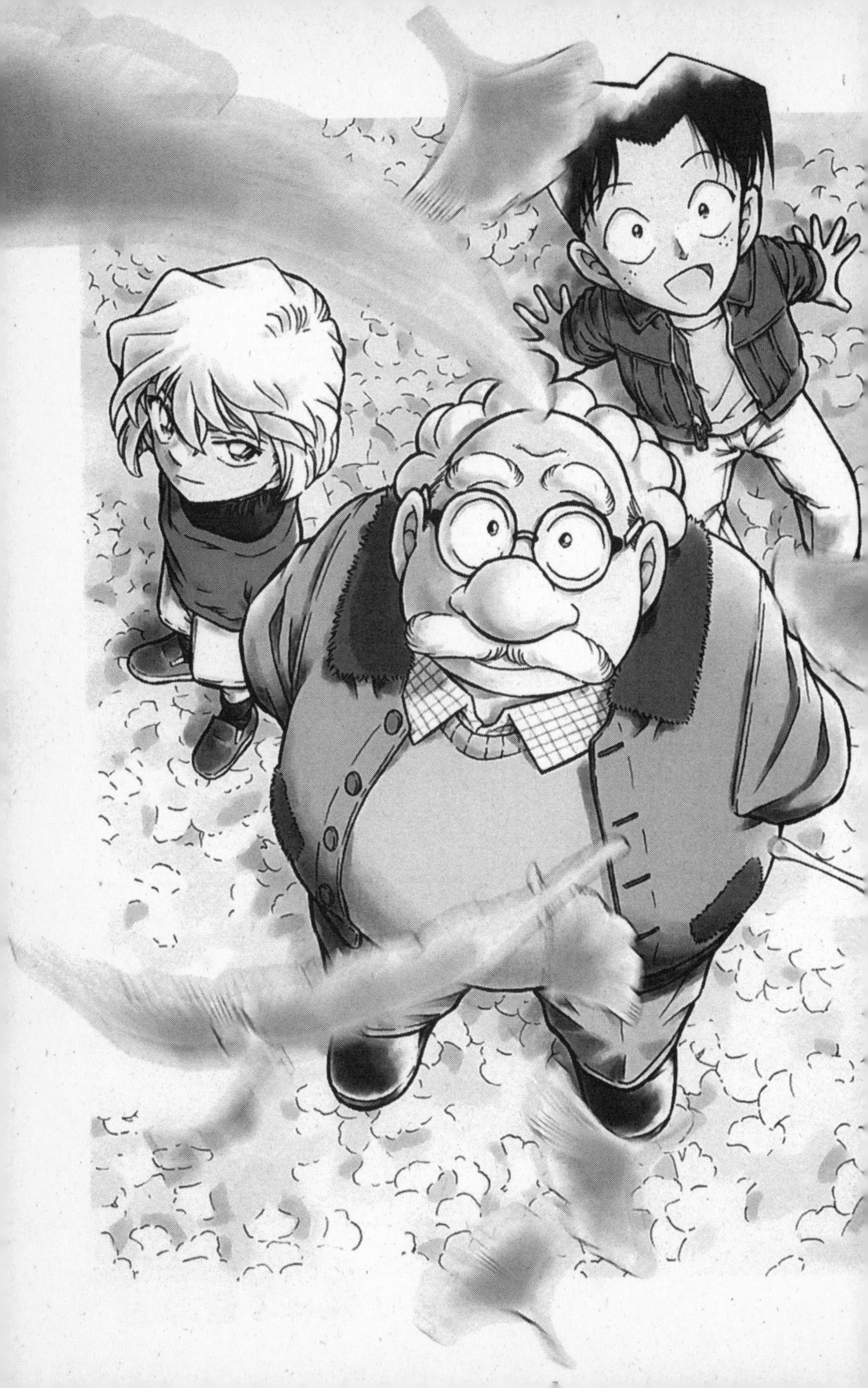

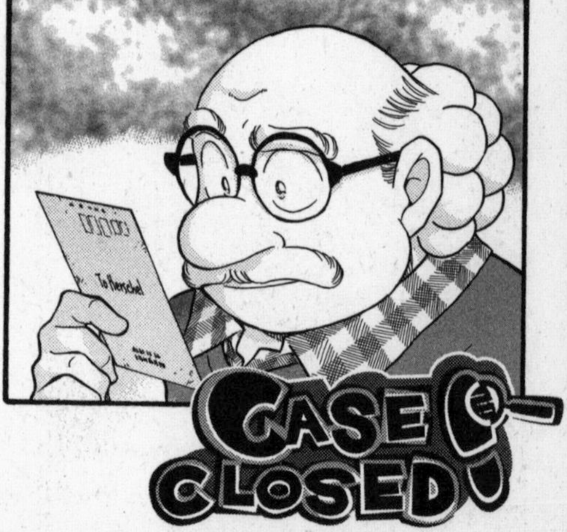
To Herschel
CASE CLOSED

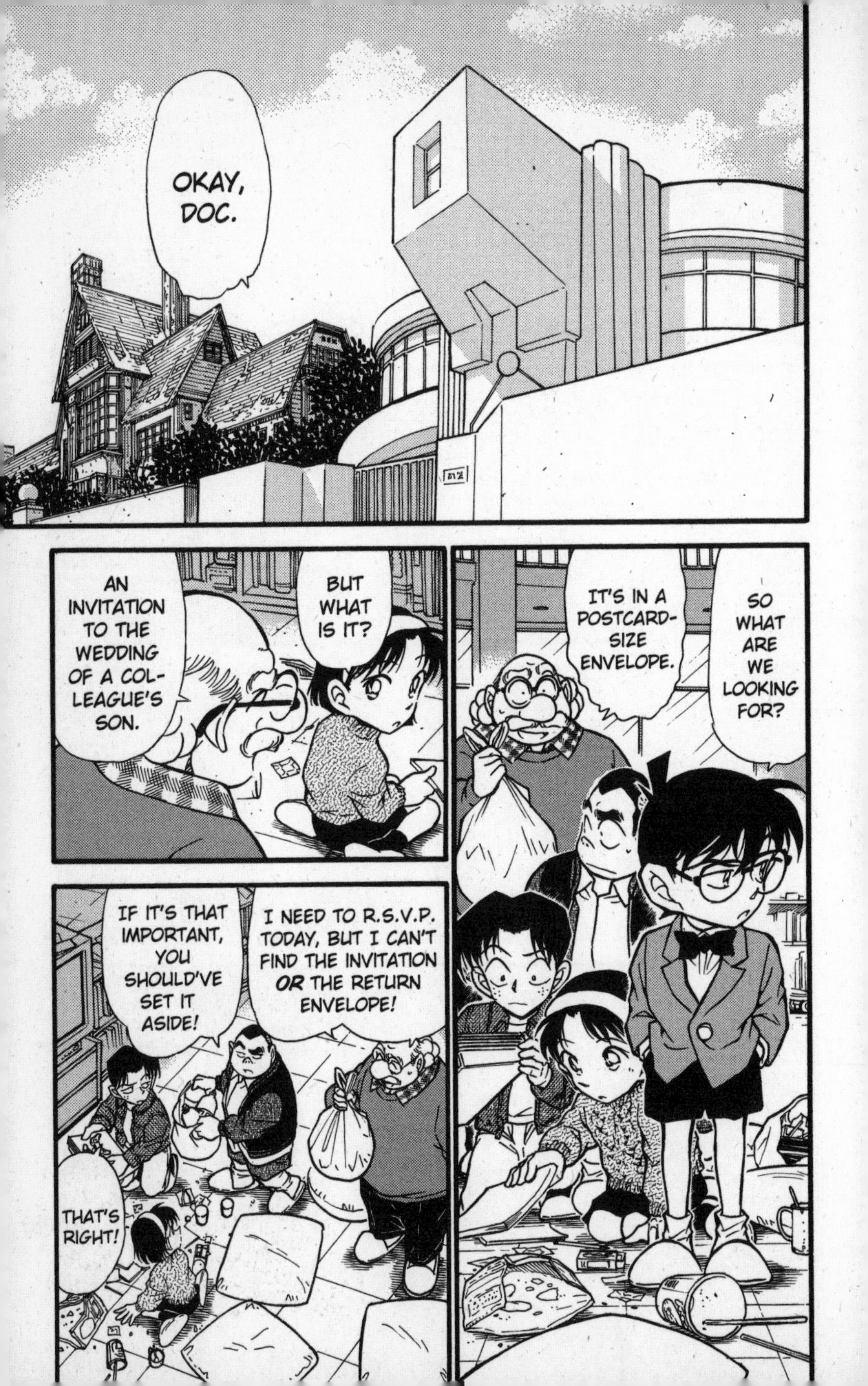
OKAY, DOC.
SO WHAT ARE WE LOOKING FOR?
IT'S IN A POSTCARD-SIZE ENVELOPE.
BUT WHAT IS IT?
AN INVITATION TO THE WEDDING OF A COL-LEAGUE'S SON.
I NEED TO R.S.V.P. TODAY, BUT I CAN'T FIND THE INVITATION *OR* THE RETURN ENVELOPE!
IF IT'S THAT IMPORTANT, YOU SHOULD'VE SET IT ASIDE!
THAT'S RIGHT!

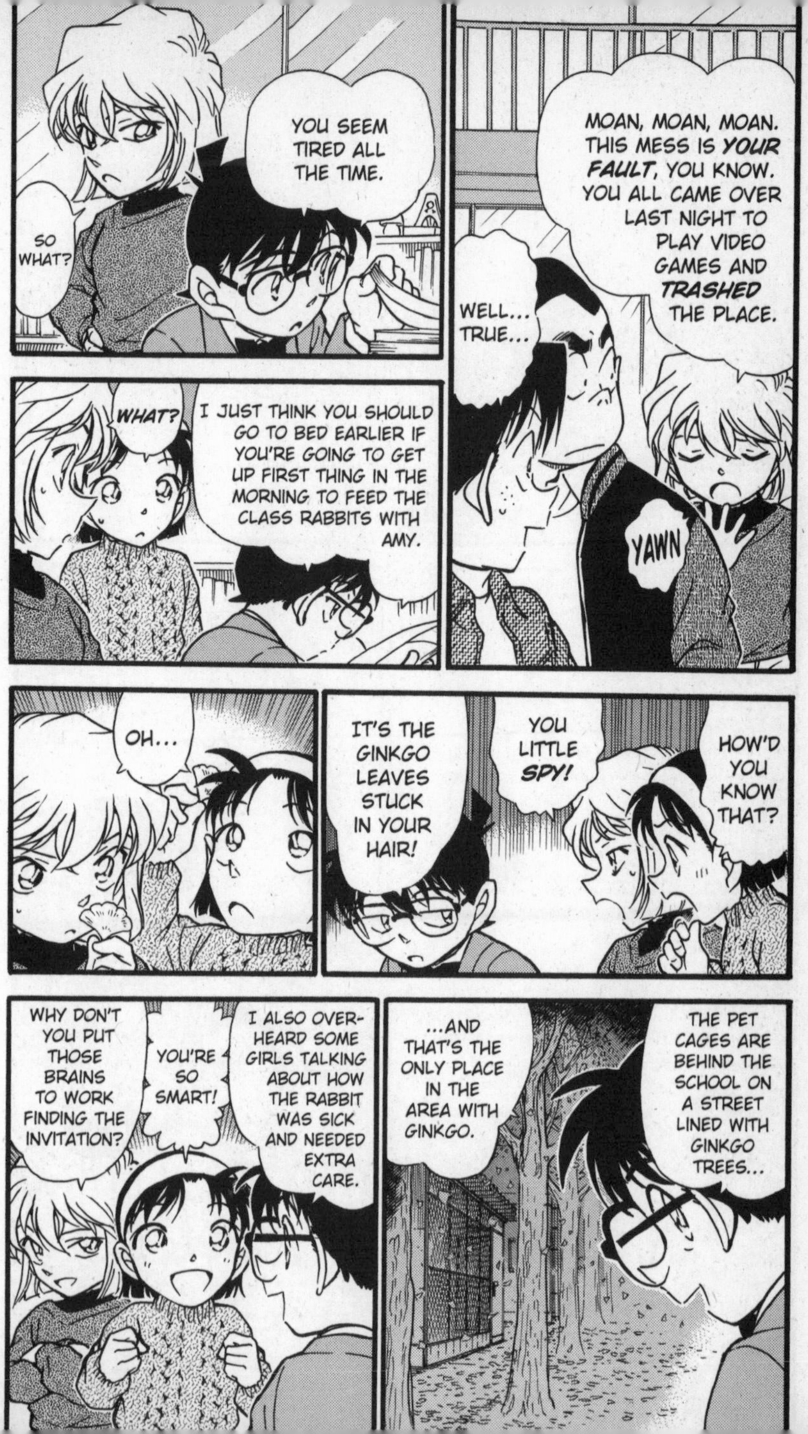
MOAN, MOAN, MOAN. THIS MESS IS ***YOUR FAULT***, YOU KNOW. YOU ALL CAME OVER LAST NIGHT TO PLAY VIDEO GAMES AND ***TRASHED*** THE PLACE.
WELL... TRUE...
YAWN
YOU SEEM TIRED ALL THE TIME.
SO WHAT?
I JUST THINK YOU SHOULD GO TO BED EARLIER IF YOU'RE GOING TO GET UP FIRST THING IN THE MORNING TO FEED THE CLASS RABBITS WITH AMY.
WHAT?
HOW'D YOU KNOW THAT?
YOU LITTLE ***SPY!***
IT'S THE GINKGO LEAVES STUCK IN YOUR HAIR!
OH...
THE PET CAGES ARE BEHIND THE SCHOOL ON A STREET LINED WITH GINKGO TREES...
...AND THAT'S THE ONLY PLACE IN THE AREA WITH GINKGO.
I ALSO OVER-HEARD SOME GIRLS TALKING ABOUT HOW THE RABBIT WAS SICK AND NEEDED EXTRA CARE.
YOU'RE SO SMART!
WHY DON'T YOU PUT THOSE BRAINS TO WORK FINDING THE INVITATION?

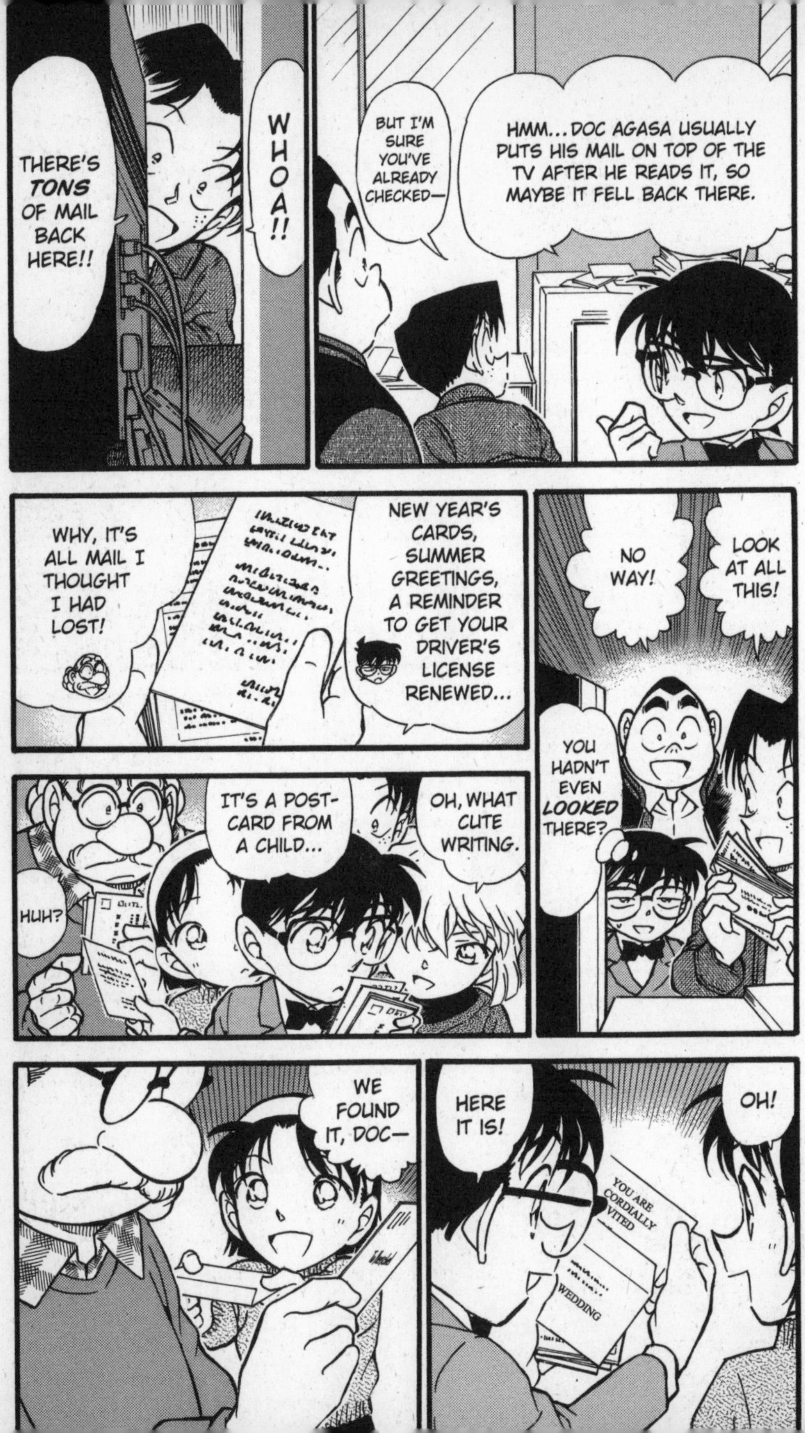
HMM... DOC AGASA USUALLY PUTS HIS MAIL ON TOP OF THE TV AFTER HE READS IT, SO MAYBE IT FELL BACK THERE.
BUT I'M SURE YOU'VE ALREADY CHECKED—
WHOA!!
THERE'S *TONS* OF MAIL BACK HERE!!
LOOK AT ALL THIS!
NO WAY!
YOU HADN'T EVEN *LOOKED* THERE?
NEW YEAR'S CARDS, SUMMER GREETINGS, A REMINDER TO GET YOUR DRIVER'S LICENSE RENEWED...
WHY, IT'S ALL MAIL I THOUGHT I HAD LOST!
OH, WHAT CUTE WRITING.
IT'S A POST-CARD FROM A CHILD...
HUH?
OH!
HERE IT IS!
YOU ARE CORDIALLY VITED
WEDDING
WE FOUND IT, DOC—

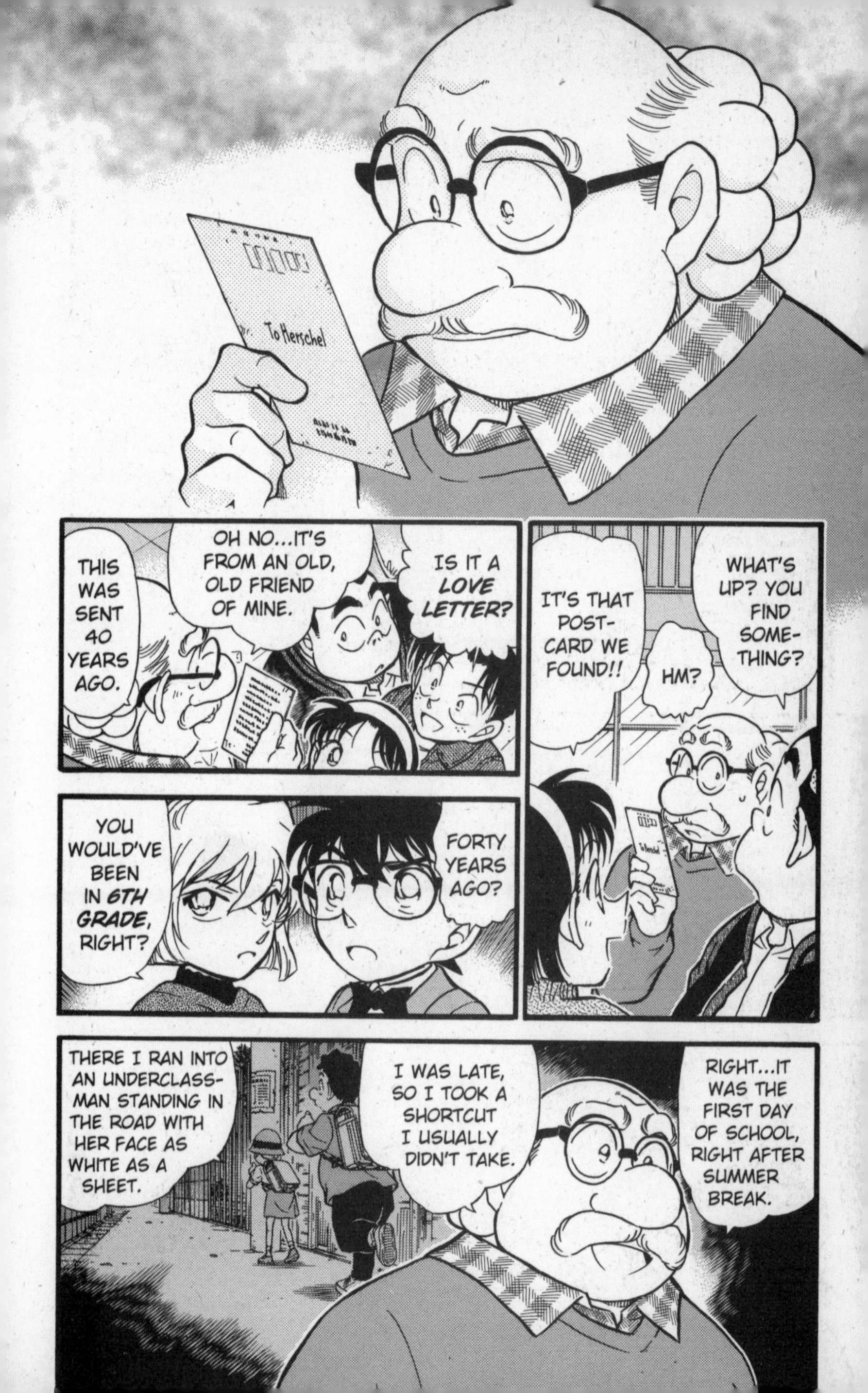
To Herschel
WHAT'S UP? YOU FIND SOME-THING?
HM?
IT'S THAT POST-CARD WE FOUND!!
IS IT A LOVE LETTER?
OH NO...IT'S FROM AN OLD, OLD FRIEND OF MINE.
THIS WAS SENT 40 YEARS AGO.
FORTY YEARS AGO?
YOU WOULD'VE BEEN IN 6TH GRADE, RIGHT?
RIGHT...IT WAS THE FIRST DAY OF SCHOOL, RIGHT AFTER SUMMER BREAK.
I WAS LATE, SO I TOOK A SHORTCUT I USUALLY DIDN'T TAKE.
THERE I RAN INTO AN UNDERCLASS-MAN STANDING IN THE ROAD WITH HER FACE AS WHITE AS A SHEET.

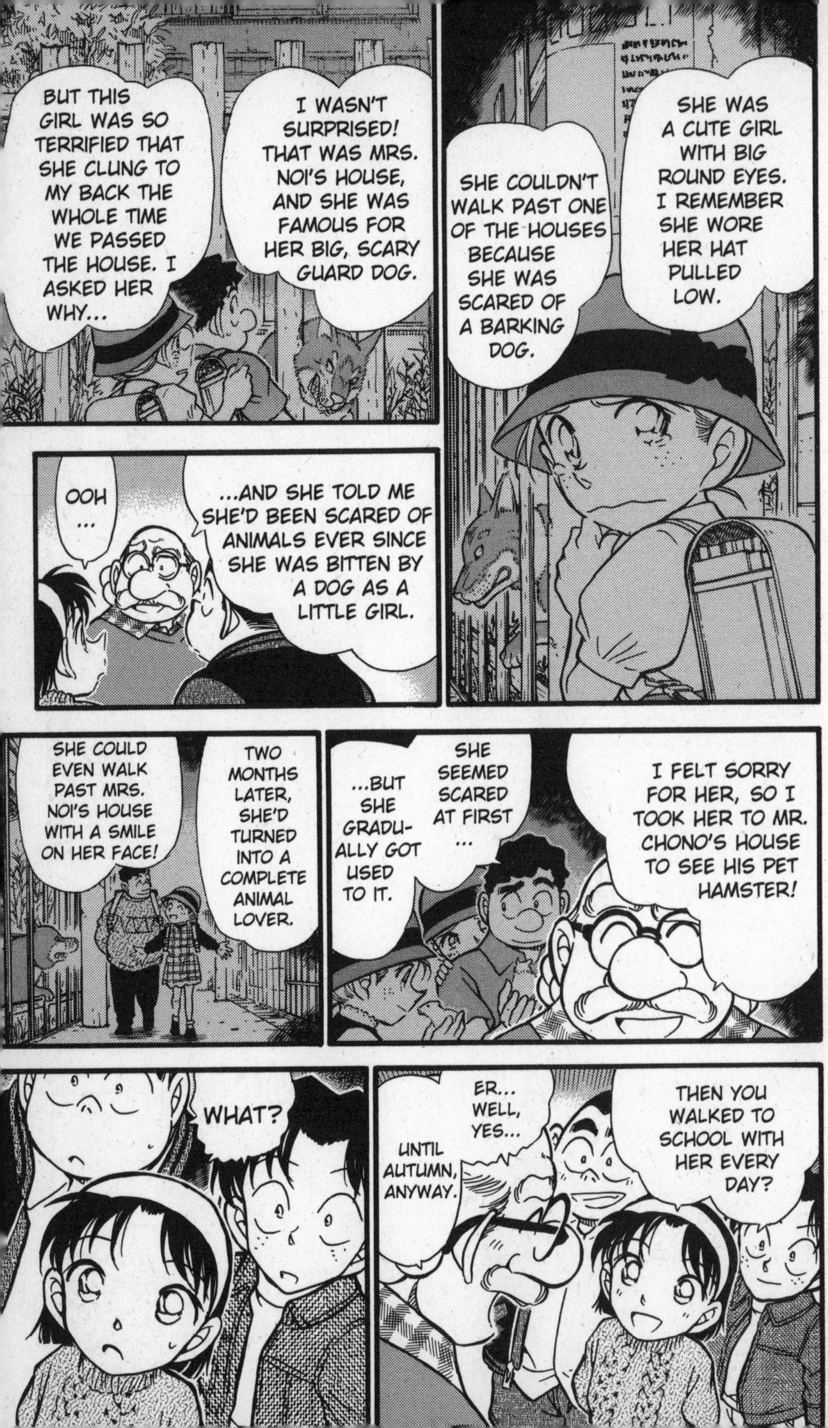
SHE WAS A CUTE GIRL WITH BIG ROUND EYES. I REMEMBER SHE WORE HER HAT PULLED LOW.
SHE COULDN'T WALK PAST ONE OF THE HOUSES BECAUSE SHE WAS SCARED OF A BARKING DOG.
I WASN'T SURPRISED! THAT WAS MRS. NOI'S HOUSE, AND SHE WAS FAMOUS FOR HER BIG, SCARY GUARD DOG.
BUT THIS GIRL WAS SO TERRIFIED THAT SHE CLUNG TO MY BACK THE WHOLE TIME WE PASSED THE HOUSE. I ASKED HER WHY...
...AND SHE TOLD ME SHE'D BEEN SCARED OF ANIMALS EVER SINCE SHE WAS BITTEN BY A DOG AS A LITTLE GIRL.
OOH ...
I FELT SORRY FOR HER, SO I TOOK HER TO MR. CHONO'S HOUSE TO SEE HIS PET HAMSTER!
SHE SEEMED SCARED AT FIRST ...
...BUT SHE GRADUALLY GOT USED TO IT.
TWO MONTHS LATER, SHE'D TURNED INTO A COMPLETE ANIMAL LOVER.
SHE COULD EVEN WALK PAST MRS. NOI'S HOUSE WITH A SMILE ON HER FACE!
THEN YOU WALKED TO SCHOOL WITH HER EVERY DAY?
ER... WELL, YES...
UNTIL AUTUMN, ANYWAY.
WHAT?

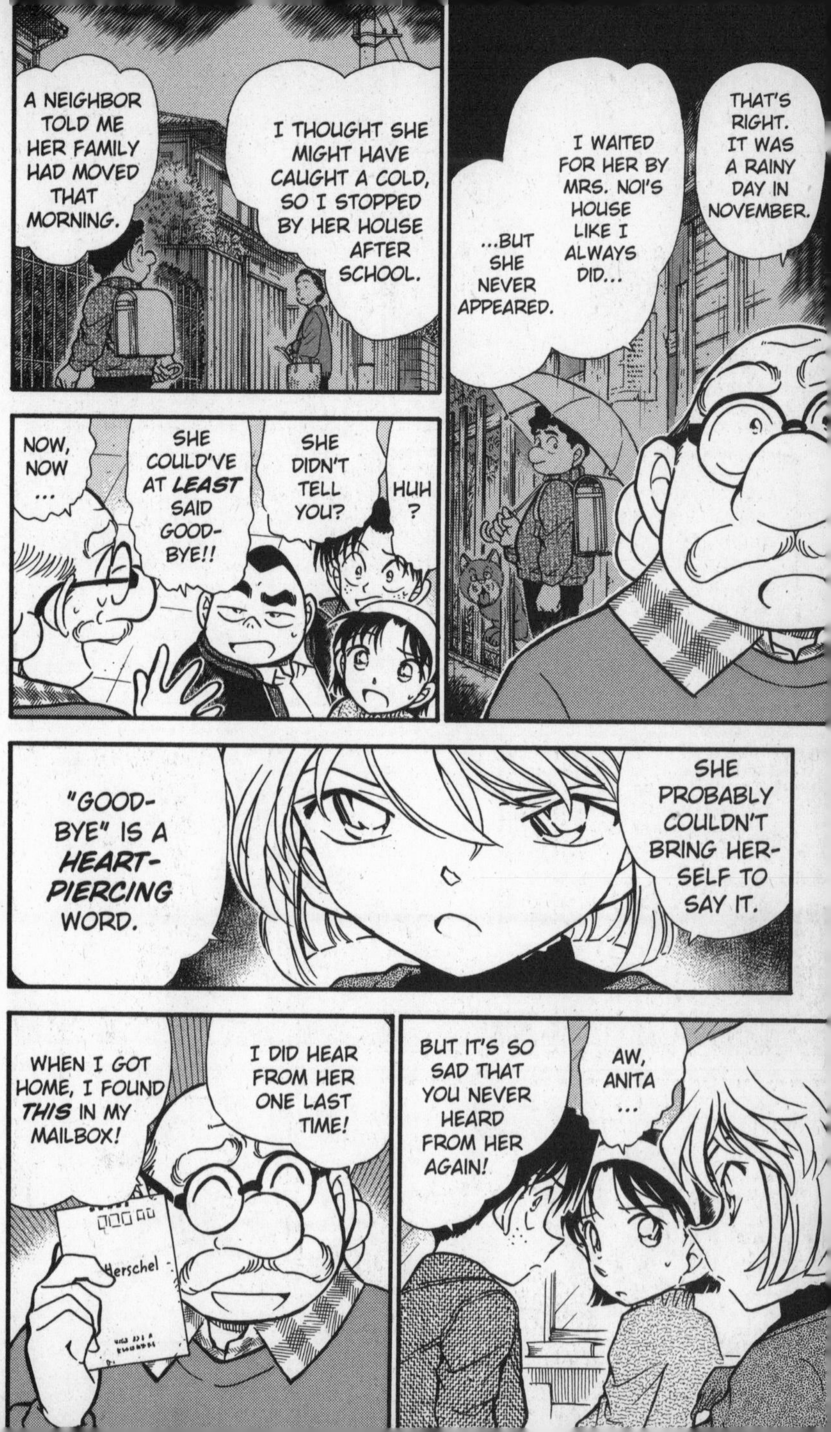
THAT'S RIGHT. IT WAS A RAINY DAY IN NOVEMBER.
I WAITED FOR HER BY MRS. NOI'S HOUSE LIKE I ALWAYS DID...
...BUT SHE NEVER APPEARED.
I THOUGHT SHE MIGHT HAVE CAUGHT A COLD, SO I STOPPED BY HER HOUSE AFTER SCHOOL.
A NEIGHBOR TOLD ME HER FAMILY HAD MOVED THAT MORNING.
HUH?
SHE DIDN'T TELL YOU?
SHE COULD'VE AT *LEAST* SAID GOOD-BYE!!
NOW, NOW ...
SHE PROBABLY COULDN'T BRING HERSELF TO SAY IT.
"GOOD-BYE" IS A *HEART-PIERCING* WORD.
AW, ANITA ...
BUT IT'S SO SAD THAT YOU NEVER HEARD FROM HER AGAIN!
I DID HEAR FROM HER ONE LAST TIME!
WHEN I GOT HOME, I FOUND *THIS* IN MY MAILBOX!
Herschel

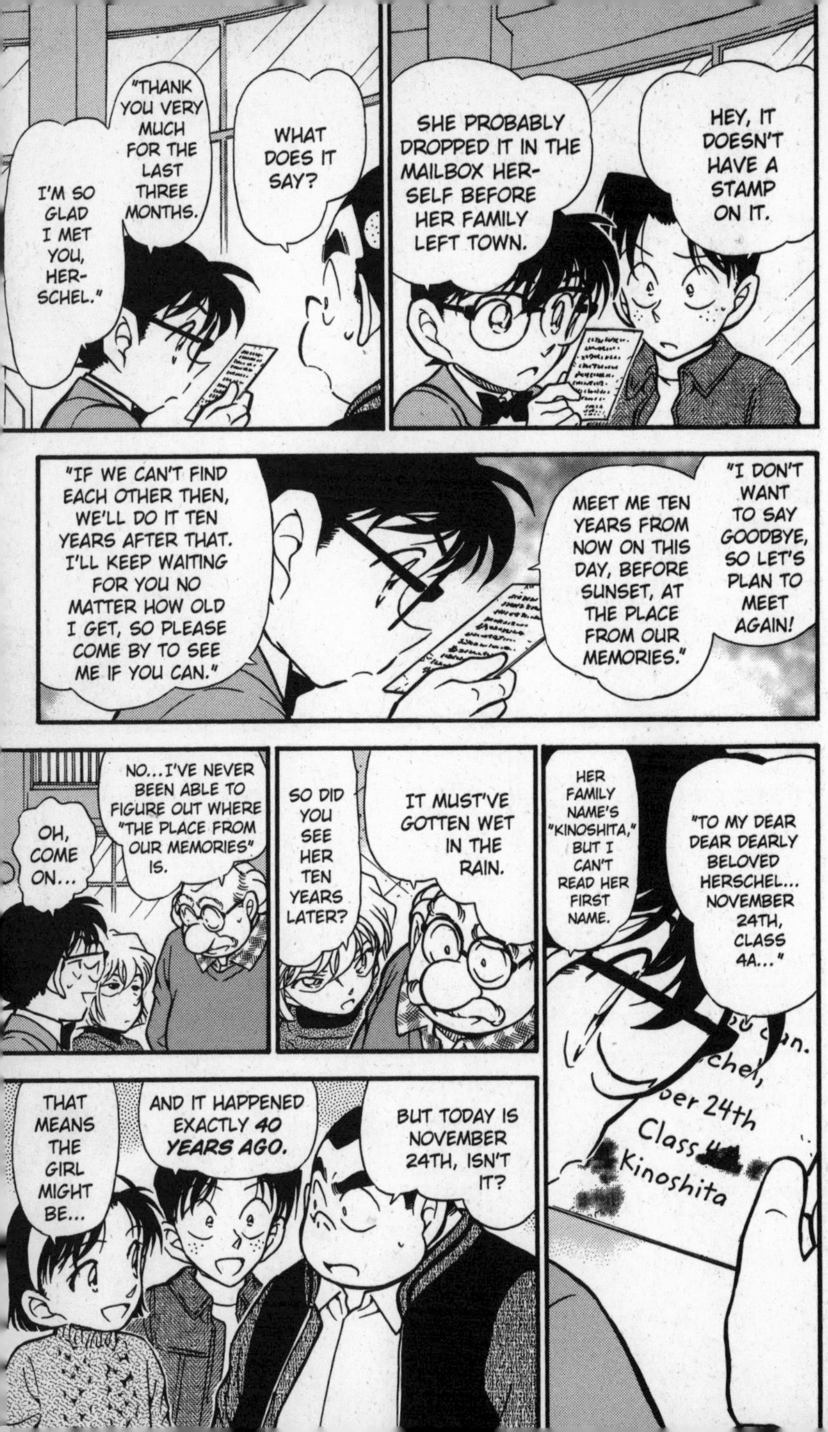
HEY, IT DOESN'T HAVE A STAMP ON IT.
SHE PROBABLY DROPPED IT IN THE MAILBOX HER-SELF BEFORE HER FAMILY LEFT TOWN.
WHAT DOES IT SAY?
"THANK YOU VERY MUCH FOR THE LAST THREE MONTHS.
I'M SO GLAD I MET YOU, HER-SCHEL."
"I DON'T WANT TO SAY GOODBYE, SO LET'S PLAN TO MEET AGAIN!
MEET ME TEN YEARS FROM NOW ON THIS DAY, BEFORE SUNSET, AT THE PLACE FROM OUR MEMORIES."
"IF WE CAN'T FIND EACH OTHER THEN, WE'LL DO IT TEN YEARS AFTER THAT. I'LL KEEP WAITING FOR YOU NO MATTER HOW OLD I GET, SO PLEASE COME BY TO SEE ME IF YOU CAN."
"TO MY DEAR DEAR DEARLY BELOVED HERSCHEL... NOVEMBER 24TH, CLASS 4A..."
HER FAMILY NAME'S "KINOSHITA," BUT I CAN'T READ HER FIRST NAME.
Kinoshita
IT MUST'VE GOTTEN WET IN THE RAIN.
SO DID YOU SEE HER TEN YEARS LATER?
NO...I'VE NEVER BEEN ABLE TO FIGURE OUT WHERE "THE PLACE FROM OUR MEMORIES" IS.
OH, COME ON...
BUT TODAY IS NOVEMBER 24TH, ISN'T IT?
AND IT HAPPENED EXACTLY ***40 YEARS AGO.***
THAT MEANS THE GIRL MIGHT BE...

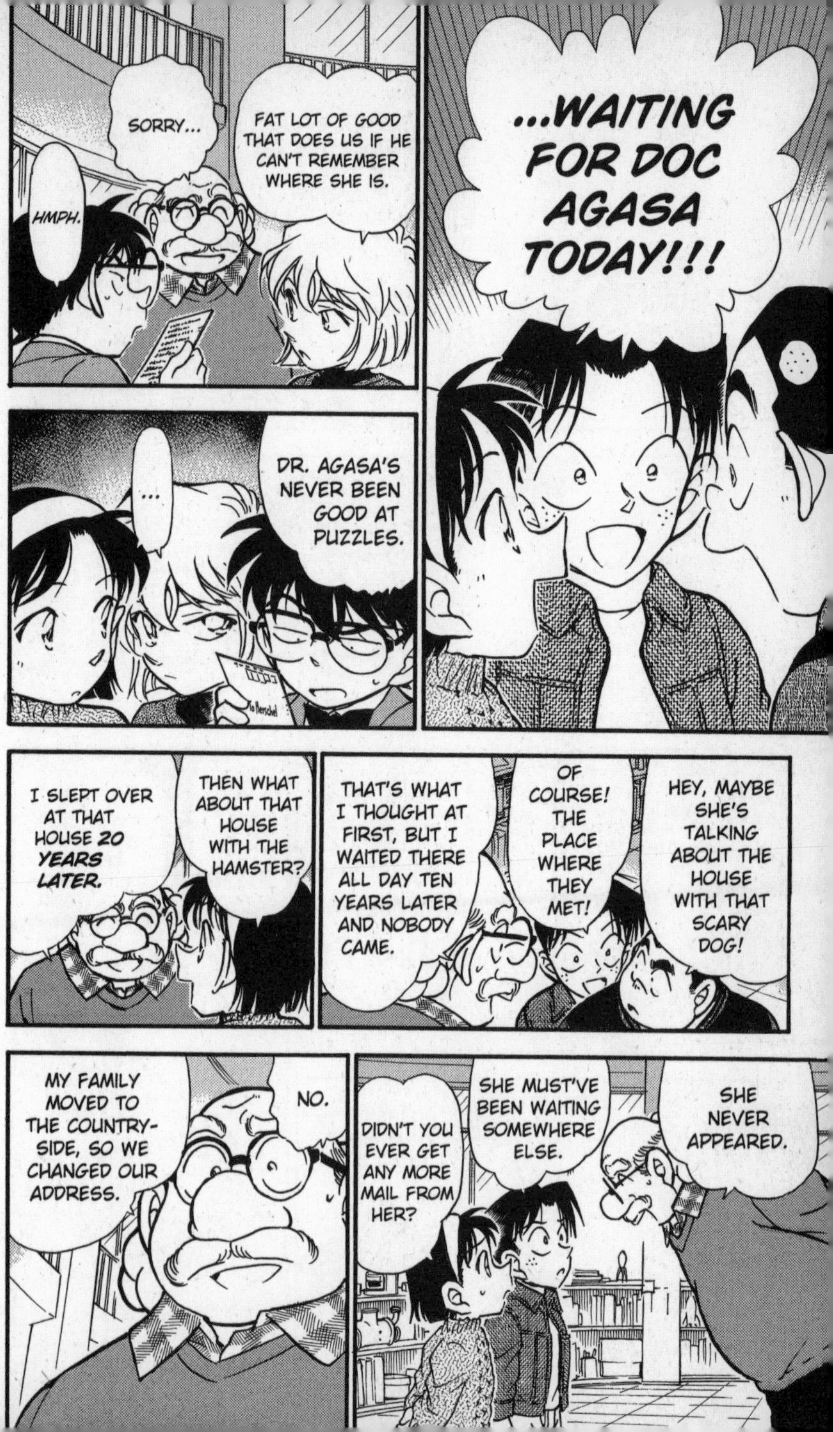
...WAITING FOR DOC AGASA TODAY!!!
FAT LOT OF GOOD THAT DOES US IF HE CAN'T REMEMBER WHERE SHE IS.
SORRY...
HMPH.
DR. AGASA'S NEVER BEEN GOOD AT PUZZLES.
...
HEY, MAYBE SHE'S TALKING ABOUT THE HOUSE WITH THAT SCARY DOG!
OF COURSE! THE PLACE WHERE THEY MET!
THAT'S WHAT I THOUGHT AT FIRST, BUT I WAITED THERE ALL DAY TEN YEARS LATER AND NOBODY CAME.
THEN WHAT ABOUT THAT HOUSE WITH THE HAMSTER?
I SLEPT OVER AT THAT HOUSE 20 YEARS LATER.
SHE NEVER APPEARED.
SHE MUST'VE BEEN WAITING SOMEWHERE ELSE.
DIDN'T YOU EVER GET ANY MORE MAIL FROM HER?
NO.
MY FAMILY MOVED TO THE COUNTRYSIDE, SO WE CHANGED OUR ADDRESS.

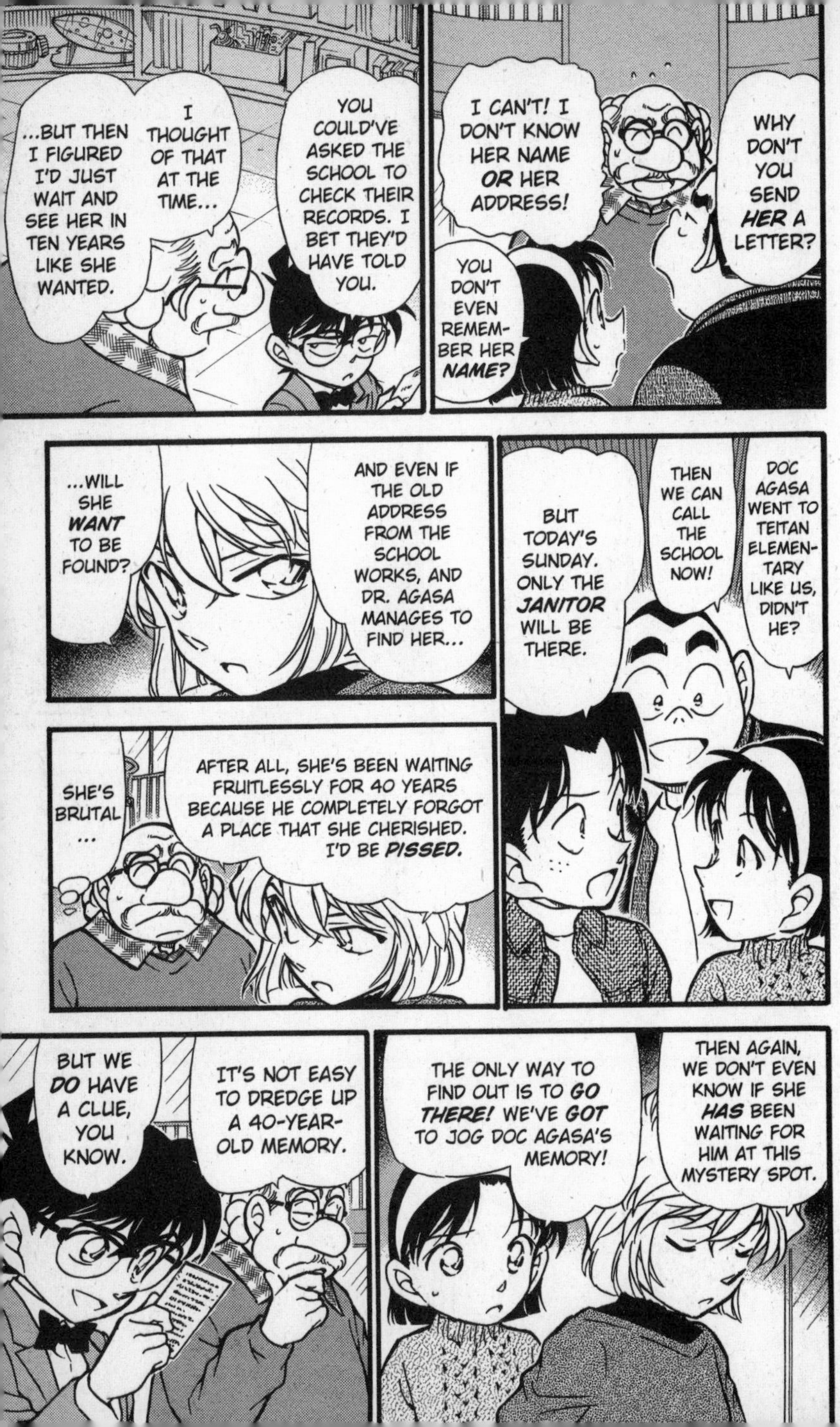
WHY DON'T YOU SEND **HER** A LETTER?
I CAN'T! I DON'T KNOW HER NAME **OR** HER ADDRESS!
YOU DON'T EVEN REMEMBER HER **NAME?**
YOU COULD'VE ASKED THE SCHOOL TO CHECK THEIR RECORDS. I BET THEY'D HAVE TOLD YOU.
I THOUGHT OF THAT AT THE TIME...
...BUT THEN I FIGURED I'D JUST WAIT AND SEE HER IN TEN YEARS LIKE SHE WANTED.
DOC AGASA WENT TO TEITAN ELEMENTARY LIKE US, DIDN'T HE?
THEN WE CAN CALL THE SCHOOL NOW!
BUT TODAY'S SUNDAY. ONLY THE **JANITOR** WILL BE THERE.
AND EVEN IF THE OLD ADDRESS FROM THE SCHOOL WORKS, AND DR. AGASA MANAGES TO FIND HER...
...WILL SHE **WANT** TO BE FOUND?
AFTER ALL, SHE'S BEEN WAITING FRUITLESSLY FOR 40 YEARS BECAUSE HE COMPLETELY FORGOT A PLACE THAT SHE CHERISHED. I'D BE **PISSED.**
SHE'S BRUTAL...
THEN AGAIN, WE DON'T EVEN KNOW IF SHE **HAS** BEEN WAITING FOR HIM AT THIS MYSTERY SPOT.
THE ONLY WAY TO FIND OUT IS TO **GO THERE!** WE'VE **GOT** TO JOG DOC AGASA'S MEMORY!
IT'S NOT EASY TO DREDGE UP A 40-YEAR-OLD MEMORY.
BUT WE **DO** HAVE A CLUE, YOU KNOW.

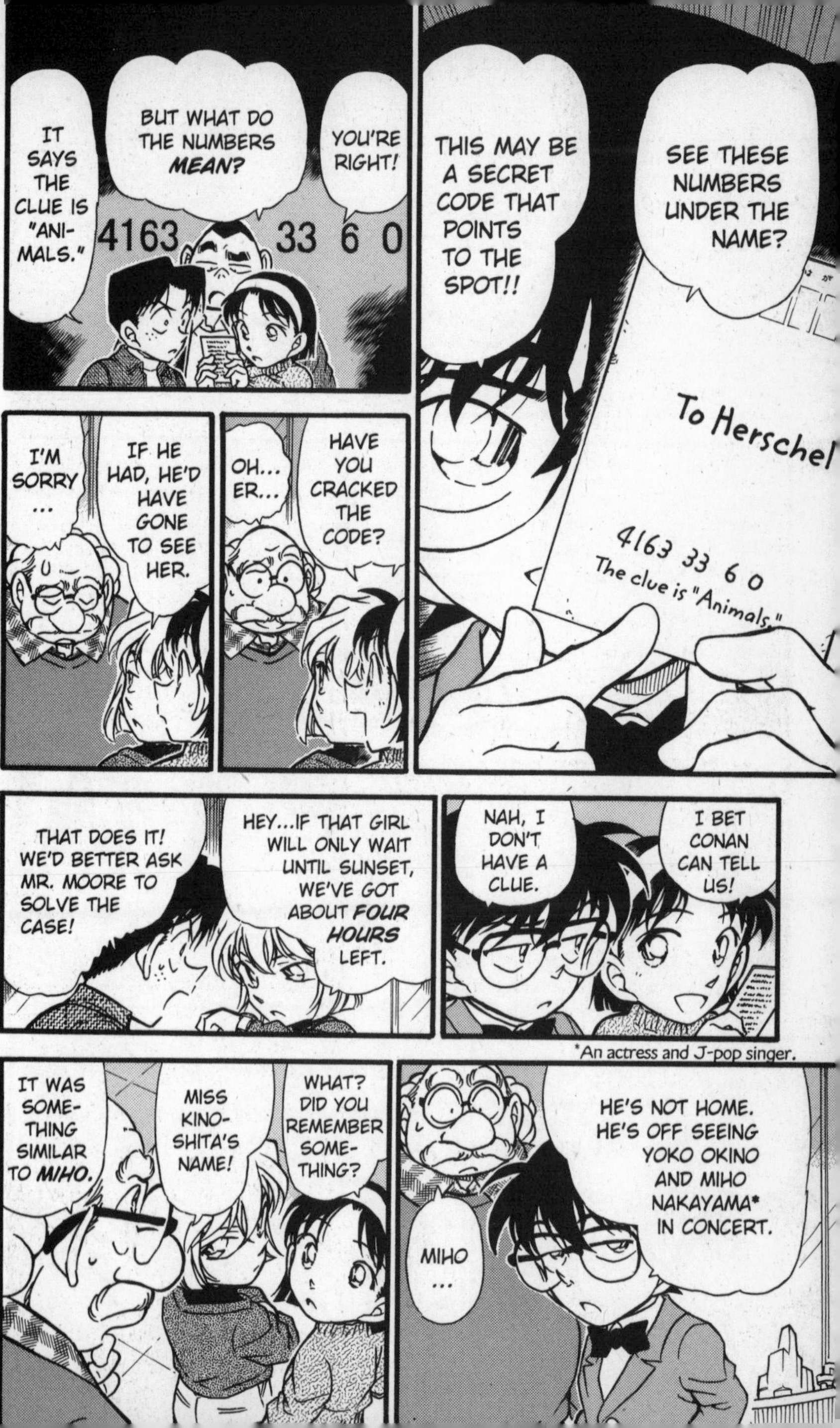
SEE THESE NUMBERS UNDER THE NAME?
THIS MAY BE A SECRET CODE THAT POINTS TO THE SPOT!!
To Herschel
4163 33 6 0
The clue is "Animals."
YOU'RE RIGHT!
BUT WHAT DO THE NUMBERS MEAN?
IT SAYS THE CLUE IS "ANIMALS."
4163 33 6 0
HAVE YOU CRACKED THE CODE?
OH... ER...
IF HE HAD, HE'D HAVE GONE TO SEE HER.
I'M SORRY...
I BET CONAN CAN TELL US!
NAH, I DON'T HAVE A CLUE.
HEY...IF THAT GIRL WILL ONLY WAIT UNTIL SUNSET, WE'VE GOT ABOUT FOUR HOURS LEFT.
THAT DOES IT! WE'D BETTER ASK MR. MOORE TO SOLVE THE CASE!
HE'S NOT HOME. HE'S OFF SEEING YOKO OKINO AND MIHO NAKAYAMA* IN CONCERT.
MIHO...
WHAT? DID YOU REMEMBER SOMETHING?
MISS KINOSHITA'S NAME!
IT WAS SOMETHING SIMILAR TO MIHO.

*An actress and J-pop singer.

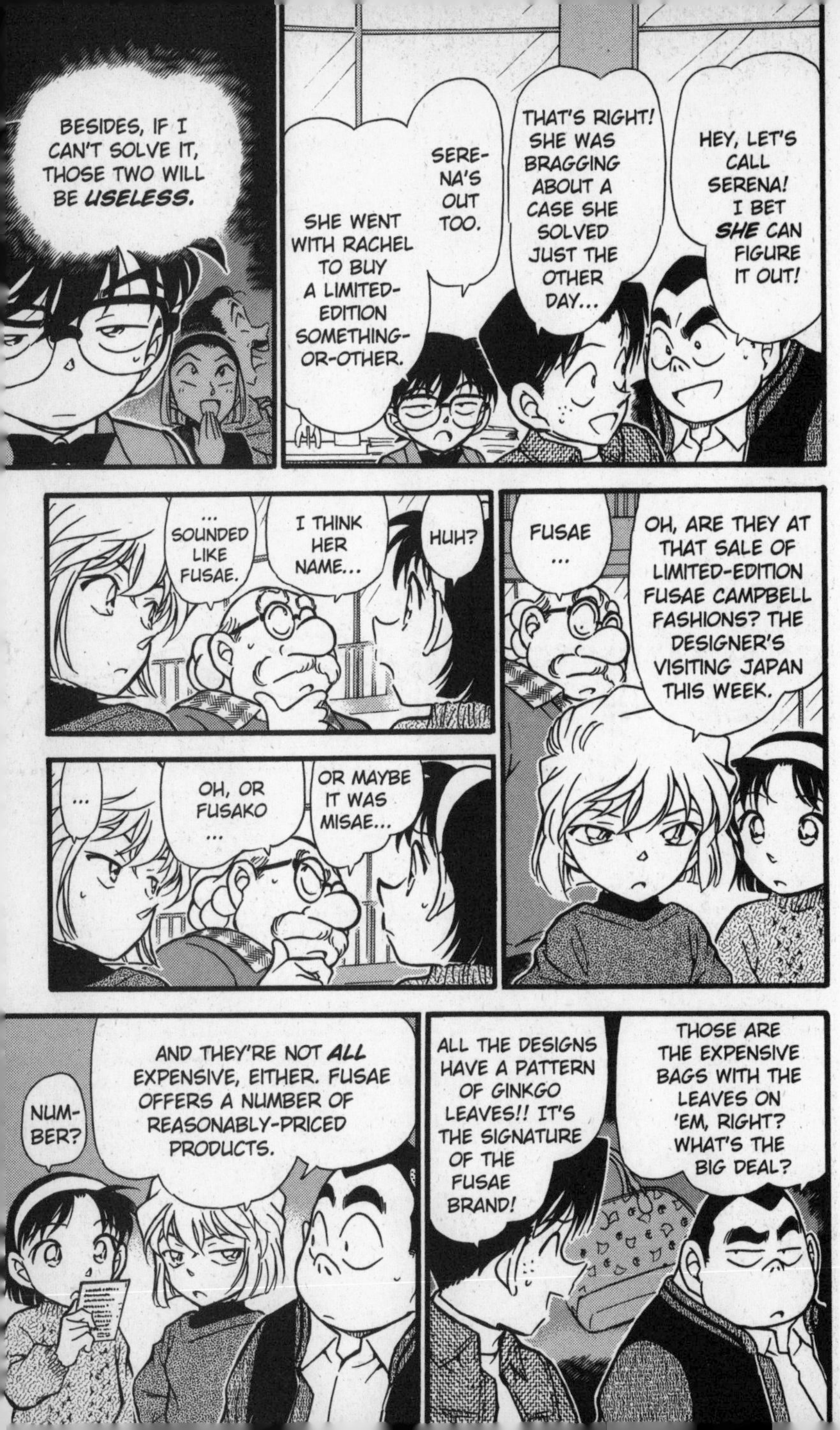
HEY, LET'S CALL SERENA! I BET SHE CAN FIGURE IT OUT!
THAT'S RIGHT! SHE WAS BRAGGING ABOUT A CASE SHE SOLVED JUST THE OTHER DAY...
SERE-NA'S OUT TOO.
SHE WENT WITH RACHEL TO BUY A LIMITED-EDITION SOMETHING-OR-OTHER.
BESIDES, IF I CAN'T SOLVE IT, THOSE TWO WILL BE USELESS.
OH, ARE THEY AT THAT SALE OF LIMITED-EDITION FUSAE CAMPBELL FASHIONS? THE DESIGNER'S VISITING JAPAN THIS WEEK.
FUSAE ...
HUH?
I THINK HER NAME...
... SOUNDED LIKE FUSAE.
OR MAYBE IT WAS MISAE...
OH, OR FUSAKO ...
...
THOSE ARE THE EXPENSIVE BAGS WITH THE LEAVES ON 'EM, RIGHT? WHAT'S THE BIG DEAL?
ALL THE DESIGNS HAVE A PATTERN OF GINKGO LEAVES!! IT'S THE SIGNATURE OF THE FUSAE BRAND!
AND THEY'RE NOT ALL EXPENSIVE, EITHER. FUSAE OFFERS A NUMBER OF REASONABLY-PRICED PRODUCTS.
NUM-BER?

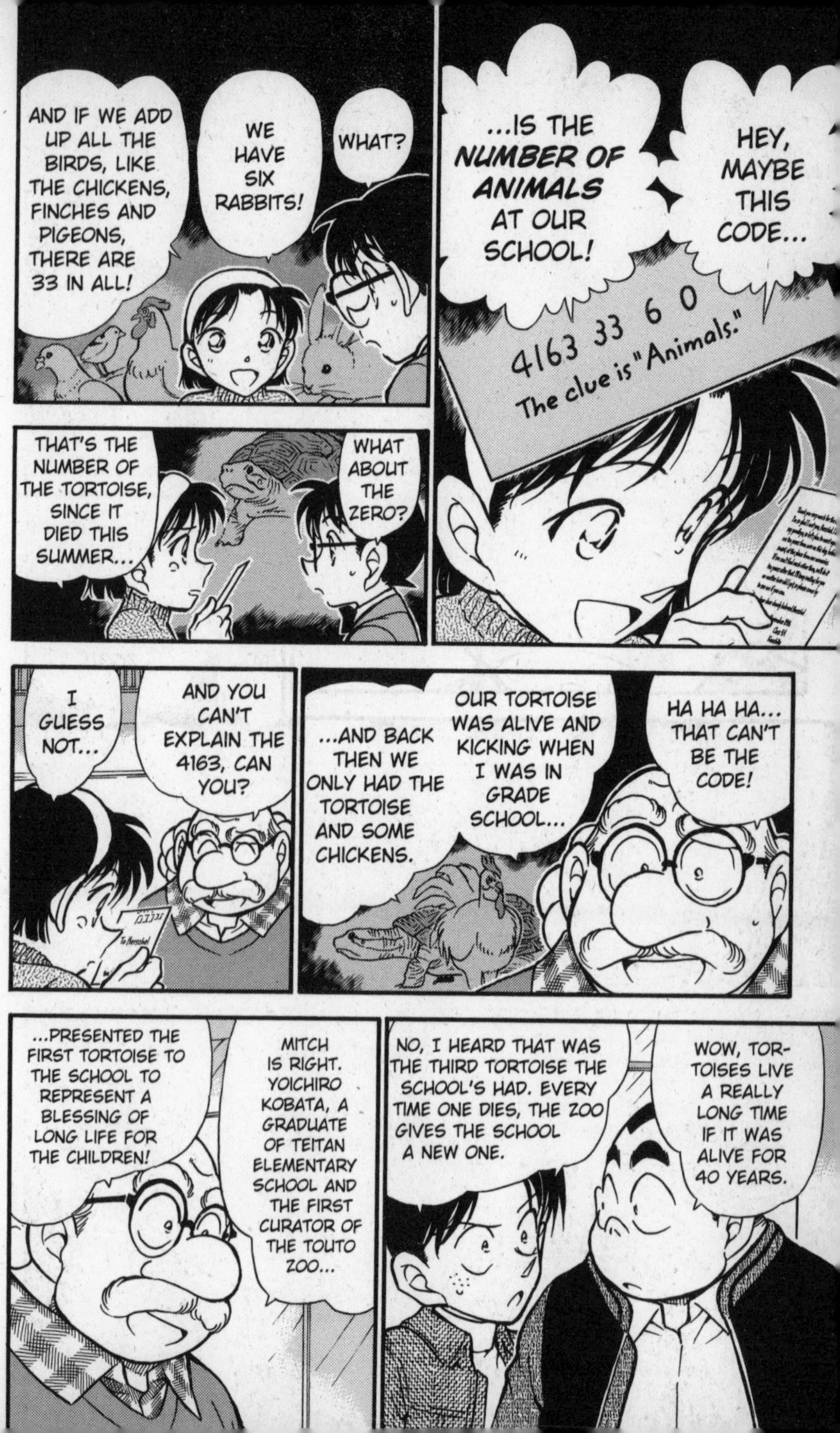
HEY, MAYBE THIS CODE...
...IS THE *NUMBER OF ANIMALS* AT OUR SCHOOL!
4163 33 6 0
The clue is "Animals."
WHAT?
WE HAVE SIX RABBITS!
AND IF WE ADD UP ALL THE BIRDS, LIKE THE CHICKENS, FINCHES AND PIGEONS, THERE ARE 33 IN ALL!
WHAT ABOUT THE ZERO?
THAT'S THE NUMBER OF THE TORTOISE, SINCE IT DIED THIS SUMMER...
HA HA HA... THAT CAN'T BE THE CODE!
OUR TORTOISE WAS ALIVE AND KICKING WHEN I WAS IN GRADE SCHOOL...
...AND BACK THEN WE ONLY HAD THE TORTOISE AND SOME CHICKENS.
AND YOU CAN'T EXPLAIN THE 4163, CAN YOU?
I GUESS NOT...
To Herschel
WOW, TOR- TOISES LIVE A REALLY LONG TIME IF IT WAS ALIVE FOR 40 YEARS.
NO, I HEARD THAT WAS THE THIRD TORTOISE THE SCHOOL'S HAD. EVERY TIME ONE DIES, THE ZOO GIVES THE SCHOOL A NEW ONE.
MITCH IS RIGHT. YOICHIRO KOBATA, A GRADUATE OF TEITAN ELEMENTARY SCHOOL AND THE FIRST CURATOR OF THE TOUTO ZOO...
...PRESENTED THE FIRST TORTOISE TO THE SCHOOL TO REPRESENT A BLESSING OF LONG LIFE FOR THE CHILDREN!

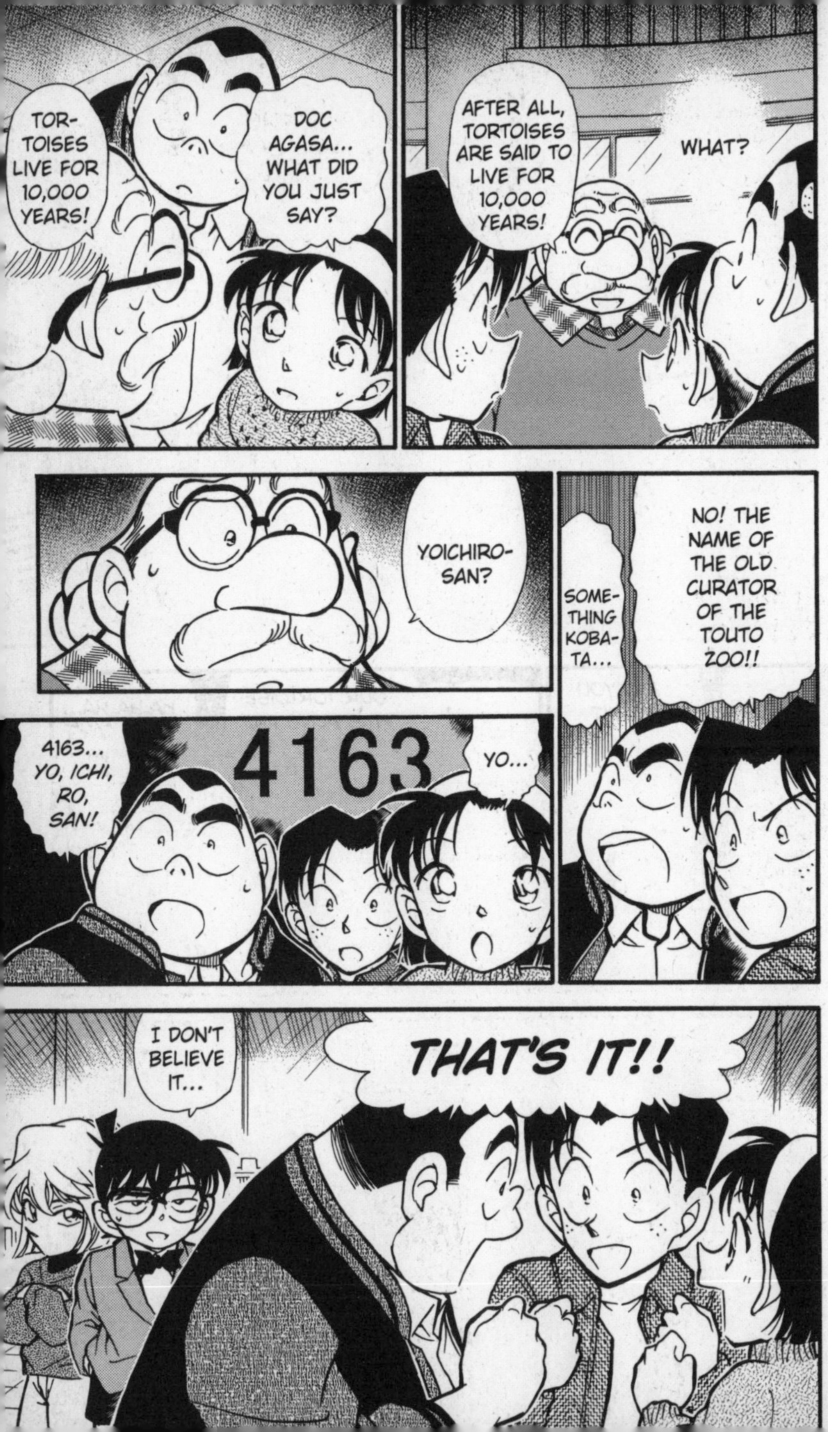
WHAT?
AFTER ALL, TORTOISES ARE SAID TO LIVE FOR 10,000 YEARS!
DOC AGASA... WHAT DID YOU JUST SAY?
TOR-TOISES LIVE FOR 10,000 YEARS!
NO! THE NAME OF THE OLD CURATOR OF THE TOUTO ZOO!!
SOME-THING KOBA-TA...
YOICHIRO-SAN?
4163
YO...
4163... YO, ICHI, RO, SAN!
THAT'S IT!!
I DON'T BELIEVE IT...

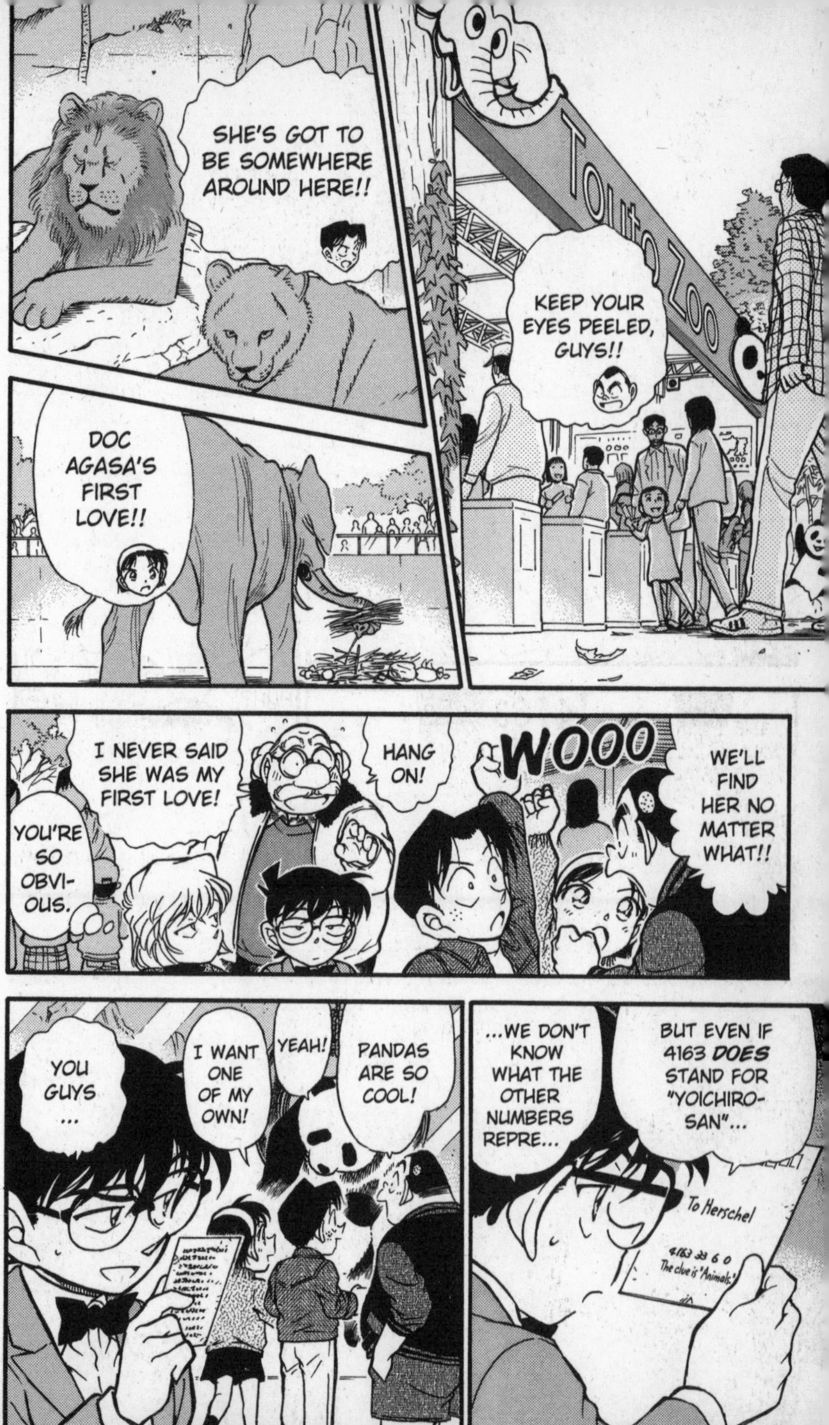
Touto Zoo
KEEP YOUR EYES PEELED, GUYS!!
SHE'S GOT TO BE SOMEWHERE AROUND HERE!!
DOC AGASA'S FIRST LOVE!!
WOOO
WE'LL FIND HER NO MATTER WHAT!!
HANG ON!
I NEVER SAID SHE WAS MY FIRST LOVE!
YOU'RE SO OBVIOUS.
BUT EVEN IF 4163 DOES STAND FOR "YOICHIRO-SAN"...
...WE DON'T KNOW WHAT THE OTHER NUMBERS REPRE...
To Herschel
4163 33 6 0
The clue is "Animals"
PANDAS ARE SO COOL!
YEAH!
I WANT ONE OF MY OWN!
YOU GUYS...

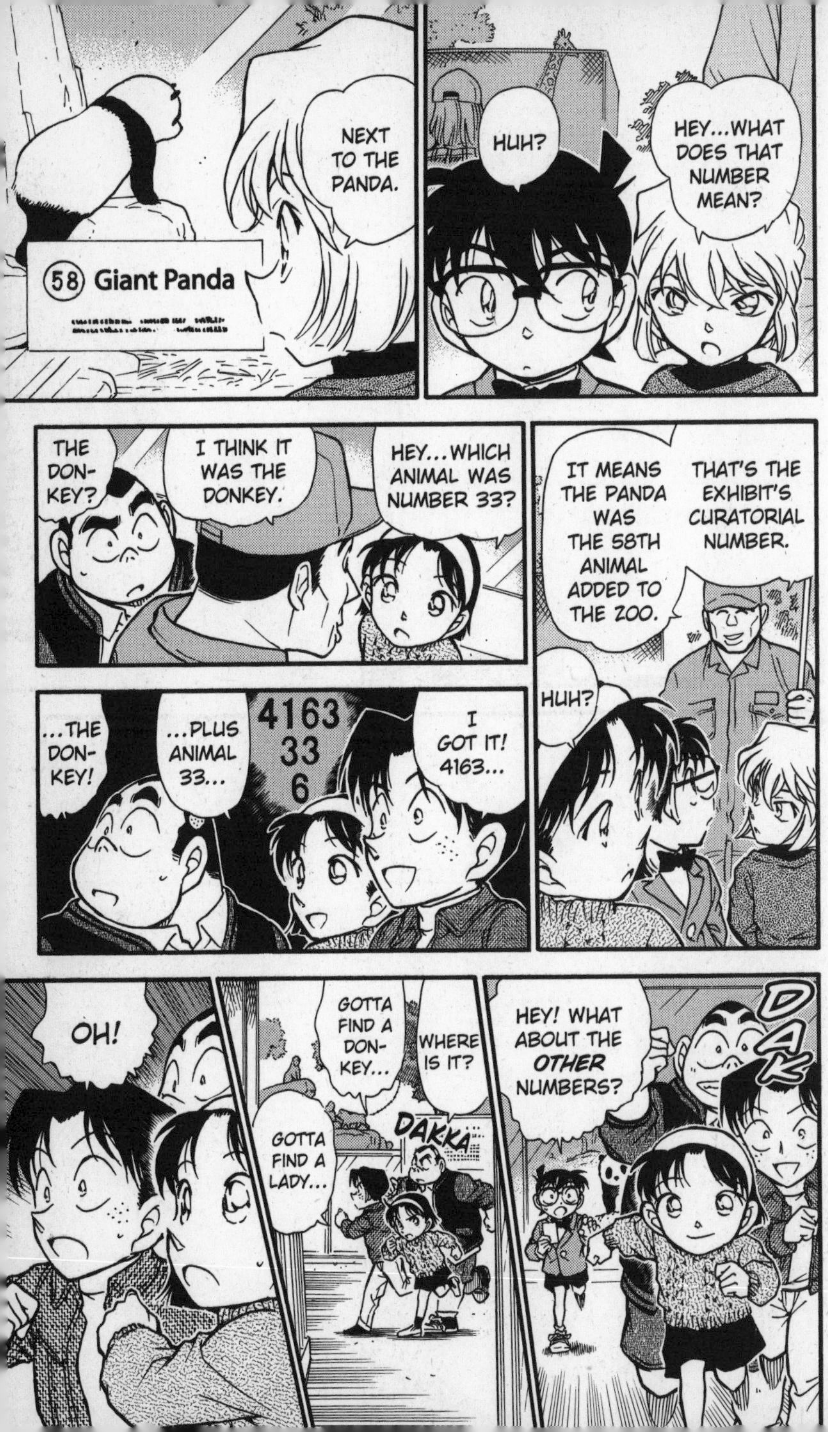
HEY...WHAT DOES THAT NUMBER MEAN?
HUH?
NEXT TO THE PANDA.
58 Giant Panda
THAT'S THE EXHIBIT'S CURATORIAL NUMBER.
IT MEANS THE PANDA WAS THE 58TH ANIMAL ADDED TO THE ZOO.
HUH?
HEY...WHICH ANIMAL WAS NUMBER 33?
I THINK IT WAS THE DONKEY.
THE DON-KEY?
I GOT IT! 4163...
4163 33 6
...PLUS ANIMAL 33...
...THE DON-KEY!
DAK
HEY! WHAT ABOUT THE *OTHER* NUMBERS?
WHERE IS IT?
GOTTA FIND A DON-KEY...
DAKKA
GOTTA FIND A LADY...
OH!

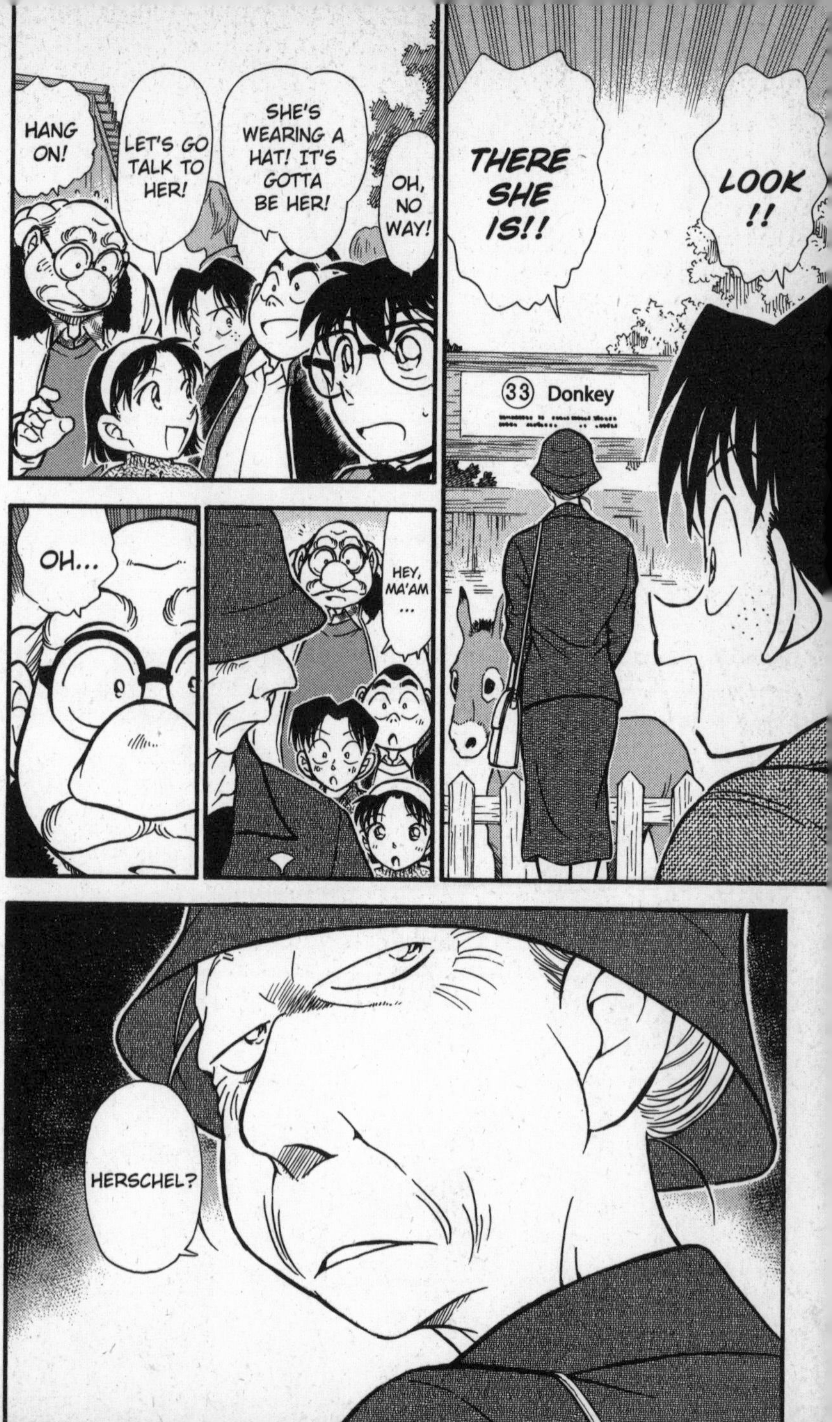
LOOK!!
THERE SHE IS!!
33 Donkey
OH, NO WAY!
SHE'S WEARING A HAT! IT'S GOTTA BE HER!
LET'S GO TALK TO HER!
HANG ON!
HEY, MA'AM...
OH...
HERSCHEL?

FILE 8: THAT MEMORABLE PLACE

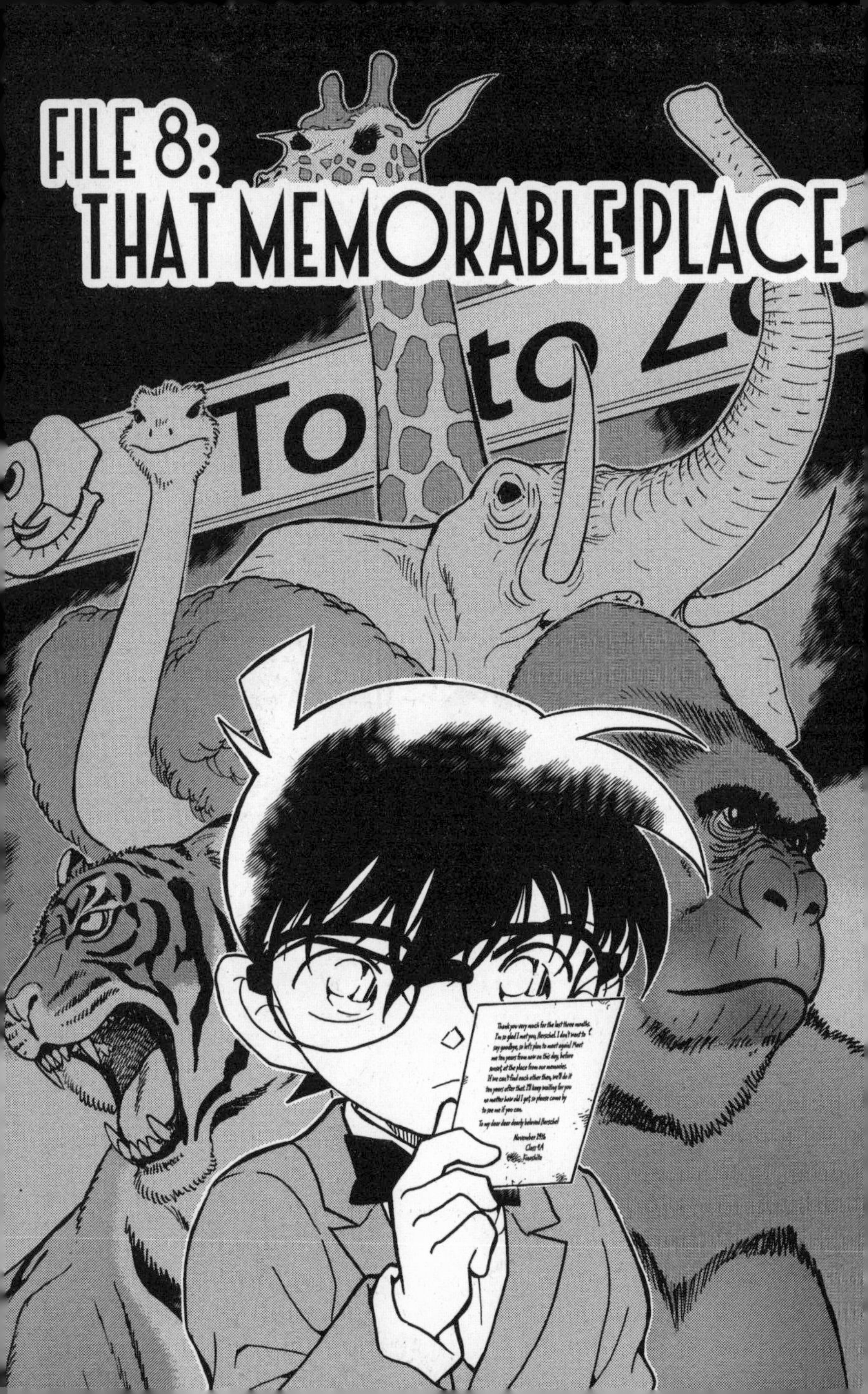
Thank you very much for the last three months.
I'm so glad I met you, Herschel. I don't want to
say goodbye, so let's plan to meet again! Meet
me ten years from now on this day, before
sunset, at the place from our memories.
If we can't find each other then, we'll do it
ten years after that. I'll keep waiting for you
no matter how old I get, so please come by
to see me if you can.
To my dear dear dearly beloved Herschel
November 29th
Class 4A

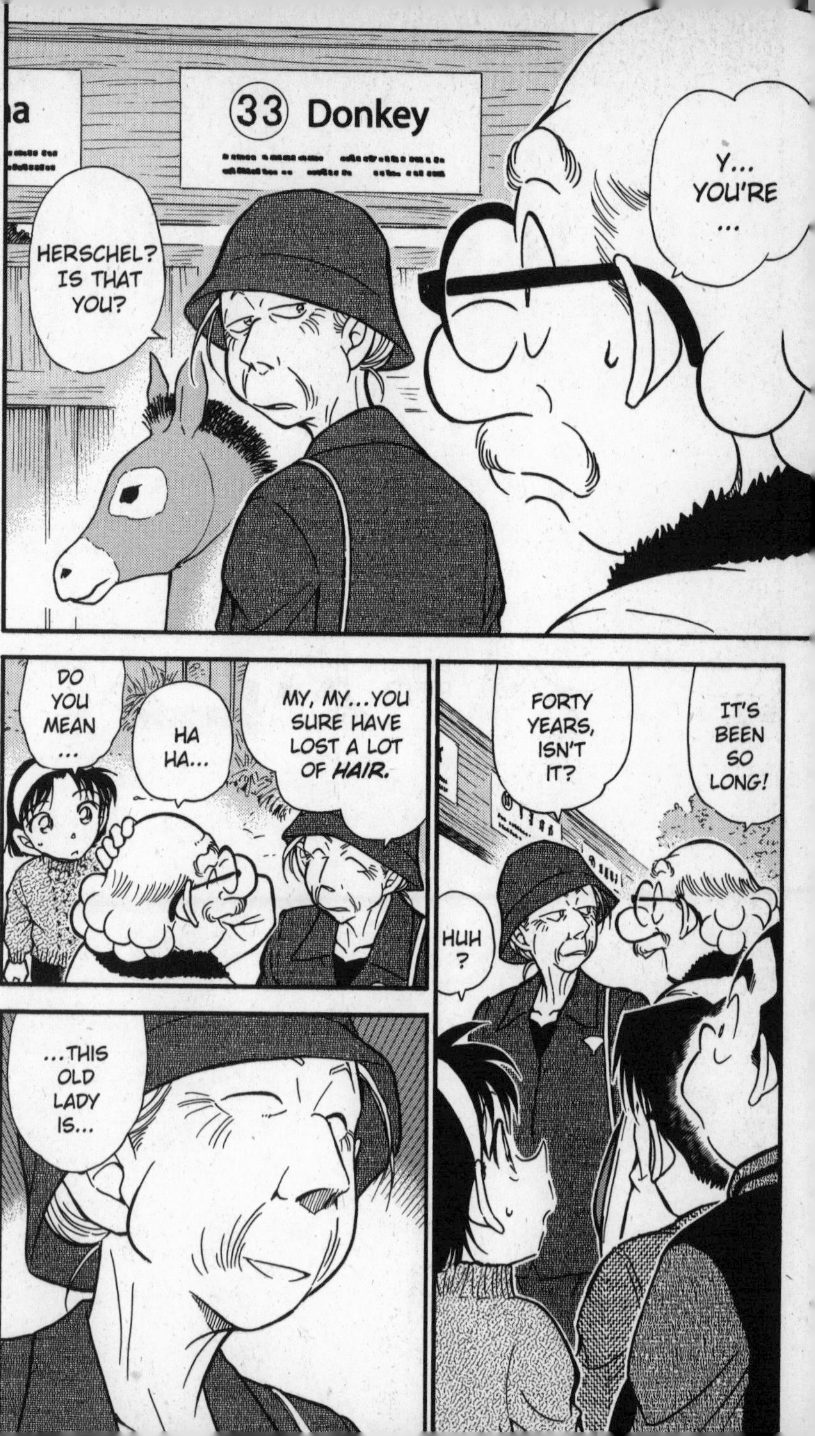
33 Donkey
Y... YOU'RE ...
HERSCHEL? IS THAT YOU?
IT'S BEEN SO LONG!
FORTY YEARS, ISN'T IT?
HUH?
MY, MY...YOU SURE HAVE LOST A LOT OF *HAIR.*
HA HA...
DO YOU MEAN ...
...THIS OLD LADY IS...

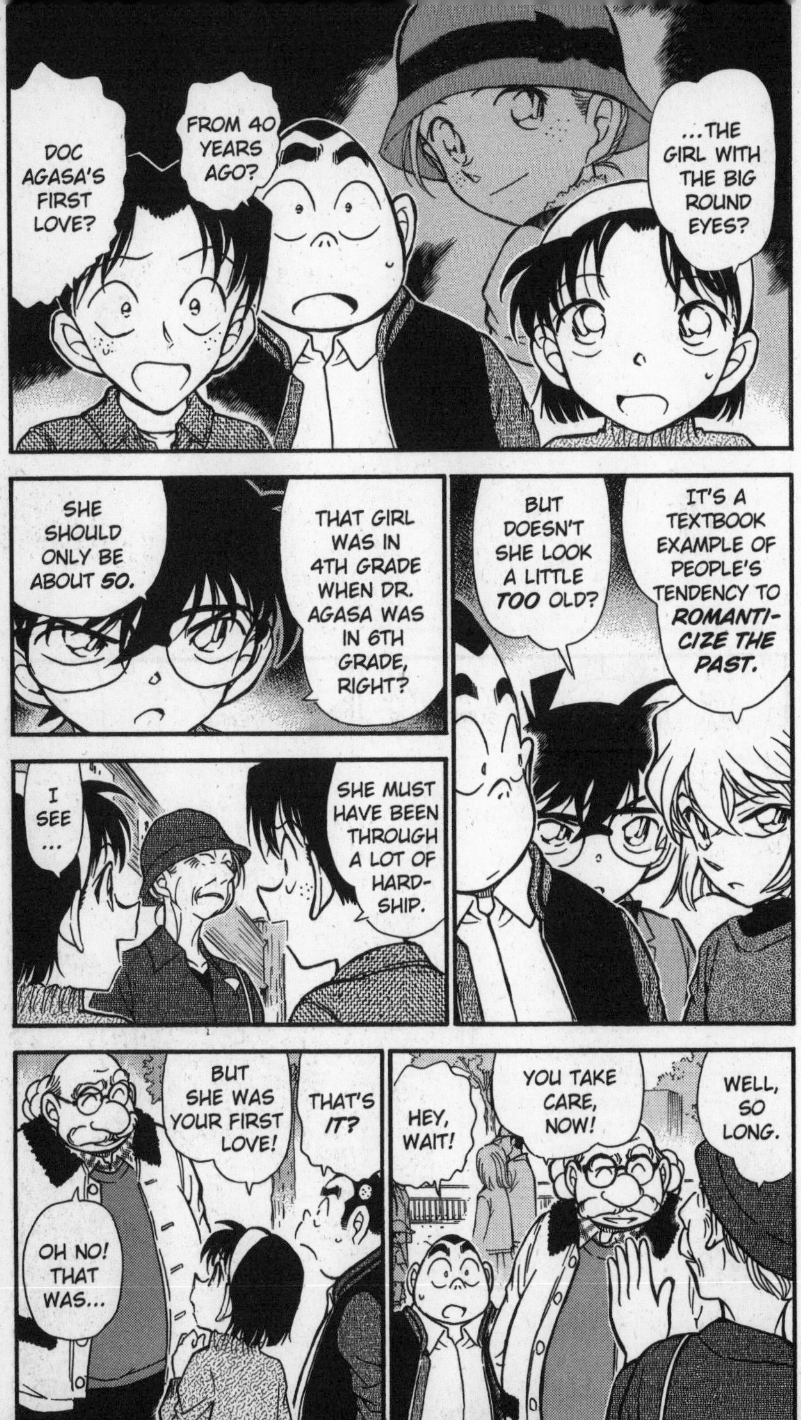
...THE GIRL WITH THE BIG ROUND EYES?
FROM 40 YEARS AGO?
DOC AGASA'S FIRST LOVE?
IT'S A TEXTBOOK EXAMPLE OF PEOPLE'S TENDENCY TO ROMANTICIZE THE PAST.
BUT DOESN'T SHE LOOK A LITTLE TOO OLD?
THAT GIRL WAS IN 4TH GRADE WHEN DR. AGASA WAS IN 6TH GRADE, RIGHT?
SHE SHOULD ONLY BE ABOUT 50.
SHE MUST HAVE BEEN THROUGH A LOT OF HARDSHIP.
I SEE...
WELL, SO LONG.
YOU TAKE CARE, NOW!
HEY, WAIT!
THAT'S IT?
BUT SHE WAS YOUR FIRST LOVE!
OH NO! THAT WAS...

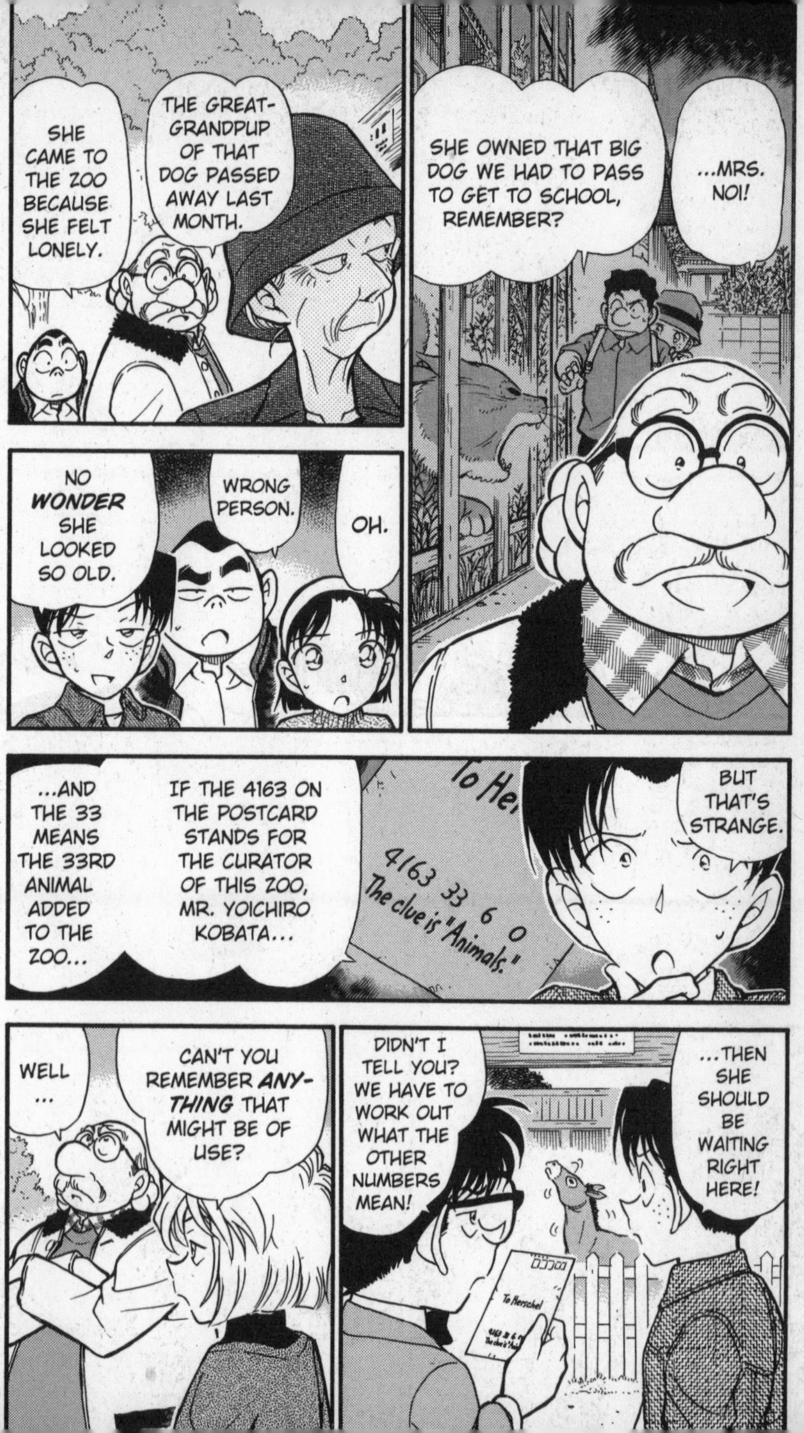
...MRS. NOI!
SHE OWNED THAT BIG DOG WE HAD TO PASS TO GET TO SCHOOL, REMEMBER?
THE GREAT-GRANDPUP OF THAT DOG PASSED AWAY LAST MONTH.
SHE CAME TO THE ZOO BECAUSE SHE FELT LONELY.
OH.
WRONG PERSON.
NO *WONDER* SHE LOOKED SO OLD.
BUT THAT'S STRANGE.
To Her
4163 33 6 0
The clue is "Animals."
IF THE 4163 ON THE POSTCARD STANDS FOR THE CURATOR OF THIS ZOO, MR. YOICHIRO KOBATA...
...AND THE 33 MEANS THE 33RD ANIMAL ADDED TO THE ZOO...
...THEN SHE SHOULD BE WAITING RIGHT HERE!
DIDN'T I TELL YOU? WE HAVE TO WORK OUT WHAT THE OTHER NUMBERS MEAN!
To Herschel
CAN'T YOU REMEMBER *ANYTHING* THAT MIGHT BE OF USE?
WELL ...

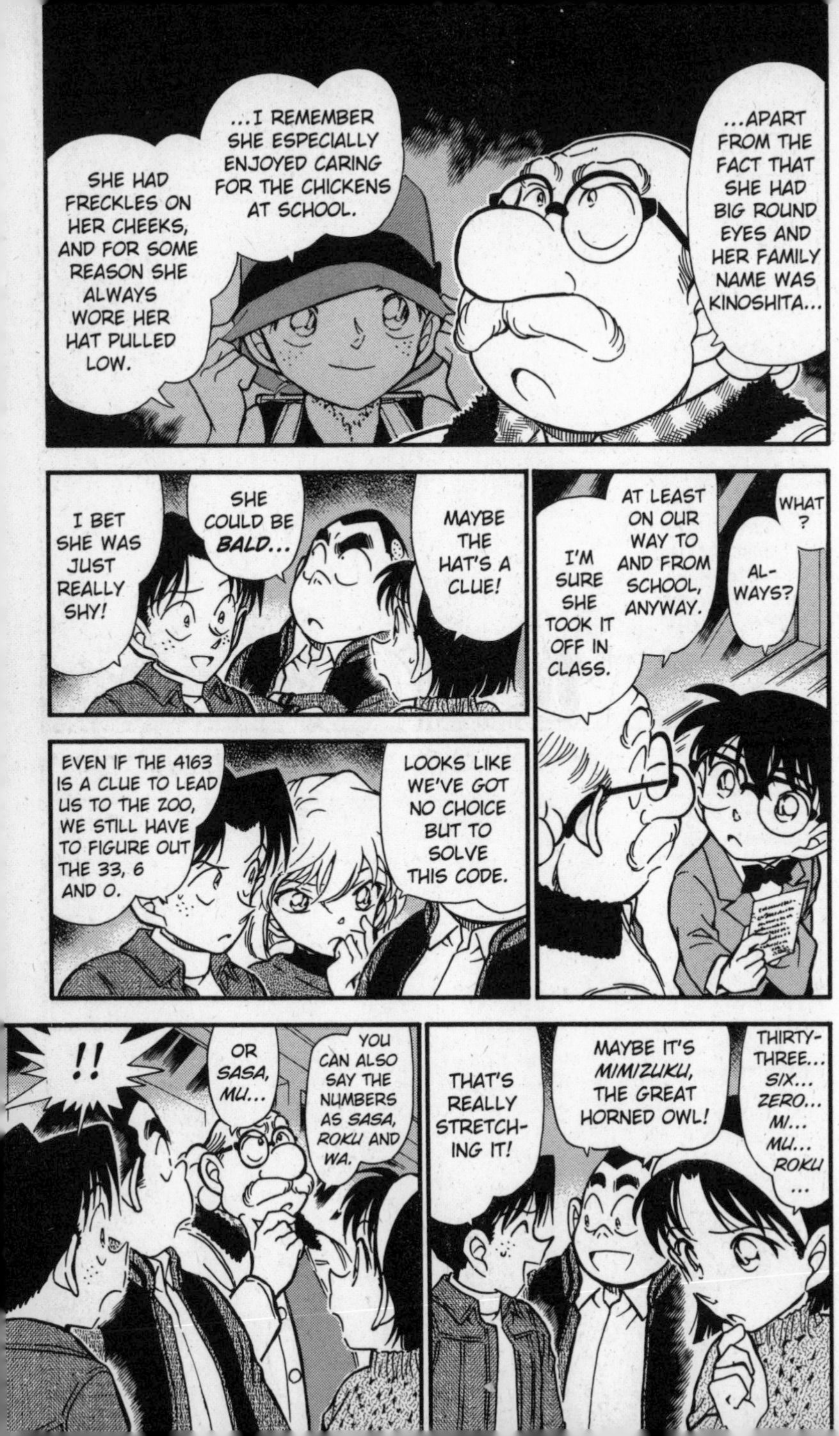

...APART FROM THE FACT THAT SHE HAD BIG ROUND EYES AND HER FAMILY NAME WAS KINOSHITA...
...I REMEMBER SHE ESPECIALLY ENJOYED CARING FOR THE CHICKENS AT SCHOOL.
SHE HAD FRECKLES ON HER CHEEKS, AND FOR SOME REASON SHE ALWAYS WORE HER HAT PULLED LOW.
WHAT?
ALWAYS?
AT LEAST ON OUR WAY TO AND FROM SCHOOL, ANYWAY.
I'M SURE SHE TOOK IT OFF IN CLASS.
MAYBE THE HAT'S A CLUE!
SHE COULD BE *BALD...*
I BET SHE WAS JUST REALLY SHY!
LOOKS LIKE WE'VE GOT NO CHOICE BUT TO SOLVE THIS CODE.
EVEN IF THE 4163 IS A CLUE TO LEAD US TO THE ZOO, WE STILL HAVE TO FIGURE OUT THE 33, 6 AND 0.
THIRTY-THREE... *SIX... ZERO... MI... MU... ROKU...*
MAYBE IT'S *MIMIZUKU*, THE GREAT HORNED OWL!
THAT'S REALLY STRETCHING IT!
YOU CAN ALSO SAY THE NUMBERS AS *SASA, ROKU* AND *WA.*
OR *SASA, MU...*
!!

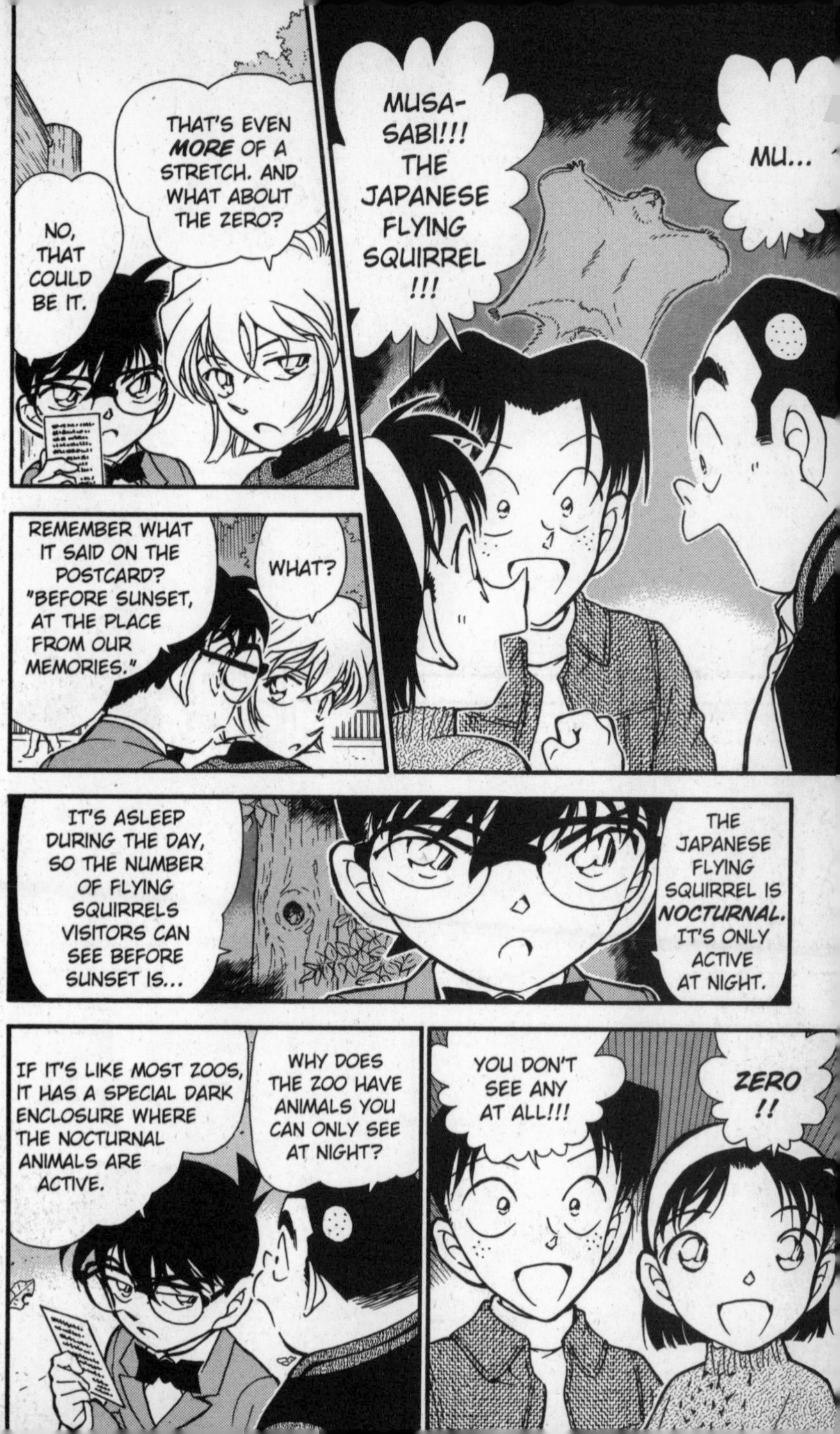
MU...
MUSA-SABI!!! THE JAPANESE FLYING SQUIRREL !!!
THAT'S EVEN **MORE** OF A STRETCH. AND WHAT ABOUT THE ZERO?
NO, THAT COULD BE IT.
WHAT?
REMEMBER WHAT IT SAID ON THE POSTCARD? "BEFORE SUNSET, AT THE PLACE FROM OUR MEMORIES."
THE JAPANESE FLYING SQUIRREL IS **NOCTURNAL.** IT'S ONLY ACTIVE AT NIGHT.
IT'S ASLEEP DURING THE DAY, SO THE NUMBER OF FLYING SQUIRRELS VISITORS CAN SEE BEFORE SUNSET IS...
ZERO !!
YOU DON'T SEE ANY AT ALL!!!
WHY DOES THE ZOO HAVE ANIMALS YOU CAN ONLY SEE AT NIGHT?
IF IT'S LIKE MOST ZOOS, IT HAS A SPECIAL DARK ENCLOSURE WHERE THE NOCTURNAL ANIMALS ARE ACTIVE.

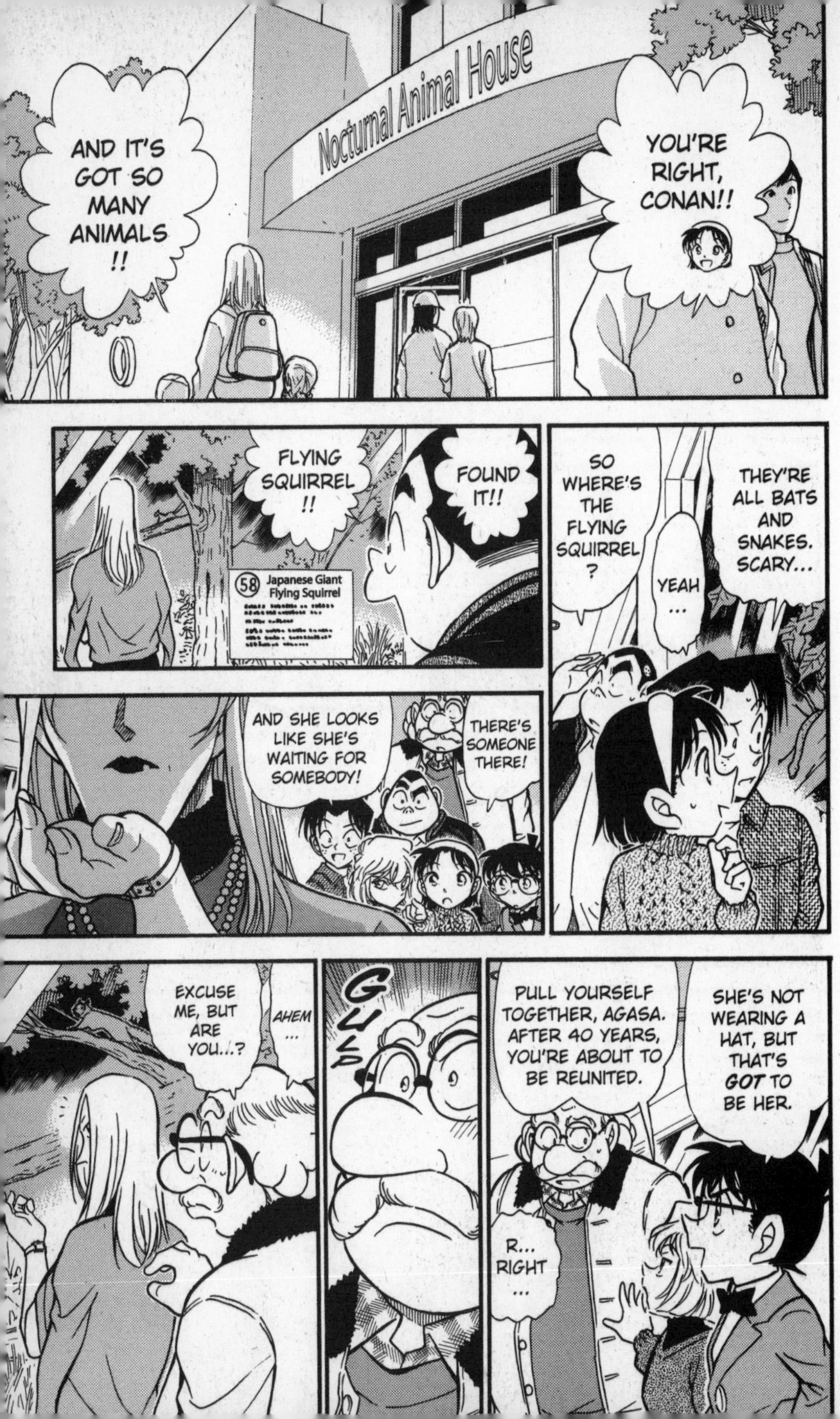
Nocturnal Animal House
YOU'RE RIGHT, CONAN!!
AND IT'S GOT SO MANY ANIMALS!!
THEY'RE ALL BATS AND SNAKES. SCARY...
YEAH...
SO WHERE'S THE FLYING SQUIRREL?
FOUND IT!!
FLYING SQUIRREL!!
58 Japanese Giant Flying Squirrel
THERE'S SOMEONE THERE!
AND SHE LOOKS LIKE SHE'S WAITING FOR SOMEBODY!
SHE'S NOT WEARING A HAT, BUT THAT'S GOT TO BE HER.
PULL YOURSELF TOGETHER, AGASA. AFTER 40 YEARS, YOU'RE ABOUT TO BE REUNITED.
R... RIGHT...
GULP
AHEM...
EXCUSE ME, BUT ARE YOU...?

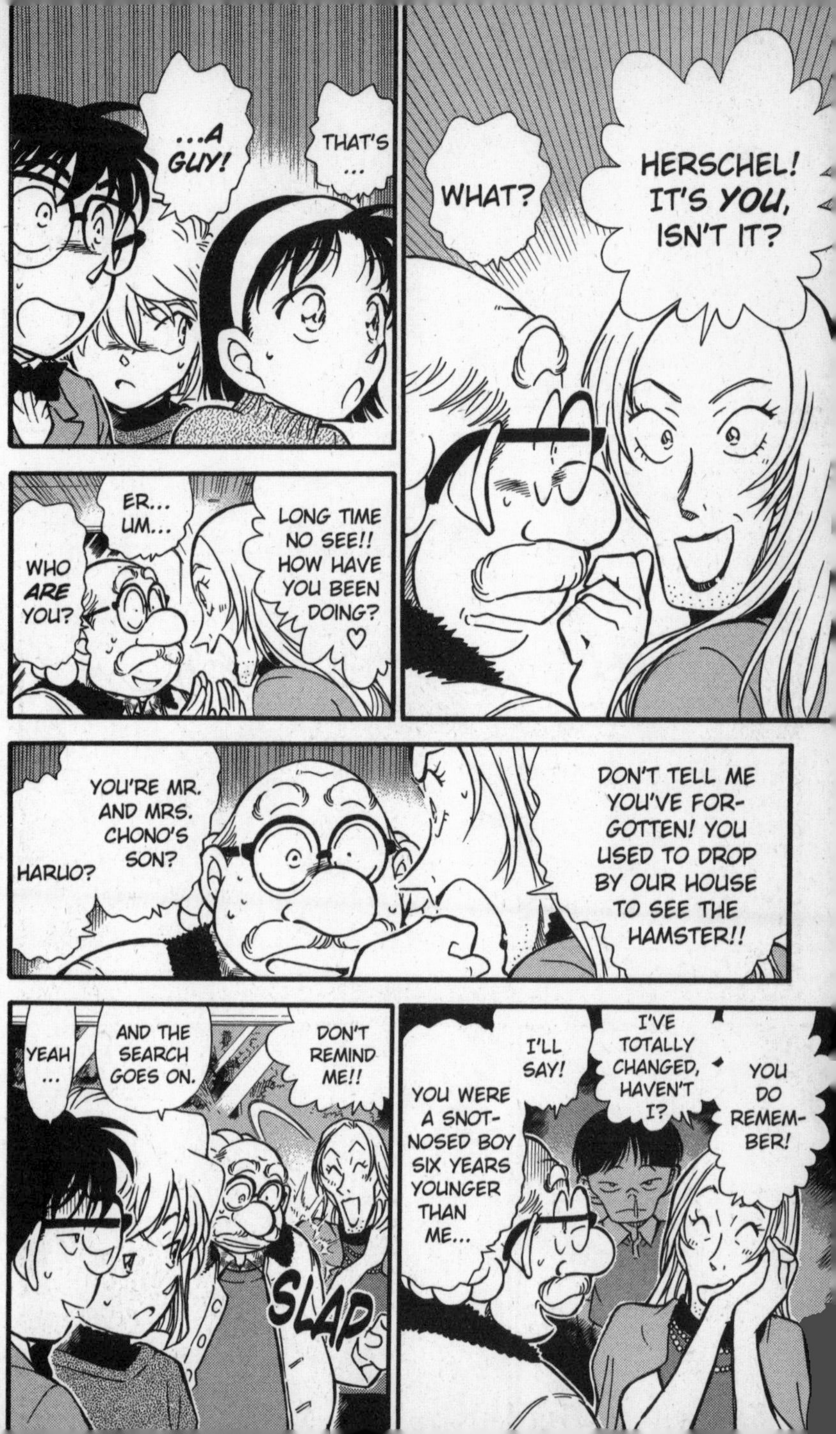
HERSCHEL! IT'S YOU, ISN'T IT?
WHAT?
THAT'S ...
...A GUY!
LONG TIME NO SEE!! HOW HAVE YOU BEEN DOING? ♡
ER... UM...
WHO ARE YOU?
DON'T TELL ME YOU'VE FOR-GOTTEN! YOU USED TO DROP BY OUR HOUSE TO SEE THE HAMSTER!!
YOU'RE MR. AND MRS. CHONO'S SON?
HARUO?
YOU DO REMEM-BER!
I'VE TOTALLY CHANGED, HAVEN'T I?
I'LL SAY!
YOU WERE A SNOT-NOSED BOY SIX YEARS YOUNGER THAN ME...
DON'T REMIND ME!!
SLAP
AND THE SEARCH GOES ON.
YEAH ...

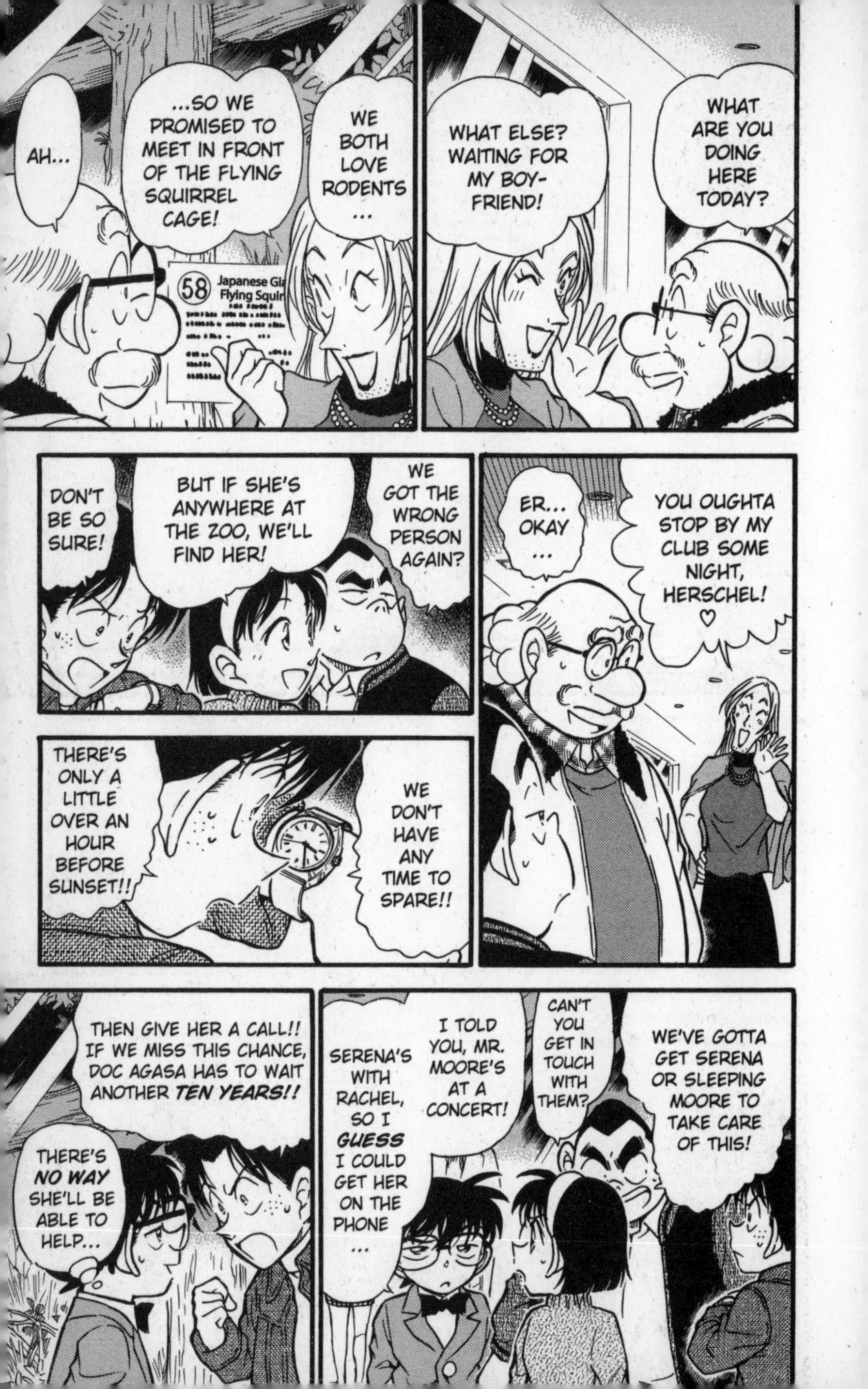
WHAT ARE YOU DOING HERE TODAY?
WHAT ELSE? WAITING FOR MY BOY-FRIEND!
WE BOTH LOVE RODENTS...
...SO WE PROMISED TO MEET IN FRONT OF THE FLYING SQUIRREL CAGE!
AH...
58
YOU OUGHTA STOP BY MY CLUB SOME NIGHT, HERSCHEL! ♡
ER... OKAY...
WE GOT THE WRONG PERSON AGAIN?
BUT IF SHE'S ANYWHERE AT THE ZOO, WE'LL FIND HER!
DON'T BE SO SURE!
WE DON'T HAVE ANY TIME TO SPARE!!
THERE'S ONLY A LITTLE OVER AN HOUR BEFORE SUNSET!!
WE'VE GOTTA GET SERENA OR SLEEPING MOORE TO TAKE CARE OF THIS!
CAN'T YOU GET IN TOUCH WITH THEM?
I TOLD YOU, MR. MOORE'S AT A CONCERT!
SERENA'S WITH RACHEL, SO I *GUESS* I COULD GET HER ON THE PHONE...
THEN GIVE HER A CALL!! IF WE MISS THIS CHANCE, DOC AGASA HAS TO WAIT ANOTHER *TEN YEARS!!*
THERE'S *NO WAY* SHE'LL BE ABLE TO HELP...

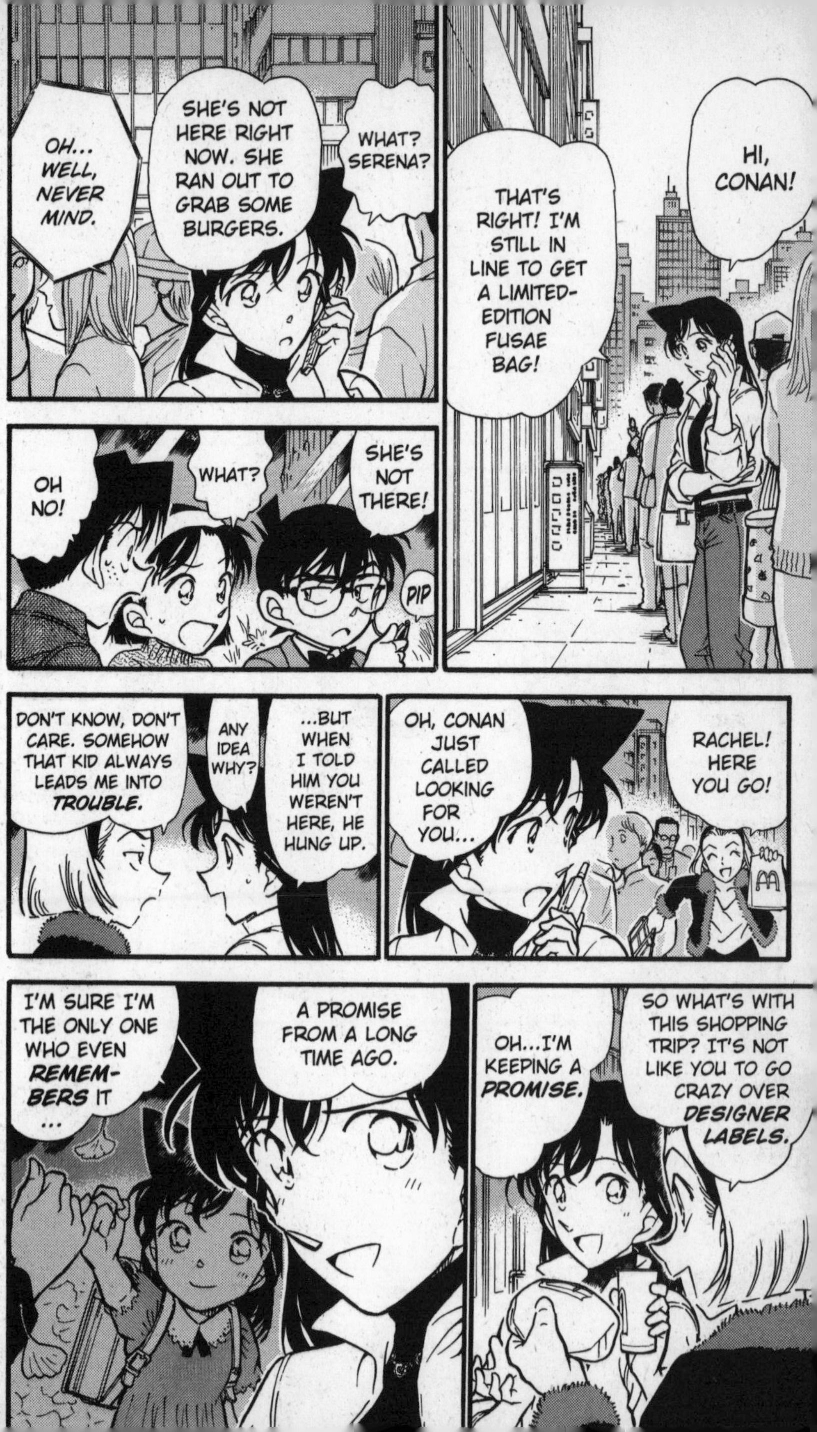
HI, CONAN!
THAT'S RIGHT! I'M STILL IN LINE TO GET A LIMITED-EDITION FUSAE BAG!
WHAT? SERENA?
SHE'S NOT HERE RIGHT NOW. SHE RAN OUT TO GRAB SOME BURGERS.
OH... WELL, NEVER MIND.
SHE'S NOT THERE!
PIP
WHAT?
OH NO!
RACHEL! HERE YOU GO!
OH, CONAN JUST CALLED LOOKING FOR YOU...
...BUT WHEN I TOLD HIM YOU WEREN'T HERE, HE HUNG UP.
ANY IDEA WHY?
DON'T KNOW, DON'T CARE. SOMEHOW THAT KID ALWAYS LEADS ME INTO *TROUBLE.*
SO WHAT'S WITH THIS SHOPPING TRIP? IT'S NOT LIKE YOU TO GO CRAZY OVER *DESIGNER LABELS.*
OH...I'M KEEPING A *PROMISE.*
A PROMISE FROM A LONG TIME AGO.
I'M SURE I'M THE ONLY ONE WHO EVEN *REMEMBERS* IT ...

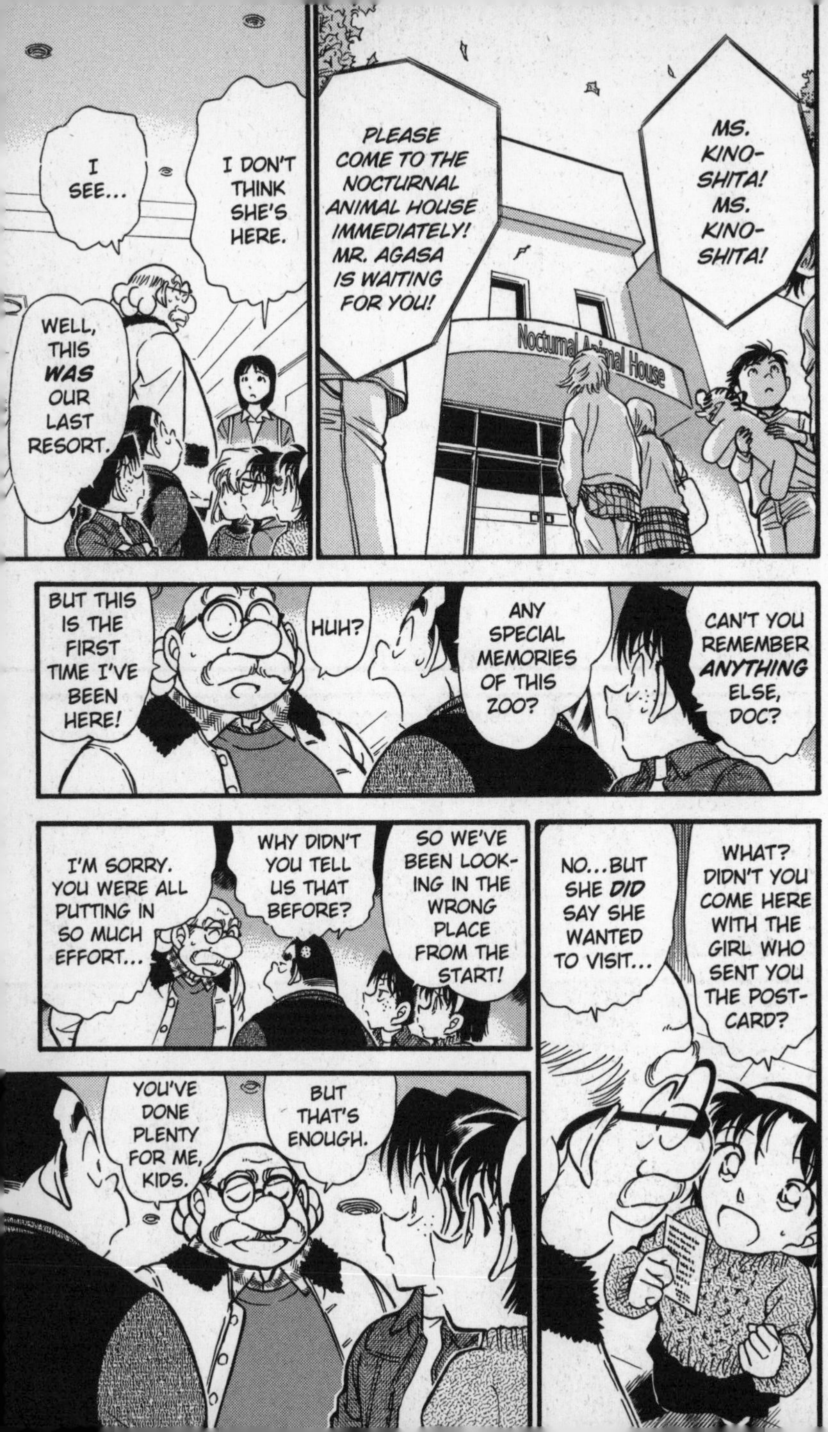
MS. KINO-SHITA! MS. KINO-SHITA!
PLEASE COME TO THE NOCTURNAL ANIMAL HOUSE IMMEDIATELY! MR. AGASA IS WAITING FOR YOU!
I DON'T THINK SHE'S HERE.
I SEE...
WELL, THIS ***WAS*** OUR LAST RESORT.
CAN'T YOU REMEMBER ***ANYTHING*** ELSE, DOC?
ANY SPECIAL MEMORIES OF THIS ZOO?
HUH?
BUT THIS IS THE FIRST TIME I'VE BEEN HERE!
WHAT? DIDN'T YOU COME HERE WITH THE GIRL WHO SENT YOU THE POST-CARD?
NO...BUT SHE ***DID*** SAY SHE WANTED TO VISIT...
SO WE'VE BEEN LOOK-ING IN THE WRONG PLACE FROM THE START!
WHY DIDN'T YOU TELL US THAT BEFORE?
I'M SORRY. YOU WERE ALL PUTTING IN SO MUCH EFFORT...
YOU'VE DONE PLENTY FOR ME, KIDS.
BUT THAT'S ENOUGH.

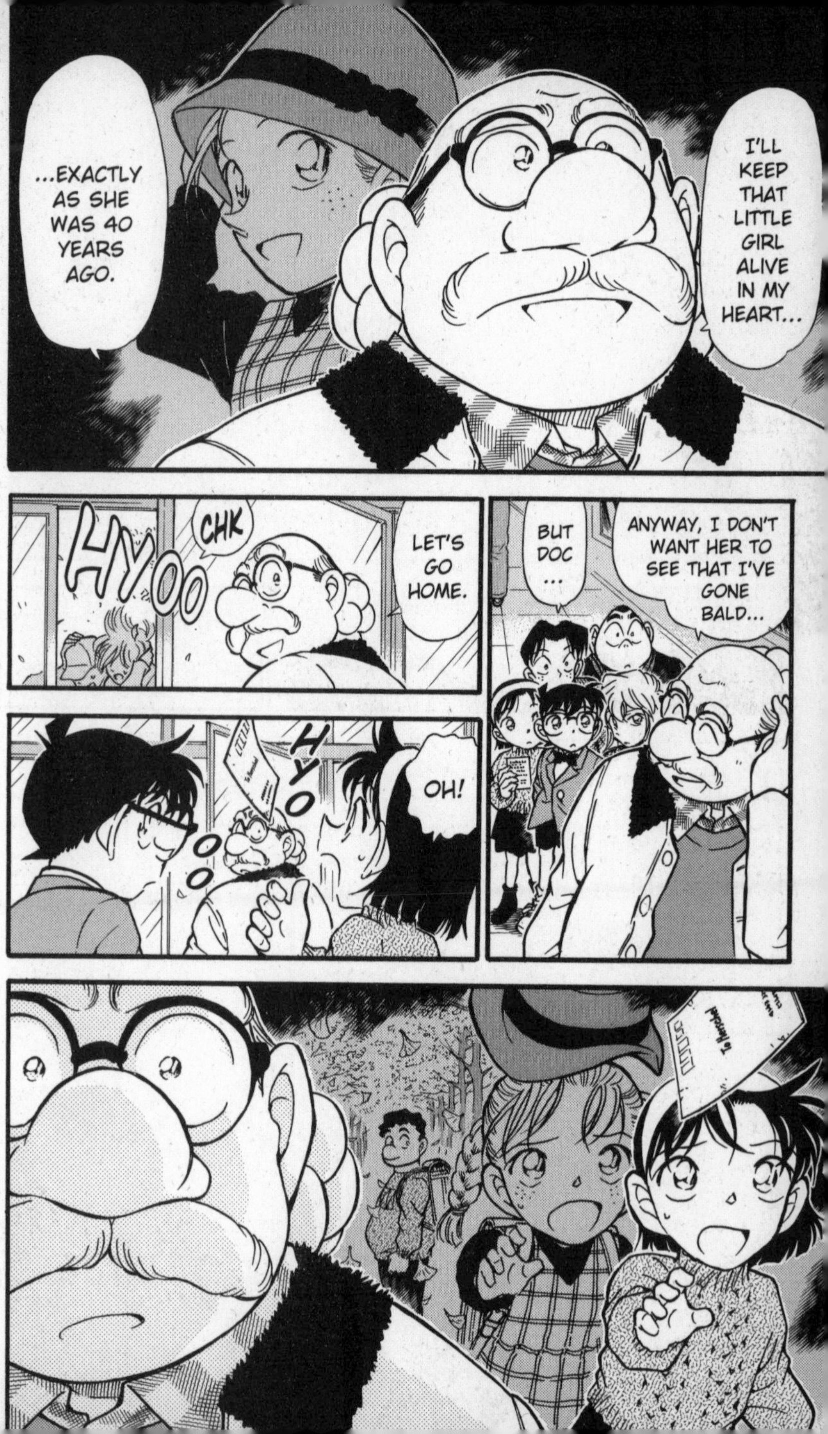
I'LL KEEP THAT LITTLE GIRL ALIVE IN MY HEART...
...EXACTLY AS SHE WAS 40 YEARS AGO.
ANYWAY, I DON'T WANT HER TO SEE THAT I'VE GONE BALD...
BUT DOC...
LET'S GO HOME.
CHK
HYOO
OH!
HYOOO

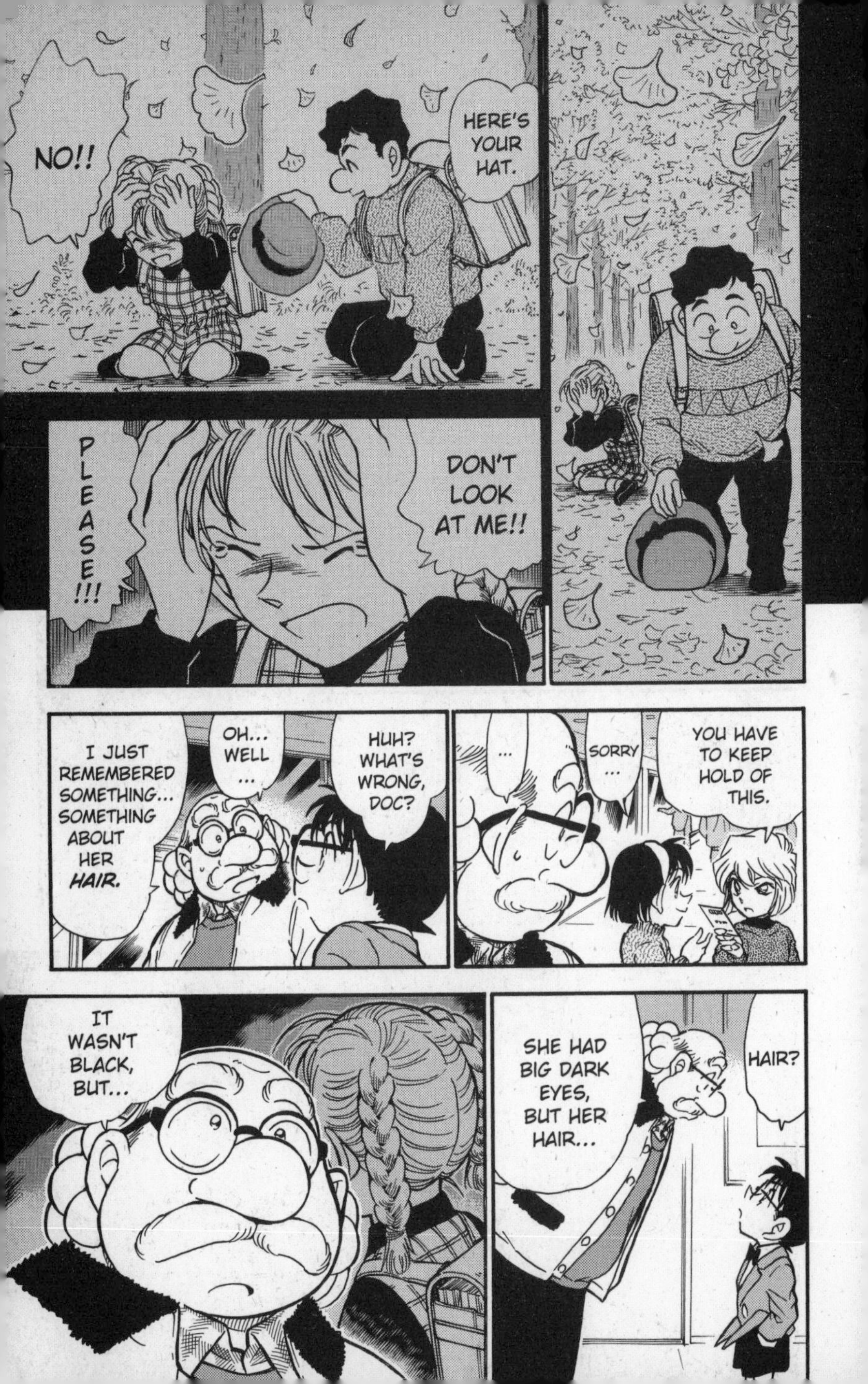
HERE'S YOUR HAT.
NO!!
DON'T LOOK AT ME!!
PLEASE!!!
YOU HAVE TO KEEP HOLD OF THIS.
SORRY ...
...
HUH? WHAT'S WRONG, DOC?
OH... WELL ...
I JUST REMEMBERED SOMETHING... SOMETHING ABOUT HER *HAIR*.
HAIR?
SHE HAD BIG DARK EYES, BUT HER HAIR...
IT WASN'T BLACK, BUT...

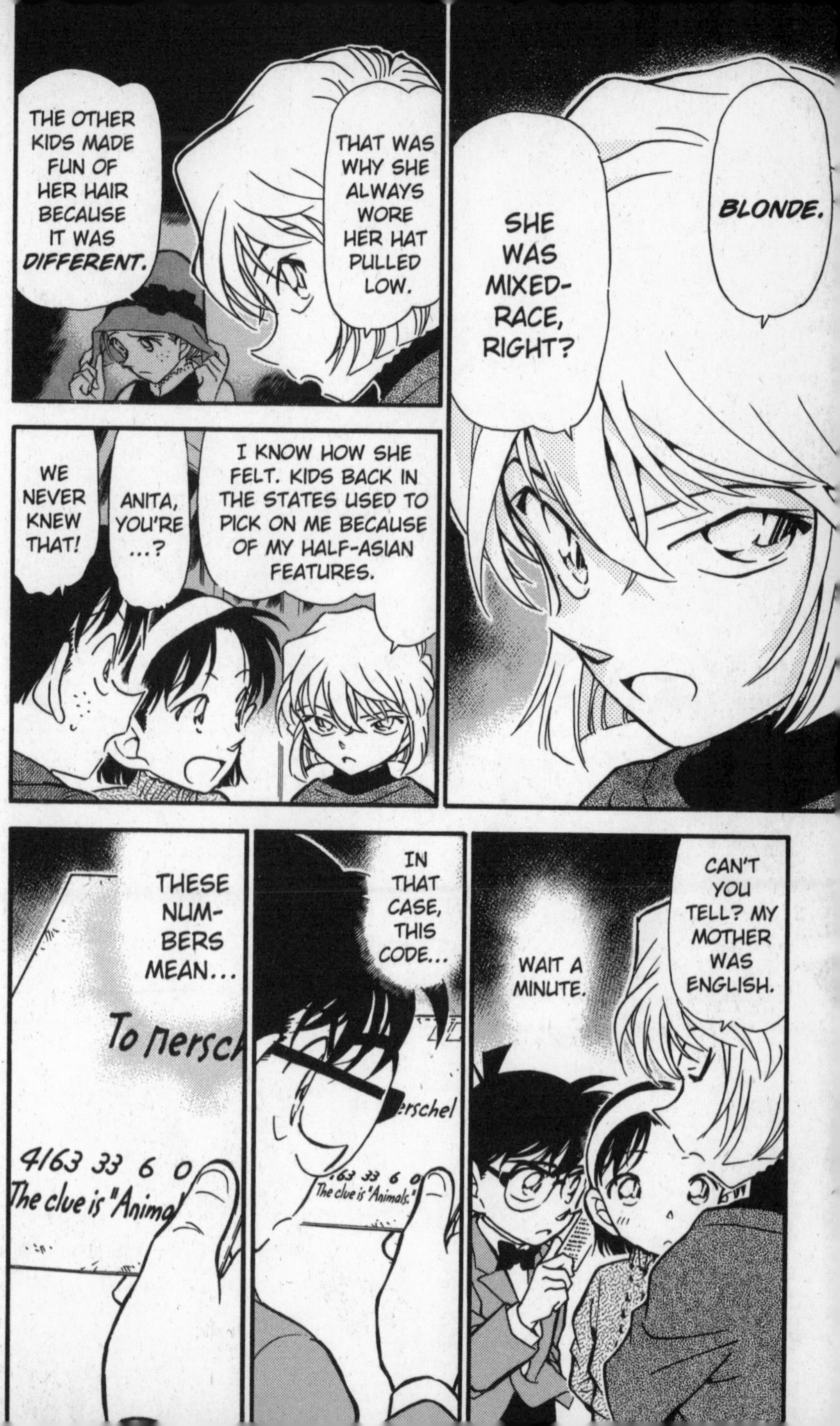
BLONDE.
SHE WAS MIXED-RACE, RIGHT?
THE OTHER KIDS MADE FUN OF HER HAIR BECAUSE IT WAS DIFFERENT.
THAT WAS WHY SHE ALWAYS WORE HER HAT PULLED LOW.
I KNOW HOW SHE FELT. KIDS BACK IN THE STATES USED TO PICK ON ME BECAUSE OF MY HALF-ASIAN FEATURES.
ANITA, YOU'RE ...?
WE NEVER KNEW THAT!
CAN'T YOU TELL? MY MOTHER WAS ENGLISH.
WAIT A MINUTE.
IN THAT CASE, THIS CODE...
4163 33 6 0
The clue is "Animals."
THESE NUMBERS MEAN...

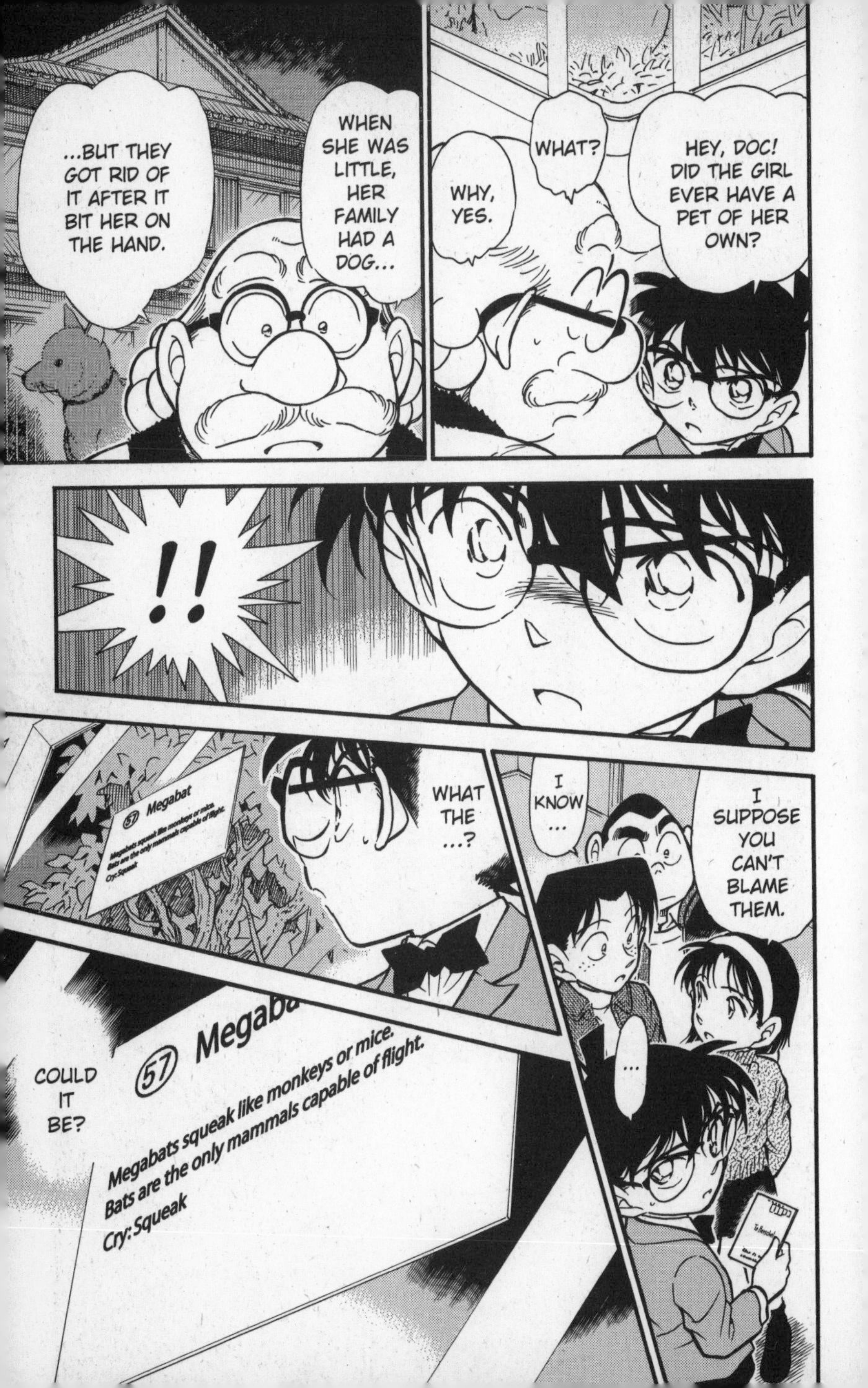
HEY, DOC! DID THE GIRL EVER HAVE A PET OF HER OWN?
WHAT?
WHY, YES.
WHEN SHE WAS LITTLE, HER FAMILY HAD A DOG...
...BUT THEY GOT RID OF IT AFTER IT BIT HER ON THE HAND.
!!
I SUPPOSE YOU CAN'T BLAME THEM.
I KNOW...
...
WHAT THE ...?
57 Megabat
57 Megaba
Megabats squeak like monkeys or mice.
Bats are the only mammals capable of flight.
Cry: Squeak
COULD IT BE?

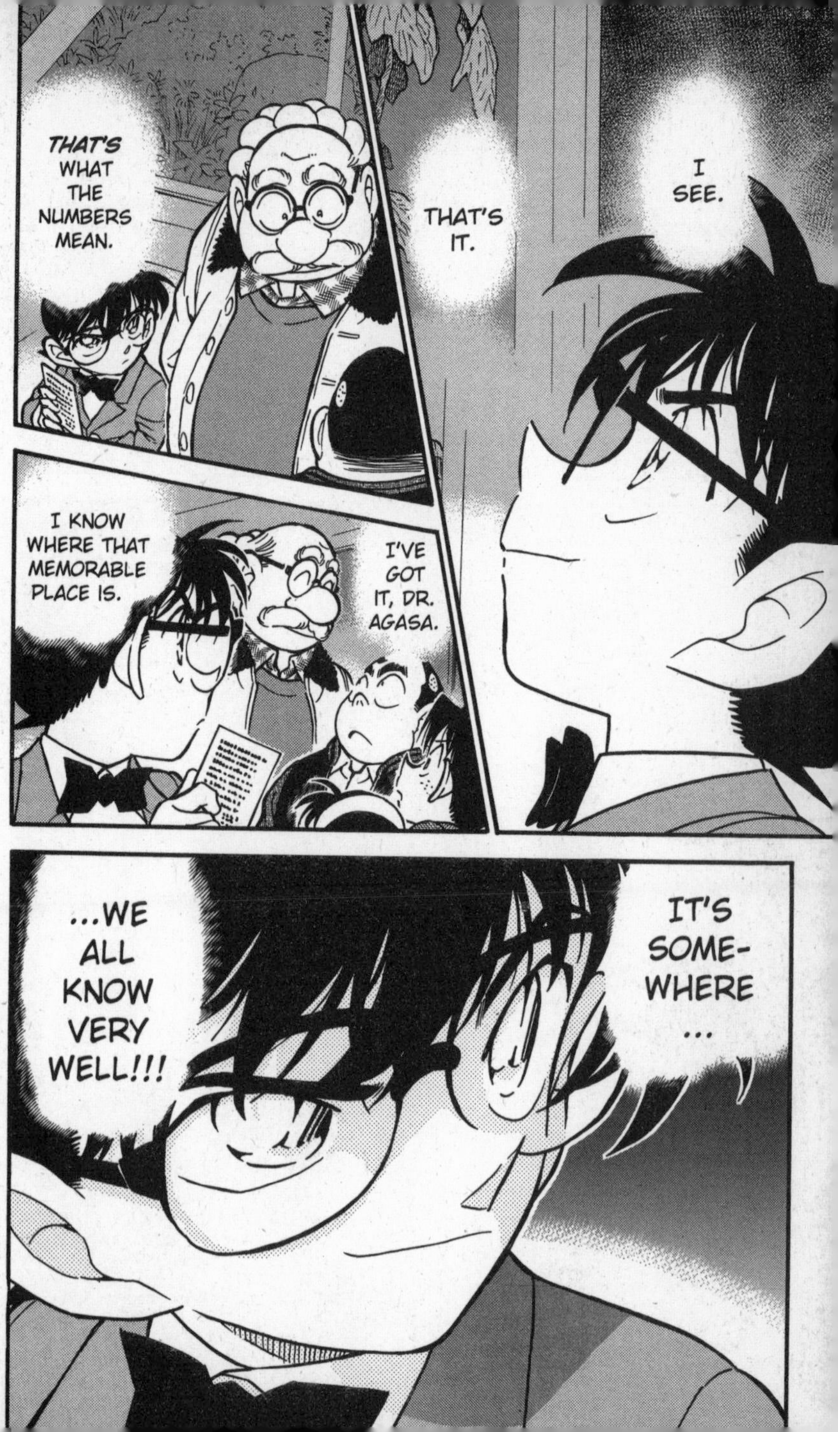
I SEE.
THAT'S IT.
THAT'S WHAT THE NUMBERS MEAN.
I'VE GOT IT, DR. AGASA.
I KNOW WHERE THAT MEMORABLE PLACE IS.
IT'S SOME-WHERE...
...WE ALL KNOW VERY WELL!!!

FIRST LOVE · REUNION · FAREWELL

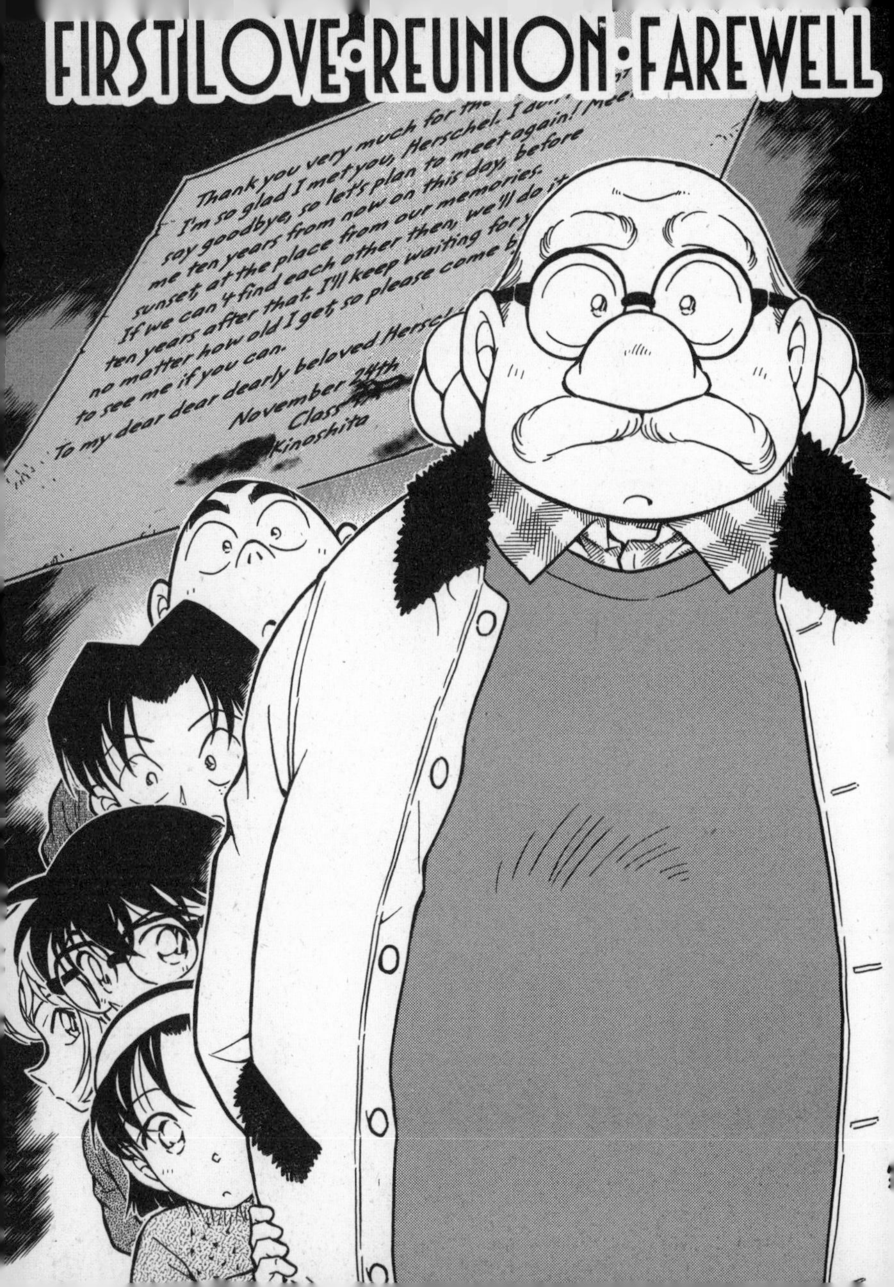

Thank you very much for the
I'm so glad I met you, Herschel.
say goodbye, so let's plan to meet again! Meet
me ten years from now on this day, before
sunset at the place from our memories.
If we can't find each other then, we'll do it
ten years after that. I'll keep waiting for y
no matter how old I get, so please come b
to see me if you can.
To my dear dear dearly beloved Hersch
November 24th
Class
Kinoshita

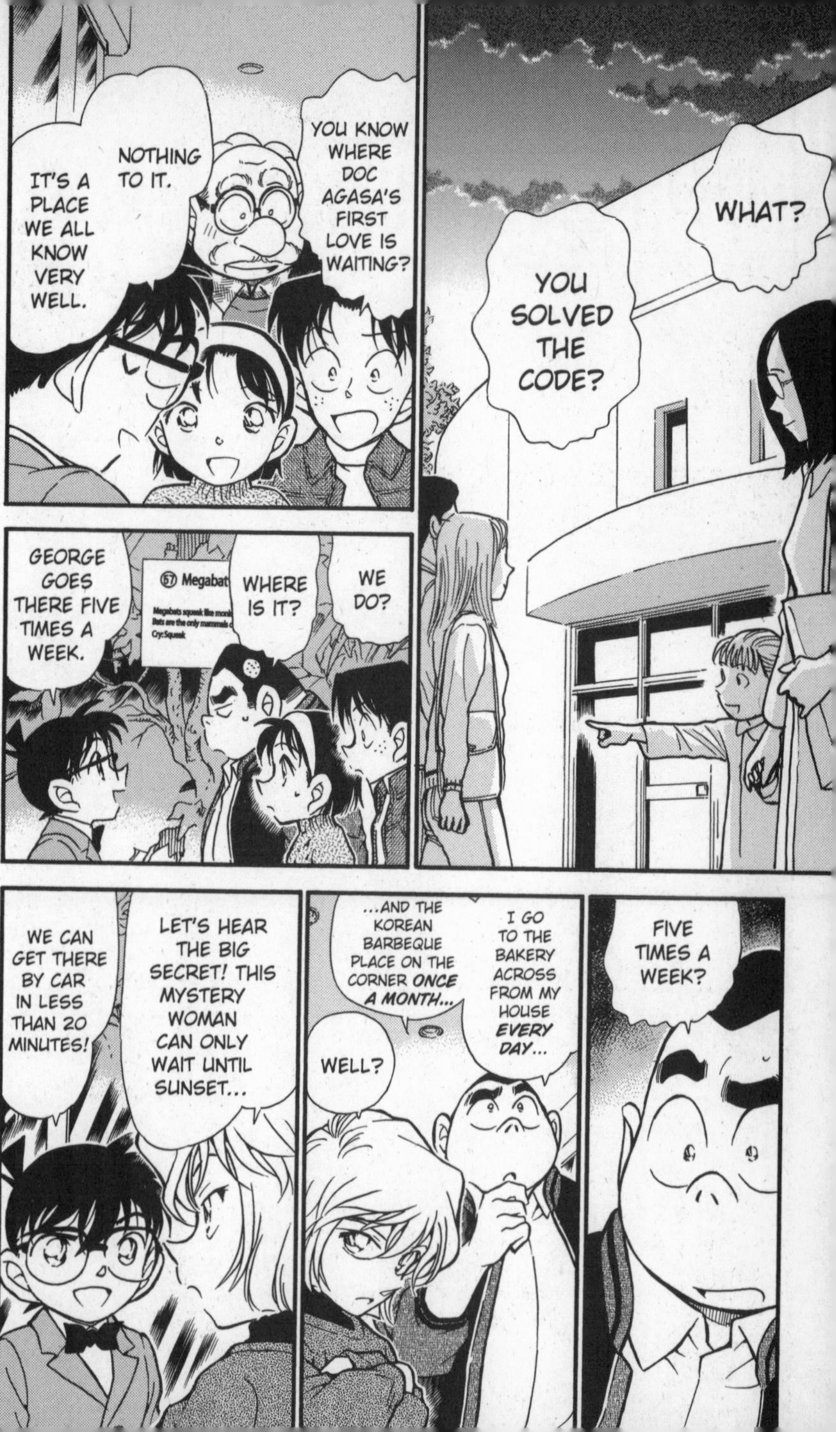
WHAT?
YOU SOLVED THE CODE?
YOU KNOW WHERE DOC AGASA'S FIRST LOVE IS WAITING?
NOTHING TO IT.
IT'S A PLACE WE ALL KNOW VERY WELL.
WE DO?
WHERE IS IT?
57 Megabat
GEORGE GOES THERE FIVE TIMES A WEEK.
FIVE TIMES A WEEK?
I GO TO THE BAKERY ACROSS FROM MY HOUSE *EVERY DAY*...
...AND THE KOREAN BARBEQUE PLACE ON THE CORNER *ONCE A MONTH*...
WELL?
LET'S HEAR THE BIG SECRET! THIS MYSTERY WOMAN CAN ONLY WAIT UNTIL SUNSET...
WE CAN GET THERE BY CAR IN LESS THAN 20 MINUTES!

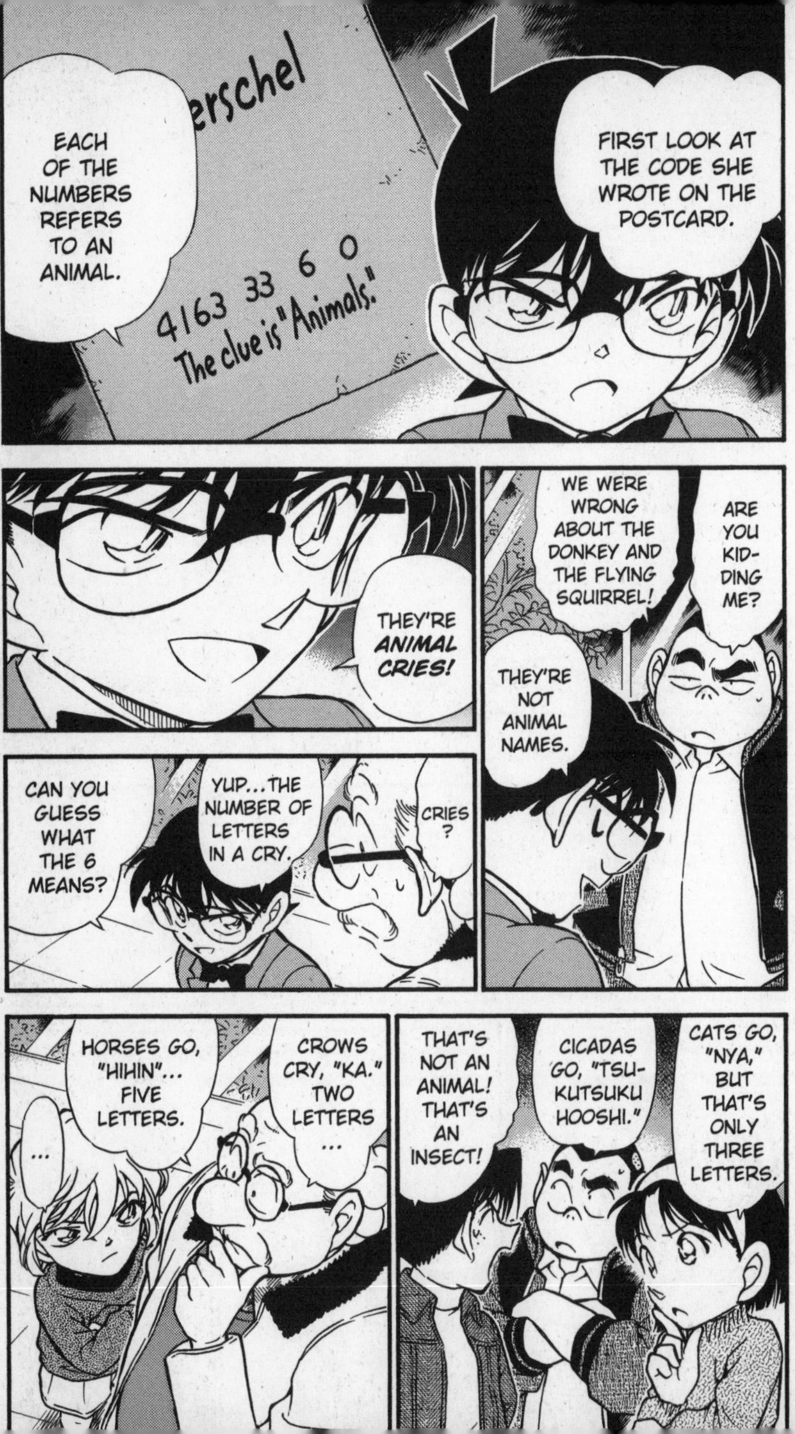

FIRST LOOK AT THE CODE SHE WROTE ON THE POSTCARD.
EACH OF THE NUMBERS REFERS TO AN ANIMAL.
erschel
4163 33 6 0
The clue is "Animals."
ARE YOU KID-DING ME?
WE WERE WRONG ABOUT THE DONKEY AND THE FLYING SQUIRREL!
THEY'RE NOT ANIMAL NAMES.
THEY'RE *ANIMAL CRIES!*
CRIES?
YUP...THE NUMBER OF LETTERS IN A CRY.
CAN YOU GUESS WHAT THE 6 MEANS?
CATS GO, "NYA," BUT THAT'S ONLY THREE LETTERS.
CICADAS GO, "TSU-KUTSUKU HOOSHI."
THAT'S NOT AN ANIMAL! THAT'S AN INSECT!
CROWS CRY, "KA." TWO LETTERS ...
HORSES GO, "HIHIN"... FIVE LETTERS.
...

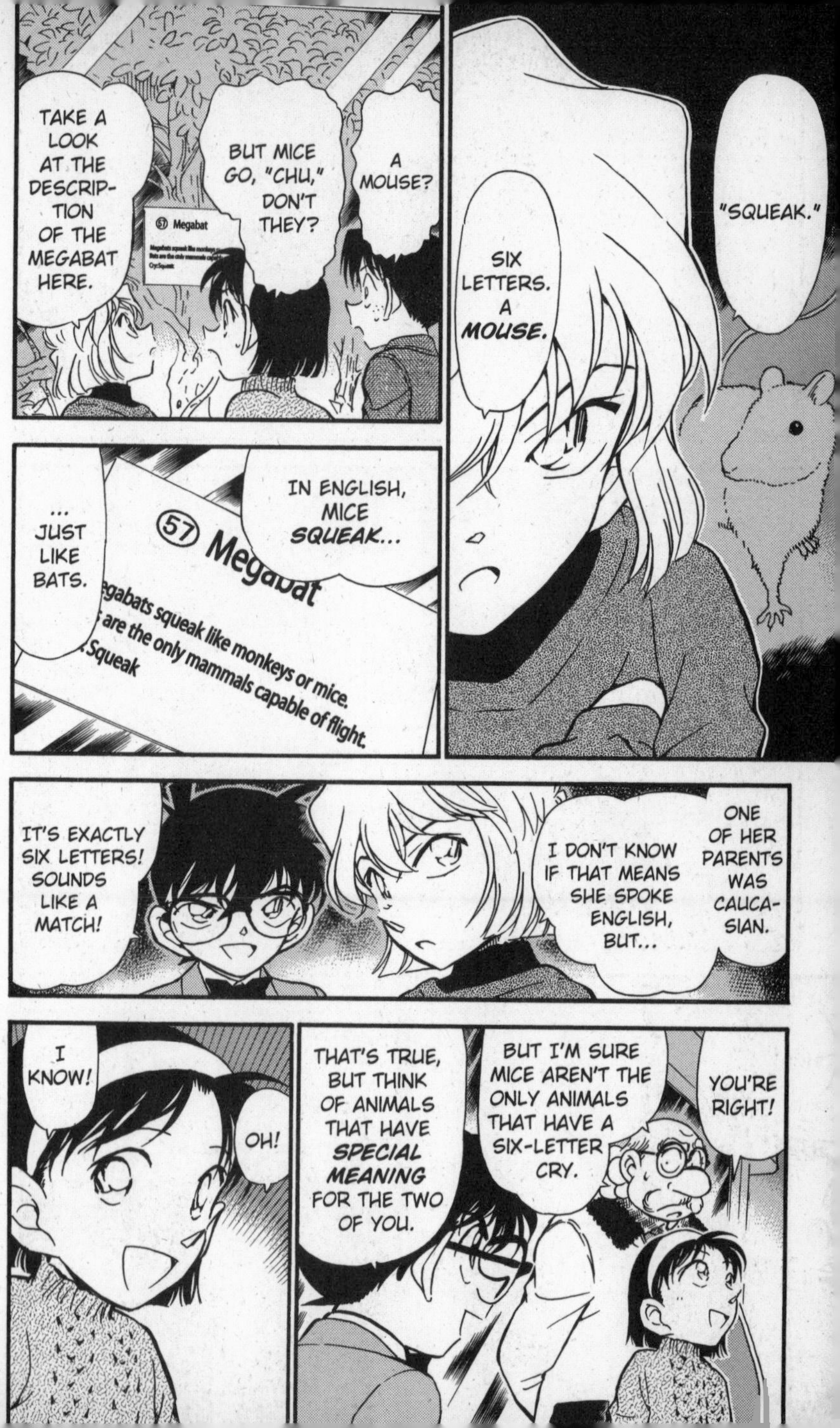
"SQUEAK."
SIX LETTERS. A *MOUSE.*
A MOUSE?
BUT MICE GO, "CHU," DON'T THEY?
TAKE A LOOK AT THE DESCRIPTION OF THE MEGABAT HERE.
57 Megabat
IN ENGLISH, MICE *SQUEAK...*
... JUST LIKE BATS.
57 Megabat
egabats squeak like monkeys or mice.
are the only mammals capable of flight.
Squeak
ONE OF HER PARENTS WAS CAUCASIAN.
I DON'T KNOW IF THAT MEANS SHE SPOKE ENGLISH, BUT...
IT'S EXACTLY SIX LETTERS! SOUNDS LIKE A MATCH!
YOU'RE RIGHT!
BUT I'M SURE MICE AREN'T THE ONLY ANIMALS THAT HAVE A SIX-LETTER CRY.
THAT'S TRUE, BUT THINK OF ANIMALS THAT HAVE *SPECIAL MEANING* FOR THE TWO OF YOU.
OH!
I KNOW!

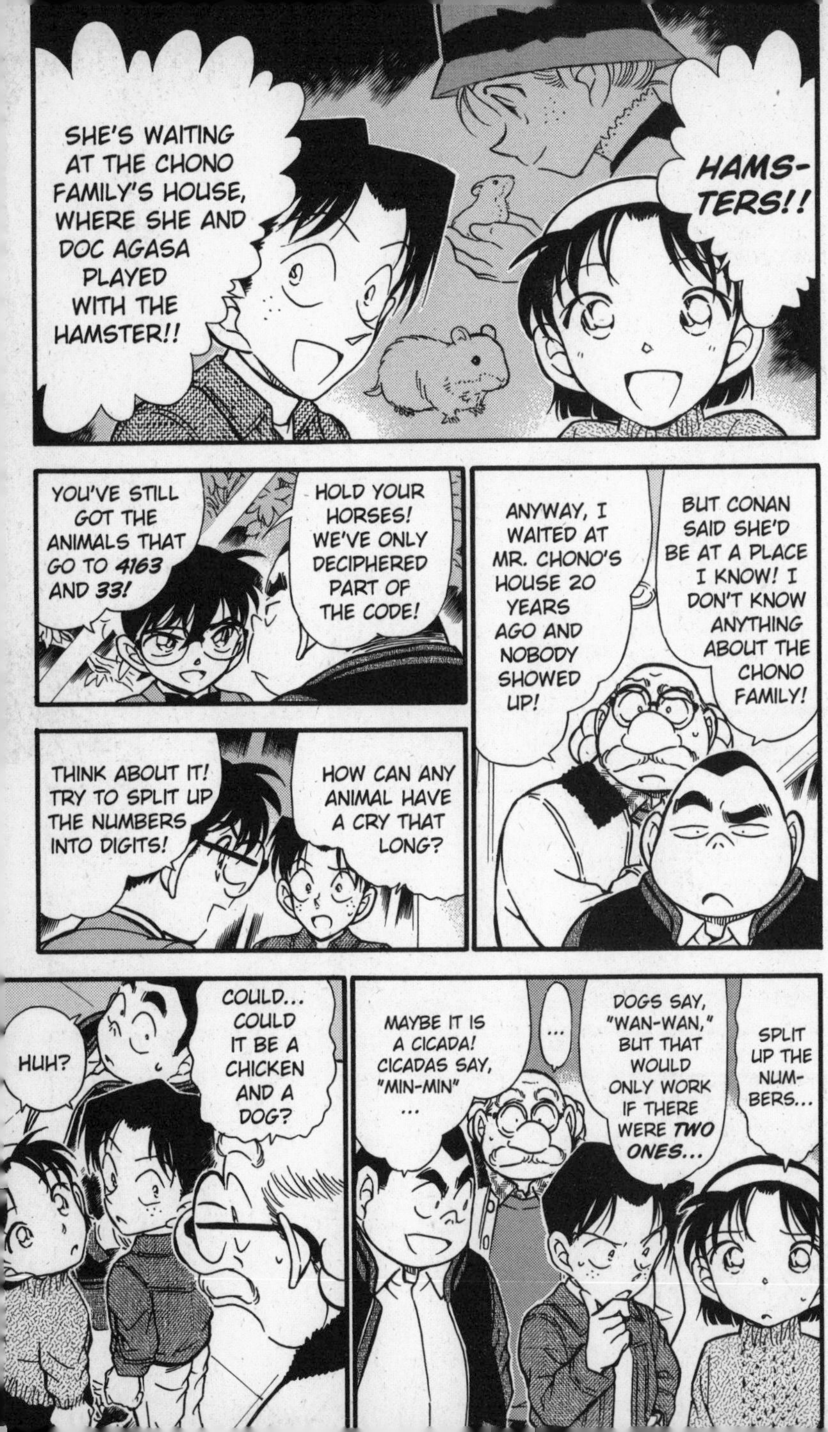
HAMSTERS!!
SHE'S WAITING AT THE CHONO FAMILY'S HOUSE, WHERE SHE AND DOC AGASA PLAYED WITH THE HAMSTER!!
BUT CONAN SAID SHE'D BE AT A PLACE I KNOW! I DON'T KNOW ANYTHING ABOUT THE CHONO FAMILY!
ANYWAY, I WAITED AT MR. CHONO'S HOUSE 20 YEARS AGO AND NOBODY SHOWED UP!
HOLD YOUR HORSES! WE'VE ONLY DECIPHERED PART OF THE CODE!
YOU'VE STILL GOT THE ANIMALS THAT GO TO 4163 AND 33!
HOW CAN ANY ANIMAL HAVE A CRY THAT LONG?
THINK ABOUT IT! TRY TO SPLIT UP THE NUMBERS INTO DIGITS!
SPLIT UP THE NUMBERS...
DOGS SAY, "WAN-WAN," BUT THAT WOULD ONLY WORK IF THERE WERE TWO ONES...
...
MAYBE IT IS A CICADA! CICADAS SAY, "MIN-MIN" ...
COULD... COULD IT BE A CHICKEN AND A DOG?
HUH?

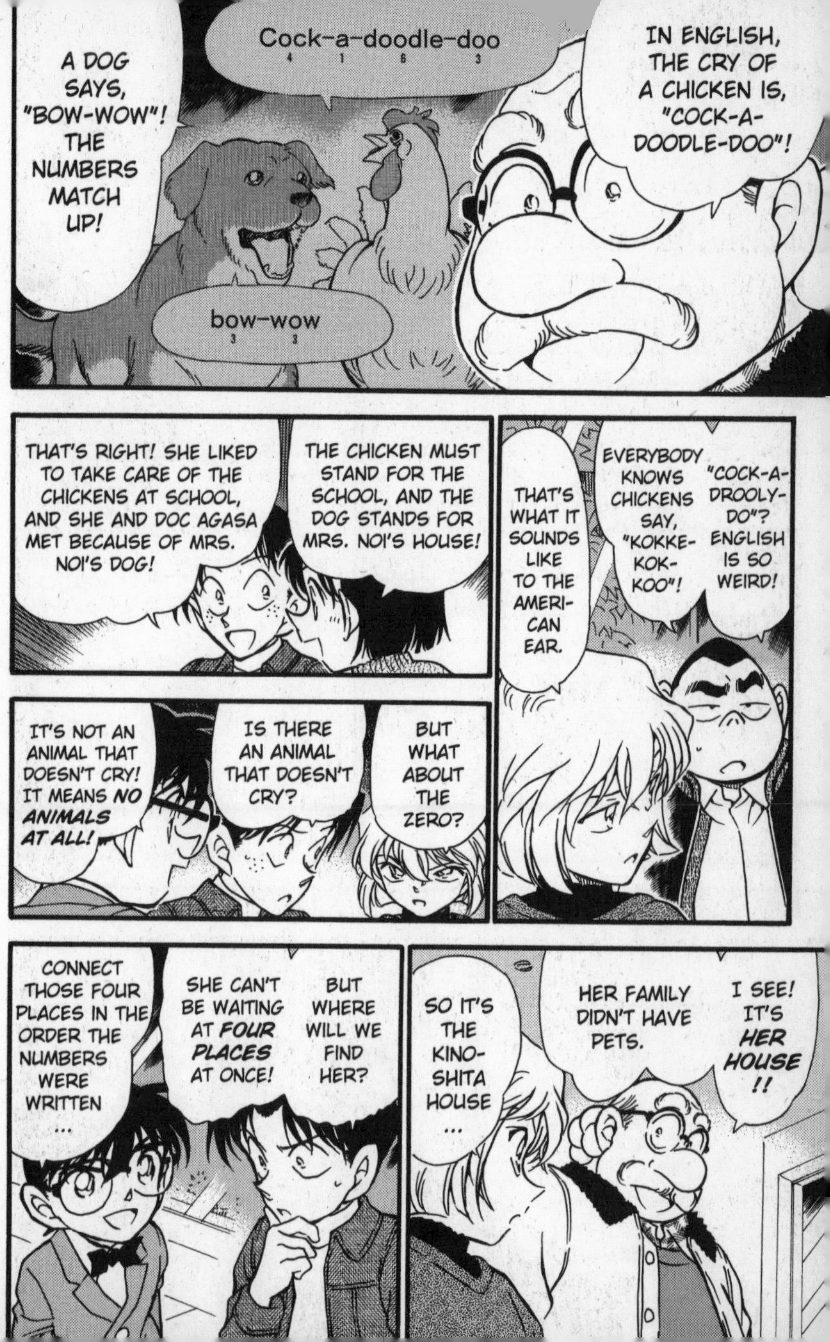
IN ENGLISH, THE CRY OF A CHICKEN IS, "COCK-A-DOODLE-DOO"!
Cock-a-doodle-doo
4 1 6 3
A DOG SAYS, "BOW-WOW"! THE NUMBERS MATCH UP!
bow-wow
3 3
"COCK-A-DROOLY-DO"? ENGLISH IS SO WEIRD!
EVERYBODY KNOWS CHICKENS SAY, "KOKKE-KOK-KOO"!
THAT'S WHAT IT SOUNDS LIKE TO THE AMERICAN EAR.
THE CHICKEN MUST STAND FOR THE SCHOOL, AND THE DOG STANDS FOR MRS. NOI'S HOUSE!
THAT'S RIGHT! SHE LIKED TO TAKE CARE OF THE CHICKENS AT SCHOOL, AND SHE AND DOC AGASA MET BECAUSE OF MRS. NOI'S DOG!
BUT WHAT ABOUT THE ZERO?
IS THERE AN ANIMAL THAT DOESN'T CRY?
IT'S NOT AN ANIMAL THAT DOESN'T CRY! IT MEANS *NO ANIMALS AT ALL!*
I SEE! IT'S *HER HOUSE*!!
HER FAMILY DIDN'T HAVE PETS.
SO IT'S THE KINOSHITA HOUSE...
BUT WHERE WILL WE FIND HER?
SHE CAN'T BE WAITING AT *FOUR PLACES* AT ONCE!
CONNECT THOSE FOUR PLACES IN THE ORDER THE NUMBERS WERE WRITTEN...

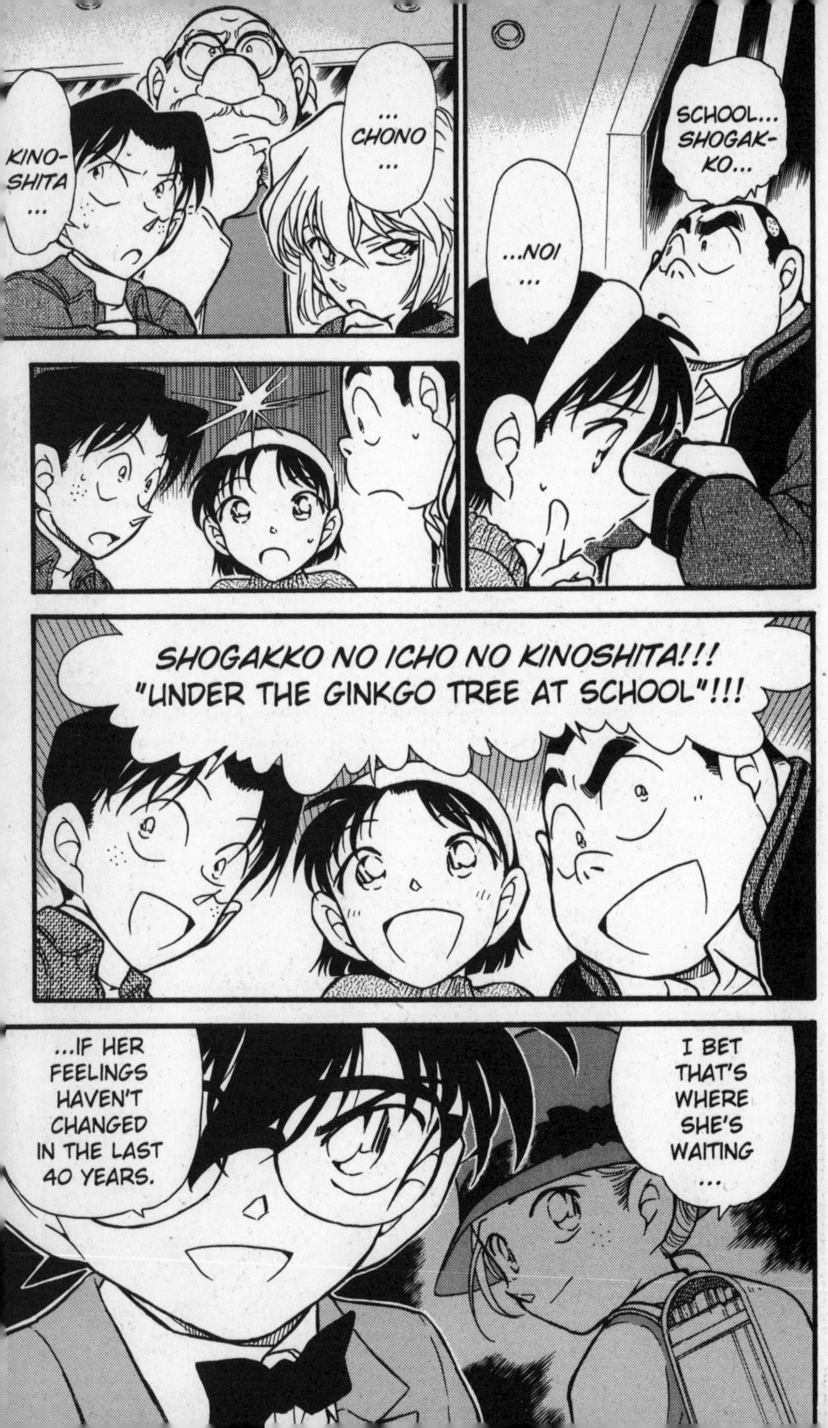
SCHOOL... SHOGAK-KO...
...NOI...
... CHONO ...
KINO-SHITA ...
SHOGAKKO NO ICHO NO KINOSHITA!!! "UNDER THE GINKGO TREE AT SCHOOL"!!!
I BET THAT'S WHERE SHE'S WAITING ...
...IF HER FEELINGS HAVEN'T CHANGED IN THE LAST 40 YEARS.

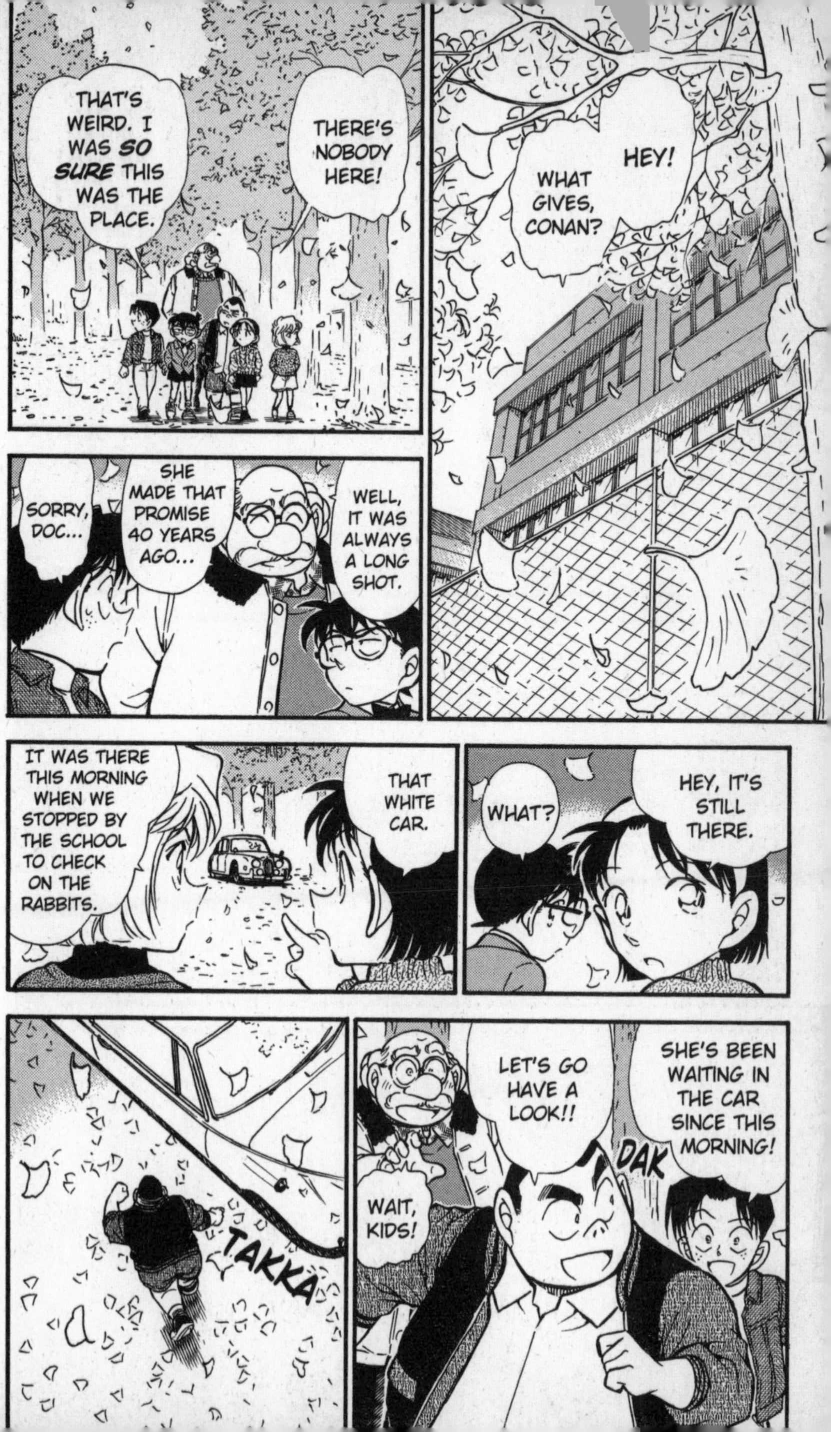
HEY!
WHAT GIVES, CONAN?
THERE'S NOBODY HERE!
THAT'S WEIRD. I WAS **SO SURE** THIS WAS THE PLACE.
WELL, IT WAS ALWAYS A LONG SHOT.
SHE MADE THAT PROMISE 40 YEARS AGO...
SORRY, DOC...
HEY, IT'S STILL THERE.
WHAT?
THAT WHITE CAR.
IT WAS THERE THIS MORNING WHEN WE STOPPED BY THE SCHOOL TO CHECK ON THE RABBITS.
SHE'S BEEN WAITING IN THE CAR SINCE THIS MORNING!
DAK
LET'S GO HAVE A LOOK!!
WAIT, KIDS!
TAKKA

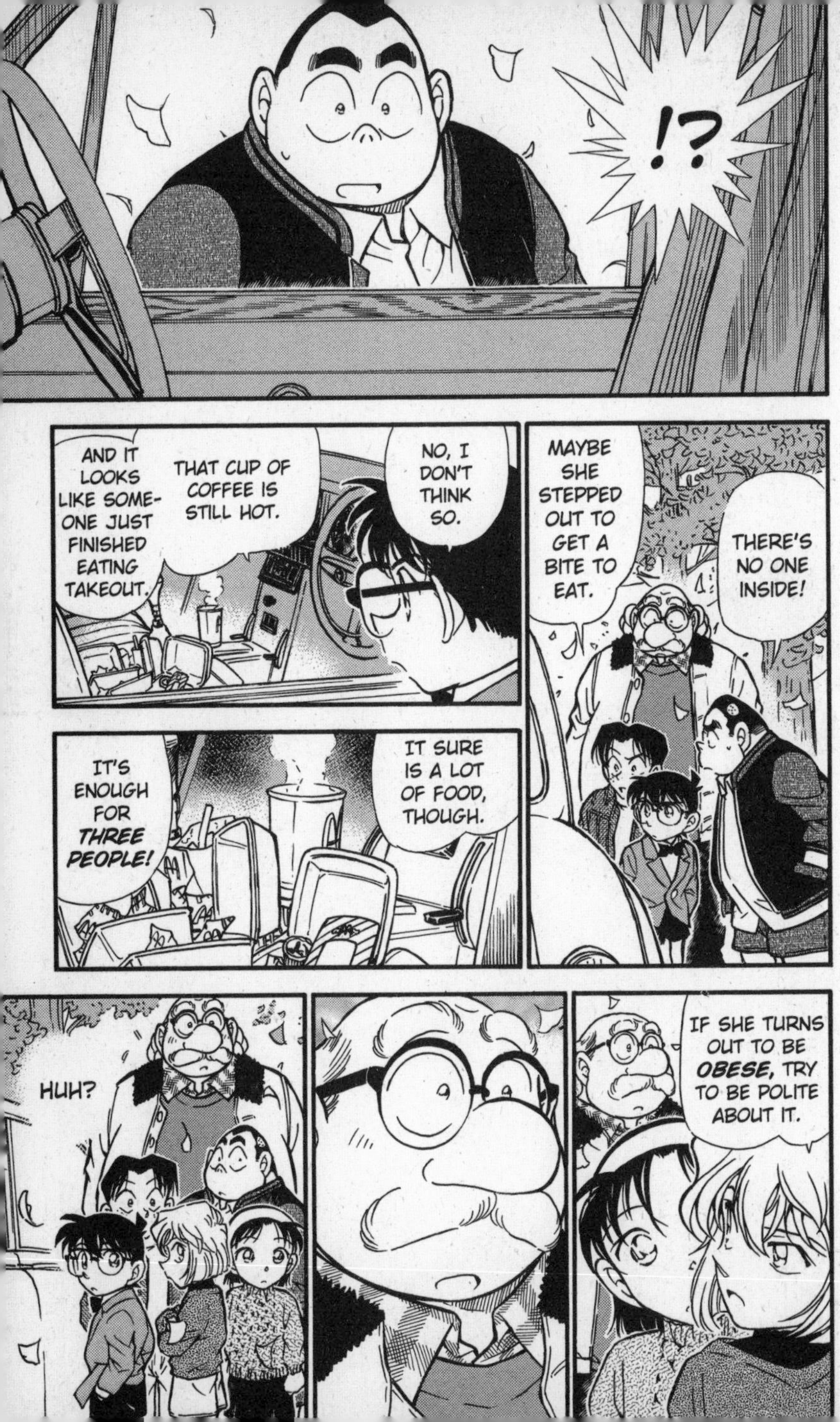
!?
THERE'S NO ONE INSIDE!
MAYBE SHE STEPPED OUT TO GET A BITE TO EAT.
NO, I DON'T THINK SO.
THAT CUP OF COFFEE IS STILL HOT.
AND IT LOOKS LIKE SOME-ONE JUST FINISHED EATING TAKEOUT.
IT SURE IS A LOT OF FOOD, THOUGH.
IT'S ENOUGH FOR THREE PEOPLE!
IF SHE TURNS OUT TO BE OBESE, TRY TO BE POLITE ABOUT IT.
HUH?

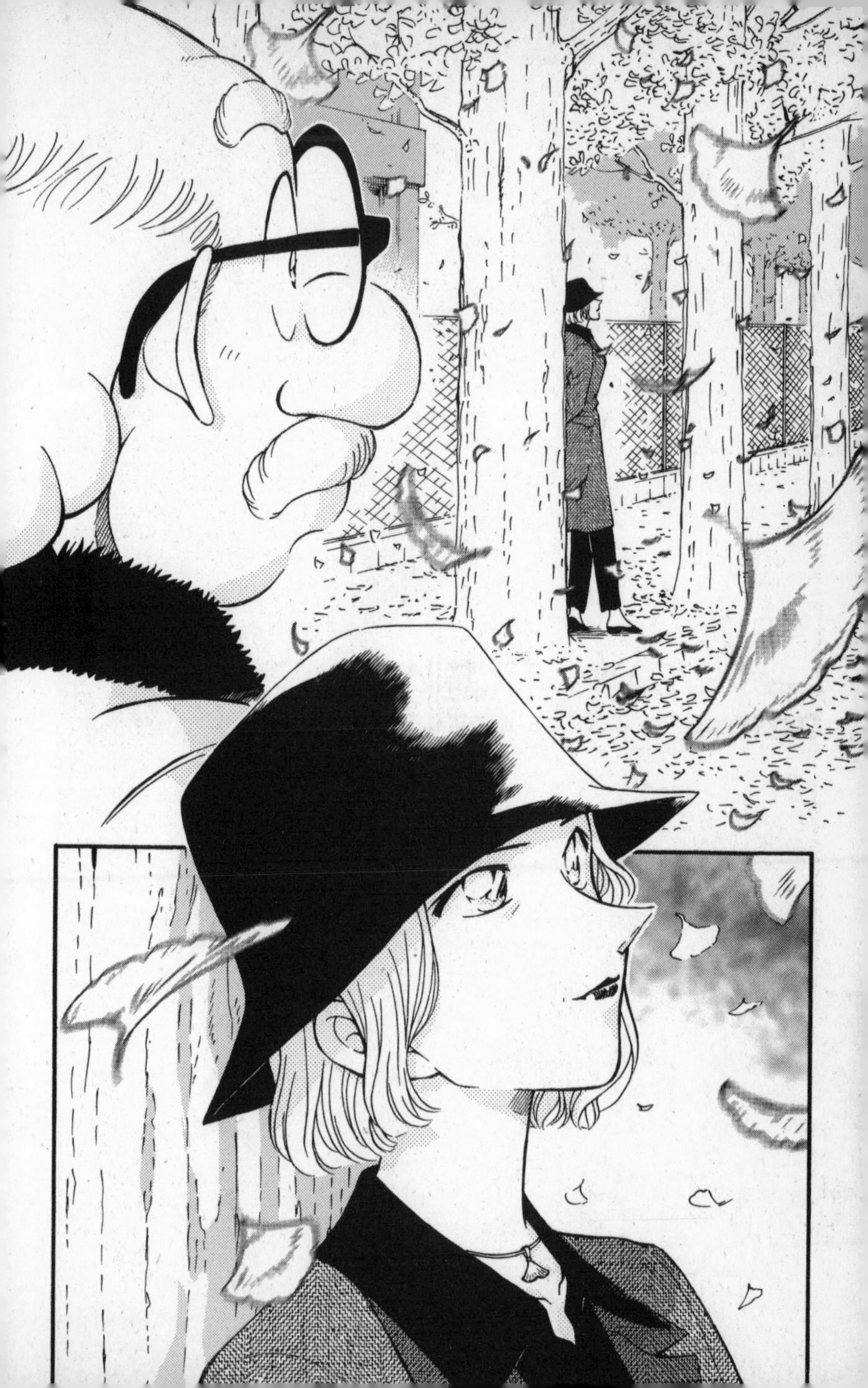

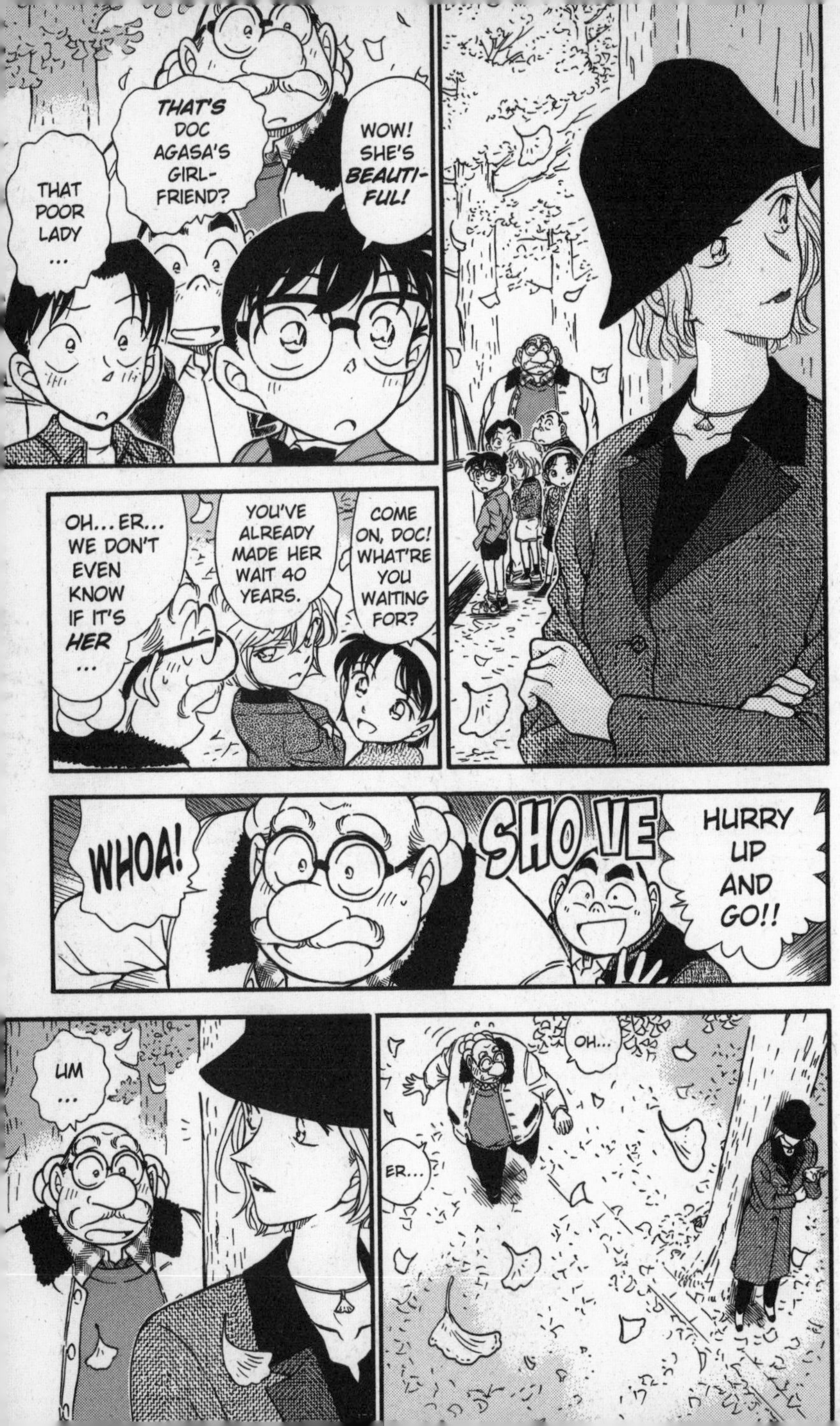
WOW! SHE'S *BEAUTIFUL!*
THAT'S DOC AGASA'S GIRLFRIEND?
THAT POOR LADY ...
COME ON, DOC! WHAT'RE YOU WAITING FOR?
YOU'VE ALREADY MADE HER WAIT 40 YEARS.
OH...ER... WE DON'T EVEN KNOW IF IT'S *HER* ...
HURRY UP AND GO!!
SHOVE
WHOA!
OH...
ER...
UM ...

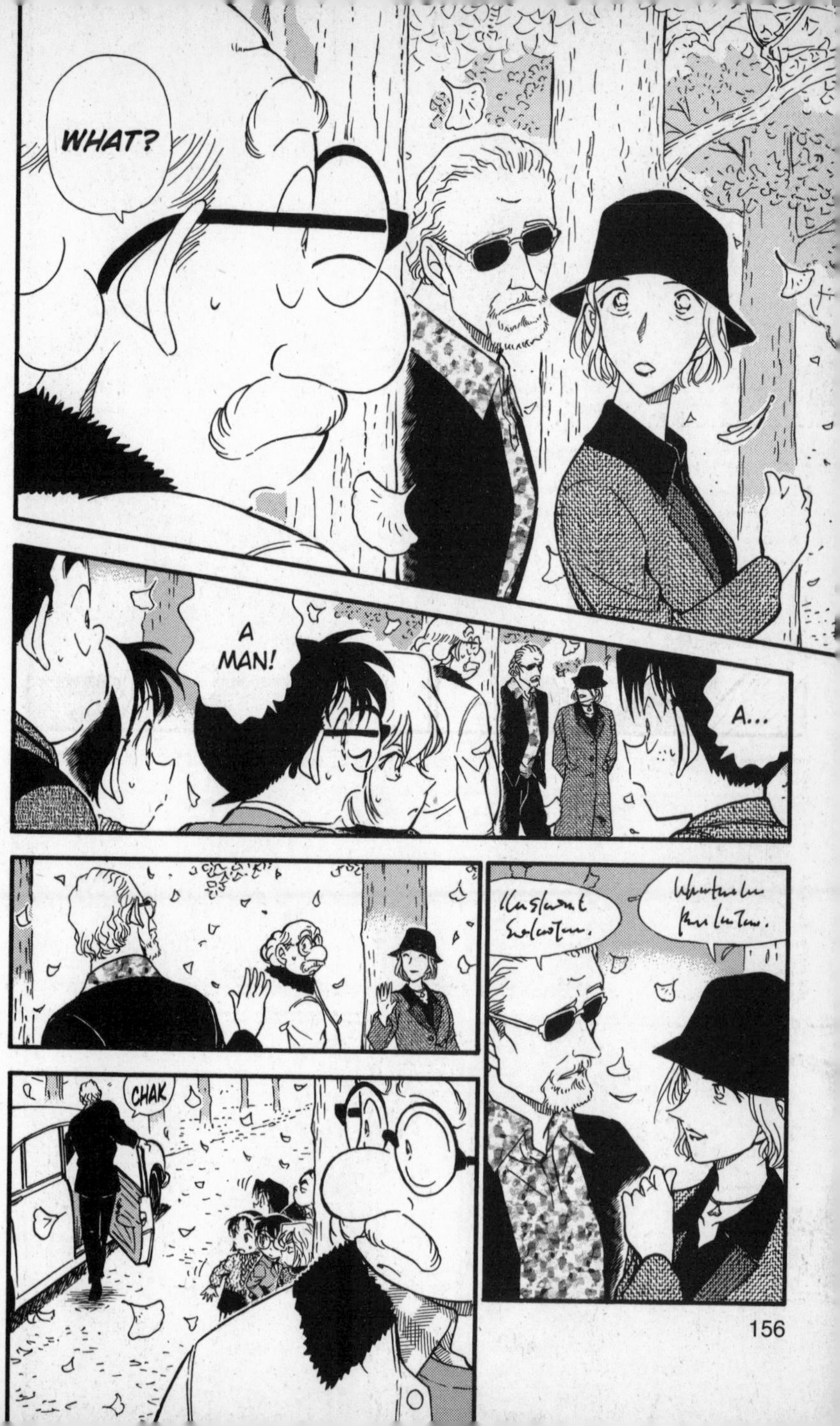
WHAT?
A...
A MAN!
CHAK

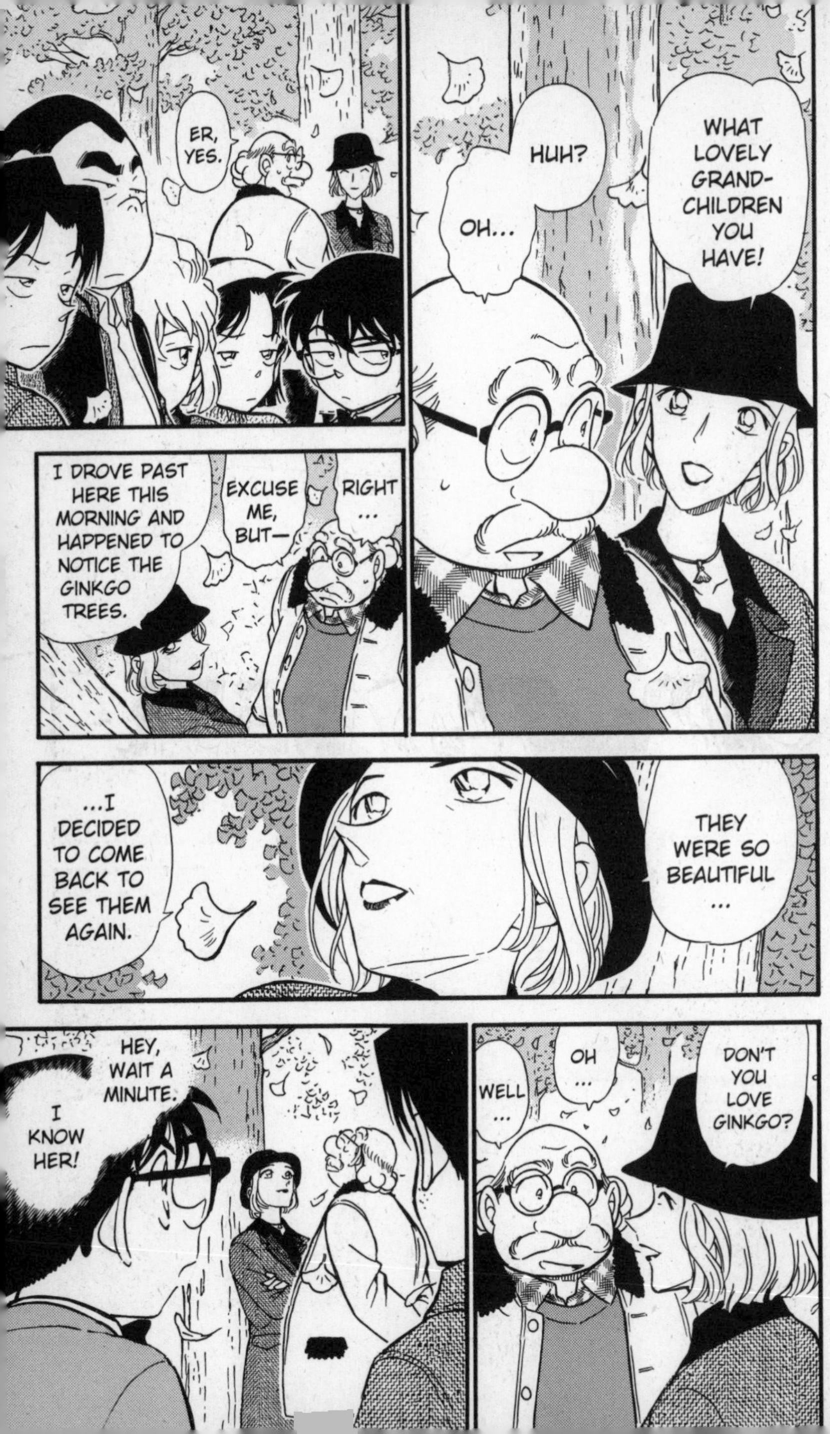
WHAT LOVELY GRAND-CHILDREN YOU HAVE!
HUH?
OH...
ER, YES.
RIGHT ...
EXCUSE ME, BUT—
I DROVE PAST HERE THIS MORNING AND HAPPENED TO NOTICE THE GINKGO TREES.
THEY WERE SO BEAUTIFUL ...
...I DECIDED TO COME BACK TO SEE THEM AGAIN.
DON'T YOU LOVE GINKGO?
OH ...
WELL ...
HEY, WAIT A MINUTE.
I KNOW HER!

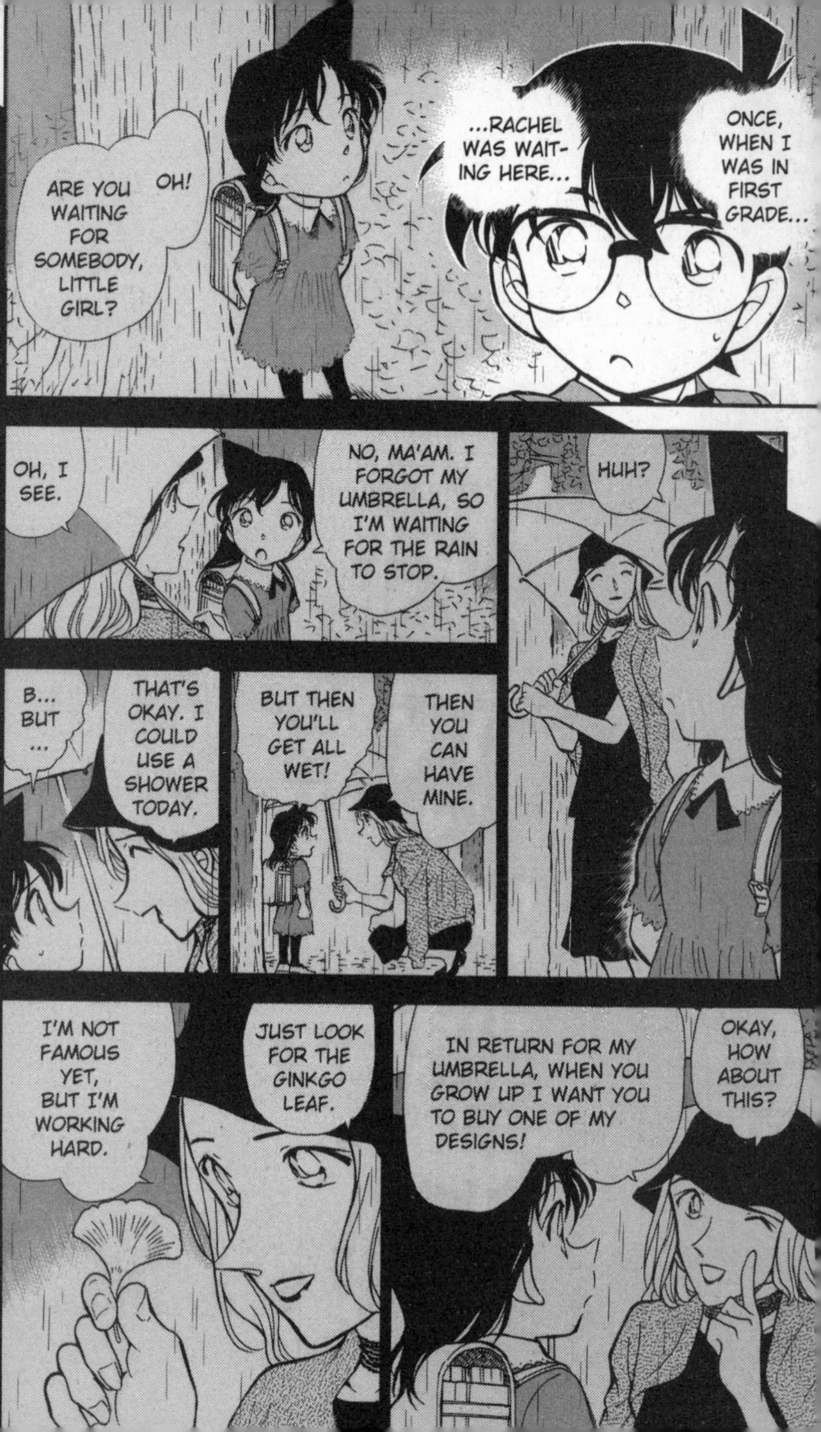
ONCE, WHEN I WAS IN FIRST GRADE...
...RACHEL WAS WAITING HERE...
OH!
ARE YOU WAITING FOR SOMEBODY, LITTLE GIRL?
HUH?
NO, MA'AM. I FORGOT MY UMBRELLA, SO I'M WAITING FOR THE RAIN TO STOP.
OH, I SEE.
THEN YOU CAN HAVE MINE.
BUT THEN YOU'LL GET ALL WET!
THAT'S OKAY. I COULD USE A SHOWER TODAY.
B... BUT ...
OKAY, HOW ABOUT THIS?
IN RETURN FOR MY UMBRELLA, WHEN YOU GROW UP I WANT YOU TO BUY ONE OF MY DESIGNS!
JUST LOOK FOR THE GINKGO LEAF.
I'M NOT FAMOUS YET, BUT I'M WORKING HARD.

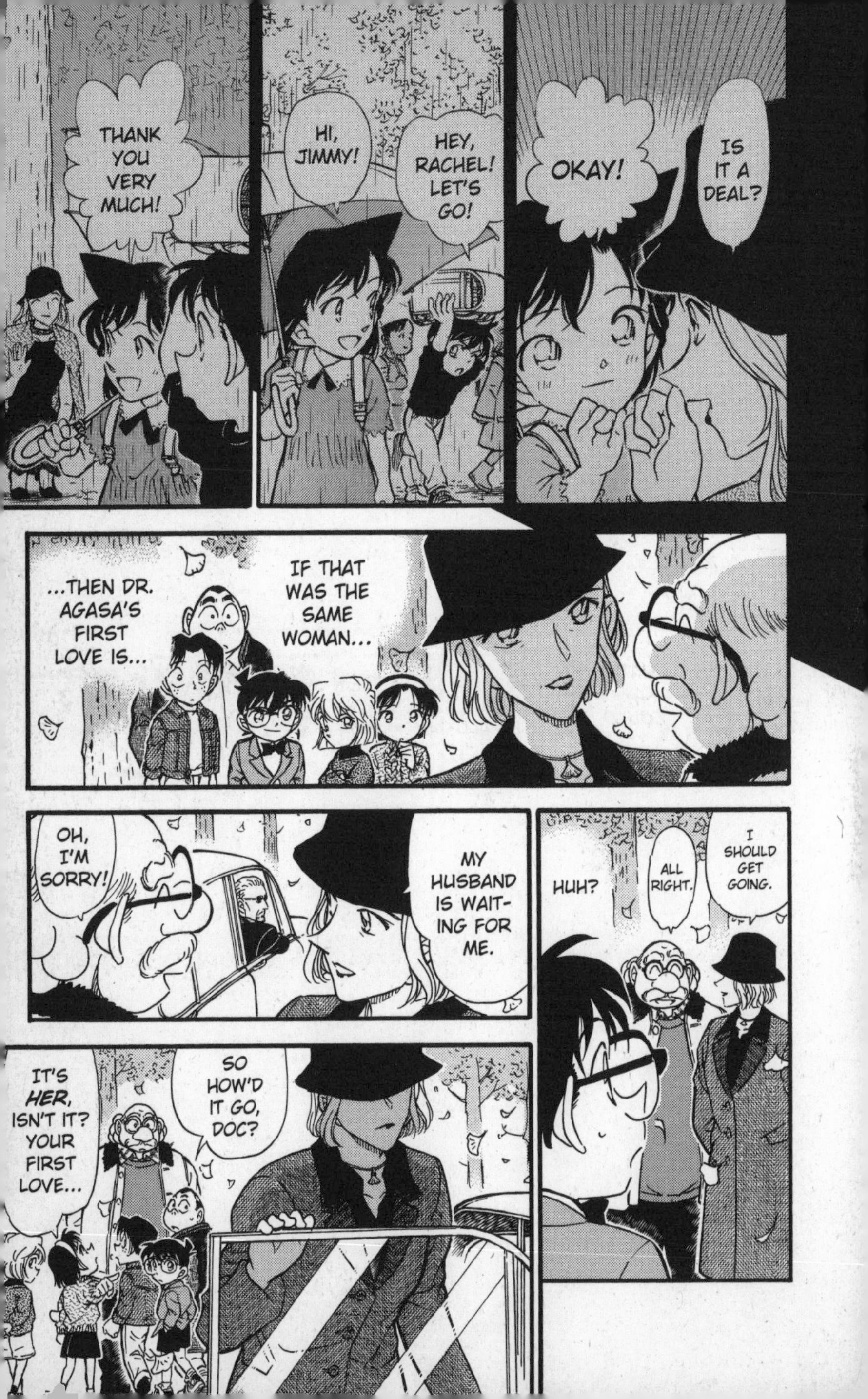
IS IT A DEAL?
OKAY!
HEY, RACHEL! LET'S GO!
HI, JIMMY!
THANK YOU VERY MUCH!
IF THAT WAS THE SAME WOMAN...
...THEN DR. AGASA'S FIRST LOVE IS...
I SHOULD GET GOING.
ALL RIGHT.
HUH?
MY HUSBAND IS WAIT-ING FOR ME.
OH, I'M SORRY!
SO HOW'D IT GO, DOC?
IT'S *HER*, ISN'T IT? YOUR FIRST LOVE...

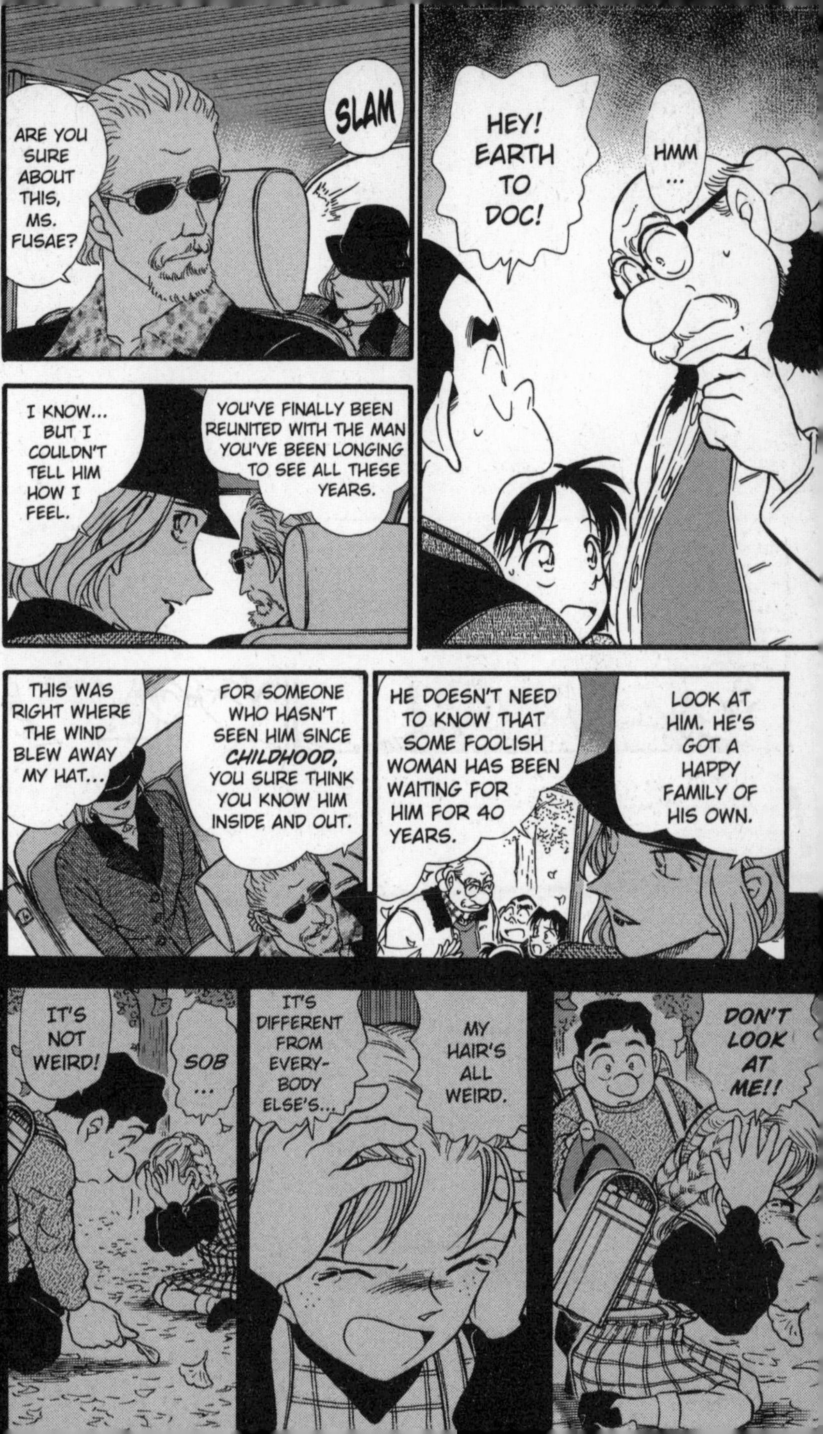
HMM ...
HEY! EARTH TO DOC!
SLAM
ARE YOU SURE ABOUT THIS, MS. FUSAE?
YOU'VE FINALLY BEEN REUNITED WITH THE MAN YOU'VE BEEN LONGING TO SEE ALL THESE YEARS.
I KNOW... BUT I COULDN'T TELL HIM HOW I FEEL.
LOOK AT HIM. HE'S GOT A HAPPY FAMILY OF HIS OWN.
HE DOESN'T NEED TO KNOW THAT SOME FOOLISH WOMAN HAS BEEN WAITING FOR HIM FOR 40 YEARS.
FOR SOMEONE WHO HASN'T SEEN HIM SINCE *CHILDHOOD,* YOU SURE THINK YOU KNOW HIM INSIDE AND OUT.
THIS WAS RIGHT WHERE THE WIND BLEW AWAY MY HAT...
DON'T LOOK AT ME!!
MY HAIR'S ALL WEIRD.
IT'S DIFFERENT FROM EVERY-BODY ELSE'S...
SOB ...
IT'S NOT WEIRD!

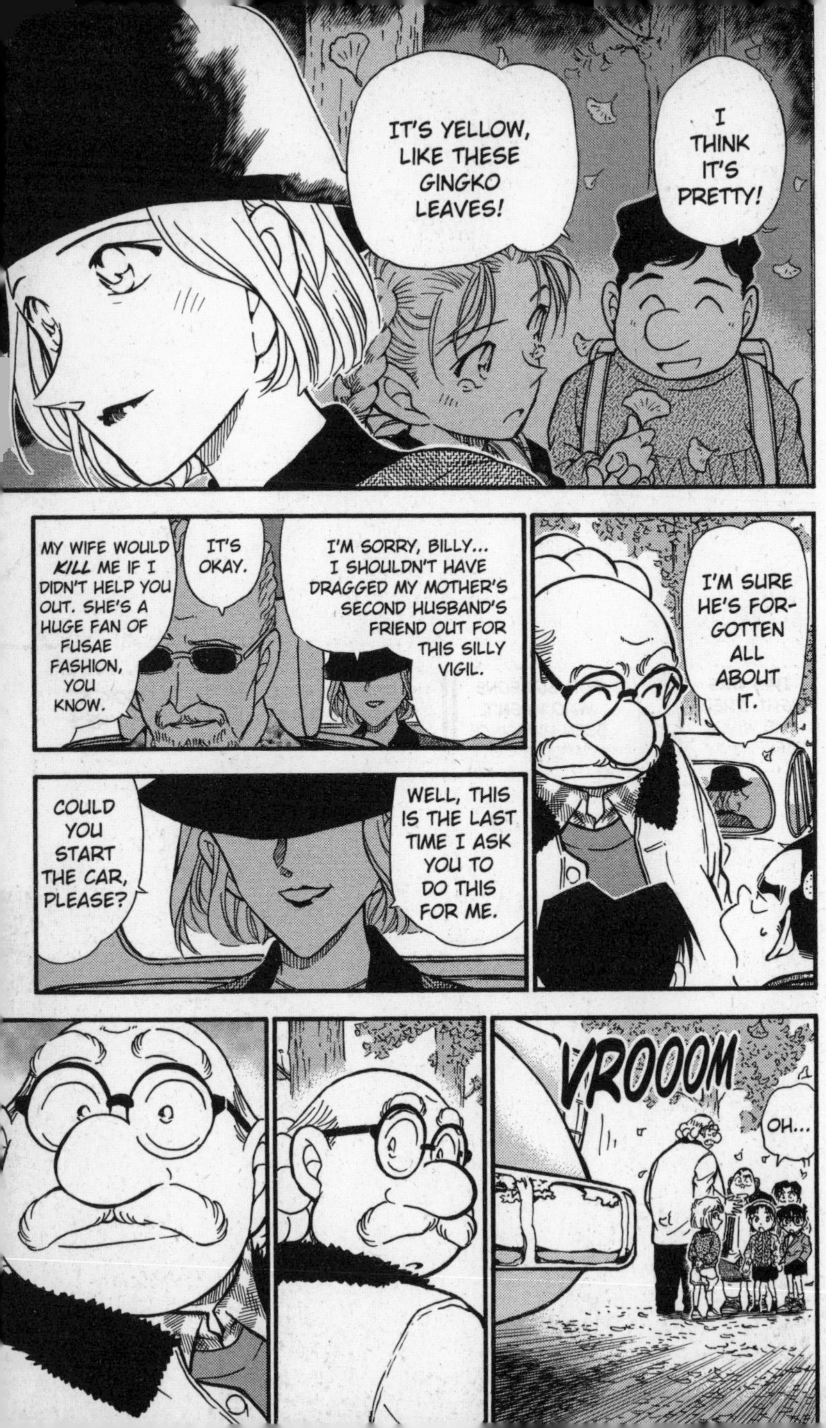
I THINK IT'S PRETTY!
IT'S YELLOW, LIKE THESE GINGKO LEAVES!
I'M SURE HE'S FOR-GOTTEN ALL ABOUT IT.
I'M SORRY, BILLY... I SHOULDN'T HAVE DRAGGED MY MOTHER'S SECOND HUSBAND'S FRIEND OUT FOR THIS SILLY VIGIL.
IT'S OKAY.
MY WIFE WOULD *KILL* ME IF I DIDN'T HELP YOU OUT. SHE'S A HUGE FAN OF FUSAE FASHION, YOU KNOW.
WELL, THIS IS THE LAST TIME I ASK YOU TO DO THIS FOR ME.
COULD YOU START THE CAR, PLEASE?
VROOOM
OH...

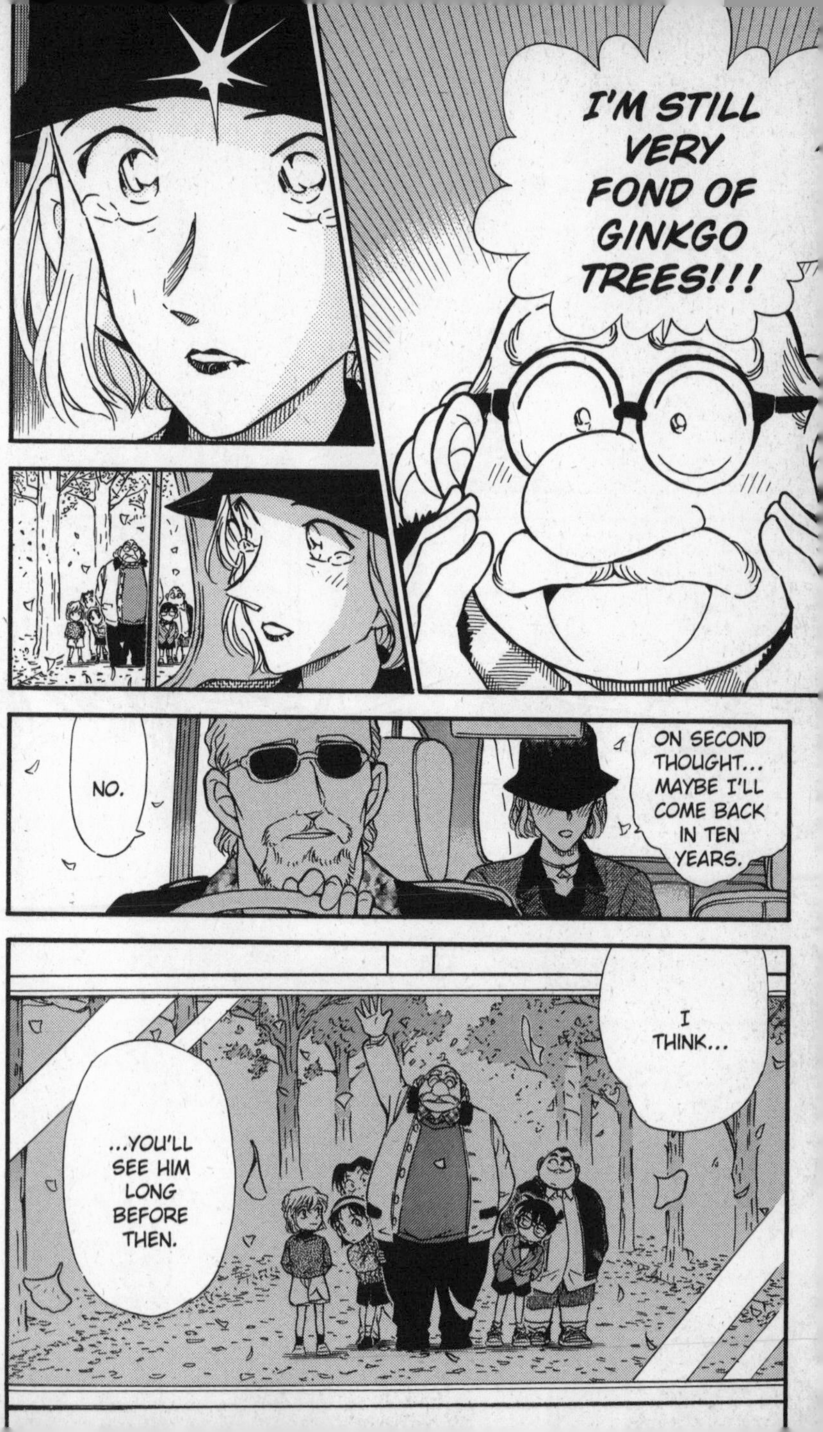
I'M STILL VERY FOND OF GINKGO TREES!!!
ON SECOND THOUGHT... MAYBE I'LL COME BACK IN TEN YEARS.
NO.
I THINK...
...YOU'LL SEE HIM LONG BEFORE THEN.

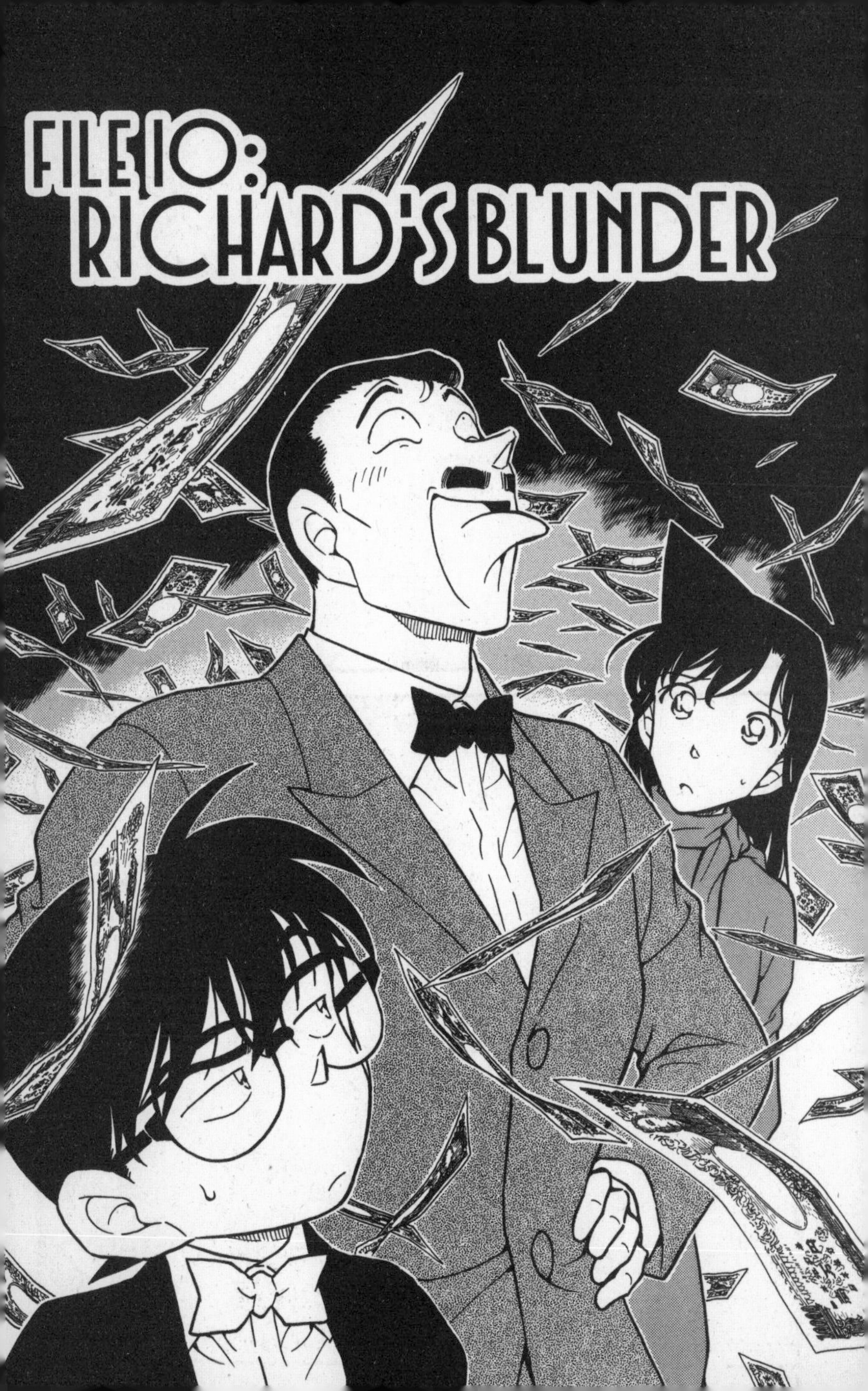
FILE 10:
RICHARD'S BLUNDER

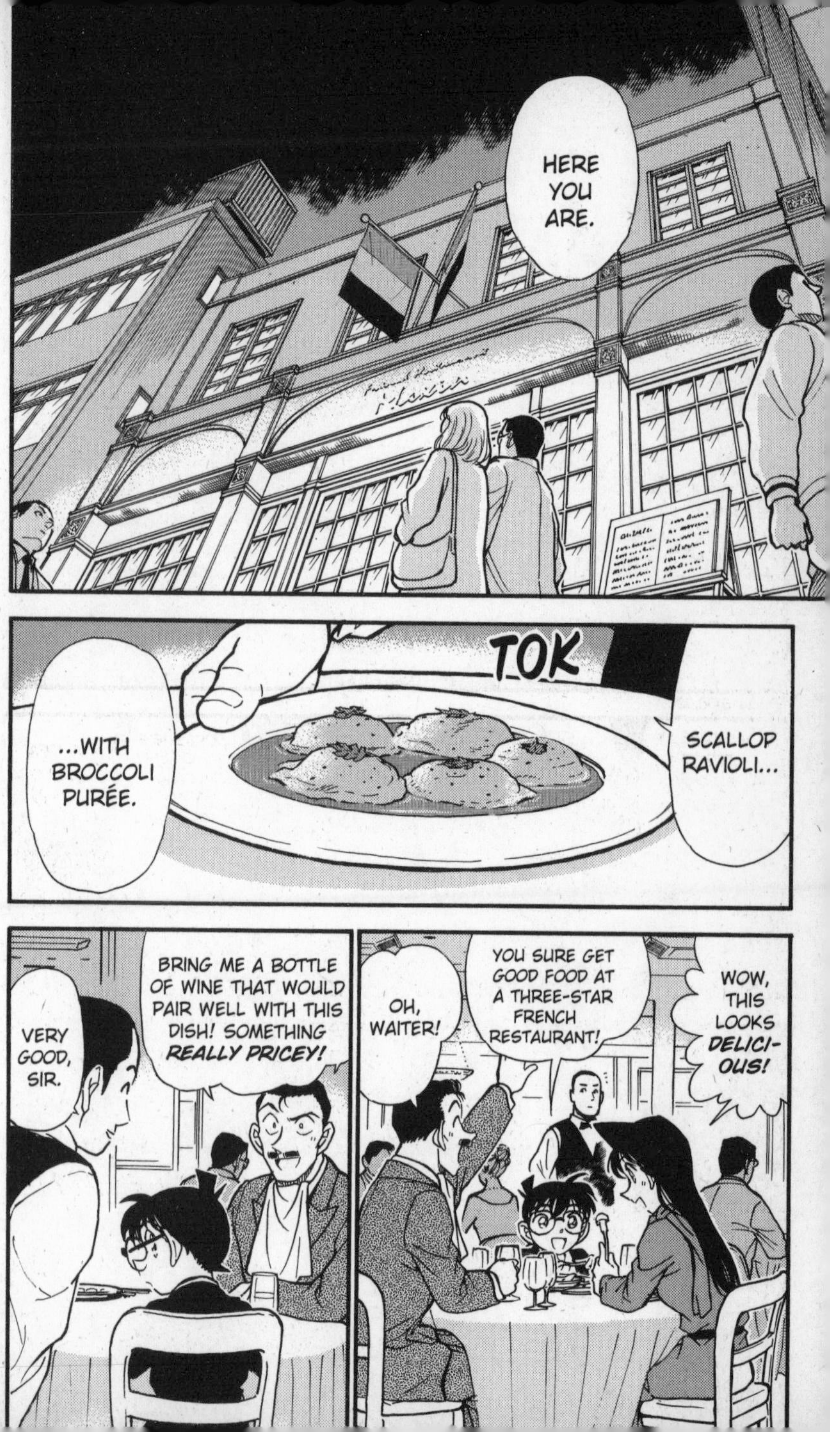
HERE YOU ARE.
TOK
SCALLOP RAVIOLI...
...WITH BROCCOLI PURÉE.
WOW, THIS LOOKS DELICIOUS!
YOU SURE GET GOOD FOOD AT A THREE-STAR FRENCH RESTAURANT!
OH, WAITER!
BRING ME A BOTTLE OF WINE THAT WOULD PAIR WELL WITH THIS DISH! SOMETHING REALLY PRICEY!
VERY GOOD, SIR.

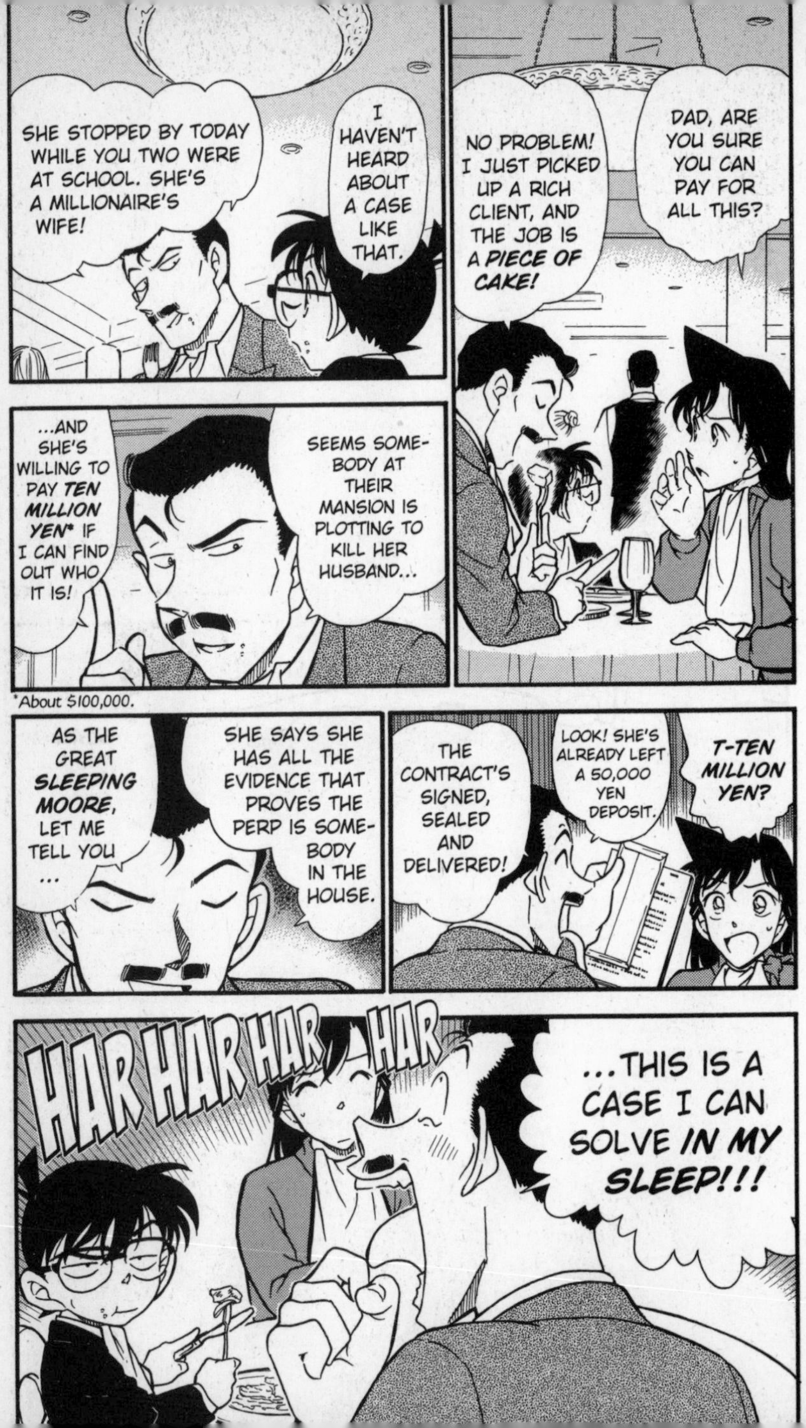
DAD, ARE YOU SURE YOU CAN PAY FOR ALL THIS?
NO PROBLEM! I JUST PICKED UP A RICH CLIENT, AND THE JOB IS A PIECE OF CAKE!
I HAVEN'T HEARD ABOUT A CASE LIKE THAT.
SHE STOPPED BY TODAY WHILE YOU TWO WERE AT SCHOOL. SHE'S A MILLIONAIRE'S WIFE!
SEEMS SOME-BODY AT THEIR MANSION IS PLOTTING TO KILL HER HUSBAND...
...AND SHE'S WILLING TO PAY TEN MILLION YEN* IF I CAN FIND OUT WHO IT IS!
T-TEN MILLION YEN?
LOOK! SHE'S ALREADY LEFT A 50,000 YEN DEPOSIT.
THE CONTRACT'S SIGNED, SEALED AND DELIVERED!
SHE SAYS SHE HAS ALL THE EVIDENCE THAT PROVES THE PERP IS SOME-BODY IN THE HOUSE.
AS THE GREAT SLEEPING MOORE, LET ME TELL YOU ...
...THIS IS A CASE I CAN SOLVE IN MY SLEEP!!!
HAR HAR HAR HAR

*About $100,000.

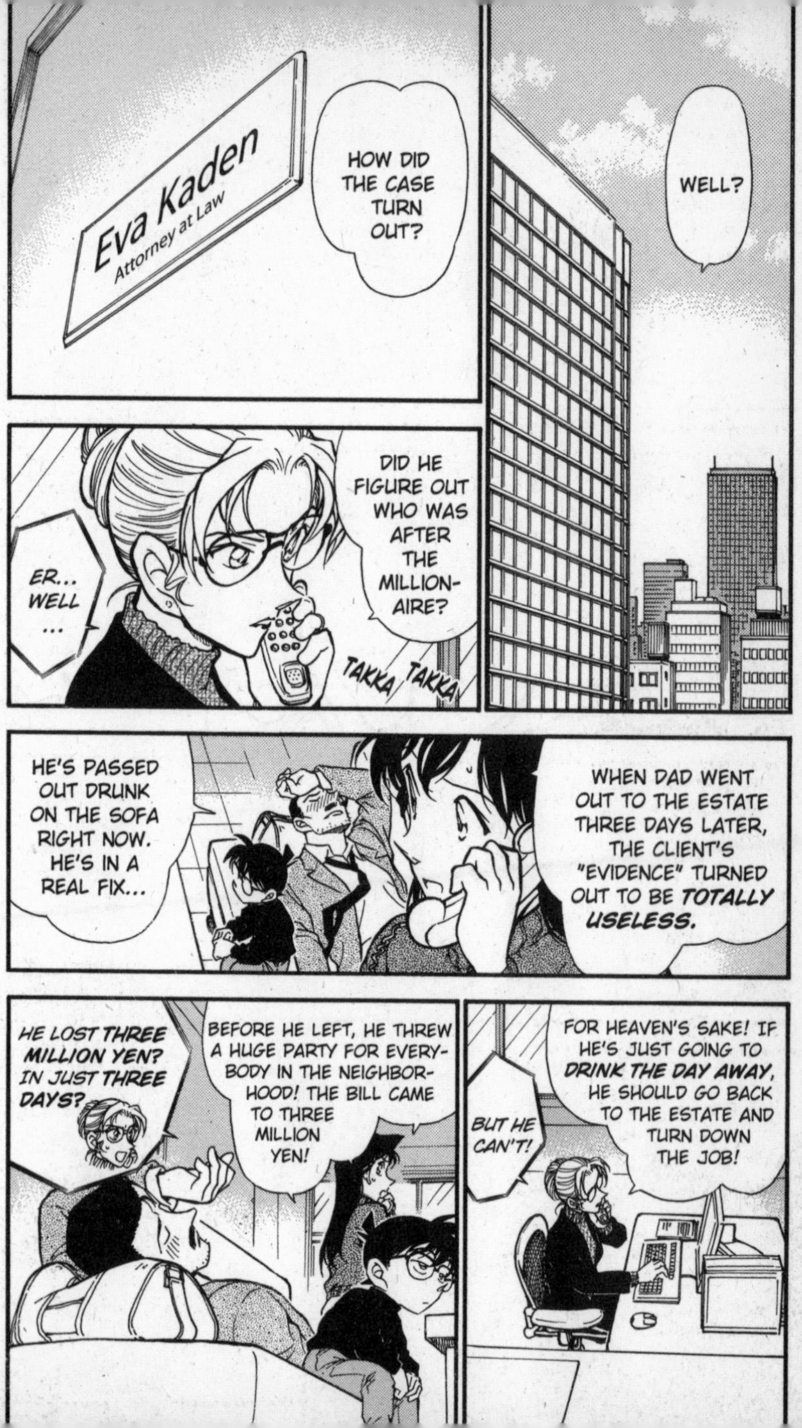
WELL?
Eva Kaden
Attorney at Law
HOW DID THE CASE TURN OUT?
DID HE FIGURE OUT WHO WAS AFTER THE MILLION-AIRE?
TAKKA TAKKA
ER... WELL...
WHEN DAD WENT OUT TO THE ESTATE THREE DAYS LATER, THE CLIENT'S "EVIDENCE" TURNED OUT TO BE TOTALLY USELESS.
HE'S PASSED OUT DRUNK ON THE SOFA RIGHT NOW. HE'S IN A REAL FIX...
FOR HEAVEN'S SAKE! IF HE'S JUST GOING TO DRINK THE DAY AWAY, HE SHOULD GO BACK TO THE ESTATE AND TURN DOWN THE JOB!
BUT HE CAN'T!
BEFORE HE LEFT, HE THREW A HUGE PARTY FOR EVERY-BODY IN THE NEIGHBOR-HOOD! THE BILL CAME TO THREE MILLION YEN!
HE LOST THREE MILLION YEN? IN JUST THREE DAYS?

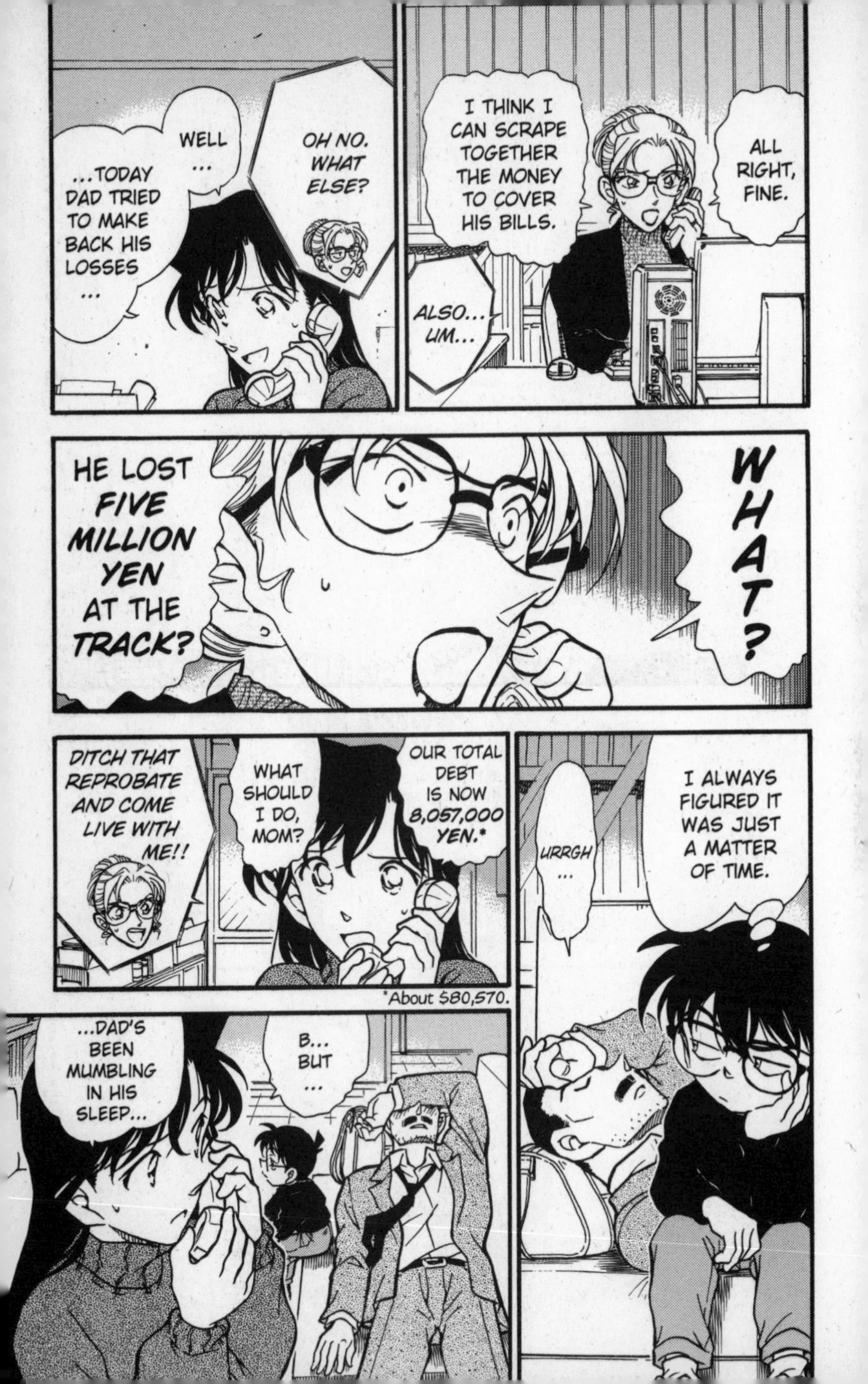
ALL RIGHT, FINE.
I THINK I CAN SCRAPE TOGETHER THE MONEY TO COVER HIS BILLS.
ALSO... UM...
OH NO. WHAT ELSE?
WELL ...
...TODAY DAD TRIED TO MAKE BACK HIS LOSSES ...
WHAT?
HE LOST FIVE MILLION YEN AT THE TRACK?
I ALWAYS FIGURED IT WAS JUST A MATTER OF TIME.
URRGH ...
OUR TOTAL DEBT IS NOW 8,057,000 YEN.*
WHAT SHOULD I DO, MOM?
DITCH THAT REPROBATE AND COME LIVE WITH ME!!
B... BUT ...
...DAD'S BEEN MUMBLING IN HIS SLEEP...
*About $80,570.

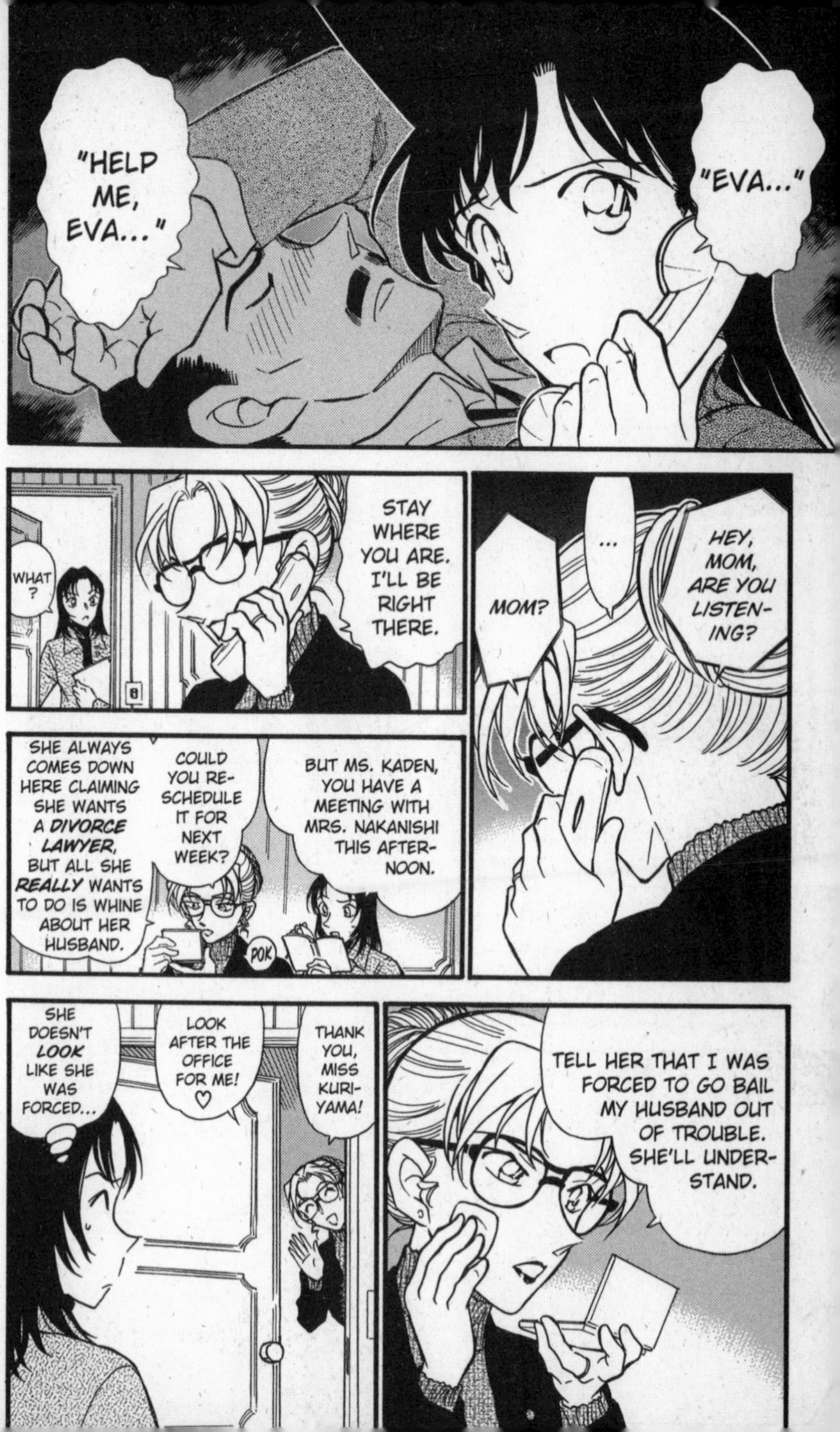
"EVA..."
"HELP ME, EVA..."
HEY, MOM, ARE YOU LISTENING?
...
MOM?
STAY WHERE YOU ARE. I'LL BE RIGHT THERE.
WHAT?
BUT MS. KADEN, YOU HAVE A MEETING WITH MRS. NAKANISHI THIS AFTERNOON.
COULD YOU RESCHEDULE IT FOR NEXT WEEK?
SHE ALWAYS COMES DOWN HERE CLAIMING SHE WANTS A *DIVORCE LAWYER*, BUT ALL SHE *REALLY* WANTS TO DO IS WHINE ABOUT HER HUSBAND.
POK
TELL HER THAT I WAS FORCED TO GO BAIL MY HUSBAND OUT OF TROUBLE. SHE'LL UNDERSTAND.
THANK YOU, MISS KURIYAMA!
LOOK AFTER THE OFFICE FOR ME! ♡
SHE DOESN'T **LOOK** LIKE SHE WAS FORCED...

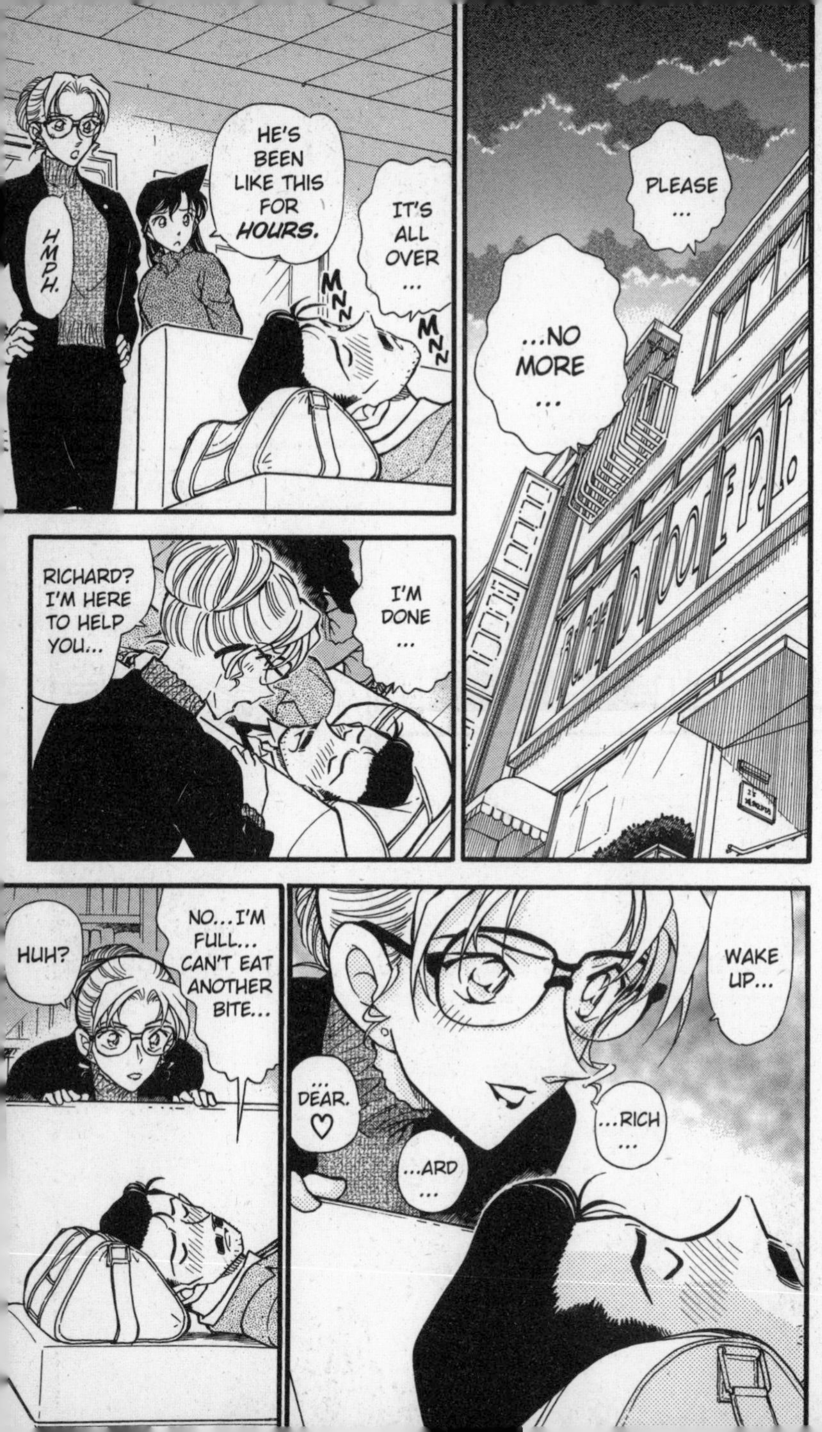
PLEASE...
...NO MORE...
IT'S ALL OVER...
MNN MNN
HE'S BEEN LIKE THIS FOR **HOURS.**
HMPH.
I'M DONE...
RICHARD? I'M HERE TO HELP YOU...
WAKE UP...
...RICH...
...ARD...
...DEAR. ♥
NO... I'M FULL... CAN'T EAT ANOTHER BITE...
HUH?

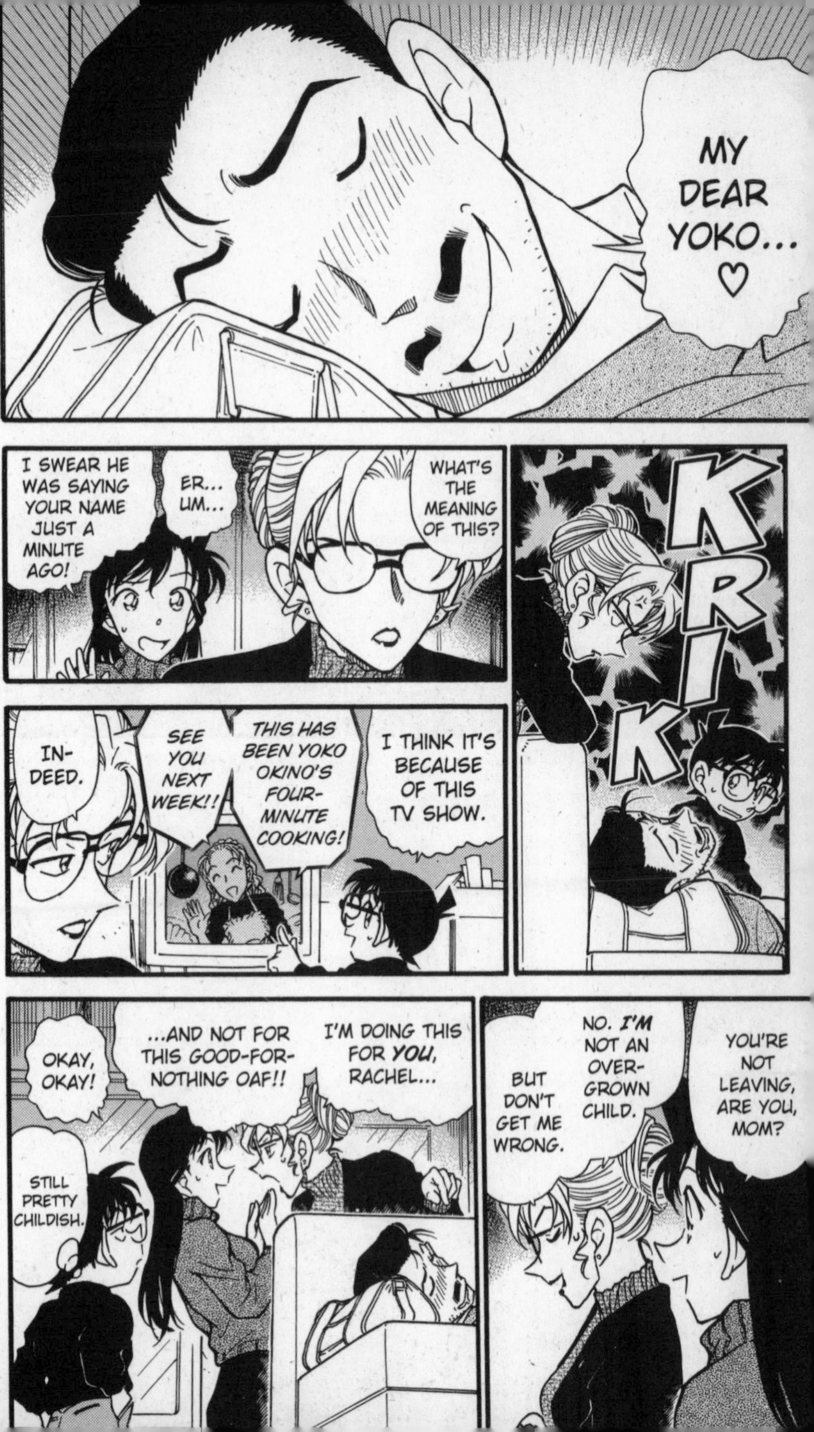
MY DEAR YOKO... ♡
KRIK
WHAT'S THE MEANING OF THIS?
ER... UM...
I SWEAR HE WAS SAYING YOUR NAME JUST A MINUTE AGO!
I THINK IT'S BECAUSE OF THIS TV SHOW.
THIS HAS BEEN YOKO OKINO'S FOUR-MINUTE COOKING!
SEE YOU NEXT WEEK!!
IN-DEED.
YOU'RE NOT LEAVING, ARE YOU, MOM?
NO. *I'M* NOT AN OVER-GROWN CHILD.
BUT DON'T GET ME WRONG.
I'M DOING THIS FOR *YOU*, RACHEL...
...AND NOT FOR THIS GOOD-FOR-NOTHING OAF!!
OKAY, OKAY!
STILL PRETTY CHILDISH.

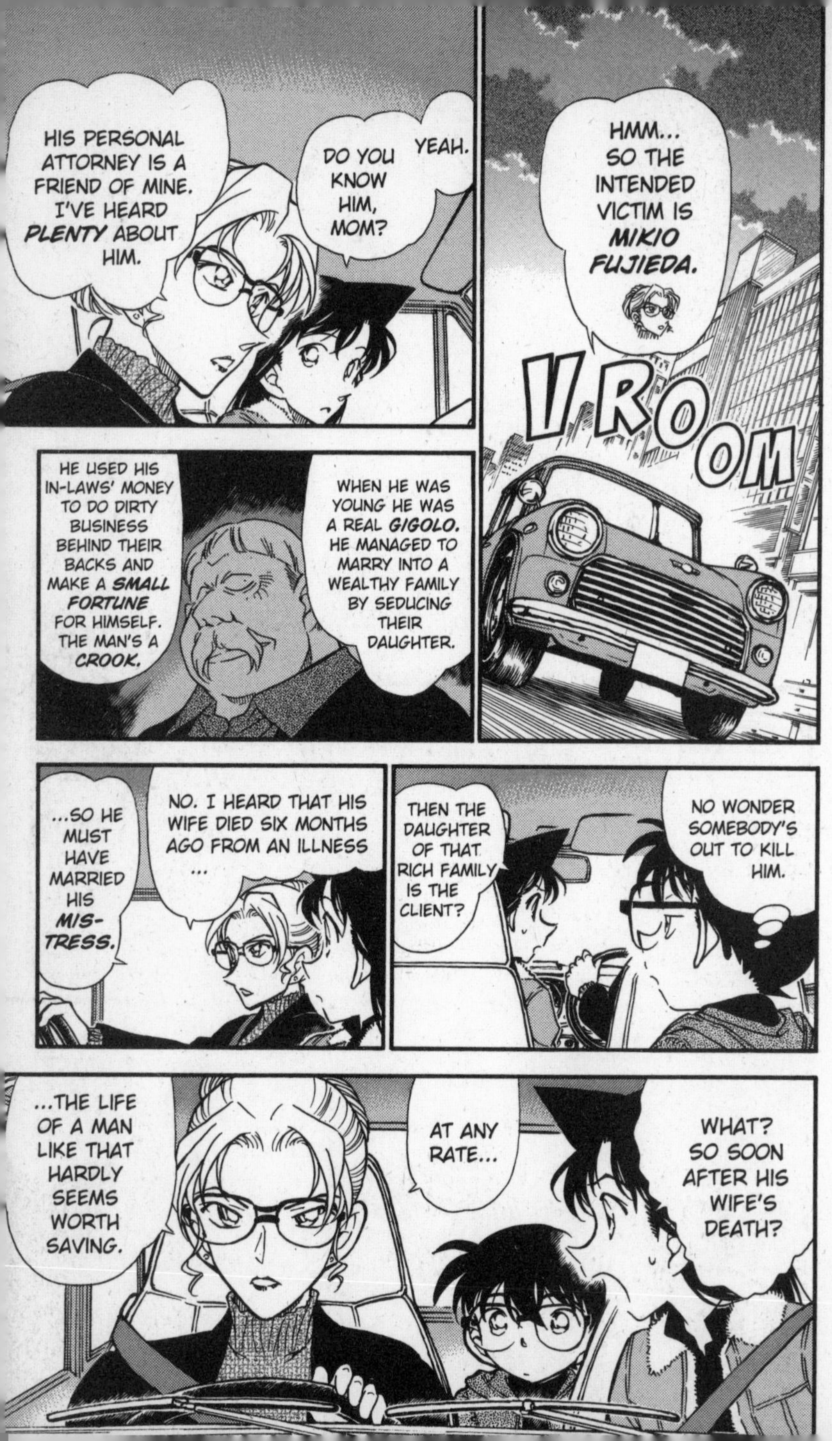
HMM... SO THE INTENDED VICTIM IS **MIKIO FUJIEDA.**
VROOM
YEAH.
DO YOU KNOW HIM, MOM?
HIS PERSONAL ATTORNEY IS A FRIEND OF MINE. I'VE HEARD **PLENTY** ABOUT HIM.
WHEN HE WAS YOUNG HE WAS A REAL **GIGOLO.** HE MANAGED TO MARRY INTO A WEALTHY FAMILY BY SEDUCING THEIR DAUGHTER.
HE USED HIS IN-LAWS' MONEY TO DO DIRTY BUSINESS BEHIND THEIR BACKS AND MAKE A **SMALL FORTUNE** FOR HIMSELF. THE MAN'S A **CROOK.**
NO WONDER SOMEBODY'S OUT TO KILL HIM.
THEN THE DAUGHTER OF THAT RICH FAMILY IS THE CLIENT?
NO. I HEARD THAT HIS WIFE DIED SIX MONTHS AGO FROM AN ILLNESS ...
...SO HE MUST HAVE MARRIED HIS **MIS-TRESS.**
WHAT? SO SOON AFTER HIS WIFE'S DEATH?
AT ANY RATE...
...THE LIFE OF A MAN LIKE THAT HARDLY SEEMS WORTH SAVING.

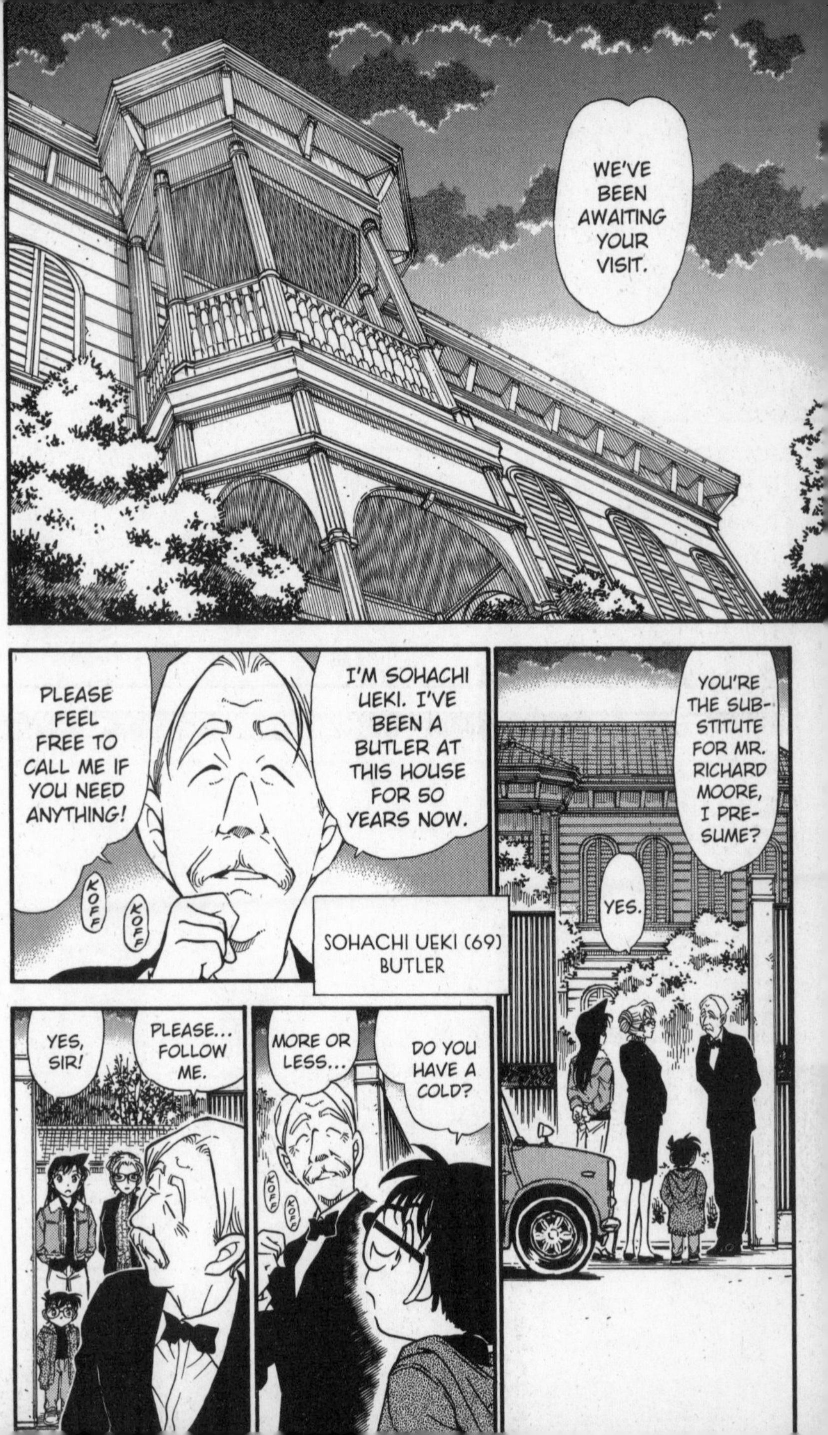
WE'VE BEEN AWAITING YOUR VISIT.
YOU'RE THE SUB-STITUTE FOR MR. RICHARD MOORE, I PRE-SUME?
YES.
I'M SOHACHI UEKI. I'VE BEEN A BUTLER AT THIS HOUSE FOR 50 YEARS NOW.
SOHACHI UEKI (69) BUTLER
PLEASE FEEL FREE TO CALL ME IF YOU NEED ANYTHING!
KOFF
KOFF
DO YOU HAVE A COLD?
MORE OR LESS...
KOFF
KOFF
PLEASE... FOLLOW ME.
YES, SIR!

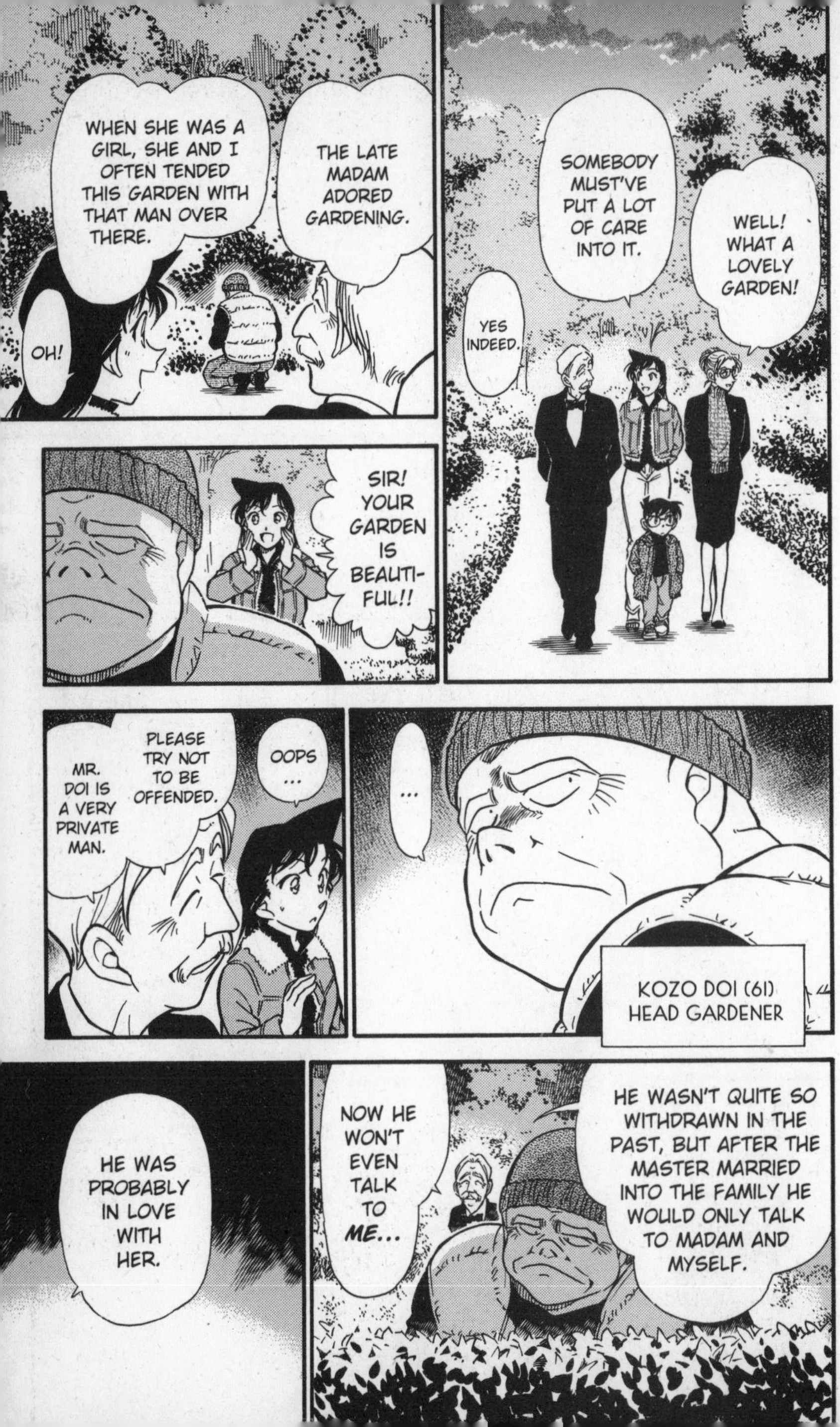
WELL! WHAT A LOVELY GARDEN!
SOMEBODY MUST'VE PUT A LOT OF CARE INTO IT.
YES INDEED.
THE LATE MADAM ADORED GARDENING.
WHEN SHE WAS A GIRL, SHE AND I OFTEN TENDED THIS GARDEN WITH THAT MAN OVER THERE.
OH!
SIR! YOUR GARDEN IS BEAUTIFUL!!
...
KOZO DOI (61) HEAD GARDENER
OOPS ...
PLEASE TRY NOT TO BE OFFENDED.
MR. DOI IS A VERY PRIVATE MAN.
HE WASN'T QUITE SO WITHDRAWN IN THE PAST, BUT AFTER THE MASTER MARRIED INTO THE FAMILY HE WOULD ONLY TALK TO MADAM AND MYSELF.
NOW HE WON'T EVEN TALK TO ME...
HE WAS PROBABLY IN LOVE WITH HER.

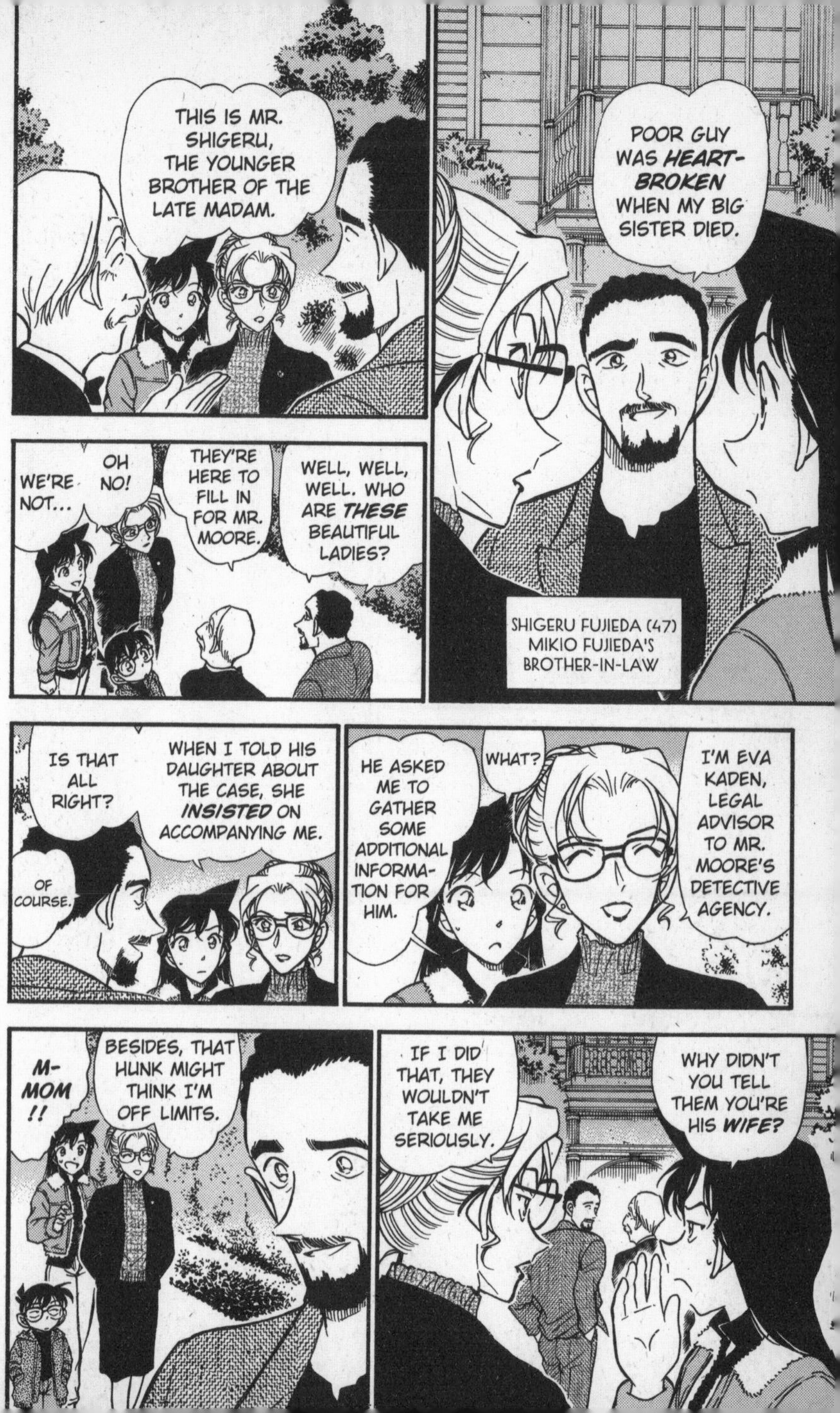
POOR GUY WAS **HEART-BROKEN** WHEN MY BIG SISTER DIED.
SHIGERU FUJIEDA (47) MIKIO FUJIEDA'S BROTHER-IN-LAW
THIS IS MR. SHIGERU, THE YOUNGER BROTHER OF THE LATE MADAM.
WELL, WELL, WELL. WHO ARE ***THESE*** BEAUTIFUL LADIES?
THEY'RE HERE TO FILL IN FOR MR. MOORE.
OH NO!
WE'RE NOT...
I'M EVA KADEN, LEGAL ADVISOR TO MR. MOORE'S DETECTIVE AGENCY.
WHAT?
HE ASKED ME TO GATHER SOME ADDITIONAL INFORMATION FOR HIM.
WHEN I TOLD HIS DAUGHTER ABOUT THE CASE, SHE ***INSISTED*** ON ACCOMPANYING ME.
IS THAT ALL RIGHT?
OF COURSE.
WHY DIDN'T YOU TELL THEM YOU'RE HIS ***WIFE?***
IF I DID THAT, THEY WOULDN'T TAKE ME SERIOUSLY.
BESIDES, THAT HUNK MIGHT THINK I'M OFF LIMITS.
M-MOM!!

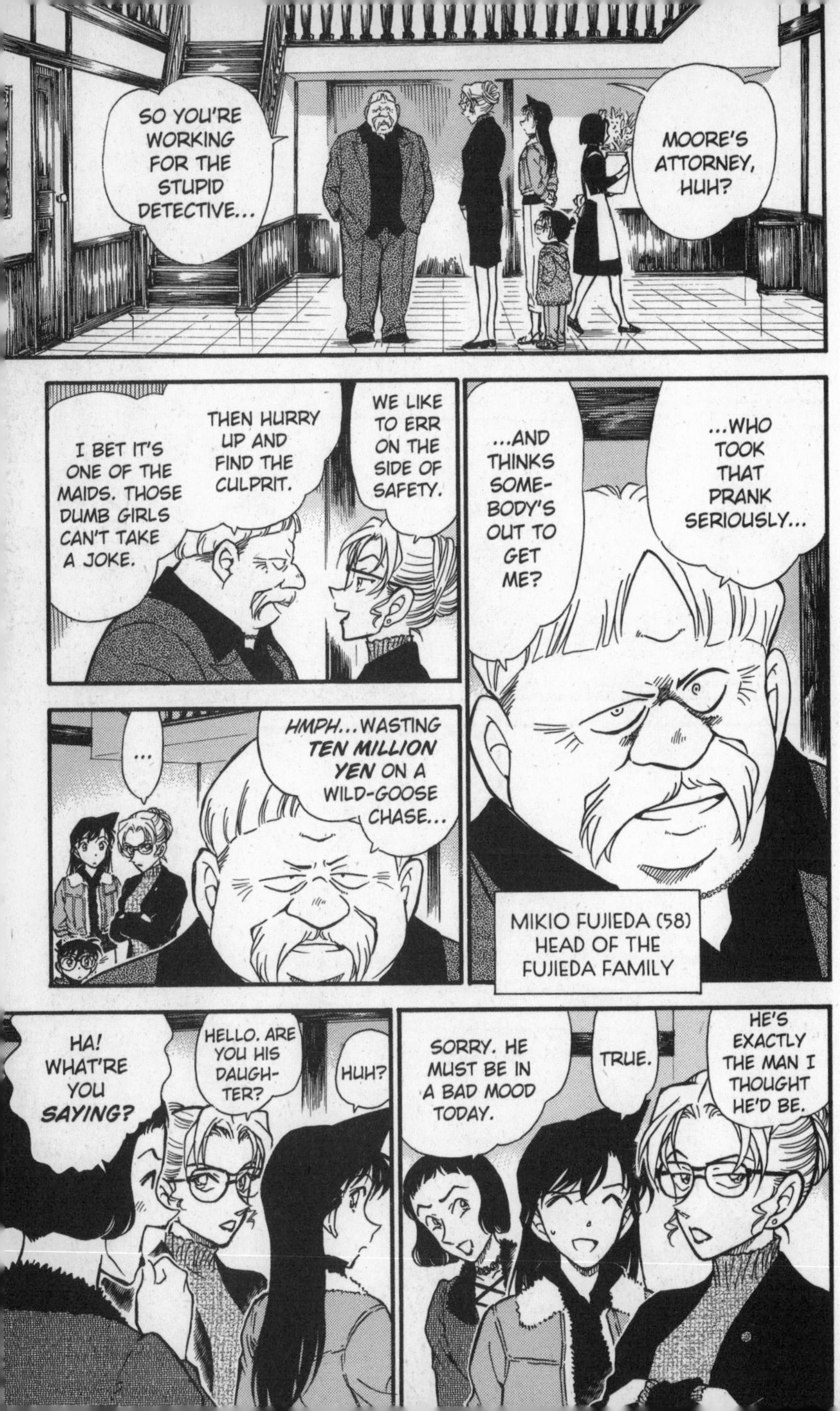
MOORE'S ATTORNEY, HUH?
SO YOU'RE WORKING FOR THE STUPID DETECTIVE...
...WHO TOOK THAT PRANK SERIOUSLY...
...AND THINKS SOMEBODY'S OUT TO GET ME?
MIKIO FUJIEDA (58) HEAD OF THE FUJIEDA FAMILY
WE LIKE TO ERR ON THE SIDE OF SAFETY.
THEN HURRY UP AND FIND THE CULPRIT.
I BET IT'S ONE OF THE MAIDS. THOSE DUMB GIRLS CAN'T TAKE A JOKE.
HMPH... WASTING TEN MILLION YEN ON A WILD-GOOSE CHASE...
...
HE'S EXACTLY THE MAN I THOUGHT HE'D BE.
TRUE.
SORRY. HE MUST BE IN A BAD MOOD TODAY.
HUH?
HELLO. ARE YOU HIS DAUGHTER?
HA! WHAT'RE YOU SAYING?

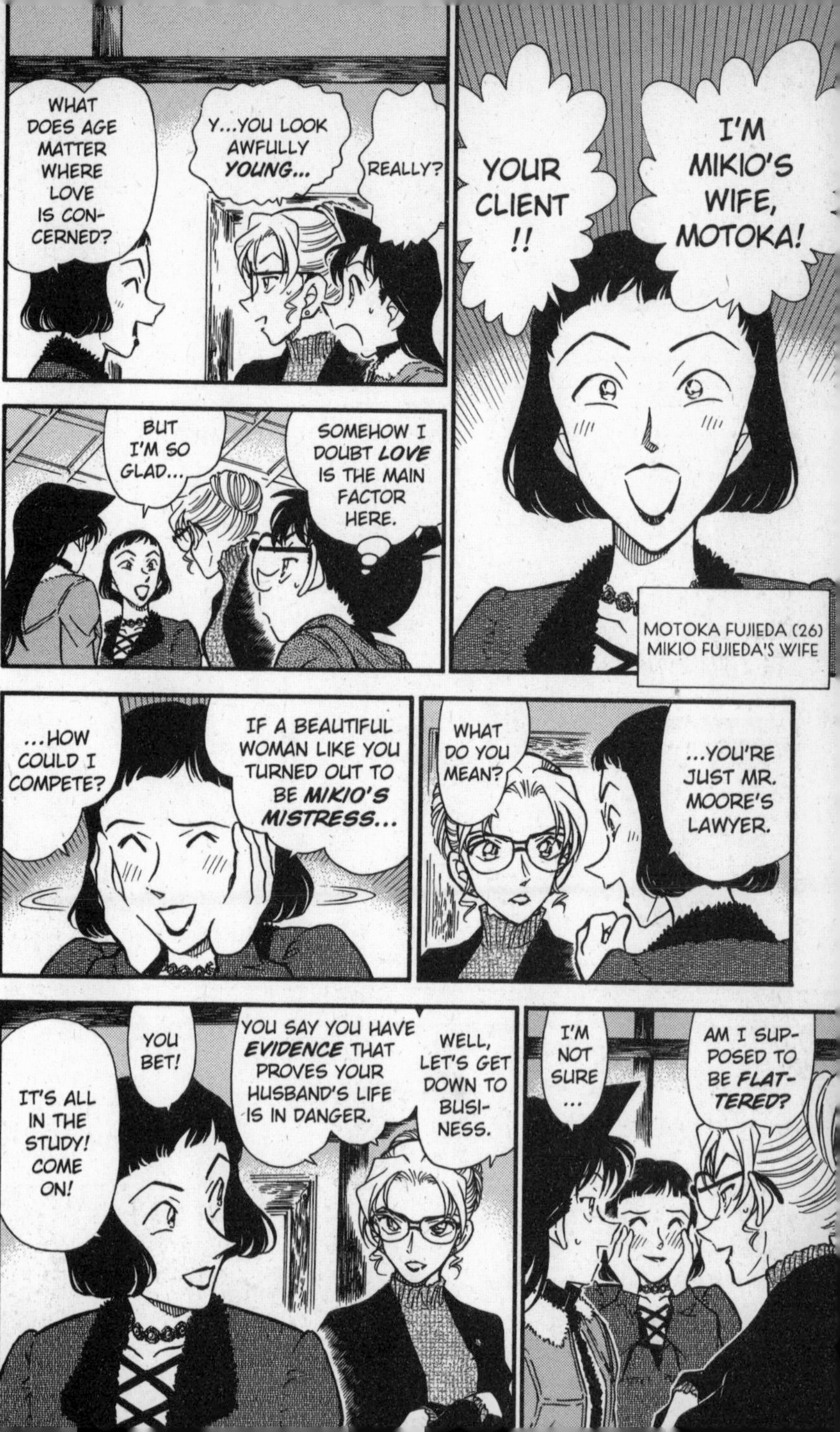
I'M MIKIO'S WIFE, MOTOKA!
YOUR CLIENT !!
MOTOKA FUJIEDA (26) MIKIO FUJIEDA'S WIFE
REALLY?
Y...YOU LOOK AWFULLY YOUNG...
WHAT DOES AGE MATTER WHERE LOVE IS CONCERNED?
SOMEHOW I DOUBT LOVE IS THE MAIN FACTOR HERE.
BUT I'M SO GLAD...
...YOU'RE JUST MR. MOORE'S LAWYER.
WHAT DO YOU MEAN?
IF A BEAUTIFUL WOMAN LIKE YOU TURNED OUT TO BE MIKIO'S MISTRESS...
...HOW COULD I COMPETE?
AM I SUPPOSED TO BE FLATTERED?
I'M NOT SURE ...
WELL, LET'S GET DOWN TO BUSINESS.
YOU SAY YOU HAVE EVIDENCE THAT PROVES YOUR HUSBAND'S LIFE IS IN DANGER.
YOU BET!
IT'S ALL IN THE STUDY! COME ON!

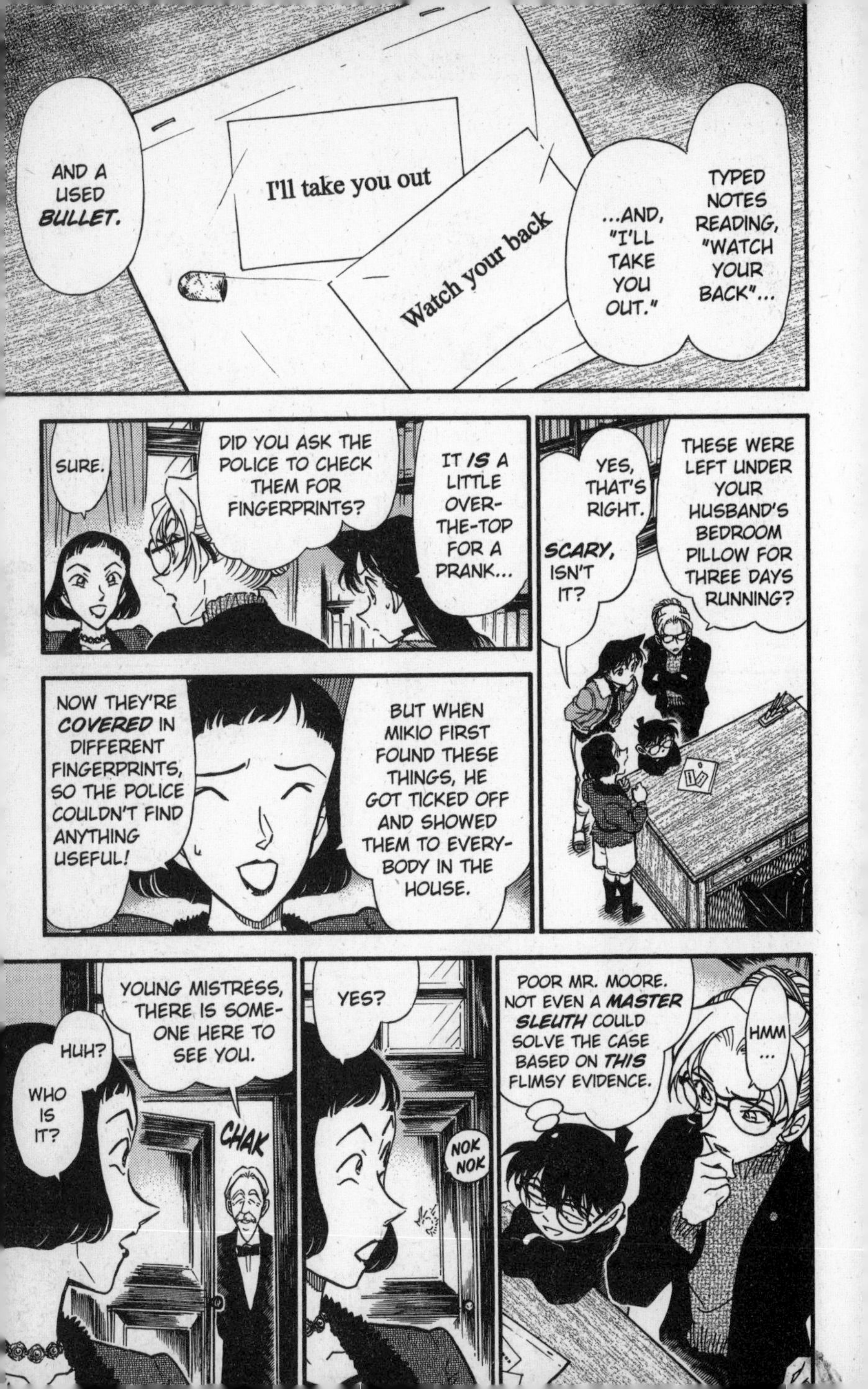
TYPED NOTES READING, "WATCH YOUR BACK"...
...AND, "I'LL TAKE YOU OUT."
Watch your back
I'll take you out
AND A USED *BULLET.*
THESE WERE LEFT UNDER YOUR HUSBAND'S BEDROOM PILLOW FOR THREE DAYS RUNNING?
YES, THAT'S RIGHT.
SCARY, ISN'T IT?
IT *IS* A LITTLE OVER-THE-TOP FOR A PRANK...
DID YOU ASK THE POLICE TO CHECK THEM FOR FINGERPRINTS?
SURE.
BUT WHEN MIKIO FIRST FOUND THESE THINGS, HE GOT TICKED OFF AND SHOWED THEM TO EVERY-BODY IN THE HOUSE.
NOW THEY'RE *COVERED* IN DIFFERENT FINGERPRINTS, SO THE POLICE COULDN'T FIND ANYTHING USEFUL!
POOR MR. MOORE. NOT EVEN A *MASTER SLEUTH* COULD SOLVE THE CASE BASED ON *THIS* FLIMSY EVIDENCE.
HMM ...
NOK NOK
YES?
YOUNG MISTRESS, THERE IS SOME-ONE HERE TO SEE YOU.
CHAK
HUH?
WHO IS IT?

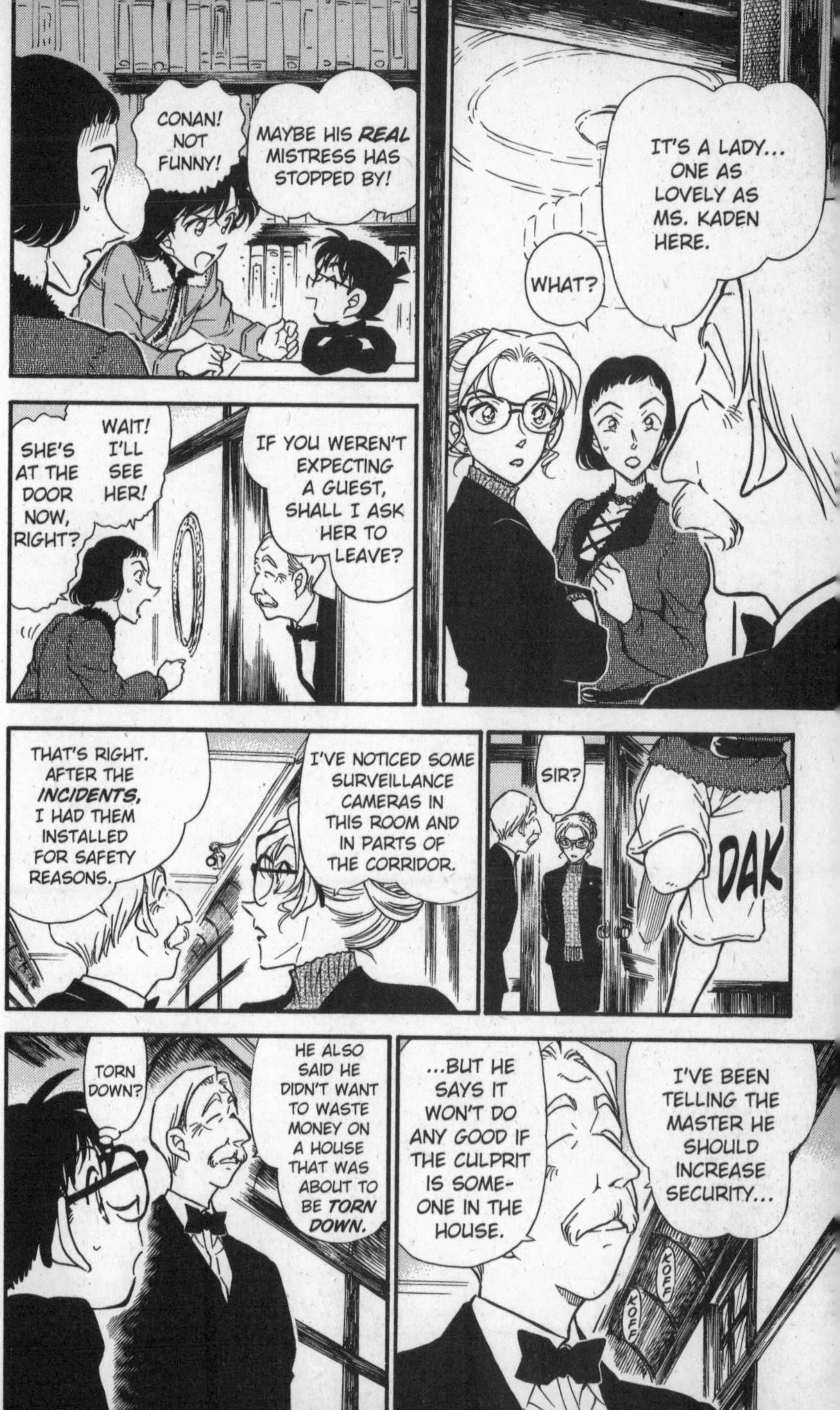
IT'S A LADY... ONE AS LOVELY AS MS. KADEN HERE.
WHAT?
MAYBE HIS *REAL* MISTRESS HAS STOPPED BY!
CONAN! NOT FUNNY!
IF YOU WEREN'T EXPECTING A GUEST, SHALL I ASK HER TO LEAVE?
WAIT! I'LL SEE HER!
SHE'S AT THE DOOR NOW, RIGHT?
SIR?
DAK
I'VE NOTICED SOME SURVEILLANCE CAMERAS IN THIS ROOM AND IN PARTS OF THE CORRIDOR.
THAT'S RIGHT. AFTER THE *INCIDENTS,* I HAD THEM INSTALLED FOR SAFETY REASONS.
I'VE BEEN TELLING THE MASTER HE SHOULD INCREASE SECURITY...
...BUT HE SAYS IT WON'T DO ANY GOOD IF THE CULPRIT IS SOME-ONE IN THE HOUSE.
KOFF
KOFF
HE ALSO SAID HE DIDN'T WANT TO WASTE MONEY ON A HOUSE THAT WAS ABOUT TO BE *TORN DOWN.*
TORN DOWN?

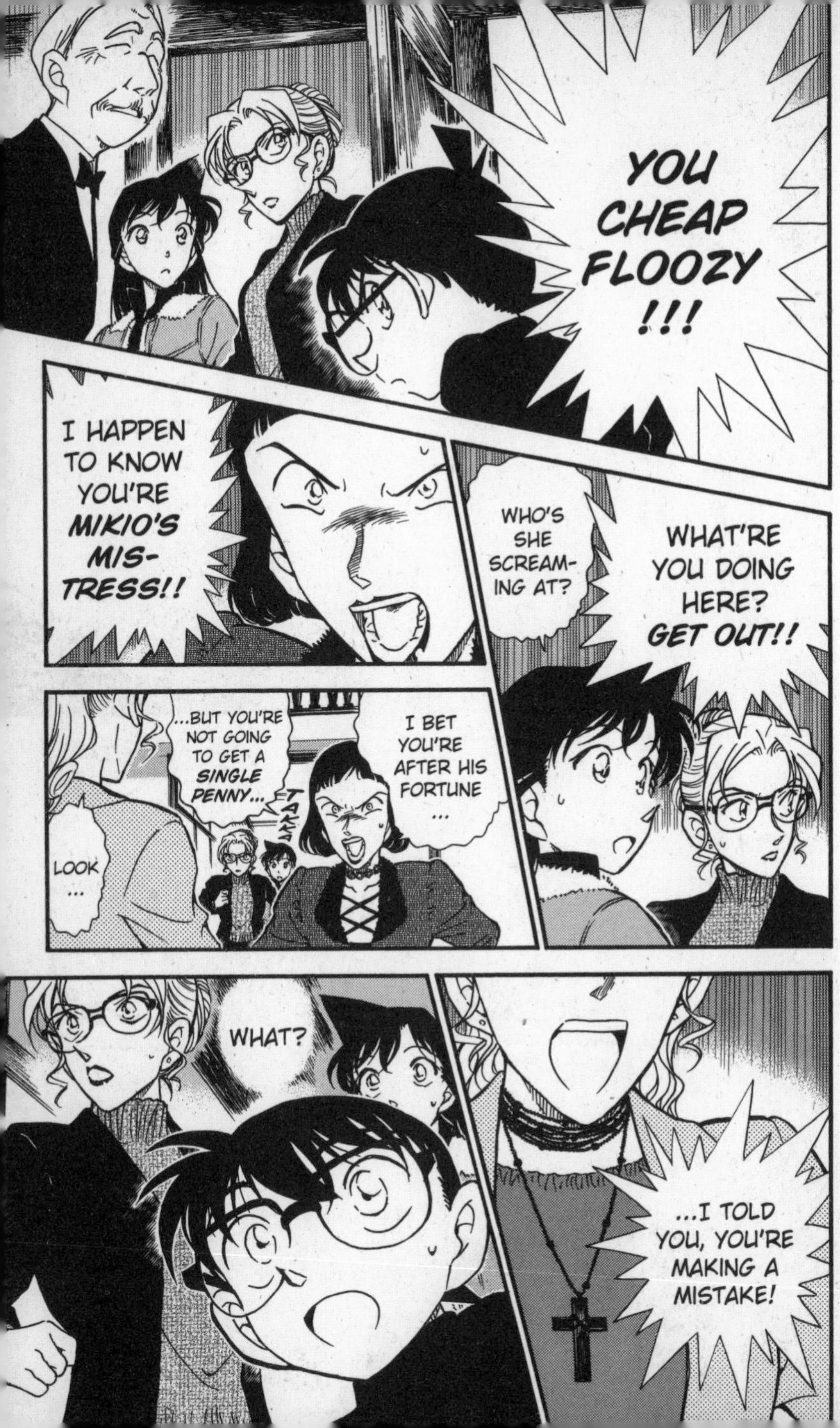
YOU CHEAP FLOOZY !!!
WHAT'RE YOU DOING HERE? GET OUT!!
WHO'S SHE SCREAMING AT?
I HAPPEN TO KNOW YOU'RE MIKIO'S MISTRESS!!
I BET YOU'RE AFTER HIS FORTUNE ...
...BUT YOU'RE NOT GOING TO GET A SINGLE PENNY...
TAKKA
LOOK ...
...I TOLD YOU, YOU'RE MAKING A MISTAKE!
WHAT?

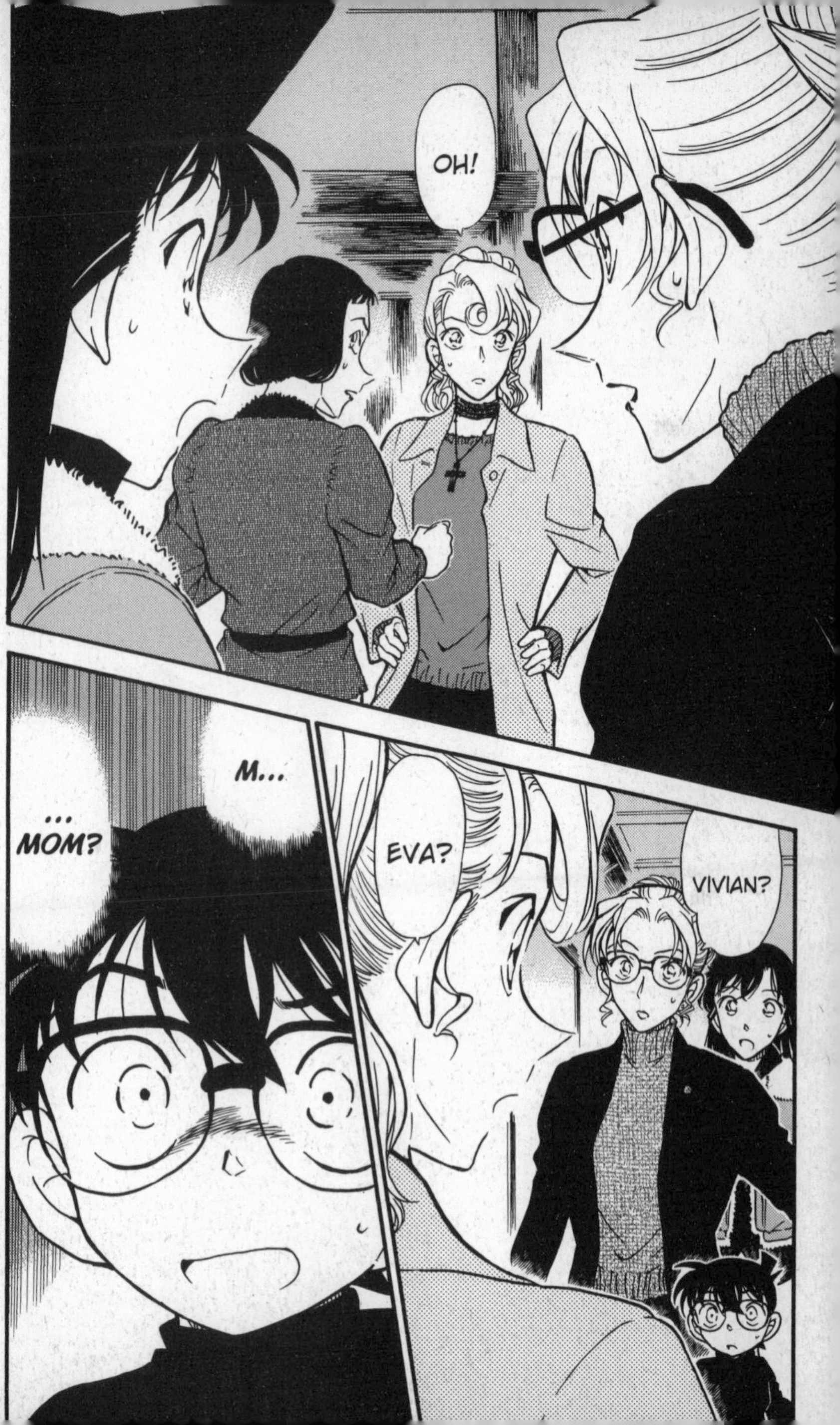
OH!
VIVIAN?
EVA?
M...
...MOM?

Hello, Aoyama here.

So she's finally made her appearance: Dr. Agasa's first love!
I came up with this story some time ago, but since it's set in
autumn I haven't had the chance to write it until now.

I guess the secret code turned out to be pretty tough to solve.
Let's just say that's because a child came up with it...heh.

Gosho Aoyama's
Mystery Library

40

KIYOSHI MITARAI

Many master sleuths are considered eccentrics, and Kiyoshi Mitarai, to whom I am about to introduce you, is one of those. An astrologer with an office in Yokohama, he's tall and definitely good-looking, but has an extreme case of bipolar disorder. Add to this his cynical, antisocial attitude and ability to remember people's birthdates but never their names, and it's no surprise that his only friend is his assistant, Ishioka.

Naturally, Mitarai has an extensive knowledge of fortune-telling techniques, but he's also an expert in mathematics and psychiatry. He studied at Harvard and speaks English fluently. Once he inputs the data of a case into his head, he becomes engrossed in the mystery and doesn't eat, sleep or talk to other people...which is another reason everyone around him sees him as an eccentric. Incidentally, his creator, Soji Shimada, worked as an astrologer when he was young too. As for me, I'm just hooked on zoological fortune-telling...heh.

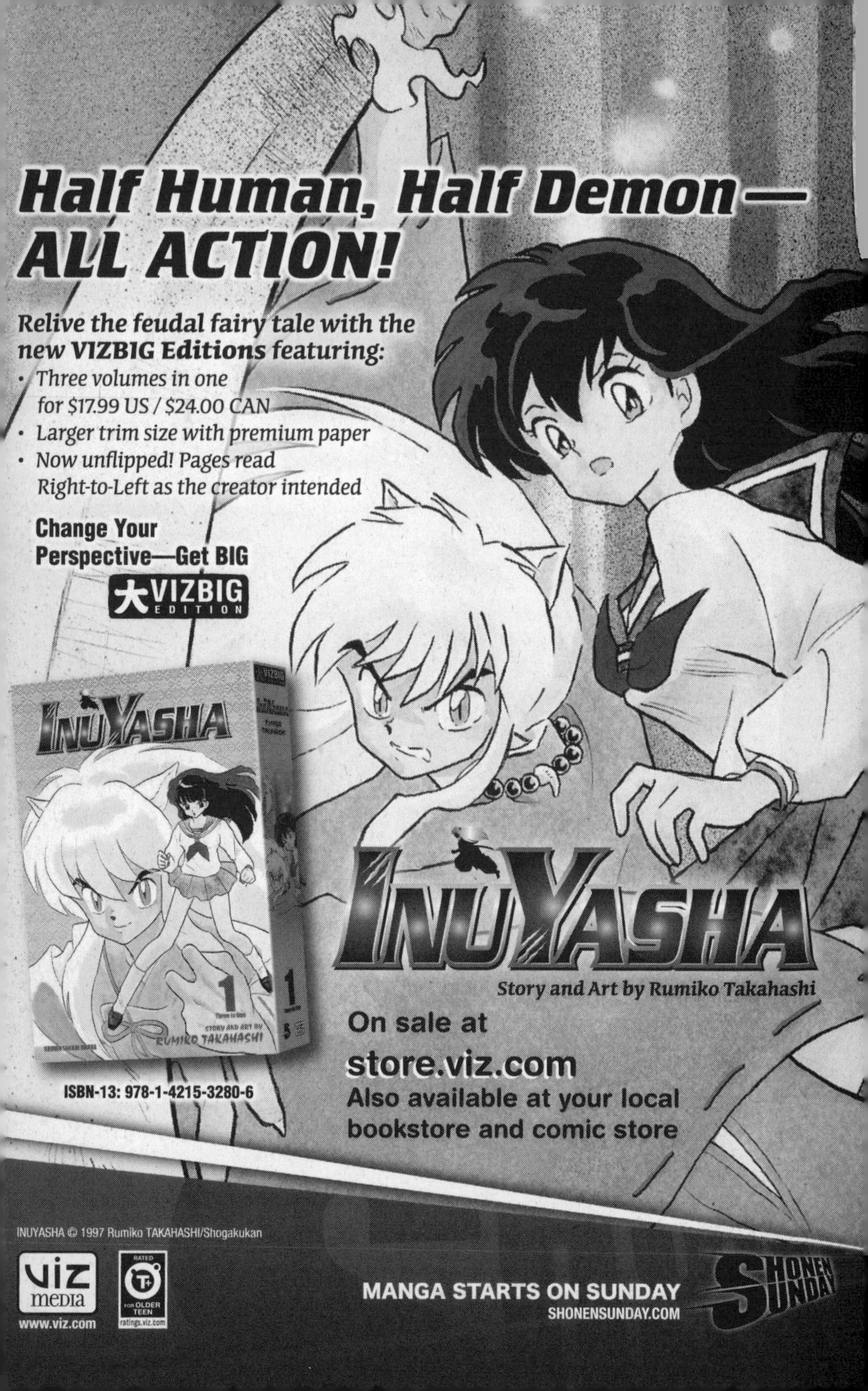
Half Human, Half Demon—
ALL ACTION!
Relive the feudal fairy tale with the new VIZBIG Editions featuring:
• Three volumes in one for $17.99 US / $24.00 CAN
• Larger trim size with premium paper
• Now unflipped! Pages read Right-to-Left as the creator intended
Change Your Perspective—Get BIG
大 VIZBIG EDITION
INUYASHA
1
STORY AND ART BY RUMIKO TAKAHASHI
ISBN-13: 978-1-4215-3280-6
INUYASHA
Story and Art by Rumiko Takahashi
On sale at
store.viz.com
Also available at your local bookstore and comic store
INUYASHA © 1997 Rumiko TAKAHASHI/Shogakukan
VIZ media
www.viz.com
RATED T+ FOR OLDER TEEN
ratings.viz.com
MANGA STARTS ON SUNDAY
SHONENSUNDAY.COM
SHONEN SUNDAY